Paul Georg von Möllendorff, Otto Franz von Möllendorff

Manual of Chinese Bibliography

Being a List of Works and Essays Relating to China

Paul Georg von Möllendorff, Otto Franz von Möllendorff

Manual of Chinese Bibliography
Being a List of Works and Essays Relating to China

ISBN/EAN: 9783337167820

Printed in Europe, USA, Canada, Australia, Japan

Cover: Foto ©Thomas Meinert / pixelio.de

More available books at **www.hansebooks.com**

OF

CHINESE BIBLIOGRAPHY,

BEING A LIST OF WORKS AND ESSAYS RELATING TO

CHINA.

BY

P. G. & O. F. von MÖLLENDORFF,

Interpreters to H. I. G. M.'s Consulates at Shanghai and Tientsin.

SHANGHAI: KELLY & WALSH.

LONDON: TRÜBNER & CO., LUDGATE HILL.

GÖRLITZ, GERMANY: H. TZSCHASCHEL.

SHANGHAI:

PRINTED AT THE "CELESTIAL EMPIRE" OFFICE.

1876.

DIE Zusammenstellung aller über China erschienenen Arbeiten ist für den im fernen Osten wohnenden Fremden schon längst ein unabweisbares Bedürfniss. Gab es auch über einzelne Zweige, wie namentlich die sprachwissenschaftlichen, geschichtlich-erdbeschreibenden Schriften, ziemlich genaue bibliographische Zusammenstellungen, so ist doch die Litteratur über das Gesammtgebiet des chinesischen Reiches niemals erschöpfend behandelt worden.

Es wird gewagt erscheinen, dass eine solche Arbeit in China selbst, wo nur mässige Privatbibliotheken zu Gebote standen, unternommen worden ist, und sind wir uns der dadurch unabwendbar gebliebenen Mängel der nachstehenden Blätter wohlbewusst. Die Hauptlücken werden die kleineren Aufsätze aus Fachzeitschriften treffen, von welchen einzelne gar nicht, viele nur bändeweise eingesehn werden konnten; viele Titel haben nur aus zweiter Hand citirt werden können und dürften zahlreiche Ungenauigkeiten enthalten.

Dennoch treten wir mit der quasi unfertigen Arbeit an die Oeffentlichkeit, um einmal die empfindliche Lücke für das wissenschaftliche Publikum hier auszufüllen, und weil wir hoffen dürfen, dass durch die Veröffentlichung unsres Materials der Anstoss zu einer erschöpfenden Bibliographie Chinas gegeben werden wird. Es dürfte ferner die unsres Wissens zum ersten Mal versuchte Uebersicht des in Zeit-

iv

schriften zerstreuten Materials, namentlich in den in China und in den englischen Colonien erschienenen, welche in Europa noch wenig bekannt und wenig zugänglich sind, auch für das europäische Publikum nicht ohne Nutzen sein. Die wenigen Zusätze und Bemerkungen haben wir, sowie die Ueberschriften, englisch gegeben, da das Publikum, für welches wir unser Buch hauptsächlich bestimmten, in überwiegender Majorität aus Engländern besteht.

PROGRESS in science can only be achieved by making use of the materials collected, and by building upon foundations already laid. A knowledge of the literature becomes therefore an indispensable necessity. The present work is an effort to meet a desideratum in this respect, which as yet is unsupplied.

We have made use of the works mentioned under part I and have to thank N. B. Dennys, Ph. D., of Hongkong, for the liberal manner, in which he has placed the commencement of a similar work of his own at our disposal.

We are not aware, that any important work has been omitted, but should such be the case, criticism ought to be lenient, considering that the work was compiled in the centre of China (at Kiukiang and Peking) and with access to none but private libraries.

TABLE OF CONTENTS.

I.

List of Works which formed the foundation of the present compilation.

1 MEUSELIUS, J. G., Bibliotheca historica. Lipsiae, 1784-1802, 11 vols., 8vo.; Vol. II, pars. II on China.
2 TERNAUX-COMPANS, H., Bibliothèque asiatique et afriquaine. Paris, 1841, 8vo.
3 WILLIAMS, S. W., List of foreign works upon China. Chinese Repository, XVIII, pp. 402-657.
4 KONER, W., Repertorium über die von 1800-1850 in akad. Abhandlungen, etc. auf dem Gebiete der Geschichte erschienenen Aufsätze. Berlin, 1852, 8vo. Continuation of No. 1, Meuselius.
5 ZENKER, J. T., Bibliotheca orientalis. Manuel de bibliographie orientale. Leipzig, 1861, 2 vols., 8vo.
6 ANDREAE, V. and GEIGER, J., Bibliotheca sinologica. Uebersichtliche Zusammenstellung als Wegweiser durch das Gebiet der sinologischen Literatur. Frankfurt a/m, 1864, 8vo.
   See J. Mohl, Journ. As., III, 370, 1864.
   A selection of European publications up to 1863.
7 Catalogue of books relating to China and the East, 8vo. This is the catalogue of A. Wylie's library, now in the R. A. S., Shanghai.

8   DENNYS, N. B., Catalogue of books on China (other than philological) in Treaty Ports (No. 1213). Appendix, pp. 1-26.

9   For the publications of protestant missionaries up to 1867, see A. Wylie's Memorials, No. 3650.

10 KISTNER, O., Buddha and his doctrines, a bibliographical essay. Leipzig, 1869, 4to.
> See Notes and queries, III, 95; Chinese Recorder, III, 228.

11 The "Wissenschaftlichen Jahresberichte der deutschen morgenl. Gesellschaft," by Fleischer, Rödiger and Arnold. But especially the excellent one by R. Gosche (Professor at Halle a/s), 1862-67. Leipzig, 1871, 8vo.

12 DUDGEON, J., List of Russian works on China, Chinese Recorder, IV, 207.

13 CORDIER, H., Catalogue of the library of the N. C. B. of the R. A. S., Shanghai. Shanghai, 1872, 8vo.
> Besides these works, nearly all the serials under IX have been extracted.

A.

Chinese Language and Literature.

II.

Grammars.

14 VARO, F., Arte de la lengua madarina, acrecentato y reducido de la mejor forma P. N. St. Pedro de la Pinuela. Anadiose un confesionario muy util y provechoso para alivio de los nuevos ministros. Canton, 1703, 4to.
> Printed on blocks, without Chinese characters.

15 FOURMONT, S., Meditationes sinicae. Paris, 1737, fol.

16 — — Linguae Sinarum manderinicae et hieroglyphicae grammatica duplex, latine et cum characteribus Sinensium. Item Sinicorum regiae bibliothecae librorum catalogus. Parisiis, 1742, fol.
See Chin. Repos., X, p. 672; XVIII, p. 403.

17 BAYER, T. S., Musaeum sinicum. Petropoli, 1780, 2 vols., 8vo.
Contains also a translation of the first part of the Ta-hsio with Chinese text; grammar of the Ts'in-ts'iu dialect, I, pp. 137-67.

18 HAGER, J., Elements of the Chinese language. London, 1806, 2 vols., 8vo.
See As. Mag., II, 79, 1803.

19 MARSHMAN, J., Clavis sinica. Elements of Chinese Grammar, with a dissertation on the characters and the colloquial medium of the Chinese and an appendix containing the Ta hyoh of Confucius with a translation. Serampore, 1814, 4to.
See A. Rémusat, Mél. as., II, 132; Chin. Repos., VII, p. 115; IX, p. 587.

20 MORRISON, R., A grammar of the Chinese language. Serampore, 1815, 4to.
See A. Rémusat, Mél. as., II, p. 152.

21 RÉMUSAT, A., Elémens de la grammaire chinoise ou principes généraux du kou-wen ou style antique et du kouan-hoa, c'est-à-dire de la langue commune. Paris, 1822, 8vo.; 2nd ed. by L. de Rosny. Paris, 1853, 8vo.
The preface contains critical notes on all preceding works.
See S. de Sacy, Notice de l'ouvrage intitulé: Eléments, etc. Paris, 1822, 4to.

22 GONÇALVEZ, J. A., Arte China, constante de Alphabeto e grammatica, comprehendendo modelos das differentes composiçoens. Macao, 1829, 4to.
See Chin. Repos., XV, p. 71.

The extracts from histories and fables translated by J. Bowring, Chin. Repos., XX, p. 94, p. 122, p. 194; and Chin. and Jap. Repos., Dec., 1863, Jan.-Ap., 1864.

23 PREMARE, P., Notitia linguae Sinicae. Malacca, 1831, 4to.

See A. Rémusat, Jour. des Savans, Sept.,1831. E. C. Bridgman, Chin. Repos., I, p. 152; XVI, p. 266.

The proverbs selected from it Chin. Repos., XV, p. 140.

Translated into English by J. G. Bridgman. Canton, 1847, 8vo.

For a notice of the manner, in which this valuable work was prepared and sent to Fourmont, see Chin. Repos., X., p. 671.

24 HYACINTHE BITCHOURIN, Kitaiskaya grammatika (Chinese grammar.) St. Petersburg, 1838, 243 pp., lithogr., 4to. (in Russian.)

25 (GUTZLAFF, K.) Philosinensis: Notices on Chinese grammar. Batavia, 1842, 8vo.

See E. C. Bridgman, Chin. Repos., XI, p. 317.

26 ENDLICHER, S., Anfangsgründe der chinesischen Grammatik. Wien, 1845, 8vo.

27 Premiers rudiments de la langue Chinoise. Paris, 1844, 12mo.

28 EDKINS, J., A grammar of colloquial Chinese, as exhibited in the Shanghae dialect. Shanghai, 1853, 8vo.; 2nd, ed., 1868, VIII, 225 pp., 8vo.

29 — — A grammar of the Chinese colloquial language, commonly called the Mandarin dialect. Shanghai, 1857, 8vo.; 2nd ed., 1864, 8vo.

30 BAZIN, A., Grammaire Mandarine ou principes généraux de la langue chinoise parlée. Paris, 1856, 8vo.

See T. Pavie, Grammaire mandarine par Bazin, J. as., 5me. série, X, p. 558; see also No. 531.

31 SCHOTT, W., Chinesische Sprachlehre. Berlin, 1857, 4to.

32 — — Zur Chinesischen Sprachlehre. Berlin, 1868, 4to.
  Contains additions and corrections to the preceding work.

33 SUMMERS, J., Handbook of the Chinese language. Oxford, 1863, 8vo.
  Grammar and Chrestomathy.

34 LOBSCHEID, W., Grammar of the Chinese language. Hongkong, 1864, 8vo.
  For the dialect of Canton.

35 ISAIAH, J., Wwedenie w russko—kitaiskii slovar. Peking, 1869, 16mo., 69 pp. (in Russian.)
  Grammatical introduction to the author's Russian-Chinese vocabulary.

36 CASTAÑEDA, B., Grammatica elemental de la lengua China, dialecto Cantonés. Hongkong, 1869, 8vo.
  See Notes and queries, III, p. 160.

37 JULIEN, S., Han-wen-tchi-nan, Syntaxe nouvelle de la langue Chinoise, fondée sur la position des mots. Paris, 1869, 2 vols., 8vo.
  See Ch. Review, I, p. 110.
      Vol. I : grammatical observations, monographies on the most difficult prepositions, particles, etc.; table of idiotisms, fables, legends, etc., translated verbally.
      Vol. II : Reprint of critiques against Pauthier, a vocabulary of difficult expressions of the Chinese novel 玉嬌梨 Yü-tshiau-li (see Wylie's notes, p. 163), a verbal translation of the first 3 acts of the "Orphelin de la Chine."

38 RUDY, C., The Chinese Mandarin language after Ollendorf's new method. Ban-zai-sau by Turretini. Senève, 1872, 8vo.

39 ROSNY, L. de, A grammar of the Chinese language, London, 1874.

III.

Dictionaries.

40 COLLADI, D., Dictionarium linguae sinensis cum explicatione latina et hispana. Romae, 1632, 4to. See A. Rémusat, mél. as., II, p. 65.

41 DIAZ, F., Vocabulario de letra China con la explicacion castellana, hecho con gran propriedad y abundancia de palabras. Manuscript in the R. libr. of Berlin, c. 1647, fol., 598 pp.; another copy at Paris, 4to., 396 pp.

42 DALQUIÉ, F. S., Dictionnaire chinois et français, in the French edition of Kirchner's China illustrata. Amsterdam, 1670, fol., appendix, p. 324-367, in roman letters.

43 RAPER, M., A Chinese and English dictionary, translated from the Latin Macao dictionary. London, 1807.

44 DEGUIGNES (fils), Dictionnaire chinois, français et latin. Paris, 1813, fol.
    Reprinted : Dictionarium sinico-latinum auctore M. de Guignes ; meliori ordine digestum labore, cura ac diligentia F. H. Mangieri. Hongkong, 1853, 4to.
    The original is the M. S. dictionary of P. Basile de Glemona. See A. Rémusat, Mél. as., II, p. 71.

45 KLAPROTH, J., Supplément au dictionnaire chinois-latin publié par M. de Guignes. Paris, 1819, fol., I, fasc.
    Only to rad. 61, the " examen critique " in the preface is by A. Rémusat.
    See A. Rémusat, Mél. as., II, p. 217-242.

46 MORRISON, R., Dictionary of the Chinese language, divided into 3 parts. I, Chinese and English, arranged according to the Radicals, 3 vols.; II,

Chinese and English, arranged alphabetically, 2 vols.; III, English and Chinese, 1 vol. Macao, 1819-22, 6 vols., 4to.

> The 2nd part, arranged alphabetically, is reprinted in 2 vols. Shanghai, 1865, 8vo.

> See J. Klaproth, Allg. Litt. zeit., No. 29, 1828, and Dernier mot sur le dictionnaire du Dr. R. Morrison. Paris, 1830, 8vo.

> A. Rémusat, Mél. as., II, p. 157-216. This monument of literary labor was published at the expense of the East India Company. The first vol. of part I is the best, the others are excelled by modern works.

47 — — Vocabulary of the Canton dialect. Macao, 1828, 3 parts, 8vo.

> I, English-Chinese; II, Chinese-English; III, Chinese words and phrases.

48 — — An English and Chinese vocabulary, the latter in the Canton dialect. Calcutta, 1840, 12mo.

49 GONÇALVEZ, J. A., Diccionario Portuguez-China. Macao, 1831, 4to.

50 — — Diccionario China-Portuguez. Macao, 1833, 4to.

> The author has reduced the number of 214 radicals to a system of his own, which is, however, easily mastered.

51 — — Vocabularium latino-sinicum. Macao, 1836, 8vo.

52 — — Lexicon manuale latino-sinicum. Macao, 1839, 8vo.

53 — — Lexicon magnum latino-sinicum. Macao, 1841, 4to.

54 MEDHURST, W. H. (sen.), Dictionary of the Hokkëën dialect of the Chinese language, according to the reading and colloquial idioms. Macao, 1832, 4to., LXIV, 860 pp.

> See Chin. Repos., VI, p. 142.

55 MEDHURST, W. H. (sen.), Chinese and English dictionary. Batavia, 1842-43, 2 vols., 8vo.

56 — — English and Chinese dictionary. Shanghai, 1847-48, 2 vols., 8vo.

See E. C. Bridgman, Chin. Repos., XII, p. 496.

57 — — Comparative vocabulary of the Chinese, Corean and Japanese languages, to which is added the Thousand-characters classic in Chinese and Corean, accompanied by indexes of all Chinese and English words. Batavia, 1835, 8vo.

58 DAVIS, J. F., Commercial vocabulary, English-Chinese. Macao, 1834, 12mo.

59 DYER, D., Vocabulary of the Hokkien dialect. Singapore, 1338, 8vo., without Chinese characters.

60 SIEBOLD, P. F. von, Lui Hö, sive vocabularium sinense in Kôraïanum conversum, opus sinicum origine in peninsula Kôraï impressum in lapide exaratum a Sinensi Ko....annexa appendice vocabulorum Kôraïanorum, japonicorum et sinensium comparativa. Lugduni Batavorum, 1838, fol.

61 CALLERY, J. M., Systema phoneticum scripturae sinicae. Macao, 1841, 8vo.

See G. T. Lay, Chin. Repos., XII, p. 253 and Callery's reply, ibid, p. 371.

62 CALLERY, J. M., Dictionnaire encyclopédique de la langue Chinoise. Paris et Macao, 1845, part I, fasc., 1, 4to.

For prospectus and preface, see Chin. Repos., XII, p. 300; XIV, p. 137.

The beginning of the translation of the 佩 文 韻 府 pëi-wen-yün-fu (see Wylie's notes, p. 11.)

63 LEGGE, J., A lexilogus of the English, Malay and Chinese languages, comprehending the vernacular idioms of the last in the Hok-keen and Canton dialects. Malacca, 1841, 8vo.

See Chin. Repos., XI, p. 389.

64 THOM, R., Chinese-English vocabulary. Canton, 1843, 8vo.

65 WILLIAMS, S. W., An English and Chinese vocabulary in the Court dialect. Macao, 1844, 8vo.
    See E. C. Bridgman, Chin. Repos., XV, p. 145.

66 — — Tonic dictionary of the Chinese language in the Canton dialect. Canton, 1856, 8vo.
    A new edition of this work by J. Eitel is soon expected.

67 — — A syllabic dictionary of the Chinese language, arranged according to the Wu-fang Yuan-yin, with the pronunciation of the characters as heard in Peking, Canton, Amoy and Shanghai. Shanghai, 1874, 1252 pp., 4to.
    See Chin. Recorder, V, p. 226-228; China Review, III, p. 138-142; W. P. Groenevelt, ibid, p. 226-241; Ibid, IV, p. 318-322.

68 SCHOTT, W., Vocabularium sinicum. Berlin, 1844, 4to.
    A collection of Chinese types, brought to Berlin by K. Gützlaff, with Latin translation.

69 GODDART, J., A Chinese and English vocabulary in the Tie-chiu dialect. Bangkok, 1847, 8vo.
    In the dialect of Chaochou fu (local pronunciation: tïe-tshiu) in the province of Kuang-tung.

70 CHALMERS, J., Chinese phonetic vocabulary, containing all the most common characters with their sounds in the Canton dialect. Hongkong, 1855, 8vo.

71 — — English and Cantonese pocket dictionary. Hongkong, 1859, 12o., 4th ed., 1873.
    See China Review, II, p. 126.

72 HOBSON, B., Medical vocabulary in English and Chinese. Shanghai, 1858, 8vo.

73 MACGOWAN, J., Chinese and English vocabulary. Shanghai, 1862, 2 vols., 8vo.
74 ISAIAH, J., Russko-kitaiski slovar (Russian-Chinese vocabulary.) Peking, 1867, 535 pp., 16mo. (in Russian.)
    Supplement, Peking, 1871, 16mo.
75 WASSILYEFF, W., Kitaiski-russko slovar (Chinese Russian dictionary.) St. Petersburg, 1867, 456 pp., fol.
76 PAUTHIER, G., Dictionnaire étymologique Chinois-Annamite Latin-Français. Paris, 1867, 4to.
77 LOBSCHEID, W., English and Chinese dictionary, with the Punti and Mandarin pronunciation. Hongkong, 1866-69, 4 vols., 4to.
    See China Mag., 1869, p. 112.
78 — — Chinese and English dictionary. Hongkong, 1871, 8vo.
79 Kwong Tsun Tuk, An English and Chinese lexicon. Hongkong, 1868, 8vo., 326 pp. and Chinese and English index, 66 pp. Expressions, 3 pp.; short sentences, 24 pp.
    In Cantonese.
80 EDKINS, J., A vocabulary of the Shanghai dialect. Shanghai, 1869, VI, 151 pp., 8vo.
    See Phoenix, II, p. 32.
81 PERNY, P., Dictionnaire Français-Latin-Chinois, de la langue Mandarine parlée. Paris, vol. I, 459 pp., 1869; vol. II, 1872, 4to.
    Vol. II has the separate title: Appendice du dictionnaire Français-Latin-Chinois, and is composed of essays on various subjects relating to China.
82 MACLAY, R. S. and BALDWIN, C. C., Alphabetic dictionary of the Chinese language, in the Foochow dialect. Foochow, 1871, 1107 pp., 8vo.
    See Chin. Recorder, III, p. 132; Phoenix, I, p. 222.

83 STENT, G. C., A Chinese and English vocabulary
   in the Pekingese dialect. Shanghai, 1871, 8vo.;
   smaller edition: A Chinese and English pocket
   dictionary. Shanghai, 1874, 8vo.
   See Chin. Recorder, V, p. 55.

84 DOOLITTLE, J., Vocabulary and handbook of the
   Chinese language. Foochow, 1872, 2 vols., 4to.
   See China Review, I, p. 269.
   Vol. I is an English-Chinese vocabulary;
   Vol. II contains useful lists and transla-
   tions by various authors.

85 DOUGLAS, C., A Chinese and English dictionary
   of the vernacular or spoken language of Amoy
   with the principal variations of the Chang-chew
   and Chin-chew dialects. London, 1873, lex. 8vo.,
   XIX, 612 pp.
   Without Chinese characters.
   See China Review, II, p. 129; Trübner's Record, June, 1873; Chin. Recorder, V, p.
   50-53; Lit. Centralblatt, 1874, p. 304.

86 GILES, H. A., A dictionary of colloquial idioms in
   the Mandarin dialect. Shanghai, 1873, 4to.
   See North Ch. Herald, 1st Dec., 1873, p. 527.

87 LEMAIRE, G. et GIQUEL, P., Dictionnaire de po-
   che Français-Chinois suivi d'un dictionnaire tech-
   nique des mots usités à l'arsenal de Foutcheou.
   Shanghai, 1874, 421 pp., 12mo.
   See Chin. Recorder, V, p. 169.

88 MORRISON, W. T., An Anglo-Chinese vocabulary
   of the Ningpo dialect. Shanghai, 1876, XV, 559
   pp., 8vo.
   See Chin. Recorder, VII, p. 145-46.

IV.

Dialogues, Handbooks, &c.

89 DUFAYEL, Recueil de pièces utiles pour faciliter

l'étude et l'intelligence de la langue Chinoise. Rouen, en XI fol.

90 MORRISON, R., Dialogues and detached sentences in the Chinese language with a free and verbal translation in English. Macao, 1816, 8vo.
The pronunciation is in the Court dialect.

91 The English and Chinese student's assistant or colloquial phrases, letters, &c. in English and Chinese. Malacca, 1826, 8vo.
See Chin. Repos., XVIII, p. 107.

92 DEAN, S., First lessons in Tie-chiu. Bangkok, 1841, 4to.
See note to No. 69.

93 BRIDGMAN, E. C., Chinese chrestomathy in the Canton dialect with English translation and notes. Macao, 1841, 4to.
See Chin. Repos., XI, p. 157-161; p. 226-230.

94 WILLIAMS, S. W., Easy lessons in Chinese or progressive exercises to facilitate the study of that language, especially adapted to the Canton dialect. Macao, 1842, 8vo.
See Chin. Repos., XIV, p. 339.

95 MEDHURST, W. H. (sen.), Chinese dialogues. Shanghai, 1844; 2nd edition, 1861, 8vo.
See Chin. Repos., XIV, p. 396.

96 — — Lessons in Chinese. Shanghai, 1846, 8vo.

97 Han-Tseu-Thso-Yao, Exercises progressifs sur les clefs et les phonétiques de la langue Chinoise, suivis de phrases familières et de dialogues. Paris, 1845, 8vo.

98 THOM, R., The Chinese speaker or extracts from works written in the Mandarin language as spoken at Peking. Ningpo, 1846, 8vo.
See Chin. Repos., XVI, p. 236.
There exists a Chinese edition in 4 vols., 16mo., without the translation, for Cantonese.

99 ROCHET, L. de, Manuel pratique de la langue Chinoise vulgaire contenant un choix de dialogues familiers, de différents morceaux de littérature, précédés d'une introduction grammaticale et suivis d'un vocabulaire. Paris, 1846, 8vo.

100 — — Textes faciles en langue Chinoise. Paris, 1864, 12mo.

101 PILAY, STRENASSA, A manual for youth and students or Chinese vocabulary and dialogue, Ningpo dialect. Chusan, 1846, 8vo.

102 DEVAN, T. T., Beginner's first book in the Chinese language, Canton vernacular. Hongkong, 1847, 8vo.

103 — — The household companion and student's first assistant with many additions, corrections, &c. by Rev. W. Lobscheid. Hongkong, 1867, 8vo.

In the Cantonese dialect.

104 HOBSON, B., Chinese dialogues in the Canton dialect with English translations. Canton, 1850, 8vo.

105 LOBSCHEID, W., Spelling and reading assistant for the Government schools of Hongkong. Hongkong, 1850, 8vo.

106 — — Beginner's first book or vocabulary in the Canton dialect. Hongkong, 1858, 8vo.

107 — — Tourist's guide and merchant's manual. Hongkong, 1864, 8vo.

108 — — Select phrases and reading lessons in the Canton dialect. Hongkong, 1864, 8vo.

109 EDKINS, J., Chinese conversations. Shanghai, 1852, 8vo.

110 — — Progressive lessons in the Chinese spoken language. Shanghai, 1862, 8vo.; 2nd edition, 1864; 3rd edition, 1869.

Translated into German by J. Haas, Shanghai, 1871, 8vo.

111 DOTY, E., Anglo-Chinese manual with romanized colloquial in the Amoy dialect. Canton, 1853, 8vo, XV, 214 pp.

112 Chinese manual, Recueil de phrases Chinoises composées de 4 caractères. London and Paris, 1854, fol.

113 BONNAY, S. W., A vocabulary with colloquial phrases in the Canton dialect. Canton, 1854, 8vo.

114 HERNISZ, S., A guide to conversation in the English and Chinese languages. Boston, 1855, 8vo.

115 Chinese and English graduated reading, comprising a circle of knowledge in 200 lessons. Hongkong, 1856, 8vo.

116 DABRY, P., Guide des armées alliées en Chine ou dialogues en trois langues : Français, Anglais, Chinois ; suivi d'un vocabulaire Chinois-Français-Anglais. Paris, 1859, 12mo.

117 WADE, T. F., Hsin Ching-Lu, or book of experiments. Hongkong, 1859, 3 vols., fol.

118 — — Yü-yen Tzü-erh Chi, A progressive course designed to assist the student of colloquial Chinese. London, 1867, with Peking syllabary and writing exercises, 4 vols., 4to.
See Notes and queries, I, p. 114, p. 149.

119 — — Wên-chien Tzü-erh Chi, A series of papers selected as specimens of documentary Chinese, with key. London, 1867, 2 vols., 4to.

120 T'ong Ting-kü, The Chinese and English instructor. Canton, 1862, 6 vols., 8vo.
In Cantonese.

121 MACGOWAN, J., A collection of phrases in the Shanghai dialect, systematically arranged. Shanghai, 1862, V, 193 pp., 8vo.

122 — — A manual of the Amoy colloquial. Hongkong, 1869, 8vo., IV, 200 pp.
See Chin. Recorder, II, p. 54 ; Notes and queries, III, p. 96.

123 Daily lessons for children in Chinese, 4to.

124 MARTIN, W. P. A., Analytical reader. Shanghai, 1863, 8vo.

125 JULIEN, S., Ji-tch'ang-k'eou-t'eou-hoa, Dialogues

Chinoises à l'usage de l'école speciale des langues orientales, publiés avec une traduction et un vocabulaire. Paris, 1863, 8vo.

126 Dialogi latino-sinenses, Dialogues français-chinois, alumni seminarii S. Josephi Tcheli meridio-orientalis typis mandabant. Hokien (Chili), 1864, 8vo.

127 Sau mang-yian, Tones of the Mandariu dialect are given in English and Chinese. Canton, 1865, 8vo.

128 RUBERY, H., Easy phrases in the Canton dialect. Canton, 1866, 4to.

129 LANCTOT, B., Chinese and English phrase books. San Francisco, 2nd edition, 1867, 12mo.

130 WASSILYEFF, W., Chinese chrestomathy (in Russian.)

131 ISAIAH, J., Chinese-Russian dialogues (in Russian.)

132 HERVEY DE SAINT-DENYS, Marquis d', Recueil de textes faciles et gradués en chinois moderne. Paris, 1869, 8vo.

133 BALDWIN, C. C., A manual of the Foochow dialect. Foochow, 1871, 8vo.

134 YATES, M. T., First lessons in Chinese (Shanghai dialect.) Shanghai, 1872, 8vo.

135 PERNY, P., Dialogues chinois-latins. Paris, 1872, 8vo.

136 GILES, H. A., Chinese without a teacher. Shanghai, 1872, 8vo.
See China Review, I, p. 203.

137 MAYERS, W. F., The Chinese reader's manual, a handbook of biographical, historical, mythological and general literary reference. Shanghai, 1874, 8vo., XXI, 640 pp.
See Chin. Recorder, V, p. 166-169; E. J. Eitel, China Review, III, p. 176-181; Lit. Centrabl., 1875, p. 910-911.

V.

Translations.

a. With Chinese Text.

138 COSTA, J. DE, Ta hio, in Latin. Kienchang fu (Kiangsi), 1662.

139 INTORCETTA, P., Sinarum scientia politico-moralis.

140 KOEGLER, J., Litterae patentes imperatoris Sinarum Kanghi. Sinice et latine, cum interpretatione et tabula aenea edidit C. G. von Murr. Norimbergae et Altdorfii, 1702.

141 BAYER, T. S., Translation of the first book of the Ch'un Ch'iu in Latin, Commentaria academiae petropolitanae, Vol. VII, p. 398.

142 Chineesche geschiedeniss. Amsterdam, 1767, 8vo.

143 HAGER, J., Monument de Yu, ou la plus ancienne inscription de la Chine, suivie de 32 formes d'anciens, caractères chinois. Paris, 1802, fol.
See As. Magaz., II, p. 473, 1803.

144 — — Epigrafi cinesi di Quang-ceu ossia della città Canton. Milano, 1828, 2nd edition.

145 MARSHMAN, J., The works of Confucius, containing the original text with a translation, to which is prefixed a dissertation on the Chinese language and characters. Serampore, 1809, 4to.
Contains the first half of the Lun-yü.
See A. Rémusat, mél. as., II, p. 277-97.

146 WESTON, S., An imperial poem in Chinese with a translation. London, 1809, 8vo.

147 — — The Conquest of the Miao-tse, an imperial poem by Kien-lung. London, 1810, 8vo.

148 — — Fan-hy-cheu, a tale in Chinese and English, with notes and a short grammar of the Chinese language. London, 1815, 8vo.

149 — — A Chinese poem, inscribed on porcelain, A. D. 1776, with a double translation and notes. London, 1816, 8vo.

150 KLAPROTH, J., Inschrift des Yü, übersetzt und erklärt. Halle, 1811, 4to.
See A. Rémusat, mél. as., II, p. 272.

151 MORRISON, R., Esop's fables, translated into the Chinese language with a free and verbal translation. Macao, 1816, 8vo.

152 — — The Chinese miscellany, consisting of original extracts from Chinese authors in the native character. London, 1825, 4to., with plates.

153 RÉMUSAT, A., L'invariable milieu, ouvrage moral de Tseu-sse, en Chinois et en Mandchou, avec une version littérale latine, traduction française et des notes; précédé d'une notice sur les quatre livres moraux communément attribués à Confucius. Paris, 1817, 4to.; also in Vol. X of Notices et Extraits des MS. de la bibl. du Roi.

154 DAVIS, Sir J. F., Hien-wan-shoo, Chinese moral maxims, with a free and verbal translation. London, Macao, 1823, 8vo.

155 THOMS, P. P., Hua-tsien, Chinese courtship in verse, Chinese and English, to which is added an appendix treating of the revenue of China. London, Macao, 1824, 8vo., p. 324.
See A. Rémusat, mél. as., II, p. 334.
German by H. Kurz, Das Blumenblatt. St. Gallen, 1836, 8vo.

156 JULIEN, S., Meng-tseu vel Mencium, inter Sinenses philosophos ingenio, doctrina nominisque claritate Confucio proximum, sinice edidit et latina interpretatione ad interpretationem tartaricam utramque recensita instruxit et perpetuo commentario sinicis deprompto illustravit. Lutetiae Parisiorum, 1824-29, 2 vols., 8vo.
See A. Rémusat, mél. as., II, p. 298-310.

157 — — Le livre des récompenses et des peines, en

chinois et en français; accompagné de quatre cents légendes, anecdotes et histoires. Paris, 1835, 8vo.

> Translation of the Kan-ying-pien (see Wylie's notes, p. 179), reprinted without the legends, etc., with an English translation in Doolittle's vocabulary, II.

158 — — Lao-tseu-tao-te-king, Le livre de la voie et de la vertu, composé dans le VI siècle avant l'ère chrétienne. Paris, 1842, 8vo.

> See Wylie's notes, p. 173.

159 — — Thsien-tseu-wen, le livre des mille mots. Paris, 1864, 8vo.

160 — — San-tseu-king ou livre de phrases de trois mots, en chinois, latin et en anglais. Paris, 1864, 8vo.

> Reprinted in Turretini's Ban Zai Sau, vol. II, 1872.

161 HYACINTHE BITSHURIN, San-tsi-king translated. St. Petersburg, 1829, 4to. (in Russian.)

162 KIDD, S., The 1,000 character classic, report of the Anglo-Chinese college, 1831.

163 SIEBOLD, P. F. von, Tsian-dsu-wen sive 1,000 literae ideogr. opus sinicum. Leyden, 1833, fol.

> Translated into German by J. Hoffmann, 1840.

164 NEUMANN, K. F., Lehrsaal des Mittelreiches, enthaltend die Encyclopaedie der chinesischen Jugend und das Buch des ewigen Geistes und der ewigen Materie. München, 1836, 4to.

165 PAUTHIER, G., Le Ta-hio, ou la grande étude, traduit en français, avec une version latine et le text chinois. Paris, 1837, 8vo.

166 — — Le Tao-te-king ou le livre révéré de la Raison suprême et de la Vertu, par Lao-tseu. Paris, 1838, 8vo., 1st fasc.

167 — — L'inscription Syro-chinoise de Si-ngan-fou, monument nestorien, élevé en Chine l'an 781 et découvert en 1625. Paris, 1858, 8vo.

168 THOM, R., Esop's fables, written in Chinese by the learned Mun Mooy Seen-shang. Canton, 1840, 4to.

    See Chin. Repos., IX, p. 201; Bazin (sen.), jour. as, 4 sér., I, No. 3, 1843, p. 268.

169 SHUCK, J. L., Portfolio chinensis, or a collection of authentic Chinese State Papers, illustrative of the history of the present position of affairs in China. Macao, 1840, 8vo.

170 DYER, S. and STRONACH, J., Esop's fables rendered into Hok-kien and Tie-chiu colloquial. Singapore, 1843, 3 parts, 8vo.

    See Chin. Repos., XIII, p. 98.

171 MEDHURST, W. H. (sen.), Ancient China, The Shooking or the historical classic. Shanghai, 1846, 8vo.

172 Monument et inscription de Si-gan-fou. Paris, 1849, 8vo.

173 CALLERY, J. M., Si-ki ou mémorial des rites, traduit pour la première fois du chinois. Turin, 1853, 4to.

    See jour. as., 4 sér., VIII, p. 76.

174 JENKINS, B., The three character classic. Shanghai, 1860, 8vo.

175 — — The 1000 character classic. Shanghai, 1860, 8vo.

176 LEGGE, J., The Chinese classics, with a translation, critical and exegetical notes, prolegomena and copious indexes.

    Vol. I, Confucian analects, Great learning and the doctrine of the Mean. Hongkong, 1861, 8vo.

        See Pfizmayer, Lit. Centralbl., 1865, No. 51, p. 1399; Max Müller, Chips I, p. 300; J. Mohl in jour. as, 5 sér., XVII, p. 533.

    Vol. II, The works of Mencius. Hongkong, 1861-62, 8vo.

See Lit. Centralbl., 1866, No. 16.
Mag. f. d. Lit. d. Ausl., vol.
XLIV, No. 35, 1875.
Vol. III, part 1 and 2, The Shooking. Hongkong, 1865, 2 vols., 8vo.
P. 105-183, translation of the annals of the Bamboobook, see
Wylie's notes, p. 19.
Vol. IV, part 1 and 2, The She king or the
book of poetry. Hongkong, 1871, 2
vols., 8vo.
See E. J. Eitel, China Review, I,
p. 2.
Vol. V, part 1 and 2, The Chun Tsew, with
the Tso Chuen. Hongkong, 1872, 8vo.
177 ROSNY, L. DE, L'Épouse d'outre tombe, conte chinois. Paris, 1864, 16mo. Translation, 44 pp.;
Chinese text, 31 pp.
Story from the Lung-tu-kung-an. See jour.
as., Fév. 1864.
178 HERVEY DE SAINT-DENYS, Marquis d', Le Li-
sao, poëme du IIIe. siècle avant notre ère, traduit
et publié avec le texte original. Paris, 1870, 8vo.
See Wylie's notes, p. 181; Lit. Centralbl.,
1871, p. 109; China Review, I, p. 60;
Comp. Pfizmayer, No. 308.
179 STENT, G. C., Chinese lyrics, J. N. C. B. of the
R. A. S., 1873; separately, Shanghai, 1873, 8vo.
Translated into German verses by Adolf Seu-
bert, Chinesische Gedichte. Leipzig,
1875, 16mo.; in Reclam's Universal bibliothek, No. 738.
179a McCLATCHIE, T., Confucian cosmogony, a translation of sect. XLIX of the complete works of the
philosopher Choo-foo-tze, with explanatory notes.
Shanghai, 1874, 8vo., XVIII, 161 pp.
180 SCARBOROUGH, W., A collection of Chinese proverbs, translated and arranged with an introduc-

tion, notes and copious index. Shanghai, 1875,
XXXVI, 478 pp., 8vo.
> See Chin. Recorder, VI, p. 301.

V. .

Translation.

b. Without Chinese Text.

181 NAVARETTE, F. DE, Spanish translation of the
明心寶鑑 ming-hsin-pau-tshien in his Tradados,
1676.
> See Plath, No. 328.

182 INTORCETTA, P., HERDTRICH, C., ROUGE-
MONT, F., COUPLET, P., Confucius Sinarum
philosophus, sive scientia sinensis latine exposita.
Adjecta est tabula chronologica sinensis monarchiae. Parisiis, 1687, fol.
> Translation of Ta-hsio, Tshung-yung and
> Lun-yü. The appended chronology is
> by Couplet, see No. 909.

183 NOEL, F., Sinensis imperii libri classici sex, nimi-
rum adultorum schola, immutabile medium, liber
sententiarum, Mencius, filialis observantia, parvu-
lorum schola, e sinico idiomate in latinum tra-
ducti. Pragae, 1711, fol.
> This contains a latin translation, besides the
> four books of the Hsiau-tshing and the
> Hsiau-hsio. See Wylie's notes, p. 7,
> p. 68.
> French by Pluquet, Les livres classiques de
> l'empire de la Chine. Paris, 1783-86,
> 7 vols., 16mo.

184 PRÉMARE, J. H., Tchao-chi-cou-culh ou l'Orphelin de la maison de Tchao, tragédie chinoise. Paris, 1755, 12mo.
> Also in Du Halde's Descr., III, p. 339 ; Eng-

lish in Miscell. pieces rel. to China, I, p.
101. Compare Voltaire's versification
of Prémare's translation and Julien's,
No. 244.

185 PERCY, T., Hau kiou chuan or the pleasing
history of Hau kiou. London, 1761, 4 vols.,
8vo.
> Translation of the novel 好 逑 傳 hau-t'shiu-
> tshuan, see Wylie's notes, p. 163.
> German by C. G. von Murr. Leipzig, 1766,
> 8vo.; new edition: Tieh und Pinsing,
> ein chinesischer Familienroman von
> Haoh-kjöh. Bremen, 1869, 8vo.; French
> by Eidous. Lyon, 1766, 4 vols., 12mo.,
> and Paris, 1828, 12mo.; Dutch. Ams-
> terdam, 1767, 12mo.

186 GAUBIL, A., Le Chouking, un des livres sacrés des
Chinois, qui renferme les fondements de leur ancienne histoire. Révu et corrigé par M. de Guignes. Paris, 1770, 4to.
> 1st part, Yü-chong, translated into German,
> as. Magaz., I, p. 455-477.

187 AMIOT, P., Eloge de la ville de Moukden et de ses
environs, poëme composé par Kien-long, empereur de la Chine. Paris, 1770, 8vo.
> See Mém. conc., IX, p. 2; Klaproth, Mém.
> rel. à l'Asie, III, p. 48.

188 — — Art militaire des Chinois, ou recueil d'anciens traités sur la guerre, révu et publié par M.
de Guignes. Paris, 1772, 4to.; 2nd edition, 1782;
also in Mém. conc., VII and VIII, p. 327.
> See Wylie's notes, p. 72, 73.

189 CIBOT, Ta-hsio and Tshung-yung, translated into
French, Mém. conc., I, p. 436, 459, 1776.

190 MAILLA, J. A. M. DE, Histoire générale de la Chine ou annales de cet empire, traduites du Tong-
kien-kang-mou, publiées par M. l'abbé Grosier.
Paris, 1777, 12 vols., 4to.

Translation of the 通鑑綱目 t'ung-tshien-kang-mu, see Wylie's notes, p. 20.

191 LEONTIEF, A., Description of cities, revenue, etc. of the Chinese empire, translated into Russian from the Chinese geography. St. Petersburg, 1778, 8vo.
German in Büsching's Mag., XIV, p. 409-556.

192 — — Sy-chou-gheï to yest tshetyrie knighi (the four books with commentaries from the Chinese and Mantshu.) St. Petersburg, 1780, 8vo. (in Russian.)

193 — — Translation of the statutary rules of the Li-fan-yüan. St. Petersburg, 1790, 8vo. (in Russian.)

194 ROSSOTSCHIN, Altaische Gebirgsbeschreibung aus dem Chinesischen. Pallas, N. Nord. Beitr., I, p. 223, 1781.

195 Hiao king ou livre canonique sur la piété filiale, Mém. conc., IV, p. 28.
See Mém. conc., IX, p. 65; X, p. 145.

196 AGAFONOFF, A., Translation of the Sacred edict. St. Petersburg, 1788, 8vo. (in Russian.)
See Wylie's notes, p. 71.

197 Das Buch des Fo aus der chinesischen Sprache in Samml. as. Originalschr, I. Zürich, 1791. Translated from Deguignes Hist. des Huns.

198 JACQUES, P., Entretiens d'un lettré chinois et d'un docteur Européen sur la vraie idée de Dieu, Lettr. éd. et cur., XXV, p. 143.
See Wylie's notes, p. 138.

199 GRAMMONT, J. DE, Testament de Khanghy, traduit et enrichi de notes, Mag. encyclop. 1799 (A. S.), VI, p. 1-29.

200 Fragmente einer chinesischen Comödie übersetzt, As. Mag., I, p. 91-97, 1802.

201 STAUNTON, Sir G. T., Ta tsing leu lee, being the fundamental laws and a selection from the sup-

plementary statutes of the penal code of China. London, 1810, 4to.

> See E. C. Bridgman, Chin. Repos., II, p. 10; Wylie's notes, p. 57.
>
> French by F. Benouard de St. Croix. Paris, 1812, 2 vols., 8vo.

202 — — Translations from the original Chinese with notes. Canton, 1815, 8vo.

> Contains mostly official documents, 18 despatches from 1795-1805.
>
> Also as appendix to the following work.

203 — — Narrative of the Chinese embassy to the Khan of the Toungouth Tartars, in the years 1772, 73, 74 and 75, by the Chinese ambassador. London, 1821, 8vo.

> See Journal des Savans, 1821, p. 260, and compare P. Gaubil, Mém. conc., II, p. 407; Observ. math., I, p. 148; Müller, Samml. Russ. Gesch., I, p. 327; A. Rémusat, Mél. as., II, p. 413.

204 — — Extracts from Peking gazettes, Transact. of R. A. S., I, part II, p. 254-258; also sep., 1828, 4to.

205 MORRISON, R., Horae sinicae, translations from the popular literature of the Chinese. London, 1812, 8vo.

> Translation of the 三字經 san-tsy-tshing, the 大學 ta-hsio and miscellaneous fragments, republished by Montucci in Parallels.

206 — — On government with sincerity. As. Jour., II, p. 571; IV, p. 377.

207 — — Testament of Kiakhing. Indochin. Gleaner, XV; also As. Journ., XI, p. 525.

> French by Landresse, J. as., I, p. 175-181.

208 — — Translation of a singular proclamation. Transact. R. A. S., I, p. 44, 1824.

209 DAVIS, Sir J. F., San-yü-low, the three dedicated

rooms, a tale translated from the Chinese. Canton, 1815, 8vo.

Also in Sir J. F. Davis, Chinese novels, No. 211.

French in A. Rémusat, Contes chinois, No. 219.

210 — — Lao-seng-urh, or an heir in his old age, a Chinese drama. London, 1817, 12mo.

French in A. Rémusat, Contes chinois, No. 219.

See A. Rémusat, Mél. as., II, p. 320.

Translated from the 元人百種曲 Yüan-jen pai-tshung-t'shü, see Wylie's notes, p. 206.

211 — — Chinese novels, translated from the originals, to which are added proverbs and moral maxims, collected from their classical books and other sources. London, 1822, 8vo.

Contains: The shadow in the water, The twin sisters, The three dedicated chambers.

French in A. Rémusat, Contes chinois, No. 219.

See A. Rémusat, Mél. as., II, p. 335.

212 — — The fortunate union, a romance with notes; Han-koong-tsew, or the sorrows of Han, a Chinese tragedy. London, 1829, 2 vols., 8vo.

French by Guillard d'Arcy. Paris, 1842, 8vo. The novel is a translation of the 好逑傳 Hau-t'shiu-tshuan, see Wylie's notes, p. 163; compare the translation of the same novel by Percy (No. 185.) The tragedy is taken from the 元人百種曲 Yüan-jen pai-tshung t'shü, see Wylie's notes, p. 206.

See Klaproth, J., Réponse à quelques passages de la préface du roman chinois Hao-khicou-tchouan traduit par J. F. Davis. Paris, 1830, 8vo.

213 RÉMUSAT, A., Le livre des récompenses et des
peines, avec des notes et des éclaircissements.
Paris, 1816, 8vo.
> Retranslated by S. Julien, No. 157.

214 — — Description du royaume de Camboge, par
un voyageur chinois, précédé d'une notice chronologique sur le même pays, extraite des annales de
la Chine. Paris, 1819, 8vo.
> Translation of the 眞臘風土記 tshen-la-feng
> t'u-tshi, see Wylie's notes, p. 47.
> Also in Nouv. Annales des voy., III, and in
> Nouv. Mél. as., II.

215 — — Histoire de la ville de Khotan, tirée des
annales de la Chine. Paris, 1820, 8vo.

216 — — Relation de l'expédition d'Hou langou au
travers de la Tartarie, traduite du chinois. Nouv.
Mél. as., I, p. 171.

217 — — Sur quelques peuples du Tibet et de la
Boukharie, traduit du Ma Touan-lin; ibid, I, p. 186.

218 — — Ju-kiao-li ou les deux cousines, roman chinois. Paris, 1826, 2 vols., 12mo.
> See S. Julien's translation of the same novel,
> No. 256.

219 — — Contes chinois, traduits par M. M. Davis,
Thoms, le P. d'Entrecolles, etc., publiés par A.
Rémusat. Paris, 1827, 3 vols., 16mo.
> In German, Leipzig, 1827, 8vo.

220 — — Foe-koue-ki ou relation des royaumes bouddhiques, voyage dans la Tartarie, etc.; ouvrage
posthume revu, complété et augmenté par J. Klaproth et Landresse. Paris, 1836, 4to.
> The original is the 佛國記 Fo-kuo-tshi, see
> Wylie's notes, p. 46.
> English by J. W. Laidley. Calcutta, 1848,
> 8vo.; also in Charton's voyageurs anc.
> et mod., I, 1862.
> See H. W. Sykes in Journ. of R. A. S., VI,
> 1841.

J. as., IX, p. 317, and A. Rémusat, Histoire de Khotan, p. 11.

221 FRESNEL, F., Hoa-thou-youen-tchouen ou histoire de la caste peinte, roman en seize livres. J. as., 1e. sér., I, p. 202; III, p. 129.
Only translation of the first two chapters.

222 MILNE, W. C., The sacred edict. London, 1817, 8vo.; 2nd ed., Shanghai, 1870, 8vo.
Translation of the 聖 諭 廣 訓 Sheng-yü-kuang-hsün, see Wylie's notes, p. 71.
See Chin. Repos., I, p. 297; A. Rémusat, Mél. as., II, p. 311-319.

223 THOMS, P. P., The affectionate pair or the history of Sung-kin, a Chinese tale. London, 1820, 8vo.
French in A. Rémusat, Contes chinois, No. 219.

224 BARGINET, A., Histoire véritable de Tcheu Tcheou-li, mandarin lettré. Paris, 1822, 8vo.

225 LIPOFZOFF, E., History of the Ming dynasty, translated into Russian. St. Petersburg, 1823, 2 vols., 8vo.
See J. as., II, p. 251.

226 — — Institutions of the Li-fan-yüan. St. Petersburg, 1824, 4to. (in Russian.)

227 SCHOTT, W., Werke des tschinesischen Weisen Kung-fu-dsü und seiner Schüler. Halle, 1826, 8vo., and Berlin, 1832, 8vo.
See J. Klaproth, Dr. W. Schott's vorgebliche Uebersetzung der Werke des Confucius aus der Ursprache. Leipzig, 1828, 8vo.; C. Landresse, Réflexions sur l'ouvrage intitulé Werke, etc. Paris, 1828, 8vo.

228 COLLIE, D., The Chinese classical works, commonly called the four books. Malacca, 1828.

229 KLAPROTH, J., Fookoua siriak ou traité sur l'origine des richesses du Japon, traduit du chinois. Paris, 1828, 8vo.

230 — — Description de la Russie, traduite du chinois, Mém. rel. à l'Asie, I.

231 — — Description du Tubet, traduite du chinois en russe par le p. Hyacinthe et du russe en français par M...., soigneusement revue et corrigée sur l'original chinois. Paris, 1831, 8vo.

> See Wylie's notes, p. 52, and Hyacinthe's original translation, No. 233.

232 — — Aperçu général des trois royaumes, traduit du Japonais-chinois. Paris, 1832, 8vo.

233 HYACINTHE BITCHOURIN, Opissanie tibeta w nynieshnem yewo sostoyanii (description of Tibet in its actual state.) St. Petersburg, 1828, 8vo., with map and a coloured lithograph of the great buddhist temple at Hlassa (in Russian.)

> Translation of the 衛藏圖識 wei-tsang-t'u-tshy, see Wylie's notes, p. 52, and Klaproth, No. 231.

234 — — Opissanie pekina i yewo okrestnostei (Description of Peking and its environs.) St. Petersburg, 1829, 8vo., with plan (in Russian.)

> Translation of part of the 宸垣識畧 t'shen-yüan-tshy-lio.
> French by Ferry de Pigny. St. Petersburg, 1829, 8vo., 175 pp.

235 — — Istoriya pervykh tshetyrokh khanu iz doma Tsingissova (History of the first four Khans of the house of Chinghiskhan.) St. Petersburg, 1829, 8vo., 440 pp.

> The first three chapters of the *Yüan-shy* and the *Kang-mu*.

236 — — Opissanie djungarii i vostotshnova turkestan w drevnëm i nyneishnëm sostoyanii (Description of Dsungaria and oriental Turkestan in their old and modern state.) St. Petersburg, 8vo., 270 pp. (in Russian.)

> Translation of the 西域聞見錄 hsi-yü-wen-tshien-lu, see Wylie's notes, p. 52.

237 — — Istoriya tibeta i khukhunora (History of Tibet and Kukunoor.) St. Petersburg, 1835, 2 vols., 8vo., 516 pp., with map (in Russian.)
>Translated from the Chinese, to the year 1227.

238 BROSSET, Relation du pays de Ta-ouan. Paris, 1829, 8vo.

239 KIDD, S., The thousand character classic. Malacca, 1829.
>Supplement to the report of the Anglo-Chinese college.

240 LACHARME, P., Confucii Chi-king sive liber carminum. Ex latina P. Lacharmi interpretatione edidit J. Mohl. Stuttgartiae et Tubingae, 1830, 8vo.
>German: F. Rückert, Schi-king, chinesische Lieder gesammelt von Confucius. Altona, 1838, 8vo.; Gesammelte Werke, Vol. VI.
>J. Cramer, Schi-king oder chinesische Lieder. Crefeld, 1844, 8vo.

241 JULIEN, S., Thse-hiong-hiong-ti ou les deux frères de sexe différent, nouvelle traduite du chinois. Paris, 1830, 4to.
>Also as appendix to L'orphelin de la Chine (No. 244), p. 263, and in Les Avadanas (No. 253), Vol. III, p. 175.

242 — — Teng-ta-yin-kuei-touan-kia-sse, nouvelle. Gazette littéraire de 9, 16, et 23 Déc. 1830.

243 — — Hoeï-lan-ki ou l'histoire du cercle du craie, drame en prose et en vers. London, 1832, 8vo.

244 — — Tchao-chi-kou-eul ou l'orphelin de la Chine, drame en prose et en vers. Paris, 1834, 8vo.
>Contains also La mort de Tong-tcho (from the San-kuo-tshy); Hing-lo-tou ou la peinture mystérieuse; Tse-hiong-hiong-ti (No. 241); and Poésies chinoises, all to be found in Les Avadanas, No. 253.
>Compare Prémare, No. 184.

245 — — Blanche et Bleue ou les deux couleuvres-fées, roman chinois. Paris, 1834, 8vo.

246 — — Résumé des principaux traités chinois sur la culture des muriers et l'éducation des vers à soie. Paris, 1837, 8vo.

    German by F. L. Lindner, Stuttgart und Tübingen, 1837, 8vo.; 2nd ed., 1844, 8vo.; Italian by M. Bonafous, Torino, 1837, 8vo.; English, Washington, 1838, 8vo.; Russian, St. Petersburg, 1840; Greek, Paris, 1847, 8vo.

    See E. Reichenbach, Ueber Seidenraupenzucht in China München, 1867, 8vo.; Isid. dell'Oro, L'educazione dei bachida seta. Milano, 1870, 16mo.

    See Wylie's notes, p. 76.

247 — — Tao-ssé ou le livre de la pureté et de la tranquillité.

    See Jaquet, J. as., déc. 1837, p. 544-599; Julien's reply, ibid, Mars 1838, p. 259-297.

248 — — Notices sur les pays et les peuples étrangers, tirées des géographies et des annales chin., J. as., 4e. sér., VIII, p. 228, p. 385; IX, p. 50, p. 189; X, p. 81.

249 — — Voyages des pélérins bouddhiques, vol. I: histoire de la vie de Hiouen-Thsang et de ces voyages dans l'Inde. Paris, 1853, 8vo.

    Vol. II and III, Mémoires sur les contrées occidentales. Paris, 1856-58, 2 vols., 8vo.

    See Wylie's notes, p. 46.

    Appendix to Vol. III, Vivien de St. Martin, Mémoire analytique sur la carte de l'Asie centrale et de l'Inde, construite d'après le Si-yu-ki et les autres relations des premiers siècles de notre ère pour les voyages de Hiouen-Thsang. Avec une carte. Paris, 1858.

Reviews : Hoffmann, Tijdschrift voor de taal-
land-en volkenkunde, 1854; J. of R. A.
S., XVI, London, 1856; A. Schiefner,
Mél. as., II. St. Petersburg, 1856; Baron d'Eckstein, J. as., 5e. série, X., 1857;
Max Müller, Buddhism and buddhist
pilgrims, Times, April 17 and 20, 1857;
also in Chips I, p. 232; H. H. Wilson, J.
of R. A. S., XVII, London, 1860; L. de
Rosny, Hiouen-Thsang, moine boud-
dhiste, Variétés Orientales, Paris, 1868.
Compare: W. Anderson, An attempt to iden-
tify some of the places mentioned in the
itinerary of Hiouen-Thsang, J. of R. A.
S. of Beng., XVI. Calcutta, 1847.
M. Kittoe, Notes on places in the province of
Behar, supposed to be those described
by Chy Fa-hian; ibid, XVI.
A. Cunningham, Verification of the itinerary
of the Chinese pilgrim Hiouen-Thsang
through Afganistan and India; ibid,
XVII, 1848.
— — Verification of the itinerary of Hiouen-Thsang through Asia and India,
ibid.
J. Fergusson, On Hiouen-Thsang's journey
from Patna to Balabbi, J. of R. A. S., n.
s., VI, part 2. London, 1873.
H. YULE, Hwen-Thsang's account of the
principalities of Tokhoristan, etc., ibid.
250 — — La visite de l'esprit du foyer à Ju-kong.
Paris, 1854, 8vo.
Reprint of one of the legends of No. 157; also
in Les Avadanas, No. 253, vol. II, p. 193.
251 — — Histoire et fabrication de la porcelaine chinoise. Ouvrage traduit du chinois. Accompagné
de notes et d'additions par M. A. Salvétat et augmenté d'un mémoire sur la porcelaine du Japon,

traduit du japonais par J. Hoffmann. Paris, 1856,
8vo., 320 pp. Carte de la Chine indiquant l'em-
placement des manufactures de porcelaine anciennes et modernes, 14 planches.

>Translation of the Tshing-te-tshen T'au-lu
in 4 vols.

252 — — Notice historique de Ma Touen-lin sur
l'Inde, J. as., X; also in Mél. géogr.

253 — — Les Avadanas, contes et apologues indiens
inconnus jusqu'à ce jour; suivis de fables, de
poésies et de nouvelles chinoises. Paris, 1859,
3 vols., 16mo., published with the title: apologues indiens traduits sur une ancienne version
chinoise, Revue orient. et am., I, p. 20; III, p.
416; IV, p. 461; V, p. 306.

>Vol. III also in the librairie Hachette. The
appendix the same as in Tchao-chi-kou-
eul, No. 244.

>The avadanas are translated from the cyclo-
paedia Yü-lin, see No. 748.

254 — — Les deux jeunes filles lettrées, roman chinois. Paris, 1860, 2 vols., 12mo.

>The original is 平山冷燕 ping-shan-leng-
yen, see Wylie's notes, p. 163.

255 — — Si-siang-ki ou l'histoire du pavillon d'occident, Comédie-opéra en 16 actes. Paris, 1861,
8vo.

>The first seven acts also in l'Europe littérai-
re, the whole reprinted in Atsume gusa,
recueil publié par F. Turretini, the Chinese text of the poetical part is given.

256 — — Yu-kiao-li ou Les deux cousines, roman
chinois. Paris, 1864, 2 vols., 12mo.

>See A. Rémusat, No. 218, Wylie's notes, p.
163.

>For a vocabulary of difficult expressions
found in this novel, see Julien's syntaxe
nouvelle, vol. II.

257 — — Documents historiques sur les, Tou-kioue
(Turcs) extraits du Pien-i-tien, J. as., 6 sér., III,
p. 325, 490; IV, p. 242, 391-430; also Paris,
1864, 8vo.
> German, Ausland, 1866, No. 12, p. 283, ss.

258 NEUMANN, K. F., History of the pirates who in-
fested the Chinese sea from 1807 to 1810. London, 1831, 8vo.

259 — — Translations from the Chinese and Arme-
nian. London, 1831, 8vo.

260 — — Catechism of the Shamans or the laws and
regulations of the priesthood of Buddha in China.
London, 1831, 8vo.
> German in Zeitschr. für hist. Theol., IV,
> 1834.
> See J. R. Morrison, Ch. Repos., I, p. 285.

261 — — Pilgerfahrten buddhistischer Priester nach
Indien. Berlin, 1833, 8vo.
> Translation of the 5th chapter of the Lo-yang
> t'shia-lan-tshi, see Wylie's notes, p. 44;
> see also Beal, No. 347.
> English by C. G. Leland. London, 1874, 8vo.

262 — — Mexico im 5 Jahrh. unserer Zeitrechnung
nach chinesischen Quellen. München, 1845, 8vo.
> See W. Schott, Berl. Jahrb. f. wiss. Krit.,
> 1845; J. Am. Or. Soc., I, p. 332.

263 SLADE, J., Record of the pacification of the seas.
Canton register, XI, No. 8.

264 PAUTHIER, G., Mémoire sur l'origine et la propagation de la doctrine du Tao, trad. du chinois.
Paris, 1831, 8vo.

265 — — Notice sur l'ile de Ceylon, J. as., Avril,
1836.
> See Julien, Lettre à M. le rédacteur du jour-
> nal asiatique. Paris, 1836.

266 — — Les livres sacrés de l'Orient, comprenant le
Chouking, les Sse-chou. les lois de Menou et le
Koran. Paris, 1840, fol.

267 — • — Examen de faits qui concernent le Thian-tchou ou l'Inde, traduits du Wen-hien-thong-khao. Paris, 1840, 8vo.

See Wylie's notes, p. 55.

See Julien, Examen critique de quelques pages de chinois relative à l'Inde, traduites par G. Pauthier. Paris, 1841.

268 — — Confucius et Mencius, les quatre livres de philosophie morale et politique de la Chine. Paris, 1841, 8vo.

German by J. Cramer. Crefeld, 1844, 8vo.

269 — — Documents statistiques et officiels sur l'empire de la Chine, traduits du Chinois. Paris, 1841, 8vo.

270 — — Documents officiels chinois sur les ambassades étrangères envoyées près de l'empereur de la Chine. Paris, 1843, 8vo.

271 — — Histoire des relations politiques de la Chine, avec les puissances occidentales, depuis les temps les plus anciens jusqu'à nos jours. Paris, 1859, 8vo.

272 — — Proclamations du mandarin Ye et du vice-roi Ho, ordonnant la liberté du culte catholique en Chine. Paris, 1860, 8vo.

273 — — Mémoire secret adressé à l'empereur Hien-foung, actuellement regnant, par un lettré chinois, sur la conduite à suivre avec les puissances européennes. Paris, 1860, 8vo.

274 — — Cérémoniel observé dans les fêtes et les grandes réceptions à la cour de Koubilaï-khan, trad. du chinois, Revue de l'Orient, XIV, 1862, p. 224.

See E. C. Bowra, Notes and Queries, I, p. 101.

275 — — Relation du voyage de Kieou dans l'Asie centrale, trad. du chinois, J. as., 1867.

276 — — Voyage de Tchang-tchun-tseu à la Mongolie occidentale, J. as., 6 sér., IX, p. 39-86.

277 — — et St. Denys, Marquis H. de, Bibliothèque
orientale : chefs d'oeuvres littéraires de l'Inde, de
la Perse, de l'Egypte et de la Chine. Paris, 1872,
2 vols, 8vo.
Contains a translation of the Shiking.

278 BRIDGMAN, E. C., Translation of the San-tze-
king, Chin. Repos., IV, p. 105.

279 — — Tsien-tze-wen or Thousand character classic, ibid, IV, p. 229.

280 — — Translation of the Odes for children, ibid,
IV, p. 287.

281 — — Translation of the Hiau-king or filial duty,
ibid, IV, p. 344.

282 — — Translation of the part I and II of the Siau-
hioh or primary lessons, ibid, V, p. 81, 305 ; VI,
p. 185, 393, 562.
See Wylie's notes, p. 68.

283 Chinese account of India, translated from the Wan-
hien-thung-kaou by Ma-touen-lin, J. of A. S. of
Beng., VI, 1837.

284 BAZIN, A., Théatre chinois ou choix de pièces de
théatre composées sous les empereurs mongols,
trad. pour la premièrefois. Paris, 1838, 8vo.
Translation of four pieces taken from the collection Yüan-jen pai-tshung-t'shü, see
Wylie's notes, p. 206.
See S. W. Williams, Chin. Repos., XVIII, p.
113, with an English translation of the
2nd piece. An extract is given in the
Ch. and Jap. Repos., I, April 1864.
Compare A. Bazin, le siècle des Youen, No.
715.

285 — — Le Pi-pa-ki ou l'histoire du luth, drame
chinois. Paris, 1841, 8vo.

286 REGIS, P., Y-king, antiquissimus Sinarum liber
quem ex latina interpretatione P. Regis aliorum-
que ex soc. J. P. P. edidit J. Mohl. Stuttgartiae
et Tubingae, 1839. 2 vols.. 8vo.

287 PAVIE, T., Choix de contes et nouvelles, trad. du
chinois. Paris, 1839, 8vo.
> Translation of seven histories taken from the
> Tshin-ku-tshi-kuan, Lung-tu-kung-an
> and Hsi-yü-tshi, see G. T. Olyphant,
> Chin. Repos., XX, p. 225.

288 — — San-koué-tchy, Ilan kouroun i pithé. Histoire des trois royaumes, roman historique traduit
sur les textes chinois et mandchou. Paris, 1845-
51, 2 vols., 8vo.
> These 2 vols. only extend to the 44th chap-
> ter, see Wylie's notes, p. 161.

289 WILLIAMS, S. W., Translation of a ballad on pick-
ing tea, Chin. Repos., VIII, p. 195.

290 SLOTH, (THOM, R.), Lasting resentment of Miss
Wang-kiaou-lwan, a Chinese tale. Canton, 1839,
8vo.
> German by A. Böttger, Wang-kiaou-loan oder
> die blutige Rache einer jungen Frau.
> Leipzig, 1847, 8vo.
> See E. C. Bridgman, Chin. Repos., VIII, p.
> 54. Taken from the collection Tshin-ku-
> tshi-kuan in 12 vols.

291 HOFFMANN, J., Tsiän dsü wen oder Buch von
1000 Wörtern, aus dem Chinesischen mit Berücksichtigung der Koraischen und Japanischen Uebersetzung ins Deutsche übertragen. Leiden,
1840, 4to.

292 BIOT, E., Traduction et examen d'un ancien ouvrage chinois intitulé Tchcou-pei, J. as.: Juin, 1841.
> See Wylie's notes, p. 86.

293 — — Tchou-chou-ki-nien ou tablettes chronologiques du livre écrit sur bambou, J. as., 4 sér.,
XVIII, p. 186. Paris, 1842.
> See Wylie's notes, p. 19.

294 — — Le Tchou-li ou rites des Tchou, tableau
des institutions et de l'état social de la Chine.
Paris, 1851, 2 vols.. 8vo.

See Wylie's notes, p. 4.

295 S...., J. L., Sketch of Kwanyin, the Chinese goddess of mercy, translated from the Sow shinke, Chin., Repos., X, p. 185, 1841-42.

296 Kin-shen, The rambles of the emperor Ching-tih in Kiang-nan, with a preface by J. Legge. London, 1843, 2 vols., 8vo.

297 LAMIOT, L., Description de la province chinoise de Sse-tchouen, traduite et résumée du Tay-tsing-tong-tchy. Paris, s. a., 8vo.

298 — — Esquisse du Sy-yu ou des pays à l'ouest de la Chine, traduite et résumée du chinois. Paris, 1852, 8vo.

299 GUTZLAFF, K., Sprüche und Erzählungen aus dem chinesischen Hausschatze. Ztschr. d. D. M. G., XVI, p. 628.

300 — — Pamphlets published by the insurgents, ibid, VII, p. 628.

301 LOWRIE, W. M., Readings in Chinese poetry, translation of 2 odes from the Shi-king, Chin. Repos., XVI, p. 454.

302 MEDHURST, W. H. (sen.), The Chinaman abroad or a desultory account of the Malayan archipelago. Shanghai, 1849, 8vo.

Chinese miscell., No. 2; Wylie's notes, p. 53.

303 — — Dissertation on the silk manufacture and the culture of the mulberry. Shanghai, 1849, 8vo.

Chinese miscell., No. 3; Wylie's notes, p. 76.

304 — — General description of Shanghai and its environs. Shanghai, 1850, 8vo.

Translation of the principal matters in the Shang-hai hsien-tshy, Ch. miscell, No. 4.

305 — — Translations from the Peking gazettes during the years 1853-56. Shanghai, 1858, 8vo.

Appeared first in N. C. Herald and afterwards in successive volumes of the Shanghai almanac for 1854-57.

306 WADE, T. F., Japan, a chapter from the Hac-kwoh-t'u chi or illustrated notice of countries beyond the seas. Hongkong, 1850, 8vo.
Also in Chin. Repos., XIX, p. 135, 206.

307 HILLIER, C. B., Translation of the Ta-heo classic, the great lesson of life, Transact. of C. B. of R. A. S. Hongkong, 1851, III, p. 11-21.

308 PFIZMAYER, A., Das Li-sao und die neun Gesänge. Zwei chinesische Dichtungen aus dem 3. Jahrhundert vor der christl. Zeitr. Wien, 1852, fol.
Translation of the first 2 poems of the Tsu-sy, see Wylie's notes, p. 181.

309 — — Gedichte aus der Sammlung der 10,000 Blätter. Wien, 1872, 4to.

310 — — Denkwürdigkeiten von den Früchten Chinas. Sitzb. K. K. Ak. d. Wiss., Wien, hist. phil. Kl., 1874, No. 21.

311 — — Denkwürdigkeiten von den Insekten Chinas, ibid, No. 26-29.

312 BOWRING, Sir J. C., Stanzas from the Chinese, Chin. Repos., XX, p. 299, p. 433.

313 — — Hwa Tsien Ki, the flowery scroll, a Chinese novel. London, 1868, 8vo.
See Notes and Queries, III, p. 15; Saturday Review, Nov. 1869.
This is only a translation from the Dutch of G. Schlegel.

314 GINGELL, W. R., The ceremonial usages of the Chinese, B. C. 1121, as described in the "Institutes of the Chow dynasty strung as pearls." London, 1852, 107 pp., 4to.
See Wylie's notes, p. 4.

315 EDKINS, J., Tseay-heue, the borrowed boots, in Chinese conversations, Shanghai, 1852, p. 1; also in China Review, II, p. 325-332.
From the collection of dramatical pieces tshui-pai-t'shin, see Wylie's notes, p. 206.

316 — — A buddhist shastra, translated from the
Chinese, with an analysis and notes, J. of S'hai
lit. soc., p. 107-128, 1858.
>The Chinese name of this abidharma is yi-
shu-lu-ka-lun, see Wylie's notes, p.
165.
317 WYLIE, A., Translation of the T'sing wan k'i
mung, a Chinese grammar of the Mandshu tartar
language. Shanghai, 1855, 8vo.
>See also under XVI, Mandshu.
318 MALAN, S. C., The threefold San-tze-king or the
triliteral classic of China, as issued, 1, by Wang-
po-keou; 2, by protestant missionaries in that
country; and 3, by the rebel-chief Tae-ping.
London, 1856, 8vo.
319 ROSNY, L. DE, Le livre de la recompense des bien
faits secrets. Paris, 1856, 8vo; and in Annales
de philosophie chrétienne, 4 sér, XIV.
>See Wylie's notes, p. 180.
320 — — Notices sur les îles de l'Asie orientale, extrait des ouvrages chinois et japonais. Paris,
1861, 8vo.
321 — — Extraits du Ti-tou-tsoung-yao relatifs aux
peuples étrangers de la Chine, Mém. de la soc.
d'ethnogr., 1873, map.
322 — — San-tsai-tou-hoci, Les peuples de l'Indo-
chine et des pays voisins, notices ethnographi-
ques trad. du chinois, Act. de la soc. d'ethnogr.,
VI, 1874; also Poissy, 1875, 8vo.
323 ZWETKOFF, P., The inscription of Si-an-fu.
Russ. Eccles. mission, III, No. 8, 1857 (in Russian.)
324 ST. DÉNYS, Marquis d'H de, Poésies de l'époque
des Thang, trad. du chinois, avec une étude sur
l'art poétique en Chine. Paris, 1862, 8vo.
>Part of the ku t'ang shy, Wylie's notes, p.
195.
325 — — Ethnographie des peuples étrangers de

Ma-touan-lin, trad. du Chinois. In "Atsume
Gusa," recueil publ. par F. Turretini. Génève,
1872, 4to., fasc. 1 and 2.

326 BIRCH, S., Chinese romance, the Elfin Fox, Ch.
and Jap. Repos., I, Sept. 1863.

327 — — The casket of gems, The Phoenix, I, 69,
88, 105; also, London, 1872, 8vo.

328 PLATH, J. H., Proben chinesischer Weisheit, nach
dem Chinesischen des Ming-sin-pao-tsien. München, 1863, 8vo.

329 GRIJS, C. F. M. DE, Geregteliike Geneeskunde.
Verh. Batav. Gen. van Kunsten en Wetensch.,
Vol. XXX. Batavia, 1863.
          Translation of hsi-yüan-lu on medical juris-
          prudence, Wylie's notes, p. 75.

330 Lui-fung-ta, Thunder-peak pagoda or the story of
Han-wan and the white serpent, Ch. and Jap.
Repos., I, Feb. 1864.

331 DELAMARRE, l'abbé, Histoire de la dynastie des
Ming, composée par l'empereur Khianloong, trad.
du Chinois. Paris, 1865, 4to., 1st vol.
          Continuation to Mailla's history, No. 190.

332 AUBARET, Histoire et description de bas Cochinchine, trad. du texte chinois. Paris, 1865, 8vo.

333 PALLADIUS, O., Ancient mongol narrative of the
life of Chinghizkhan, translated from the Yüan-
t'shan pi-shy, Russ. Eccl. mission, IV, No. 1,
1866 (in Russian.)
          See Chin. Recorder, V, p. 193, note 3.

334 — — Si-yü-ki, journey of the buddhist monk
Chang-chun to the west; ibid, No. 2 (in Russian.)

335 — — Translation of the diary of Cheng Tchui,
1248, in Records of Sib. B. of J. R. Geogr. S.
Irkutsk, 1867, X, XI, p. 582 (in Russian.)

336 — — The journey of the Chinese traveller Chang-
te-hui from Peking to the summer residence of
Kublai in western Mongolia in 1248; ibid, 1874
(in Russian.)

English by E. Schuyler, Geogr. Magazine, Jan. 1875.

337 — — Ancient Chinese narrative of the life of Chinghiskhan, translated from the Chinese Tshin-tsheng-lu, Oriental Magazine, I, No. 3, 1872 (in Russian.)
See Chin. Recorder, VI, p. 90, note 4.

338 CHALMERS, J., Translations from Chinese poetry, Notes and Queries I, p. 54; II, p. 8; China Review, I, p. 50, p. 199, p. 322, p. 393; II, p. 50.

339 — — The speculations of the old philosopher. London, 1868, 8vo.
Translation of the Tau-té-tshing, see Wylie's notes, p. 173; Notes and Queries, II, p. 143.
Compare Julien, No. 158.

340 — — Confucian cosmogony, China Review, III, p. 342-351.

341 Etiquette to be observed by officials in mutual intercourse, as prescribed and sanctioned by imperial authority, Notes and Queries, I, p. 23, p. 36, p. 68.

342 EITEL, E. J., Hiüeh pên king, translated; Ibid, II, 1868.

343 BOWRA, E. C., The dream of the red chamber, The China Magazine, Christmas vol., 1868, p. 1, 3, 33, 65, 97, 129; 1869, p. 1, 33, 65.
Translation of the first eight chapters of the Hung-lou-meng.

344 EVANS, E., Yuk-noo, the round head's daughter, a romance of 1600 years ago; Ibid, 1868, 5, p. 17, p. 37.

345 History of the Southern Sung, A translation, Chin. Recorder, I, p. 46, 103, 137, 160, 207, 229.

346 LEGGE, J., Chinese Classics, translated into English with preliminary essays and explanatory notes. Vol. I : The life and teachings of Confucius. London, 1869, 8vo.

Vol. II : The life and works of Mencius. London, 1875, 8vo.
See Ausland, 1876, No. 5, p. 93-95.

347 BEAL, S., The travels of the buddhist pilgrims Fah-hian and Sung-yun. London, 1869, 8vo.
The first part is a translation of the Fo-kuo-ki (comp. A. Rémusat, No. 220); the second part the same work as Neumann, No. 261.

348 — — A catena of buddhist scriptures from the Chinese. London, 1871, 8vo.
See the Phœnix, I, p. 222.

349 — — The sutra of 42 sections, J. of R. A. S., XIX, p. 337.
See Wylie's Notes, p. 163.

350 — — The diamond sutra ; Ibid, n. ser., I, p. 1.
See Wylie's Notes, p. 164.

351 — — The great paramitra heart sutra; Ibid, p. 25.
See Wylie's Notes, p. 164.

352 — — The amithaba sutra ; Ibid, II, p. 136.
See Wylie's Notes, p. 164.

353 — — The legend of Dipankara Buddha, translated from the Chinese ; Ibid, VI, 1873.

354 — — The romantic history of Sakya Buddha, translated from the Sanskrit into Chinese by Dju-anakuta, and from the Chinese into English. London, 1874, 8vo.

355 STRAUSS, V. von, Lao-Tsè's Taò Te King, Aus dem Chinesischen in's Deutsche übersetzt. Leipsig, 1870, 8vo.

356 — — Lieder des Schiking. Neue Monatsschrift f. Dichtk. u. Kritik Berlin, April, 1875.

357 PERNY, P., Proverbes chinois. Paris, 1870, 12mo.

358 Deathblow to corrupt doctrines, translated from the Chinese. Shanghai, 1870, 8vo.
Translation of a paper circulated against missionaries, see Chin. Recorder, III, p. 254.

359 The three brothers, a Chinese tale from the 11th century, China Mag., IV, 1870.

360 PLAENCKNER, R. von, Lao-tse Tao-te-king, der Weg zur Tugend. Leipzig, 1870, 8vo.

361 — — Confucius Ta-hio, die erhabene Wissenschaft, aus dem Chinesischen übersetzt und erklärt. Leipzig, 1874, XX, 358 pp., gr. 8vo.
See Lit. Centralbl., 1874.

362 No Cha, a Chinese fairy tale, China Mag., IV, p. 27, 1870.

363 WATTERS, T., Discourse on heresy by a Chinese emperor, Chin. Recorder, IV, p. 226.

364 PUINI, C., Novelle cinesi tolte dal Lung-tu-kung-ngan e tradotte sull' originalle cinese. Piacenza, 1871, 8vo.
Seven novels from the Lung-tu-kung-an, two of which were published 1867 in the Rivista orientale, Firenze.

365 CAROLL, C., A cure for jealousy, The Phoenix, I, p. 35, 55, 87, 112, 146, 184, 214; II, p. 5, 21, 39.

366 MacCARTEE, D. B., Translation of the inscription upon a stone tablet, J. N. C. B. of R. A. S. Shanghai, 1871, p. 173.

367 The adventures of a Chinese giant, China Review, I, p. 13, 71, 144, 220.

368 LISTER, A., A Chinese farce with an introduction; Ibid, I, p 26.

369 — — Rhymes from Chinese; Ibid, I, p. 96.

370 WODEHOUSE, H. E., Mr. Wade on China, an unpublished state paper (translation); Ibid, I, p. 38, 118.

371 (FAY, Miss L. M.), The marriage of the emperor of China, translated from the official programme. Shanghai, 1872, 16mo.

372 Eulampius, Memoir of a Chinese on Annam, 1835, translated from the Chinese Oriental Mag., I, No. 2, 1872 (in Russian).

373 A translation of the Peking gazette for 1872. Shanghai, 1873, 8vo ; the same for 1873, 1874, 8vo.; 1874, 1875, 8vo.; for 1875 with complete index and genealogical table of the imperial family of China. Shanghai, 1876, 8vo.

Appeared first in the North China Daily News.

374 BOEHM, G., Chinesische Lieder aus dem livre de jade von Judith Mendès. München, 1873, 16mo.

375 ALLEN, C. F. R., The young prodigy, a translation, China Review, II, p. 21-29, 65-74, 133-144, 197-206, 261.

376 — — Tales from the Liao-chai-chih-yi ; Ibid, II, p. 364-369 ; III, p. 18-23, 99-107, 142-149, 205-219, 284-293.

377 BROWN, Sei-yo-ki-bun, annals of Western Ocean, J. N. C. B. of R. A. S., III, p. 40-62.

378 MOULE, E. G., The obligations of China to Europe in the matter of physical science, acknowledged by eminent Chinese, being extracts from the preface of Tseng Kwo-fan's edition of Euclid, J. of N. C. B. of R. A. S., VII, p. 147.

379 STENT, G. C., Fanning the grave and the wife tested. Shanghai, 1873, 8vo.

See China Review I, p. 395.

380 — — Jên-kuei's Return, a play. Shanghai, 1873, 8vo.

381 — — The Azalea (ballad), translated. China Review, II, p. 80-88.

382 — — The Jade chaplet in 24 beads, a collection of some ballads, etc. from Chinese. London, 1874. 8vo.

See Lit. Centralbl., 1875, No. 1.

383 — — Mêng-chêng's journey to the great wall (ballad), China Review, III, p. 114-119, 149-158.

384 — — Death and funeral of Mr. Locust ; Ibid, p. 312-316.

385 — — The lamentations and death of Ch'ung-chen ; Ibid, IV, p. 294-296.

386 GARDNER, C. T., Translation of an inscription on a tablet at Hangchow, J. of N. C. B. of R. A. S., IV, p. 21-32.

387 POPOFF, P. S., The Tsung si ki lio translated into Russian.

388 GILES, H. A., The San-tzŭ-ching or three character classic, and the Ch'ien-tzŭ-wên or thousand character essay, metrically translated. Shanghai, 1873, 8vo.
See China Review, I, p. 394.

389 — — A thousand character essay, China Review, II, p. 182-185.

390 A translation of examination papers given at Wu-ch'ang, China Review, II, p. 309-314.

391 TURRETINI, F., Histoire des Taira, tirée du Nit-Pon Gwai-si, traduite du Chinois. Génève, 1875, II, 89 pp., 4to.

392 ARENDT, C., Das schöne Mädchen von Pao. Eine Erzählung aus der Geschichte Chinas im 8. Jahrh. Mitth. d. Deutschen Ges. f. Ostas. 8. Heft Sept. 1875, Yokohama. Extrabeilage fol.
From the Tung-tshou-lie-kuo-tshy, see Wylie's Notes, p. 162.

393 WEBSTER, A., Yu-pe-ya's lute. London, 1875, 8vo.
Chinese tales in English verse, see China Review, III, p. 184-186.

394 McCLATCHIE, T., A translation of the Confucian I-king or Classic of change, with notes and appendix. Shanghai, 1876, 8vo.

VI.

Philological Treatises.

395 WEBB, S., Historical essay on the probability that the language of the empire of China is the primitive language. London, 1669, 8vo.

396 MUELLER, A., Oratio dominica sinice et monumenti sinici quod A. D. 1625 in ipsa China erutum descriptio. Berolini, 1672, 4to.
397 — — Hebdomas observationum de rebus sinicis. Brandenburgiae, 1674, 4to.
398 — — Unschuld gegen die heftigen Beschuldigungen. Stettin, 1683, 4to.
399 — — De invento sinico, 4to.
400 — — De rebus Sinensium epistola. Jenae, 1689, 12mo.
401 — — Opuscula nonnulla orientalia uno volumine comprehensa. Francofurti ad Oderam, 1695, 4to., VI, 476 pp.
402 MENTZEL, K., Sylloge minutiarum lexici sinico-characteristici. Norimbergae, 1685, 4to.
    Taken from Diaz, Vocabulario della letra china, MS. of R. library of Berlin, No. 41.
403 — — Clavis sinica. Berolini, 1689, 4to.
404 Synopsis sinica in Thevenot, Relations des divers voyages, 2nd ed. Paris, 1696.
405 LEIBNITZ, G., Collectanea etymologica. Hannover, 1717, 8vo.
406 — — Epistolae ad diversos. Lipsiae, 1734-42, 8vo.
407 MASSON, P., Dissertation critique ou l'on tache de faire voir l'utilité qu'on peut tirer de la langue chinoise pour l'intelligence de divers mot de l'ancient testament.
408 BAYER, T., De horis sinicis et cyclo horario commentationes, acc. ejusdem auctoris parergon sinicum de calendariis sinicis. Petropoli, 1735, 4to.
409 FRÉRET, N., Réflexions sur la langue chinoise et sur la littérature chinoise. Acad. des inscr. et des bell. lett., III, p, 456-481.
410 HAUPT, J. F., Neue und vollständige Auslegung des von Fohi hinterlassenen Buches Yi-king. Rostock, 1753, 8vo.

411 HOWELL, Essay on the Chinese language. Aberdeen, 1753, 8vo.

412 MAIRAN, DE, Lettres au P. Parrenin, contenant diverses questions sur la Chine. Paris, 1759, 8vo.; and 1770, 8vo.

413 GUIGNES, DE (père), Mémoire dans lequel on prouve que les Chinois sont une colonie égyptienne. Paris, 1759, 4to.
> See Deshauterays, le Roux; Doutes sur la dissertation de M. de Guignes. Paris, 1759, 2 parties, 8vo. De Guignes' reply: Réponse au Doutes de Deshauterays. Paris, 1759, 12mo.

414 NEEDHAM, T., Epistola de inscriptione quadam egyptiaca Taurini inventa et charactericis egyptiis olim et sinis communibus exarata. Romae, 1761, 8vo.

415 HYDE, T., Syntagma dissertationum cum appendice de lingua sinensi; ed. G. Sharpe. Oxonii, 1767, 2 vols., 4to.

416 SHARPE, G., De lingua sinensi aliisque linguis orientalibus. Oxonii, 1767, 4to.

417 PAUX, DE, Recherches philosophiques sur les Egyptiens et les Chinois. Berlin, 1773, 2 vols., 8vo.
> English, London, 1795, 8vo.
> See Mém. conc., II, p. 365.

418 AMIOT, L., Lettre de Pékin sur le génie de la langue chinoise et sur la nature de leur écriture symbolique, comparée avec celles des anciens Egyptiens. Bruxelles, 1773, 4to.; and 1782, 8vo.
> English in Philosophical Transactions.

419 JONES, W., Poeseos asiaticae commentariorum libri VI. Londini, 1774, 8vo.; and Lipsiae, 1777, 8vo.

420 — — Discours sur les Chinois. Paris, 1776, 4to.

421 VISDELOU, C., Monument de la religion chrétienne trouvé en Chine. Herbelot, bibl. or 1776, suppl., p. 165-190.

422 — A. et Galand, C., Observations sur ce que les historiens Arabes et Persans rapportent de la Chine et de la Tartarie; ibid, p. 1-17, 134-163.

423 Essai sur l'antiquité des Chinois, Mém. conc., I, p. 1-269.

    German in No. 839.

424 L'antiquité des Chinois prouvée par les monuments; ibid, II, p. 1ss.

425 Portraits des Chinois célèbres; ibid, III, p. 1; V, p. 69; VIII, p. 1; X, p. 1.

426 Essai sur le passage de l'écriture hiéroglyphique à l'écriture alphabétique; ibid, VIII, p. 112.

427 Essai sur la langue et les caractères des Chinois; ibid, VIII, p. 133; IX, p. 282.

428 CIBOT, Essai sur la longue vie des hommes dans l'antiquité, spécialement à la Chine; ibid, XIII, p. 309.

429 — Parallèle des moeurs et usages des Chinois avec les moeurs et usages décrits dans le livre d'Esther; ibid, XIV, p. 309; XV, p. 1.

    A German extract from this: Ueber die Magie der Chinesen, As. Mag., II, p. 224.

430 WEBB, M., Some reasons for thinking that the Greek language was borrowed from the Chinese. London, 1787, 8vo.

431 PALLAS, Vocabularia totius orbis comparativa.

432 CHAMBERS, Sir W., Asiatic miscellany. Calcutta, 1787, 8vo.

433 HAGER, J., The characteristic merits of the Chinese language. London, 1801, 4to.

434 KLAPROTH, J., Asiatisches Magazin. Weimar, 1802, 2 vols., pp. 554, 557, 8vo.

435 — — Bemerkungen über die chinesische Sprache, As. Mag., II, p. 79-82.

436 — — Drei Schreiben an Herrn Sinologus Berolinensis (Montucci.) St. Petersburg, 1810, 4to.

437 — — Leichenstein auf dem Grabe der Gelehrsamkeit des Herrn J. Hager. Berlin, 1811, 8vo.

438 — — Grande exécution d'automne. 1 Weston, 2 Langlès, Pékin et Moukden, 20 année : Kinking et Saitchounga Feng-chou, 8 et 9 lune, jours malheureux. Paris, 1815, 8vo.

439 — — Abhandlung über die Sprache und Schrift der Uiguren. Paris, 1820 ; also in Verzeichniss No. 668.

440 — — Asia polyglotta (in French.)   Paris, 1823, 4to., with atlas in fol.
> German, Paris, 1831, pp. 400, 4to., with appendix : Leben Buddhas.
> See A. Rémusat, Mél. as., I, p. 267-309. Some of the ethnographical tables have been translated by G. Phillip in Doolittle's handbook, Vol. II (No. 84.)

441 — — Mémoirs relatifs à l'Asie contenant des recherches historiques, géographiques et philologiques sur les peuples de l'Orient. Paris, 1824-28, 2 vols., 8vo.

442 — — Magazin asiatique ou Recueil géographique et historique de l'Asie centrale et septentrionale. Paris, 1825, 2 vols., 8vo.

443 — — Recherches sur le pays de Fousang.

444 — — (W. Lauterbach), Méprises singulières de quelques sinologues. Paris, 1827, 8vo.

445 — — Sur les différents noms de la Chine, J. as., X, p. 53 ss.; and Mém. rel. à l'Asie, III, p. 257 ss.
> See N. J. as., XI, p. 188 ss.

446 — — Lettre à M. de Humboldt sur l'invention de la boussole. Paris, 1834, 8vo.

447 EICHHORN, J. G., Geschichte der neueren Sprachenkunde. Göttingen, 1807, 8vo.

448 GUIGNES, de (fils), Réflexions sur la langue chinoise, et sur la composition d'un dictionnaire chinois, français et latin. Paris, 1807, 8vo.; and 1810, 8vo.

449 LANJUINAIS, De la langue chinoise. Paris, 1807, 8vo.

450 MONTUCCI, A., De studiis sinicis. Berolini, 1808, 4to.

451 MARSHMAN, J., Dissertation on the characters and sounds of the Chinese language. Serampore, 1809, 4to.

Also as introduction to his "Works of Confucius," No. 145.

452 RÉMUSAT, A., Essai sur la langue et la littérature chinoise avec cinq planches contenant des textes chinois. Paris, 1811, 8vo.; and Mél. as., II, p. 1-18.

453 — — Notice sur une version chinoise de l'Evangile de St. Marc, publiée par les missionnaires anglais de Bengale. Paris, 1812, 8vo.; and Mél. as., I, p. 1-26.

454 — — Explication d'une inscription en chinois et mandchou gravée sur une plaque de jade du cabinet des antiques de Grenoble. Grenoble, 1812, 8vo.

455 — — Plan d'un dictionnaire chinois avec des notices de plusieurs dictionnaires manuscripts et des réflexions sur les travaux exécutés jusqu'à ce jour par les Européens pour faciliter l'étude de la langue chinoise. Paris, 1814, 8vo.; and Mél. as., II, p. 62-131.

456 — — Programme du cours de la langue et de la littérature chinoise et mandchoue. Paris, 1815, 8vo.

457 — — Mélanges asiatiques ou choix de morceaux critiques et de mémoires relatifs au religion, aux sciences etc. des nations orientales. Paris, 1825-26, 2 vols., 8vo.

458 — — Nouveaux mélanges asiatiques. Paris, 1829, 2 vols., 8vo.

Several of the biographies have been translated into English by Mrs. Coolidge, Chin. Repos., IX, p. 143, 210, 274; X, p. 320.

459 — — Mélanges posthumes d'histoire et de littérature orientales. Paris, 1843, 8vo.

460 — — Considérations sur la nature monosyllabi-
que attribuée communément à la langue chinoise.
Fundgruben, Vol. III; and Mél. as., II, p. 47-61.

461 — — De la philosophie chinoise, Mél. posthumes,
p. 160-205.

462 Urh-chih-tsze-tcen-se-yin-pe-kean, being a parallel
drawn between the two intended Chinese dictionaries by the Rev. R. Morrison and A. Montucci,
together with Morrison's Horae sinicae with the
text to the popular Chinese primer San-tsi-king.
London, 1817, 4to.

463 MORRISON, R., A view of China for philological
purposes. Macao, 1817, 4to.
See Rémusat, Nouv. mél. as., II, p. 325.

464 — — Chinese miscellany. London, 1825, fol.

465 — — Remarks on the language, history, etc. of
China. London, 1825, 8vo.

466 — — Titles of Chinese emperors in various dynasties, Chin. Repos., II, p. 309, 1833.

467 MYERS, T., An essay on the nature and structure
of the Chinese language. London, 1825, 8vo.

468 SCHOTT, W., De indole linguae sinicae. Halis,
1826, 8vo.

469 — — Ueber die chinesische Sprache. Enc. von
Ersch und Gruber, Theil, XVI, 1827.

470 — — Ueber die s. g. indochinesischen Sprachen.
Berlin, 1856, 4to.

471 — — Etwas über den Roman der Chinesen.
Ausland, 1856, No. 86, 87.

472 — — Ueber die chinesische Verskunst. Berlin,
1857, 4to.

473 — — Ueber Invectiven und Verwünschungen bei
den Chinesen, Monatsber. d. Berl. Ak., 1857,
Juli, p. 384.

474 HUMBOLDT, W. von, Lettre à M. A. Rémusat sur
la nature des formes grammaticales en général et
sur le génie de la langue chinoise en particulier.
Paris, 1827, 8vo.

See S. de Sacy, Notice de l'ouvrage intitulé :
Lettre etc. Paris, 1827, 4to.

475 — — Ueber die Kawi Sprache. Berlin, 1836-
39, 3 vols., 4to.

The preface of this work (p. 1-430) is a standard introduction to the science of language, new edition by Pott, 1875.

476 DAVIS, Sir J. F., Poeseos sinensis commentarii.
On the poetry of the Chinese, Transact. R. S.
London, 1827; also, London, 1829, 4to.; Macao,
1834, 8vo.; London, 1870, 4to.

See Ch. and Jap. Repos., I, 1864; Phoenix,
I, p. 17.

477 — — Chinese miscellanies, a collection of essays
and notes. London, 1865, 8vo.

See Reader, 1865, No. 152, p. 593; Athenaeum, 1866, Jan. 13, p. 51; Lit. Centralbl., 1866, No. 41, p. 105.

478 JULIEN, S., Vindiciae philologicae in linguam sinicam. Paris, 1830, 8vo.

English by G. R. Brown, Chin. Repos., X,
p. 222.

See Pauthier, Vindiciae, No. 490; and Vindiciae novae, No. 491.

479 — — Discussions grammaticales sur certaines
. règles de position, qui en chinois jouent le même
rôle que les inflexions dans les autres langues.
Paris, 1841, 8vo.

480 — — Exercises pratiques de syntaxe et de lexi-
graphie. Paris, 1842, 8vo.

481 — — Simple exposé d'un fait honorable odieu-
sement dénaturé dans un libelle récent de M.
Pauthier. Paris, 1843, 8vo.

For Nos. 478-481 see Pauthier, No. 489-491.

482 — — Lettre à M. R. Thom. Paris, 1844, 8vo.

483 — — Concordance sinico-sanscrite d'un nombre
considérable de titres d'ouvrages bouddhiques, re-
cueillis dans un catalogue chinois de l'an 1306 et

publiés, après le déchiffrement et la restitution des mots indiens, Jour. as., 4me. s. XIV, p. 353, 1849.

Also in Mélanges de géographie, No. 485.

484 — — Méthode pour déchiffrer et transcrire les noms sanscrits qui se rencontrent dans les livres chinois. Paris, 1861, 8vo.

  See J. as., 5 sér., XVII, p. 101 ss.; XVIII, p. 121 ss. Called for by the author's translation of the voyages des pélérins, No. 249. See Max Müller's Chips, I, 288.

485 — — Mélanges de géographie asiatique et de philosophie sinico-indienne. Paris, 1864, 8vo.

  Reprints of articles from the Journal asiatique, followed by a Sinico-sanscrit concordance of buddhist books, No. 483.

486 — — Réponse obligée à un prétendu ami de la justice qui se cache sous le voile de l'anonyme ; suivie de barbarismes et de solécismes latins d'un candidat qui a toutes ses sympathies. Paris, 1871.

  See Pauthier, Vindiciae sinicae novae, No. 491.

487 AMPÈRE, J. J., De la Chine et des travaux de M. Rémusat, Revue des deux mondes, VIII et 2me. s. IV, 1832.

488 PAUTHIER, G., Essai sur la poésie Chinoise, Revue encycl., Feb. 1833.

489 — — Réponse à l'examen critique de M. St. Julien. Paris, 1842, 8vo.

490a — — Vindiciae sinicae. Dernière réponse à M. St. Julien suivie d'un parallèle de sa nouvelle traduction de Lao-Tseu. Paris, 1842, 8vo.

490b — — Supplément aux vindiciae sinicae ou dernière réponse à St. Julien. Paris, 1843, 8vo.

491 — — Vindiciae sinicae novae, No. 1: Abel Rémusat, premier professeur de langue et de littéra,

ture Chinoise, défendu contre les imputations men-
songères de M. St. Julien, son élève et son suc-
cesseur. Paris, 1872, 8vo.
    For No. 489-491 see Julien, No. 478-481,
      and No. 486.

492 — — De l'authenticité de l'inscription nestorien-
ne de Si-ngan-fou. Paris, 1857, 8vo.

493 BRIDGMAN, E. C., Antiquity and study of the Chinese language, Chin. Repos., III, p. 1.

494 — — The Chinese oral language; ibid, III, p.
480.

495 — — Chinese intonations described and illustrated; ibid, VII, p. 57.

496 — — Introductory remarks on Chinese grammar; ibid, IX, p. 329, 519.

497 — — Orpen's remarks on the nature of language; ibid, XII, p. 582.

498 — — Triglot translation of the Syrian monument of Si-ngan fu; ibid, XIV, p. 202; XIX,
p. 552.

499 — — Philological diversions illustrating the word
fung or wind as used in Chinese writings; ibid,
XVIII, p. 470; XIX, p. 486.

500 MORRISON, J. R., The Chinese written language;
ibid, III, p. 14.

501 — — Features of the oral language and its dialects; ibid, III, p. 480.

502 — — New orthography of all sounds in the Chinese language; ibid, V, p. 22; VI, p. 479.

503 — — Facilities for studying the Chinese language; ibid, VII, p. 113.

504 MUIRHEAD, R., The profession of letters in China; ibid, III, p. 118.

505 TRACY, J., An alphabetic language for the Chinese;
ibid, IV, p. 167.

506 — — Remarks on the study of Chinese; ibid,
VIII, p. 338; VII, p. 204.

507 PARAVEY, C. DE, Dissertation abrégée sur le nom

antique et hiéroglyphique de l'Indée, ou traditions conservées en Chine sur l'ancien pays de Tsin. Paris, 1836. 8vo.

508 — — Documents hiéroglyphiques conservés en Chine et en Amérique sur le déluge de Noê. Paris, 1838, 8vo.

509 — — Dissertation sur les Ting-ling dont parlent les livres chinois, ou sur la véritable nation à laquelle on donnait le nom de Centaures dans l'antiquité. Paris, 1839, 8vo.

510 — — Dissertation sur les Amazones, dont le souvenir est conservé en Chine. Paris, 1840, 8vo.

511 — — Identité du déluge d'Yao et de celui de la bible. Paris, 8vo.

512 — — L'Amérique sous le nom de pays de Fou-Sang, a-t-elle été connue en Asie dès le 5. siècle? Paris, 1844, 8vo.

513 — — L'Amérique sous le nom de Fou-Sang et nouvelles preuves que le pays du Fou-Sang est l'Amérique. Paris, 1844, 8vo.

514 — — Traditions primitives. De quelques erreurs sur la Chine et Confucius professés par M. de Lamartine dans son cours de littérature. Lyon, 1863, 8vo.

515 DYER, S., Remarks on the Fuhkien dialect, Chin. Repos., IV, p. 172.

516 — — Notes on the grammatical construction of the Chinese language, Per. Misc. and Juven. Instr. I, p. 154, 181, 205, 229, 279, reprinted in Chin. Repos., VIII, p. 347-359.

517 — — On select Chinese particles, Per. Misc. and Juven. Instr. II, p. 58, 82, 102, 126, 151, 206.

518 STEWART, J. C., Remarks on Morrison's system of orthography, Chin. Repos., V, p. 65.

519 WOLFE, S., Objections to the proposed orthography of the Chinese language as applied to the dialect of Fuhkien; ibid. V. p. 481.

520 NEUMANN, K. F., Asiatische Studien. Leipzig, 1837, 8vo.

521 — — Ueber chinesische Sprüchwörter. Zeitschr. der deutsch. morg. Ges., II, p. 47.

522 — — Beurtheilung der chinesischen Bibelübersetzung von Morrison, Milne und Gützlaff; ibid, III, p. 362.

523 — — Ueber die erdichtete Inschrift von Signan-fu; ibid, IV, p. 33.

524 WILLIAMS, S. W., Chhong Se Toan with remarks on romanizing the Chinese language, Chin. Repos., VII, p. 490; XX, p. 472.

525 — — Table of sounds in 3 dialects; ibid, XI, p. 28.

526 — — On the mode of spelling Chinese, Notes and Queries, I, p. 34.

527 LAY, G. T., Remarks on the cantus of the Chinese, Chin. Repos., VI, p. 172.

528 — — New analysis of the Chinese language; ibid, VII, p. 255.

529 KIDD, S., Lecture on the nature and structure of the Chinese language. London, 1839, 8vo.

530 BAZIN, A., Mémoire sur l'organisation intérieure des écoles chinois. Paris, 1839, 8vo.

531 — — Mémoire sur les principes généraux du chinois vulgaire, J. as., 4 sér., V, 346, 469; VI, p. 89; and Paris, 1845, 8vo.

532 — — Recherches sur l'histoire, l'organisation et les travaux de l'académie impériale de Pekin. Paris, 1858, 8vo.

533 GLADISCH, A., Ueber die chinesische Sprache. Posen, 1840, 4to.

534 DEAN, W., Chinese language as used in Cochinchina, Chin. Repos., XI, p. 450.

535 BIOT, E., Mémoire sur les recensements des terres consignés dans l'histoire chinoise. Paris, 1838, 8vo.

536 — — Essai sur l'histoire de l'instruction publi-

que en Chine. Paris, 1845, 8vo.
See S. W. Williams, Chin. Repos., XVIII,
p. 57.

537 — — Mémoire sur quelques anciens monuments
de l'Asie analogues aux pierres druidiques. Paris,
8vo.

538 A., De la doctrine et des livres des Chinois. Paris,
1844, 8vo.

539 LOWRIE, W. M., On the significance of the character jen (humanity), Chin. Repos., XV, p.
329.

540 PIPER, G. O., Ueber die Bedeutung etymologischer
Forschungen in der chinesischen Sprache. Jah-
resbericht der deutsch. morg. Ges., 1847, p. 160.

541 — — Ueber die alte chinesische Sprache.
Zeitschr. d. deutsch. morg. Ges., IV, p. 114.

542 — — Meine Stellung zum chinesischen Alter-
thum und die Stellung meiner Gegner. Bern-
burg, 1857, 8vo.

543 HYACINTHE, B., Observations sur les traductions
et les critiques littéraires de M. de Klaproth, 4to.

544 GETTY, E., Notices of Chinese seals found in Ireland. London, 1850, 8vo.

545 THOMS, P. P., Remarks on the Chinese word Man.
London, 1851, 8vo.

546 — — A dissertation on the ancient Chinese vases
of the Song dynasty. London, 1851, 8vo.
See S. W. Williams, Chin. Repos., XX, p.
489.

547 BROCKHAUS, Prof., Vorschläge zur zweckmässi-
gen Einrichtung eines chinesischen Wörterbuchs.
Zeitsch. d. deut. morg. Ges., VI, p. 532.

548 MEDHURST, W. H., Remarks on the Chinese word
man. Shanghai, 1852, 4to.

549 — — Remarks on the Chinese character E.
Hongkong, 1852, 8vo.

550 — — The tablet of Yü, J. N. C. B. of R. A. S.,
1869, p. 78.

551 — — On Chinese street literature. Shanghai, 1870, 8vo.

552 PARKES, Sir H. S., Observations on the Chinese word man. Canton, 1852, 8vo.

553 LUNEVILLE, DE, La croix instructive et historique trouvée en Chine. Paris, 1853, 8vo.

554 SUMMERS, J., Lecture on the Chinese language and literature. London, 1853, 8vo.

555 — — The study of the Chinese by Europeans, Ch. and Jap. Repos., II, 26, 1864.

556 SALISBURY, E. E., On the genuiness of the so called nestorian "monument de Si-ngan-fu," J. of Am. Or. Soc., III, p. 399, 1853.
See Palladius, Chin. Recorder, VI, p. 147-148.

557 WYLIE, A., On the nestorian tablet at Se-Gan-Foo. New York, 1854, 8vo.

558 — — On an ancient inscription in Chinese and Mongol from a stone tablet in Shanghai, Transact. Ch. B. R. A. S., V, p. 65-81, 1856.

559 — — On an ancient inscription in the Neuchih language; ibid, VI, p. 137-153, 1859.

560 — — Remarks on some impressions from a lapidary inscription at Keu-yun-kwan on the great wall near Peking, J. N. C. B. of R. A. S., I, p. 133, 1865; and J. R. As. S., V, No. 1, 1871.

561 PARRAT, H., Les tons chinois sont sémitiques. Porrentruy, 1854, 4to.

562 WHITE, M. C., Chinese local dialects reduced to writing, J. Am. Or. Soc., IV, p. 327.

563 — — On Chinese philology; ibid, Vol. V.

564 — — The Chinese language spoken at Foochau, Methodist Quarterly Review, July, 1856, p. 352; also separately in 8vo.

565 RAUTENBACH, E., Die chinesische Sprache in ihren Rechten als Sprache. Darmstadt, 1855, 8vo.

566 EDKINS, J., On ancient Chinese pronunciation,

Transact. of the C. B. of R. A. S., Vol. IV, p. 51-85. Hongkong, 1855.

567 — — Connection of Chinese and Hebrew, Chin. Recorder, III, p. 203, 323; IV, p. 23, 48, 74, 102, 123, 182, 215, 245, 279, 287, 326.
See P. G. von Möllendorff, Chin. Recorder, IV, p. 253.

568 — — Curiosities of Chinese etymology, Notes and Queries, II, p. 4, 50, 65, 86, 101.

569 — — Dialect used in Chinese plays; ibid, II, p. 183.

570 — — Celtic compared with Chinese, The Phoenix, II, p. 17.

571 — — Chinese philology, Ch. Review, I, p. 181, 293.

572 — — China's place in philology. London, 1872, 8vo.
See T. Watters, China Review, I, p. 53.

573 HALDEMAN, The relation between the Chinese and Indo-European languages, 1852.

574 STEINTHAL, H., Charakteristik der hauptsächlichsten Typen des Sprachbaues. Berlin, 1860, 8vo.

575 LEPSIUS, R., Ueber chinesische und tibetanische Lautverhältnisse und über die Umschrift jener Sprachen. Berlin, 1861, 4to.

576 JENKINS, B., A list of syllables for romanizing works according to the Shanghai dialect. Shanghai, 1861, 8vo.

577 PLATH, J. H., Ueber die lange Dauer und die Entwicklung des chinesischen Reiches. München, 1861, 4to.

578 — — Die Tonsprache der alten Chinesen. München, 1862, 8vo.

579 EWALD, H., Sprachwissenschaftliche Abhandlungen. Göttingen, 1862, 4to.

580 Thoughts on the past and future of China, translated from the French of Count d'Escayrac de Lau-

ture, Chin. and Jap. Repos., July, August, 1863.

581 KROOMAN, D., Phonetic alphabet of the Canton dialect. Canton, 1863, 8vo.

582 REINAUD, J. T., Mémoire sur le Périple de la mer Erythère et sur la navigation etc. après les témoignages grecs, latins, arabes, persans, indiens et chinois. Paris, 1864, 4to.

583 Chinesen vor Columbus in America. Ausland, 1865, No. 12, p. 163.

584 ANDREE, R., War Amerika den alten Chinesen bekannt? Wo lag das Land Fusang? Globus, 1865, VIII, Heft 16, p. 346.
    From the French of V. de St. Martin, Année géogr., 1865, p. 253.

585 SEVERINI, A., Il monosillabismo della lingua Cinese, Rivista Orient., fasc. 1, 1867.

586 MUELLER, M., Chips from a German workshop. London, 1867-1875, 4 vols., 8vo.

587 CHALMERS, J., The origin of the Chinese. London, 1868, 8vo.

588 — — Chinese spelling tables, China Review, IV, p. 307-311.

589 JEANNET, P., De la langue chinoise et des moyens d'en faciliter l'usage. Paris, 1869, 8vo.

590 STRAUSS, V. von, Das 14 cap. des Taoteking. Zeitschr. der d. morg. Ges., XXIII, p. 473.

591 BASTIAN, A., Sprachvergleichende Studien. Mit besonderer Berücksichtigung der Indochinesischen Sprachen. Leipzig, 1870, 8vo.
    See China Review, I, 58.

592 BRETTSCHNEIDER, E., On the knowledge possessed by the ancient Chinese of the Arabs and Arabian colonies. London, 1871, 8vo.

593 — — Fusang or who discovered America, Chin. Recorder, III, p. 114.

594 GULICK, J. T., On the best method of representing the unaspirated mutes of the mandarin dialect; ibid, III, p. 153.

595 — — The mandarin mutes; ibid, VI, p. 414-418.

596 WATTERS, T., Tao, an essay on a word; ibid, IV, p. 1, 33, 100.

597 — — Chinese notions about pigeons and doves, J. N. C. B. of R. A. S., IV, p. 225-242.

598 — — Essays on the Chinese language, China Review, IV, p. 212, p. 271-278. .

599 Analysis of Chinese characters, Chin. Recorder, IV, p. 90, 119.

600 MAYERS, W. F., On the extended use of the Peking system of orthography for the Chinese language, Notes and Queries, I, p. 10.

601 — — Etymology of the name of the Yang tze kiang; ibid, I, p. 35.

602 — — On the term of Po sing or 100 surnames; ibid, I, p. 140.

603 — — Comparative table illustrating the Chinese scheme of physics; ibid, I, p. 146.

604 — — Chinese terms for murder and manslaughter; ibid, II, p. 44.

605 — — The term t'ang (Hall); ibid, II, p. 77.

606 — — Origin of the term niao t'siang; ibid, II, p. 142.

607 — — Specification of the term Pa hi; ibid, II, p. 152.

608 — — The term Pi hia; ibid, II, p. 170.

609 — — The Chinese word ma-tow; ibid, III, p. 127.

610 — — Authenticity of Chinese records; ibid, III, p. 167.

611 — — The name Fuh-lin; ibid, III, p. 174.

612 — — The term pang and kuo; ibid, III, p. 179.

613 LAY, W. T., On the meaning of jen in Dr. Martin's translation of Wheaton's international law; ibid, I, p. 99; Martin's reply; ibid, I, p. 157.

614 The term man-ji; ibid, I, p. 91, 108, 173.

615 The name Cathay in English titles; ibid, I, p. 123.
616 The origin of the Chinese; ibid, I, p. 152.
617 TAINTÖR, E. C., Chinese terms for murder and manslaughter; ibid, II, p. 44.
618 — — The term tyfoon; ibid, III, p. 42.
619 SCHLEGEL, G., The words Tang shan; ibid, II, p. 78.
620 — — Chinese and Egyptian hieroglyphs; ibid, III, p. 65, 81.
621 — — Sinico-Aryaca, ou recherches sur les racines primitives dans les langues chinoises et aryennes. Etude philologique. Batavia, 1872, 8vo. See Trübner's Am. and Or. Record, 1872, p. 206; China Review, I, p. 136.
622 The term "sword rack," Notes and Queries, II, p. 108, 142.
623 Pidgin English; ibid, II, p. 174.
624 SMITH, F. P., Instances of the use of the number seven by the Chinese; ibid, III, p. 7.
625 — — Identification of the names of foreign countries, mentioned in Chinese writings; ibid, III, p. 118.
626 — — The designation T'ien chuh kwoh; ibid, III, p. 152.
627 The term tyfoon; ibid, III, p. 42.
628 PHILLIPS, G., Notes on Sumatra and Po-szu; ibid, III, p. 90, 106, 119.
629 — — The Chinese names given to Arabia and Persia; ibid, III, p. 154.
630 — — A note concerning Fuhlin (El-hirah); ibid, III, p. 163.
631 A plea for a common system of orthography; ibid, III, p. 155.
632 ALABASTER, C., The word pang (country); ibid, III, p. 168.
633 TWESTEN, K., Die religiösen, politischen und sozialen Ideen der asiatischen Culturvölker. Berlin, 1872, 2 vols., 8vo.

634 LOBSCHEID, W., Evidence of the affinity of the polynesian and American Indian with the Chinese and other nations of Asia. Hongkong, 1872, 8vo.

635 SWINHOE, R., On the Chinese dialect spoken at Hainan, The Phoenix, I, p. 67, 85, 115.

636 GARDENER, C. T., Chinese verse, China Review, I, p. 248.

637 — — On the Chinese race, J. of ethnol. Soc. London, April 1870.

638 — — The tablet of Yü, p. 293-306.

639 HIRTH, F., Sinico-european similarities, China Review, I, p. 362.

640 — — Words introduced from the Chinese into European languages; ibid, II, p. 95-98.

641 EITEL, E. J., Amateur sinology; ibid, II, p. 1-8.

642 LISTER, A., On the supposed difficulty of Chinese; ibid, II, p. 103-115.

643 — — A last word about tones; ibid, III, p. 380-383.

644 Is sinology a science? ibid, II, p. 169-173.

645 The relations of the Chinese language with the languages of Central Asia. St. Petersburg, 1873, 8vo. (in Russian.)

646 St. DENYS, HERVEY de, Deux traductions du San-tseu-king et de son commentaire. Réponse à un article de la Revue Critique du 8 Nov. 1873. In Ban Zai Sau, 1873, 8vo., pp. 27.

647 — — Examens des faits mensongers contenus dans un libelle publié sous le faux nom de Léon Bertin. St. Germain, 1875, 8vo.
See P. Perny, No. 648.

648 PERNY, P., Le charlatanisme littéraire dévoilé ou la vérité sur quelques professeurs de langues étrangères à Paris. Versailles, 1874, 8vo.
See St. Denys, No. 647.

649 DOUGLAS, C., Chinese tones most important and not very difficult, China Review, III, p. 248-252.

650 PARKER, E. H., The Hankow dialect; ibid, p. 308-312.

651 HIMLY, K., Ursprung des Wortes Typhon und der Aussprache Taifun. Mitth. d. deutsch. Ges f. Ostas, VIII. Heft, 1875, p. 14-20.

652 DOUGLAS, R. K., The language and literature of China. Two lectures delivered at the R. Inst. of Great Britain. London, 1875, 8vo., pp. 118.
See Saturday Review, 1875, p. 720-722; E. J. Eitel, China Review, IV, p. 301-306.

653 PRESTON, C. F., The Chinese vernaculars, China Review, IV, p. 152-160.

VII.

Literature.

654 Variorum librorum Chinensium bibliotheca. Amstelodami, 1605.

655 REIMANNUS, J. F., Historia literaria Babyloniorum et Sinensium. Brunsvigae et Hildesiae, 1641, 8vo.

656 SPIZELIUS, T., De re literaria sinensium commentarius. Lugd. Bat., 1660, 12mo.

657 Fourmontii oratio de literatura sinica recitata Parisiis in regia Inscr. academia, die 14 Apr. 1722.

658 Catalogue des ouvrages de M. Fourmont, l'ainé. Amsterdam, 1731, 8vo.

659 GUIGNES, DE (père), Idée de la littérature chinoise, Rec. de l'ac. des inscr., XXXVI, 1774.

660 JONES, W., Sur le second livre classique des chinois. Paris, 4to.

661 Notice du livre chinois Si-yuen, Mém. conc., IV, p. 421.

662 A Chinese fragment. London, 1786, 8vo.

663 LANGLÈS, L. M., Notice des ouvrages élémentaires m. s. sur la langue chinoise que possède la

bibliothèque nationale. Paris, an. VIII, 8vo.
664 Sur le San-tsai-t'u-hoei. Not. et Extr., II, p. 160.
665 MONTUCCI, A., Account of a Chinese MS. in the British Museum. London, 1801, 8vo.
666 — — Letters to the editor of the Universal Magazine on Chinese literature, including strictures on Dr. Hager's 2 works. London, 1804, 8vo.
667 KLAPROTH, J., Abhandlung über die alte Litteratur der Chinesen, As. Mag., II, p. 89-104, 192-211, 491-557, 1803.
668 — — Verzeichniss der chinesischen und mandschuischen Bücher und Handschriften der kgl. Bibliothek. Berlin, 1822, fol.
See A. Rémusat, Mél. as., II, p. 352-371.
669 — — Rapport sur les ouvrages du P. H. Bitchourinski. Paris, 1830, 8vo.
670 — — Notice de l'Encyclopédie littéraire de Ma-Touan-Lin, intitulée Wen-Hian-Toung-khao. Paris, 1832, 8vo.
671 WESTON, S., Fragments of oriental literature. London, 1807, 8vo.
672 RÉMUSAT, A., Mémoires sur les livres chinois de la bibliothèque du Roi. Paris, 1818, 8vo.; also in Mél. as., II, p. 372-426.
673 — — Lettre sur l'état et le progrès de la littérature chinoise en Europe. Paris, 1822, 8vo.; also in Mél. as., II, p. 19-32.
674 — — Sur un vocabulaire philosophique en 5 langues imprimé à Peking, Mél. as., I, p. 153-184; II, p. 264; also Fundgruben, III.
675 — — Discours sur la littérature orientale, Mél. posth., p. 253-321.
676 Catalogue des ouvrages imprimés et manuscrits de feu M. L. M. Langlès. Paris, 1825, 8vo.
677 BROSSET, Essai sur le Chi-king. Paris, 1828, 8vo.
678 — — Sseki de Szematsien, Nouv. Journ. as., II, 1828.
679 KURZ, H., Ueber einige der neuesten Leistungen

in der chinesischen Literatur. Paris, 1830, 8vo.
680 — — Mémoire sur le Chouking, Nouv. Journ. as., VI.
681 Catalogue des livres imprimés et manuscrits de feu M. A. Rémusat. Paris, 1833, 8vo.
682 MORRISON, J. R., Review of the Ta-tsing wan-neen yi-tung king-wei yu-too, a general geographical map by Li Ming-che Tsing-lae, Chin. Repos., I, p. 33.
683 — — The sacred edict in rhyme; ibid, I, p. 244.
684 — — Notice of the Sing Pu or work on biography; ibid, I, p. 107.
685 — — Newspapers and gazettes; ibid, I, p. 492, 506.
686 — — Ballad and story hawked about the streets; ibid, I, p. 493.
    Dutch by J. Werninck, Verslag aan de volks literatur d. Chinezen uit het Engl., 8vo.
687 — — Notice of the Olea fragrans miscellany; ibid, II, p. 426.
688 NEUMANN, K. F., Coup d'oeil historique sur les peuples et la littérature de l'Orient, Nouv. J. as., XIV, 1834,
689 — — Die Sinologen und ihre Werke. Ztschr. d. D. M. G. I, p. 91, 217.
690 — — Claude Visdelou und das Verzeichniss seiner Werke; ibid, IV, p. 227.
691 — — Maigrot (Caroli) und seine Werke; ibid, IV, p. 237.
692 JULIEN, S., Lettre relative au dictionaire Ou-tché-yun-fou, J. as., 4. sér., III, p. 417.
693 — — Renseignement bibliographique sur les relations des voyages dans l'Inde, N. J. as., X, 1847.
694 GUETZLAFF, K., Character and synopsis of the Chinese classics, Chin. Repos., III, p. 97.
695 — — Notice of the San kwoh chi or history of the 3 states; ibid, VII, p. 233.

696 — — Review of the Shin-sien tung-kien or general account of gods and genii; ibid, VII, p. 505.

697 — — Review of the Shuking or book of records; ibid, VIII, p. 385.

697a — — Sack of wisdom, a story book; ibid, X, p. 450.

698 — — Ta Tsing hwang te Shing heun or sacred institution of the emperors of the Ta Tsing dynasty; ibid, p. 593.

699 — — Ping nan how chuen or an account of the latter pacification of the south, an historical work in 6 vols.; ibid, VII, p. 281.

700 — — Review of the works of the poet Su Tungpo; ibid, XI, p. 132.

701 — — Dreams of the Red Chamber; ibid, XI, p. 266.

702 — — Review of the Ta-tsing Hwei-tien or statutes and statistics of the Chinese government; ibid, XII, p. 57.

703 — — Hai-kwoh Tu-chi or Lin's geography; ibid, XVI, p. 417.

703a — — Ing hoan tschi lio, kurze Beschreibung der Umgegenden des Weltmeeres, in 6 Theilen, von Lü-ki-yü Lien-ti. Ztschr. d. D. M. G., VI, p. 565.

704 BRIDGMAN, E. C., Use of the 100 family names as a schoolbook, Chin. Repos., IV, p. 153.

705 — — Account of the Peking gazette; ibid, V, p. 1.

706 — — Chinese history, its value and character as viewed and exhibited by native historians with a notice of the work entitled History made easy; ibid, X, p. 1.

707 — — Synopsis of the Chinese chrestomathy; ibid, XI, p. 157, 223.

708 — — List of 218 dictionaries in the Chinese language; ibid, XVII, p. 433.

709 — — The Urh Ya or Ready guide, a Chinese dictionary; ibid, XVIII, p. 170.

710 — — The Chi-shing Pien Nien-shi ki, or annals
of a genealogy of the most holy sage; ibid, XVIII,
p. 254.

711 — — Shwoh Wan kiai-tsz' or the etymologicon
of Hsü Shin; ibid, XIX, p. 169.

712 PIPER, G. O., Ueber das I-king. Ztschr. d. D. M.
G., III, p. 273; V, p. 195; VII, p. 187.

713 BAZIN, A., Notice du Chan-hai-king, cosmographie
fabuleuse attribuée au Grand Yü. Paris, 1839,
8vo.

714 — — Rapport sur une version chinoise des Fables d'Esope, J. as. Paris, 1843.

715 — — Le siècle des Youan ou tableau historique
de la littérature chinoise depuis l'avénement des
empereurs mongols jusqu'à la restauration des
Ming, J. as., 4. sér., XV, p. 5, 101; XVI, p. 428;
XVII, p. 5, 163, 309, 497; XVIII, p. 247, 517;
XIX, p. 435; also Paris, 1856, 8vo.

716 Catalogue des livres manuscrits et ouvrages chinois,
tartares, japonais de M. J. Klaproth. Paris, 1839,
2 parties, 8vo.

717 BIOT, E., Table générale d'un ouvrage chinois intitulé Souan-fa-tong-tsong ou traité complet de l'art
de compter. Paris, 1839, 8vo.

718 — — Sur le chapitre Yu koung du Chouking, J.
as., 3. sér., XIV, p. 152, 1842.

719 — — Sur les manuscrits inédits du P. Gaubier
et du P. Amiot, J. as. Paris, 1850, 8vo.

720 HUNTER, W. C., Chinese theatre and translation
of a farce, Chin. Repos., VI, p. 575.

721 WILLIAMS, S. W., Review of Luhchau's Nü Hioh
or position and education of females in China;
ibid, IX, p. 545.

722 — — Ying Hwan Chi-hioh or general survey of
the Maritime circuit by Sü Kiyü; ibid, XX, p. 169.

723 — — Yung Yuen Tsiuen-tsih or collection of
garden of Banians and examination of an alleged
forgery; ibid, XX, p. 340.

724 SCHOTT, W., Verzeichniss der chinesischen und mandschuischen Handschriften und Bücher der Bibliothek zu Berlin. Berlin, 1840, 8vo.

725 — — Ueber Lao-tse's Tao-te-king. Jahrb. f. wiss. Kritik, 1842, No. 64, p. 510.

726 — — Entwurf einer Beschreibung der chinesischen Literatur. Berlin, 1854, 4to., 126 pp.

727 HELMKE, J., Ueber sinesische Sprache und Literatur. Kleve, 1840, 4to.

728 HABAKUK, Catalogue of Chinese, Mandshu, Mongolian, Tibetan and Sanscrit books and manuscripts in the Asiatic library. St. Petersburg, 1843, 8vo. (in Russian.)

729 Review of the Ming-sin-pau-kien or mirror of the mind, Chin. Repos., XVI, p. 406.

730 MILNE, W. C., Si-fang-kung-kü or public proofs of buddhism from the west; ibid, XVI, p. 448.

731 — — Shing-yü kwang-hsün or amplification of the sacred edict; ibid, XVI, p. 500.

732 BRIDGMAN, J. G., Sing Shi Pau Yen or precious words to awaken the age; ibid, XIX, p. 233.

733 Catalogue of the library of the honorable East India Company. London, 1845-51, 2 vols., 8vo.

734 SCHIEFNER, A., Bericht über die neuste Büchersendung von Peking, Mél. as. St. Petersburg, 1852, Vol. I, 8vo.

735 Catalogue des livres imprimés et manuscrits composant la bibliothèque du feu M. E. Burnouf. Paris, 1854, 8vo.

736 HARLAND, W. A., Chinese medical jurisprudence. Notice of a Chinese work: Hsi-yuan-lu, Trans. C. B. of R. A. S., IV, p. 87. See Wylie's notes, p. 75.

737 WASSILYEFF, W., Two notices on the works in oriental languages, which are found in the libraries of Kazan and St. Petersburg. 1855 (in Russian.)

738 KIDD, S., Catalogue of the Chinese library of the R. A. S. London, 8vo.

739 WYLIE, A., Catalogue of the London Mission library at Shanghai. Shanghai, 1857, 8vo.

740 — — Notes on Chinese literature. Shanghai,
1867, 4to.

See Lit. Centralbl., 1869, No. 36.

741 PAVIE, T., Etude sur le roman bouddhique chinois
Si-yeou tchin-tsuen, J. as., 5. sér., IX, p. 357;
X, p. 308.

742 ROSNY, L. DE, Remarques sur quelques dictionnaires japonais-chinois, J. as., 5. sér., XI, p. 256.

743 EDKINS, J., On the present state of science, literature and literary criticism in China, North-China
Herald, March, 1857; also Chin. and Jap. Repos., July, August, 1863.

See J. as., 5. sér., VI, p. 98; VIII, p. 79.

744 — — Notices of the character and writings of
Mch-tzï, J. of N. C. B. of R. A. S., II, p. 165,
1859.

745 MACGOWAN, D. J., Chinese bibliography; ibid,
II, p. 170-175.

746 PLATH, J. H., Ueber die Quellen zum Leben des
Confucius. München, 1863, 8vo.

See Lit. Centralbl., 1864, No. 5, p. 102.

747 — — Ueber die Sammlung chin. Werke aus
der Zeit der Dynastien Han und Wei. Sitz. b. der
Ak. der Wiss. 2. Heft, p. 241, 1868; also München, 8vo.

See Wylie's notes, p. 209.

748 ROST, R., Fables of beasts and birds in China, with
a notice of Prof. Julien's Les Avadanas, China
and Jap. Repos., I, 1864.

749 SKATCHKOFF, K., On the geographical knowledge of the Chinese. Iswestiya of Im. Russ. Geo.
Soc., II, 1866 (in Russian.)

German by P. Völkel, Petermann's geog.
Mitth., 1868.

750 MAYERS, W. F., State papers relating to Tibet,
Notes and Queries, I, p. 6.

751 — — Chronicle of the fall of the T'ang dynasty (T'san-t'ang wu tai t'süan chwan); ibid, I, p. 14.

752 — — The records of marvels or tales of genii (Liao chai chih yi); ibid, I, p. 24.

753 — — Works of travel (Nau yew ki; Shu yew jih ki; Ju shu ki); ibid, I, p. 41.

754 — — Chinese biographical dictionaries; ibid, I, p. 72.

755 — — Chinese works of fiction;
   1. Historical romances; ibid, I, p. 86, 102, 119.
   2. Romantic novels; ibid, I, p. 137, 154, 165.

756 — — Chinese version of the legend of St. George of the dragon; ibid, I, p. 148.

757 — — A Chinese collection of epigrams; ibid, III, p. 33.

758 — — Bibliographical notes on Chinese books, Phoenix, Sept. 1872.

759 ARENDT, K., Beiträge zur Kenntniss der chinesischen Literatur. Ein Abschnitt aus dem heiligen Edikt. Ausland, 1866, No. 50, p. 701.

760 — — Beiträge zur Kenntniss der neuesten chinesischen Literatur, Mitth. d. Deutschen Ges. f. Ostas. 8. Heft, 1875, p. 37-39.

761 BEAL, S., The Sûrangama sûtra, The Phoenix, II, p. 92.

762 MACY, W. A., On Chinese dictionaries, J. of A. O. S., VI.

763 WATTERS, T., The life and works of Han-yü or Han Wên Kung, J. N. C. B. of R. A. S., 1873, p. 165.

764 New Chinese literature. Iswestiya J. Russ. Geo. S. 1873, Nos. 5, 8 (in Russian.)

765 LISTER, A., Chinese Almanacs, China Review, I, p. 237.

766 — — An hour with a Chinese romance; ibid, I, p. 284, 352.

767 CHALMERS, J., Han wan kung; ibid, I, p. 275, 339.
768 NACKEN, J., A Chinese Webster, a study in Chinese lexicography; ibid, II, p. 175-182, 215-222, 354-363.
769 Kanghi's dictionaries; ibid, II, p. 335-341.
770 MARTIN, E., Examen critique des jugements portés sur la valeur des monuments philosophiques, litéraires scientifiques des Chinois, Revue de Linguist. et de Philol. comparée, VII, 1874, 1 fasc.
771 Die Chinesischen Klassiker, Mag. f. d. Lit. des Auslandes, 1875, No. 35.
772 Ein Chinesischer Roger Bacon. Das Ausland, 1875, No. 50.
773 San-kuo-chih, China Review, III, p. 191-205.
774 STUHLMANN, C. C., Chinesische Märchen. Globus, XXIX, 1876.
775 Zur Volkspoesie der Chinesen, Mag. f. d. Lit. des Auslandes, 1876, No. 4.

VIII.

Chinese Characters and Printing.

776 MUELLER, A., Besserer Unterricht von der Chinesen Schrift und Druck. Berlin, 1680, 4to.
777 — — Specimina sinica. Berolini, 1685, fol.
778 BRING, S., De praerogativis imaginum literarum chinensium. Lund, 1748, 4to.
779 SCHULZE, Der orientalische und occidentalische Sprachmeister. Leipzig, 1748, 8vo.
780 FRÉRET, N., Réflexions sur les principes généraux de l'art d'écrire et en particulier sur les fondéments de l'écriture chinoise, Mém. de Litt., IX, p. 328-369.
781 GUIGNES, DE (père), Essay historique sur le typographie orientale et grecque de l'imprimerie royale. Notices et Extraits, I, p. 79, 1789.

782 AMIOT, Lettre sur les caractères chinois, Mém. con., I, p. 275.

783 — — Origine des différents sortes de caractères chinois, dont on voit le modèle dans les 32 volumes de l'édition chinoise. Eloge de Moukden, p. 127-197.

· See No. 187.

784 BREITKOPF, J. G. L., Exemplum typographiae sinicae figuris characterum e typis mobilibus compositum. Lipsiae, 1789, 4to.

785 HÄGER, J., An explanation of the elementary character of the Chinese language. London, 1801, fol.

See As. Mag., II, 79, 1803.

786 WESTON, S., Siao-cu-lin, Chinese characters analized and decompounded. London, 1808-10, 8vo.

787 Charactères chinois clichès sur le corps de 24 points, employés aux ouvrages de A. Rémusat. Paris, 4to., s. a.

788 PARAVEY, C. DE, Essai sur l'origine des chiffres et des lettres. Paris, 1826, 8vo.

789 DAVIS, Sir J. F., Eugraphia Sinensis or the art of writing the Chinese characters with correctness. London, 1826, 4to.

790 RÉMUSAT, A., Recherches sur l'origine et la formation de l'écriture chinoise. Rec. de l'acad. des inscr., Vol. VIII ; also Paris, 1827, 4to.

791 — — Remarques sur quelques écritures syllabiques tirées des caractères chinois ; ibid, 1827.

792 LÉVASSEUR ET KUETZ, Tableau des élémens vocaux de l'écriture chinoise. Paris, 1829.

793 SIEBOLD, P. J. von, Sin-Zi-Lin Yjok-Ben, sive collectio omnium litterarum Sinensium secundum radices disposita pronunciatione japonica adscripta. Leyden, 1834, fol.

794 BRIDGMAN, E. C., Modes of printing in Chinese and desirableness of having metallic types, Ch. Repos., I, 414.

795 — — Presses in China; ibid, II, 1; III, 43.
796 — — Specimen of Dyer's large type and of Pauthier's divisible type; ibid, XIV, 124.
797 DYER'S circular respecting preparation of moveable types; ibid, II, 477.
798 — S., A selection of 3000 characters, being the most important in the Chinese language. Malacca, 1834, 12mo.
799 MEDHURST, W. H., Comparative expense of printing in Chinese on wood, on stone and with types, Ch. Repos., III, 246.
800 WILLIAMS, S. W., Notice of the Parisian font of Chinese types; ibid, III, 528.
801 — — Metallic moveable types among the Chinese; ibid, XIX, 247.
802 — — Specimen of three-line diamond Chinese type made in Hongkong and Chinese moveable types; ibid, XX, p. 281.
803 — — Moveable types for printing Chinese, Chin. Recorder, VI, p. 22-30, 1875.
804 WALL, C. W., An examination of the ancient orthography of the Jews. London, 1835-41, 3 vols., 8vo.
   On Chinese characters, Vol. III.
805 PONCEAU, P. S. du, A dissertation on the nature and character of the Chinese system of writing. Philadelphia, 1838, 8vo.
806 PAUTHIER, G., De l'origine de la formation des différents systèmes d'écritures orientales et occidentales, Encycl. nouv., s. v. écriture; also Paris, 1838, 4to.
807 — — Sinico-aegyptiaca, Essai sur l'origine et la formation des écritures figuratives chinoise et égyptienne. Paris, 1842, 8vo.
808 — — Observations sur l'alphabet de Pa-sse-pa et sur le tentative de Koubilaï-khan pour transcrire la langue figurative des Chinois au moyen d'une écriture alphabétique. Paris, 1862, 8vo.

809 MARSHMAN, J., Dissertation on the composition of the characters of the Chinese language, Chin. Repos.; IX, p. 587.

810 Characters formed by the divisible type belonging to the Chinese mission of the Presbyt. Church of America. Macao, 1844, fol.

811 R. H. S. S., Some observations and conjectures concerning the Chinese characters, 8vo.

812 LOWRIE, W. M., Specimen of the type belonging to the Chinese mission. Macao, 1844, 8vo; Ningpo, 1852, 8vo.

813 PIPER, G. O., Bezeichnungen der chinesischen Welt-und Lebensanschauungen in der chinesischen Bilderschrift. Berlin, 1846, 8vo.

814 JULIEN, S., Documens sur l'art d'imprimer à l'aide de planches en bois, de planches en pierre, et des types mobiles, inventés en Chine. Paris, 1847, 8vo.

815 AUER, A., Oratio dominica polyglotta, 815 linguis et dialectis etc. Viennae, 1847 et 1851, fol.

816 COLE, R., Specimen of the 3-line diamond Chinese type made by the London Mission Society; Hongkong, 1849, 8vo.

817 Catalogue des caractères chinois de l'imprimerie nationale, fondus sur le corps de 24 points. Paris, 1851, fol.

818 Tableau des 214 clefs Chinoises. Paris (Marcellin Legrand), 8vo.

819 STEINTHAL, H., Die Entwickelung der Schrift. Berlin, 1852, 8vo.

820 SCHLEIERMACHER, A., De l'influence de l'écriture sur le langage. Darmstadt, 1853, 8vo.

821 The Chinese radicals adapted to the Hokien dialect. Paris, 1853, 8vo.

822 Tsz-po ou 214 clefs chinoises. Paris, 1853, 8vo.

823 ANDREWS, S. P., Discoveries in Chinese or the symbolism of the primitive characters of the Chinese system of writing. New York, 1854, 8vo.

See Plath, Münch. Gel. Anz., Vol. 42, No. 20.

824 ROSNY, L. DE, Notice sur l'écriture chinoise et les
principales phases de son histoire, comprenant
une suite de spécimens de caractères chinois de
diverses époques. Paris, 1854, 8vo.

825 — — Table des principales phonétiques chinoises. Paris, 1858, 8vo.

826 — — Recherches sur l'écriture des différents
peuples, anciens et modernes. Paris, 1862,
8vo.

827 SCHUETZ, F., Propagation des sciences européennes dans l'extrême Orient. Nancy, 1856, 8vo.

828 MARELLIN-LEGRAND, Specimen de caractères
chinois gravés sur acier et fondus en types mobiles. Paris, 1859, 8vo.

829 St. AULAIRE and GROENEVELDT, Manual of
Chinese running-hand writing. Amsterdam, 1861,
4to.

830 GAMBLE, W., List of Chinese characters formed
by the combination of the divisible type of the
Berlin font. Shanghai, 1862.

831 — — 2 lists of select characters. Shanghai,
1861 and 1865.
See Doolittle's handbook, Vol. II.

832 HOFFMANN, J. J., Chinese printing types. Leiden, 1864, 4to.

833 SCHLEGEL, G., On Chinese and Egyptian hiero-
glyphics, Notes and Queries, IV.

834 JAMIESON, R. A., The hieroglyphic character of
the Chinese written language, J. N. C. B. of R.
A. S., II, p. 113-123.

835 WUTTKE, H., Geschichte der Schrift und des
Schrifttums von den rohen Anfängen des Schrei-
bens in der Tatuirung bis zur Legung elektromag-
netischer Drähte. Vol. I, Die verschiedenen
Schriftsysteme. Leipzig, 1872, XXIII, 782 pp.,
8vo.
On Chinese writing, I, p. 242-481.

IX.

Serials.

836   Journal des savants. Paris, 1665-1792, 111 vols., 4to.; 1797 and 1816, 8vo.

837   HERBELOT, d', Bibliothèque orientale ou dictionnaire universel contenant généralement tout ce qui regarde la connoissance des peuples de l' Orient. Paris, 1697, XXVIII, 1060 pp., fol.; also Maestricht, 1776, XXVI, 954 pp., fol. avec supplément par A. Visdelou et C. Galand, 284 pp.

838   Lettres édifiantes et curieuses écrites des missions étrangères. Paris, 1717-1776, 34 recueils, 8vo., chronologically arranged.

> 2nd edition, Paris, 1781-83, 26 vols., 8vo., geographically arranged; on China, vol. 16-26; also Toulouse, 1810.
> Choix des lettres édifiantes écrites des missions étrangères. Paris, 1808, 3 vols., 8vo.
> Nouvelles lettres édifiantes des missions de la Chine. Paris, 1818-1823, 8 vols., 12mo.
> See A. Rémusat, Mél. as., I, p. 51-87.
> Lettres édifiantes et curieuses publiées sous la direction de L. A. Martin. Paris, 1843, 4 vols., 8vo.

839   Mémoires concernant l'histoire, les sciences, les arts, les moeurs et les usages des Chinois par les missionnaires de Pékin (Amiot, Bourgeois, Cibot, Ko, Poirot, Gaubil), publ. par C. Batteux, de Bréguigny, de Guignes et S. de Sacy. Paris, 1776-1814, 16 vols., 4to.

> Vol. XVI is Gaubil's chronology (No. 932.)
> Vol. I, German : Meiners, C.; Abhandlungen sinesischer Jesuiten über Geschichte etc. der Chinesen. Leipzig, 1778, 8vo.

840 Miscellaneous pieces relating to the Chinese. London, 1762, 2 vols., 12mo.
841 Lettres d'un missionnaire à Pékin, Supplément aux Mémoires concernant etc. (No. 839). Paris, 1782, 4 vols., 8vo.
842 The Asiatic miscellany, consisting of original productions. Calcutta, 1785-86, 2 vols., 4to.
843 Notices et extraits des M. S. de la bibliothèque du Roi. Paris, 1787 ss., 21 vols., 4to.
844 Asiatic researches or transactions of the Society of Bengal. Calcutta, 1788-1821; and Scrampore, 1825-39, 20 vols., 4to.; index to Vol. I-XVIII. Vol. I and II in French. Paris, 1805, 4to.
845 Magazin encyclopédique ou journal des sciences, des lettres etc., réd. par Millin. Paris, 1800-1816.
846 ADELUNG, J. C., Mithridates oder allgemeine Sprachenkunde, fortgesetzt von Vater. Berlin, 1806-17, 5 vols., 8vo.
847 DALRYMPLE, Oriental Repertory, 1807 ss.
848 KLAPROTH, J., Archiv für asiatische Litteratur, Geschichte etc. St. Petersburg, 1810, 8vo.
849 Fundgruben des Orients, Mines de l'Orient, herausgegeben von J. von Hammer. Wien, 1810-19, 6 vols., fol.
850 Biographie universelle ancienne et moderne, redigée par une société de gens de lettres et de savents. Paris, 1811-28, 52 vols., 8vo.
851 Asiatic journal and monthly register for British and foreign India, China and Australasia. London, 1816 ss., 28 vols., 8vo.; from 1830-45, 31 vols., 8vo.
852 The Indo-Chinese gleaner, containing miscellaneous communications on the literature, history, etc. of the Indo-Chinese nations. Malacca, 1817-22, 4to.
Consists of contributions chiefly written by R. Morrison and Milne.
See No. 866, The periodical misc.

853 Journal asiatique, 1 série, 1822-27, 12 vols., 8vo.
        2 „ 1828-35, 16 „ „
(nouveau journ. as.)
        3 „ 1836-42, 14 „ „
        4 „ 1843-52, 20 „ „
        5 „ 1853 „
Paris, 1822 ss., 8vo.

854 Annales de la propagation de la foi, Recueil périodique, faisant suite à toutes les éditions des Lettres édifiantes. Lyon et Paris, commencé en 1823, 8vo.

855 Transactions of the R. A. S. of Great Britain and Ireland. London, 1824 ss., 4to.

856 Verhandelingen van het Bataviaasch genootschaap. Batavia, 1825-53, 20 vols., 8vo.

857 Canton miscellany, Nos. I, X. Macao, 1830, 8vo.

858 BERGHAUS, H., Annalen der Erd-Völker-und Staatenkunde. Berlin, 1830 ss.

859 The Canton Register. Canton, 1831-34, 2 vols., 8vo.

860 Revues de deux mondes. Paris, 1831 ss., 8vo.

861 Journal of the R. A. S. of Bengal. Calcutta, 1831-62, 31 vols., 8vo.

862 The Chinese Repository. Canton, 1832-51, 20 vols., 8vo.

863 MORRISON, J. R., Companion to the Anglo-Chinese calendar. Canton, 1832, 12mo.

864 The evangelist and miscellanea sinica, 4 Nos. Macao, 1833, 4to. Commenced by R. Morrison, but suspended, as contrary to the doctrines of the Roman Catholic Church.

865 The journal of the R. A. S. of Great Britain and Ireland. London, 1834 ss., 8vo.

866 EVANS, J., The periodical miscellany and juvenile instructor. Malacca, 1836-37, 8vo.
        Intended to be a successor to Milne's Indo-Chinese gleaner, No. 852.

867 Zeitschrift für die Kunde des Morgenlandes, herausg. von Ewald, Lassen, Rückert u. A., I-III, Göttin-

gen, 1837-39, IV-VII; Bonn, 1845-50, 7 vols., 8vo.

868 VATER, J. S., Analekten der Sprachkunde. Leipzig, 1840, 8vo.

869 Revue orientale, Recueil périodique par Carmoly. Bruxelles, 1841 ss.

870 Revue de l'Orient. Paris, 1843-46, 11 vols.; continuation under the title : Revue de l'Orient et de l'Algérie. Paris, 1847 ss.

871 Zeitschrift der Deutschen morgenländischen Gesellschaft. Leipzig, 1846 ss., 8vo.

872 Jahresberichte der Deutschen morgenländischen Gesellschaft. Leipzig, 1846 ss., 8vo.

873 Transactions of the China Branch of the R. A. S. Hongkong, 1848-59, 6 parts, 8vo.

874 Journal of the American Oriental Society. New York, 1849-56, Vols. I-V, 8vo.; New Haven, 1860 ss., Vols. VI ss., 8vo.

875 The Chinese miscellany. Shanghai, 1849-50, 8vo., 4 Nos.

> 1. A glance at the interior of China; 2. The Chinaman abroad; 3. Dissertation on the silk manufacture; 4. General description of Shanghai.
> This serial was begun by W. H. Medhurst, sen.

876 Evangelischer Reichsbote. Organ für den evangelischen Gesammtverein für die chinesische Mission. Berlin, 1850 ss., 4to.

877 Nachrichten der ostindischen missionsanstalt zu Halle.

878 KALKAR, C. H., Meddelelser angaande evangeliets udbredelse in China. Copenhagen, 1851 ss., 4to.

879 An Anglo-Chinese calendar. Canton, 1851 ss., 8vo.

880 Shanghai almanack and commercial guide. Shanghai, 1852 ss., 8vo.

881 Shanghai miscellany. Shanghai, 1852-56, 2 vols., 8vo.

882 Trudui tshlenow rossiskoi dukhoonoi missii w Peki-
nie (Works of the Russian ecclesiastical mission
at Peking.) St. Petersburg, 1852-66, 4 vols.,
8vo., 486 pp., 490 pp., 473 pp., 460 pp.
See J. as., XIII (1869), p. 70; Ztschr. d.
D. M. G., XXI, p. 499.
Vol. I-III German by Abel und Mecklenburg,
Arbeiten der Kaiserlich Russischen Gesandtschaft zu Peking über China. Berlin, 1858, 2 vols., 8vo.

883 PETERMANN, A., Mittheilungen aus Justus Per-
thes' geographischer Anstalt. Gotha, 1855 ss.,
4to.

884 Annuaires de la société d'ethnographie par Labarthe
et Rosny. Paris, 1855 ss., 12mo.

885 Sapiski of the Siberian branch of the J. Russian
geographical society. Irkutsk, 1856 ss., 8vo. (in
Russian.)

886 Journal of the N. C. Branch of the Royal asiatic society. Shanghai, 1858 ss., 8vo.; Vol. I Journal
of the Shanghai literary and scientific society.

887 The Chinese and Japanese repository by J. Summers. London, 1863-65, 3 vols., 8vo.

888 Notes and Queries on China and Japan, ed. by N.
B. Dennys. Hongkong, 1867-70, 4 vols., 8vo.

889 Papers on China. Hongkong, 1867-68, 8vo.

890 The Missionary recorder. Fuchow, 1867-72, 4 vols.,
8vo.
Vol. I edited by Rev. Wheeler; II by Rev. S.
L. Baldwin; III and IV by Rev. J. Doolittle. Recommenced under the title of

891 Chinese recorder and Missionary journal, ed. by A.
Wylie. Shanghai, 1874 ss., 8vo.

892 The China magazine, edited by C. Langdon Davies. Hongkong, 1868-69, 3 vols., 8vo.

893 The Phoenix, a monthly magazine for China, Japan and Eastern Asia, edited by Rev. J. Summers. London, 1871-72, 2 vols., 4to.

894 Atsume Gusa, pour servir à la connaissance de l'extrême Orient. Recueil publié par F. Turretini. Génève, 1871 ss., 4to.

895 Ban Zai San, same title, 8vo.

896 The China review or Notes and queries on the Far East, published every two months, edited by N. B. Dennys. Hongkong, 1872 ss., 8vo.
Since 1875 edited by E. J. Eitel.

897 Wostotshuy Sbornik (Oriental magazine.) St. Petersburg, 1872 ss., I, 3 Nos., 202 pp., 8vo. (in Russian.)

898 Mittheilungen der Gesellschaft für Natur-und Völkerkunde Ostasiens. Yokohama, 1873 ss.; Heft, I-IX, fol.

X.

History and Chronology.

899 MALDONADO, H., Epitome historical de Reyno de la China, 1621, 8vo.
French: Nouvelle histoire de la Chine par J. J. Bellefleur. Paris, 1622, 8vo.

900 ANGELIS, J. D', Histoire de ce qui s'est passé aux royaume de la Chine et au Japon, tirée des lettres écrites les années 1619-1621, trad. de l'Italien par P. Morin. Paris, s. a., 4to. (1624.)

901 Histoire de ce qui s'est passé aux royaumes de la Chine et du Japon tirée des lettres écrites en 1621-22 trad. de l'Italien par J. B. de Machault. Paris, 1627, 8vo.

902 MARTINIUS, M., De bello tatarico historia. Antverpiae, 1654, 8vo.; Amsterdam, 1655, 12mo.
French: Paris, 1654; Dutch: D elft, 1654.

903 — — , Sinicae historiae decas prima. München, 1658, 4to.

904 — — , Historia sinica vetus ab origine ad Christum natum. Amsterdam, 1659, 8vo.

905 PALAFOX y MENDOÇA, Historia de la conquis-
ta de la China por el Tartaro. Paris, 1670, 4to.
French by Collé. Paris, 1670, 12mo.; Ams-
terdam, 1723, 12mo.; also in Bernard,
Recueil, Vol. VI; English: 1671, 8vo.
The author who wrote in Mexico got his in-
formation from China viâ the Philippine
Islands.

906 GRESLON, A., Histoire de la Chine sous la domi-
nation des Tartares depuis 1651-69. Paris, 1671,
8vo.

907 ROUGEMONT, Fr. de, Historia tartaricosinica nova (1660-68.) Lovanii, 1673, 8vo.

908 SETTLE, E., The conquest of China by the Tartars. London, 1676. 4to.

909 COUPLET, P., Tabula chronologica monarchiae
Sinicae juxta cyclos annorum LX ab anno a. C.
2952 ad annum p. C. 1683. Paris, 1686, fol.;
Viennae, 1703, 12mo.
Also in No. 182.

910 ORLÉANS, P. J. de, Histoire des deux conquérants
tartares qui ont subjugués la Chine. Paris, 1688,
8vo.; also in Bernard, Recueil des voy., Vol.
VII.
English by Earl of Ellesmere. London,
1854, 8vo.

911 MENTZELIUS, C., Kurtze chinesische Chronologie oder Zeitregister aller chinesischen Kayser.
Berlin, 1696, 4to.

912 BOUVET, J., Portrait historique de l'empereur de
la Chine (Kanghi.) Paris, 1697, 12mo.
Latin by Leibnitz: Icon regia monarchae Sinarum nunc regnantis ex gallico versa,
1699, 8vo.

913 — — , Histoire de l'empire de la Chine. La
Haye, 1699, 12mo.
English: London, 1699, 12mo.

914 Ambassade de Scharok, fils de Tamerlan, et d'autres

princes ses voisins à l'empereur de Khatai, l'an 1419. Thévenot's Coll., pt. IV.

915 RENAUDOT, Anciennes relations des Indes et de Chine. Paris, 1718, 8vo.

916 FOUQUET, J. F., Tabula chronologica historiae sinicae. Romae, 1729.

917 Salmon und von Goch; Heutige Historie von allen Nationen, aus dem Englischen übers. Altona, 1732, 4to.

918 FRÉRET, N., De l'antiquité et de la certitude de la chronologie chinoise, Mém. de l'acad. roy. des inscr., Vol. X, 377 (1736); XV, 595 (1753); XVIII, 178 (1773); also in Fréret's oeuvres, XIII, 116-331; XIV, 1-268. Paris, 1796.

919 VOJEUX DE BRUNEM, J., Histoire de la conquête de la Chine par les Tartares mandchoux. Lyon, 1754, 2 vols., 12mo.

Extract from De Mailla's histoire générale (No. 925), which at that time was yet unpublished.

920 A history of China upon the plan of Mr. Rollin's ancient history. London, 1763.

921 GUIGNES, J. DE (père), Réflexions générales sur les liaisons et le commerce des Romains avec les Tartares et les Chinois, Rec. de l'ac. des inscr., XXXII, 1768.

922 — —, Examen critique des annales chinoises ou Mémoire sur l'incertitude des 12 premiers siècles de ces annales et de la chronologie Chinoise, Recueil de l'acad. des inscr., Vol. XXXVI, 1774.

923 — — Réflexions sur quelques passages rapportés par les missionnaires concernant la chronologie Chinoise; ibid, Vol. ILIII, 239.

924 TRAGAREL, E., De antiquitate Sinarum. Gryphisvaldiae, 1772, 4to.

925 MAILLA, A. M. DE, Histoire générale de la Chine ou Annales de cet empire traduites du Tong-kien-

kang-mu, publiées par M. l'Abbé Grosier. Paris, 1777-85, 12 vols., 4to.
See No. 190.

926 CLERC, M., Yu le Grand et Confucius, Histoire Chinoise. Soissons, 1779, 4to.

927 Sur le retour de l'empereur Kien-long, qu'on avait cru mort, Mém. conc., VIII, p. 289.

928 AMIOT, Sur les services d'Akoui et sur la mort de Pan-tchan Lama; ibid, IX, p. 441.

929 — , Abrégé chronologique de l'histoire universelle de l'empire Chinois; ibid, XIII, p. 74.

930 — , Sur la chronologie Chinoise; ibid, XV, p. 260.

931 GAUBIL, A., Abrégé de l'histoire Chinoise de la grande dynastie Tang; ibid, XV, p. 399-516, XVI.

932 — — Traité de la chronologie Chinoise, publié par M. de Sacy. Paris, 1814, 4to.; also as Vol. XVII of Mém. conc., No. 839.

933 Faits mémorables des empereurs de la Chine. Paris, 1784, 4to.

934 TITSINGH, G., Tydreekening der Chineesche kysers, 1784, fol.

935 Ambassades réciproques des Rois des Indes et de la Chine en 1412, traduits du Persan. Paris, 1788, 8vo.

936 BREITENBAUCH, G. A. von, Lebensgeschichte des jüngst verstorbenen sinesischen Kaisers Kienlung. Paris, 1788, 8vo.

937 On the festival of the 10th birthday of Kienlung, Lettr. edif., n. ed., XXIV, p. 491-500; also Mém. conc., VIII, p. 283-288; vide Murr, Journ. für Kunst und Litt., IX, p. 93.

938 KLAPROTH, J., Eroberung von China durch die Mandschus in 1644, As. mag., p. 200-220, p. 328-342; II, p. 136-144.

939 — — , Atlas historique de l'Asie. Paris, 1828.

940 — — , Tableaux historiques de l'Asie, depuis la monarchie de Cyrus jusqu'à nos jours. Paris, 1826, 4to.

941 — — , On a Japanese and Chinese chronology,
As. journal, new series, Vol. VI, p. 24, 1831.

942 — — , Notice d'une chronologie chinoise et japonaise, As. journal, new series, XII, p. 402, 1833.

943 — — , Description de la Chine sous le règne de
la dynastie Mongole, traduite du persan. Paris,
1833, 8vo.

944 BEAUMONT, DE, Beautés de l'histoire de la Chine,
du Japon et de Tartares. Paris, 1818, 2 vols.,
12mo.

945 On the Hebrew and Chinese chronology, As. Journ.,
IX, p. 433, 1820.

946 WACKERBARTH, Geschichte der letzten grossen
Revolution in Schina, 1644; Hamburg, 1821, fol.

947 (SACY, S. DE,) Résumé de l'histoire de la Chine.
Paris, 1824, 12mo.; 2nd edition, 1825.

948 LEONTIEF, A., Histoire de la guerre avec les Son-
gares sous le règne de l'empereur Kanghi, Journ.
as., Vol. V, p. 313.

949 PLATH, J. H., Geschichte Ostasiens, I, Die Völker
der Mandschurei. Göttingen, 1830-31, 2 vols.,
8vo.
History of the Liao and Kin Tartars, of the
Mandshus and their conquest of China.

950 — — , Ueber die Verfassung und Verwaltung
Chinas unter den ersten Dynastien. München,
1865, 4to.
See Lit. Centralbl. (1865), No. 51, p. 1388.

951 — — , Ueber die Glaubwürdigkeit der ältesten
chinesischen Geschichte. München, 1866, 4to.
See Lit. Centralbl. (1866), No. 1, p. 4.

952 — — , Chronologische Grundlage der alten chi-
nesischen Geschichte. München, 1867, 4to.
See Lit. Centralbl. (1868), No. 12, p. 299;
Ausland (1867), No. 44, p. 1040.

953 — — , Die Quellen der alten chinesischen Geschichte. München, 1870, 4to.

954 KURZ, H., Mémoire sur l'état politique et religieux

de la Chine, 2300 ans avant notre ère selon le
Chouking, Nouv. Journ. As., V., 1830, p. 401 ss.;
VI, p. 401 ss.

955   LJUNGSTEDT, A., Correction of an error in the
account of the last hours of Kanghi, Chin. Repos.,
I, p. 378.

956   GUETZLAFF, K., Remarks on the history and chronology of China from the earliest age down to the
present time; ibid, II, 1833, p. 74, 111.

957   — — , Charakter of Chinese historical works,
ibid, III, p. 53.

958   — — , A sketch of Chinese history. London,
1834, 2 vols., 8vo.
> German : E. Bauer. Quedlinburg, 1836, 2
> vols., 8vo.

959   — — , The eventful life of Hung woo, the foun-
der of the Ming dynasty from the Hung-woo
tseuen chuen, Chin. Repos., VII, p. 353.

960   — — , Rambles of the emperor Chingtih; ibid,
IX, p. 57.

961   — — , History of the southern Sung dynasty;
ibid, XI, p. 529.

962   — — , History of the Ming dynasty; ibid, XI,
p. 592.

963   — — , Geschichte des chinesischen Reiches, herausgegeben von K. Neumann. Stuttgart, 1847, 8vo.
> Dutch : Hague, 1852, 2 vols., 8vo.
> See Zeitschr. d. deutsch. morgenl. Ges.,
> XIII, p. 530.

964   — — , Leben des Kaisers Taokuang, Memoiren
des Hofes zu Peking. Leipzig, 1852, 8vo.
> English : London, 1852, 8vo.

965   BRIDGMAN, E. C., Character of Chinese monarchs and their wars, Ch. Repos., III, p. 516.

966   — — , Life and actions of Wu Tsih-tien, empress of the Tang dynasty; ibid, III, p. 543,

967   — — , Details of the success of Taukwang; ibid,
X, p. 87.

968 — — , Records of the three august sovereigns; ibid, X, p. 231.

969 — — , Chronology and list of all the dynasties of the Chinese monarchy; ibid, X, p. 121.

970 — — , Lifes and times of Confucius; ibid, XVIII, p. 337.

971 — — , Survey of the chronology and geography of China during the period occupied by the Chun Tsiu; ibid, XVIII, p. 393.

972 — — , The holy wars or records of the military achievements of the monarchs of the great pure dynasty; ibid, XIX, p. 241.

973 STEVENS, E., Sketch of the character of Hokwan, prime minister of China; ibid, III, p. 24.

974 INGLIS, R., Statesmen who have swayed modern China; ibid, IV, p. 59.

975 IDELER, L., Ueber die Zeitrechnung der Chinesen Verhandl. Berlin. Akadem. 1837, p. 199-369.; also Berlin, 1839, 4to.

976 DANIEL, Vse-obshtshaya istoria kitaya (General history of China), 1838, 4 fasc. (in Russian.)

977 URBAN, F. d', Histoire antediluvienne de la Chine ou histoire de la Chine jusqu' au déluge de Yao. Paris, 1840, 2 vols., 12mo.

978 — — , Discours sur l'empereur Kien-long. Paris, 1841, 12mo.

979 Points and Pickings in Chinese history. London, 1840, 8vo.

980 MILNE, W. C., Extract from the San kwoh chi, or the rebellion of the yellow caps, Ch. Repos., X, p. 98.

981 — — Extract from the San kwok chi, sketch of Kung ming; ibid, XII, p. 126.

982 SHUCK, J. L., Trial and condemnation of Ilipu; ibid, X, p. 633.

983 QUINCY, T. DE, Revolt of the Tartars or flight of Kalmuckkhan and his people from Russian territories to the frontier of China, Edinburgh magazine, complete works, IV, p 111-175.

984 SAVAGNIER, Abrégé de l'histoire de la Chine. Paris, 1844, 2 vols., 8vo., 336, 311 pp.

985 THORNTON, T., A history of China. London, 1844, 2 vols., 8vo.

986 VALROGER, Mélanges postumes de l'histoire, etc. Paris, 1844, 8vo.

987 WILLIAMS, S. W., Death of Taukwang and papers connected with the accession of Hienfung, Ch. Repos., XIX, p. 165, 231, 282.

988 MEDHURST, W. H., Memoir of the general Chin Chungmin, the hero of Wusung; ibid, XIII, p. 247.

989 BIOT, E., Étude sur les anciens temps de l'histoire chinoise, Journ. asiat., 4. sér., VI, p. 362; VII, p. 161, 389; also separately, Paris, 1846, 8vo.

990 — — , Mémoire sur la constitution politique de la Chine au XII siècle avant notre ère, Rec. des mém. de l'Ac. des Inscr. et de belles lettr., II.

991 — — , La population de la Chine et ses variations, Journ. asiat., 1856.

992 KAEUFFER, J. E. R., Das chinesische Volk vor Abraham's Zeiten, zu gutem Theile als Spiegel für die Völker des 19. Jahrh. Dresden, 1850, 8vo.

993 — — , Geschichte des ostasiatischen Reiches. Leipzig, 1860, 3 vols., 8vo.
See Lit. Centralbl., 1866, No. 16, p. 410.

994 — — , Ueberblick der Geschichte Ostasiens. Leipzig, 1864, 8vo.

995 PFIZMAYER, A., Ueber das Geschichtswerk Tsotschuen. Wien, 1851, 4to.

996 — — , Notizen aus der Geschichte des chinesischen Reiches, vom J. 590-529 v. Chr. Wien, 1856, 4 Abth., 8vo.

997 — — , Geschichte des Hauses Tschao. Wien, 1857, 4to.

998 — — , Geschichte des Hauses U. Wien, 1857, 4to.

999 — — , Leben des Prinzen Wuki. Wien, 1858, 4to.

1000 — — , Die Zeiten des Fürsten Siuen von Lu-
wen, Luhi etc. Wien, 4to.

1001 — — . Tschin-thang. Fürst-zertrümmerer von
Hu. Wiener Ak., phil. hist., 1862, p. 396.

1002 — — . Die Könige von Houi-nan aus dem Hause
Han; ibid. p. 575-618.

1003 — — . Die Heerführer Li-khuang und Li-ling;
ibid, 1863, p. 511-44; also 1864, 8vo.

1004 — — , Die Würdenträger Tsinen-pu-i, Sa-kuang,
Yu-tang-kue und deren Gesinnungsgenossen;
ibid, 1862, p. 131-163.

1005 — — , Geschichte des Hauses Thai-kung. Wien,
1863, 8vo.; ibid.

1006 — — , Die Geschichte einer Gesandtschaft bei
den Hiung-nus; ibid, 1863, p. 581-600; also separately.

1007 — — , Geschichte des Fürstenhauses Tsin; ibid,
1863, p. 74-152.

1008 — — , Geschichte des Hauses Tschen-kung;
ibid, p. 90.

1009 — — , Geschichte der Häuser Schaokung und
Khang-scho; ibid, p. 435.

1010 — — , Die Unternehmungen der früheren Han
gegen die südwestl. Fremdengebiete; ibid, Vol.
XLV (1864), p. 294-313.

1011 — — . Die Heerführer Weitsing und Ho-khiu-
ping; ibid, p. 139-180.

1012 — — , Die Eroberung der beiden Yue und des
Landes Tschao-sien durch Han; ibid, Vol. XLVI
(1864), p. 481-526.

1013 — — , Geschichte des Königlandes Tsu; ibid,
p. 68.

1014 — — , Keu-tsien, König von Yue; ibid, p. 197.

1015 — — , Ungewöhnliche Erscheinungen und Zu-
fälle in China um die Zeit der südlichen Sung,
ib., 1874; also separately, Vienna, 1874, 8vo.,
82 pp.

1016 SPEER, W., Notices of the ancient intercourse with

China through Central Asia and Chinese account of Jesus Christ, Chin. Repos., XVIII, p. 485.

1017 GORSKY, W., The beginning and first acts of the Mantschu dynasty, Russ. Eccl. Miss., I, No. 1 1852 (in Russian.)

1018 ZAKHAROFF, J., Historical sketch of the population of China; ibid, No. 3 (in Russian); English by W. Lobscheid. Hongkong, 1864, 8vo.

1019 HILARION, O., Sketch of the history of intercourse between China and Tibet; ibid, II, No. 6, 1853 (in Russian.)
German in Erman's Archiv., XV, 349-362.

1020 A history of China to the present time, including an account of the rise and progress of the present religious insurrection. London, 1854, 8vo.

1021 MERITENS, E. DE, Liste alphabétique des nien hao, Journ. as., 5. s., III, 510-536, 1854.

1022 WASSILJEFF, W., History of Eastern Asia from the 10th to the 13th century. St. Petersburg, 1857 (in Russian.)

1023 KRAPOWITZKY, M., The fall of the Ming dynasty, Russ. Eccl. Miss., III, No. 1 (1857) (in Russian.)

1024 OLIPHANT, L., China, a popular history. London, 1857, 8vo.

1025 Der Fall der Ming Dynasty und die Begründung der Mandschuherrschaft. Ausland, 1858, No. 11.

1026 NEUMANN, K. F., Ostasiatische Geschichte, vom ersten chinesischen Kriege bis zu den Verträgen, 1840-60. Leipzig, 1861, 8vo.
See Ch. and Jap. Repos., July, 1863.

1027 ROSSMANN, W., Der Eintritt Ostasiens in die moderne Gesichte. Preuss. Jahrbücher, XIII (1861), p. 256-281.

1028 Annales choisies de la dynastie Min, Revue de l'Orient, XV (1863), p. 203.

1029 REINAUD, J. T., Relations politiques et commerciales de l'empire Romain avec l'Asie Orientale, Journ. As., March, 1863; also Paris, 1863, 8vo.

1030 SUMMERS, J., The conquest of the island Tai-wan (Formosa) by the Chinese Kosenga or Cochinga, a. 1662, transl. from the "Nippon" of von Siebold, Ch. and Jap. Repos., I (1864.)

1031 — — , Sz-ma-tsien, the historian; ibid, III, p. 14-16.

1032 — — , History of the Ming dynasty; ibid, III, (1865), p. 417-424, 473-483.

1033 (FAY, Miss L. M.), Su-wu, the faithful ambassador to Tartary; ibid, II, p. 144.

1034 — — , Pan-chau, of the Han dynasty, the hero of Tibet; ibid, II, p. 98-100.

1035 — — , Ta-koo, a Chinese lady of the second century; ibid, II, p. 51-54.

1036 — — , Distinguished men of the T'ang dynasty; ibid, II, p. 19-22.

1037 — — , Memoir of Chau-woo; ibid, III, p. 545-547.

1038 — — , The favourite of Gai-wang of the Han dynasty; ibid, III, p. 102-105.

1039 — — , Noted characters in Chinese history, The Phoenix, II, p. 57.

1040 GLADISCH, A., Die Hyperboreer und die alten Schinesen. Leipzig, 1866, 4to.
See Heidelb. Jahrb., LIX, p. 422; Lit. Centralbl. (1867), p. 563.

1041 Die Mausoleen der chinesischen Kaiser aus der Ming dynastie, Globus, XII (1867), No. 11, p. 339-341.

1042 LABARTHE, C. DE, Essai critique sur les premiers temps de l'histoire de la Chine, Revue Orientale, 2. s., I, part I (1867), p. 64-71.

1043 PAUTHIER, G., Mémoires sur l'antiquité de l'histoire et de la civilisation chinoises d'après les écrivains et les monuments indigènes. Paris, 1868, 8vo., and Jour. as., 5. s., X, 197.

1044 Aperçu historique sur la Chine, par un missionnaire. Paris, 12mo.

1045 LAY, W. T., The close of the Ming dynasty, Notes and Queries, I, p. 117.

1046 MAYERS, W. F., "The western king mother;" ibid, II, p. 12.

1047 — — , Chinese chronological tables, Journ. of N. C. B. of the R. A. S., IV., Dec. 1867, p. 159-183; also in Doolittle's handbook, Vol. II, and in Chinese readers manual, p. 361-390.

1048 — — , Chinese explorations of the Indian Ocean during the 15th century, China Review, III, 219-225, 321-331; IV, 61-67, 173-190.

1049 TAINTOR, E. C., The emperor Hung-wu, Marsden's error respecting him, Notes and Queries, II, p. 52.

1050 Koxinga's name; ibid, II, p. 42; III, p. 30, 42, 58, 94.

1051 Giornale d'un ambassadore chinese spedite in Cocincina d'al imperatore Tao kwang, 1840-41, Bull. della Soc. Geogr. Ital., Aug., 1868.

1052 GREEN, D. D., Early history of Hangchou, Chin. Recorder, II, p. 156, 178.

1053 Synoptical table of Chinese dynasties; ibid, III, p. 78.

1054 BOWRA, E. C., Su Tung-p'o, China Review, I, p. 32.

1055 — — , The Manchu conquest of Canton; ibid, I, p. 86, 228.

1056 — — , The Liu family or Canton during the period of the five dynasties; ibid, I, p. 316.

1057 — — , The last of the Chinese, An episode in oriental history; ibid, III, p. 257-269.

1058 KOPSCH, H., Wang-an-shih, the "innovator," China Rev., II, p. 35-33, 74-80.

1059 OXENHAM, E. L., History of Hanyang and Hankow; ibid, I, p. 366-370; II, p. 98-103, 282-286.

1060 KINGSMILL, T. W., The mythical origin of the Chou or Djou dynasty, J. N. C. B. R. As. Soc., VII, 1873, p. 1.

1061 LEGGE, J., Two heroes of Chinese history, China Rev., I, p. 370.

1062 BRETSCHNEIDER, E., Notes on Chinese mediæval travellers to the west, Chinese Recorder, V,
1874, p. 113-126, 173-199, 237-252, 305-327;
VI, p. 1-22, 81-104; also separately, Shanghai,
1875, 8vo., with an appendix by A. Wylie.

1063 — — , Chinese intercourse with the countries of
central and western Asia during the fifteenth century, China Rev., IV, p. 312-318.

1064 ALLEN, H. J., Early relations of China and Japan;
ibid, III, p. 57-61.

1065 — — , Chinese notice of the Shogun Taikosa-
ma; ibid, III.

1066 HUGHES, G., The Japanese and China; ibid, II,
p. 369-375; III, p. 23-29.

1067 GROENEFELDT, W. P., The expedition of the
Mongols against Java in 1293, A. D., China Rev.,
IV, p. 246-255.

XI.

Geography and Travels.

a. General Geography and Topography, Population, Statistics.

1068 MUELLER, A., Disquisitio geographica et historica
de Chataja. Berolini, 1671, 4to.

1069 MARTIN MARTINIUS, Déscription géographique
de la Chine, Thévenot's collection, pt. III.

1070 D'ANVILLE, La Sérique des Anciens. Paris, 1775,
4to.

1071 AMIOT, Population de l'empire Chinois, Mém. conc.
la Chine, VI, p. 271-290.

1072 — , Introduction à la connaissance des peuples Chinois; ibid, XIV, p. 1.

1073 BOURGEOIS, Sur l'étendue de la ville de Nanquin
et la population de la Chine, Mém. conc., IX,
p. 431.

1074 Description de l'inondation de la ville de Yen-tchcou-
fou en 1742; ibid, IX, 454.

1075 GUIGNES, J. DE (père), Mémoire dans laquelle on
examine quelle fut l'étendue de l'empire de la
Chine depuis sa fondation jusqu'à l'an 249 avant
J. Ch. Rec. de l'acad. des inscr., XLII, 1786,
p. 93.

1076 JACQUEMIN, Sur l'isle de Tson-ming, prov. de
Nanking, Lettre de 1712, Lettr. éd., nouv. ed.,
XXVIII, p. 131-172.

1077 MANNERT, Serica, Handbuch der Geogr. und Reisen, IV, p. 500-528.

1078 KLAPROTH, J., Ueber die russisch-chinesische
Grenze. Arch. für as. Lit.   St. Petersburg, 1810.

1079 — —, Notice sur l'Archipel de Jean Potocki de
la Mer Jaune avec une carte.   Paris, 1820, 4to.

1080 — —, Notices géographiques et historiques du
Thai-thsing-y-thoung-tschi.   Peking, 1770; Mag.
asiat., I, 1825.

1081 — —, De la frontière russe et chinoise, notes
recueillies pendant un voyage en Sibérie en 1806;
Mém. relat. à l'Asie, I, 1826.

1082 — — Observations sur la carte de l'Asie, Journ.
As., VIII, 1826.

1083 — —, Tableau des plus hautes montagnes de la
Chine, Mag. As., II, 1826.

1084 — —, Aperçu statistique de la Chine tiré de documens originaux.
German in Hertha, X, 1827.

1085 — —, Remarques géographiques sur les provinces occidentales de la Chine décrites par M. Polo,
Nouv. Journ. As., I, 1828.

1086 — —, Recherches sur les ports de Gampou et
Zaithoum, Mém. rel. à l'Asie, II, 200.

1087 — —, Description du grand canal de la Chine;
ibid, III, 1828.

1088 — —, Recherches sur le pays de Fou-sang des
livres chinois.

1089 THOMS, P. P., Statistics of China, Macao, etc., Asiat. Journ and Monthly Reg., XX, 1825.

1090 RÉMUSAT, A., Remarques sur l'extension de l'empire chinois du côté de l'occident, Rec. de l'Acad. des Inscr., VIII, 1827, p. 124 ss. See Ritter, Erdkunde, VII, p. 560 ss.

1091 DAVIS, J. F., Geographical notice of the frontiers of the Burmese and Chinese empires, Transact. R. Soc., II. London, 1827.

1092 RITTER, K., Die Erdkunde im Verhältniss zur Natur und zur Geschichte des Menschen. Berlin, 1830-1858, 20 vols., 8vo. (Asia, Vols. II-VIII.)
Russian: Asia, I, IV, by P. Semenoff and W. Grigorieff. St. Petersburg, 1859-1869.

1093 MORRISON, J. R., General account of the division and topography of the Chinese empire, Chin Rep., I, 1832, p. 33, 113, 170.

1094 — — , Remarks on the situation of the port of Canfu; ibid, III, 1834, p. 115.

1095 — — , Description of the coast of China and places on it; ibid, V, 335; VI, 9.

1096 BERGHAUS, H., Asia. Sammlung von Denkschriften in Bez. auf die Geographie etc. Gotha, 1832.

1097 BRIDGEMAN, E. C., Population of China examined, Chin. Rep., I, p. 347, 385.

1098 — — , General division of the eighteen provinces; ibid, XI, p. 44.

1099 — — , Notices of the Peiho and passage up to Peking; ibid, XI, p. 92.

1100 — — , Topography of the provinces Chihli, Shantung, Shansi, Kiangsu, Nganhwui, Chekiang, Kiangsi, Fuhkien, Kwangtung, Kwangsi; ibid, XI, p. 101, 162, 210, 307, 374, 438, 557, 617, 651; XII, p. 88, 309, 477; XIV, p. 171.

1101 — , Notice of a visit to the cities of Kiating and Nantsiang; ibid, XVII, p. 462.

1102 GUETZLAFF, K., Remarks on the population of China, Chin. Rep., II, 1833, p. 33.

1103 — — , Navigation and course of the Yangtse kiang; ibid, II, p. 316.

1104 Yangtszekiang, nautical surveys made by H. B. M. ship "Conway" in 1840, Chin. Rep., X, 1841-42, p. 383.

1105 Coast of China, etc., Observations made by H. B. M. squadron in 1840, Chin. Rep., X, 1841-42, p. 371.

1106 HYACINTH (Bitschurin), Statistitscheskoe opisanie kitaiskoi imperii (Statistical description of the Chinese empire.) St. Petersburg, 1842, 2 vols., 8vo., 626 pp., map (in Russian.)

1107 BISCHOFF-WIDDERSTEIN, F., China oder Uebersicht der vorzüglichsten geographischen Punkte. Wien, 1843, 8vo., map.

1108 WILLIAMS, S. W., Chinese topography. Canton, 1844, 8vo.

1109 — — , Alphabetical list of all provinces, departments and districts in China, Ch. Rep., XIII, p. 320, 357, 418, 478, 513.

1110 — — , Topography of the provinces Honan, Yunnan, Kweichau, Hupeh, Hunan, Shansi, Szchuen, Kansu; ibid, XVIII, p. 525, 588; XIX, p. 97, 156, 220, 317, 394, 554; XX, p. 546.

1111 — — , Course and topography of the Chukiang or Pearl river; ibid, XX, p. 105, 113.

1112 Chinese topography. Canton, 1844, 8vo.

1113 BIOT, E., Etudes sur les montagnes et les cavernes de la Chine. Paris, 1844, 8vo.

1114 — — , Recherches sur la hauteur de quelques points remarquables du territoire chinois. Paris, 8vo.

1115 — — , Mémoire sur la géographie de la Chine ancienne. Paris, 8vo.

1116 — — , Mémoire sur les déplacements du cours inférieur du fleuve jaune, Journ. As., 4. sér., I, p. 432; II, p. 84, 307; also separately. Paris, 1844, 8vo.

1117 — — , Mémoire sur l'extension progressive des

côtes orientales de la Chine, Journ. As., 4. sér., IV, p. 408.

1118 — — , Dictionnaire des noms anciens et modernes des villes et arrondissements compris dans l'empire chinois. Paris, 1852, 8vo.

1119 MACGOWAN, D. J., The Eagre of the Tsientang river, Transact. Ch. Br. R. As. Soc., IV, 1855, p. 11-19.

1120 BOWRING, J., A letter on the population of China; ibid, V, 1856, p. 1-16.

1121 PETSCHUROFF, Aufnahme des Amurstroms im Jahre 1855 und die russisch-chinesische Grenze von 1689-1856, Peterm. Geogr. Mitth., 1856, No. 11-12.

1122 PETERMANN, A., Zur Topographie der Provinz Fu kiän. N. Zeitschr. f. allg. Erdkunde, II, p. 6, 1857.

1123 — — , Die südlichen Inselgruppen des chinesischen Reiches. "Ausland," No. 25, 1858.

1124 EDKINS, J., On the ancient mouths of the Yangtsekiang, Journ. Shanghai Lit. and Scient. Soc., I, 1858, p. 77-84.

1125 KRONE, R., A notice of the Sanon district, Transact. Ch. Br. R. As. Soc., VI, 1859, p. 71-105, map.

1126 — — , Der Lofan Berg in China, Petermann's Mitth., 1864, p. 283-292.

1127 WARD, J., Sailing directions for the Yangtze kiang from Woosung to Hankow, J. N. Ch. Br. As. Soc., I, 1859, p. 231-246.

1128 PLATH, J. H., Allgemeine Uebersicht über Asien und das chinesische Reich. Stein's Handb. der Geogr. und Statist., II, 3. Leipzig, 1860; also separately.

1129 — — , Die chinesische Provinz Shantung. "Ausland," 1873, No. 4 ss.

1130 BRAUER, J. H., Das chinesische Reich und Korea. Stein's Handb. d. Geogr. und Stat., II, 3, 1860.

1131 BARTON, A., Notes on the Yang-tsze-kiang, J. R. Geogr. Soc., 1862, p. 26-41.

1132 KONER, W., Der Yangtze-kiang von Hankow bis Pingshan. Zeitschr. f. allg. Erdk., 1862, XII, p. 87-111. "Ausland," 1862, No. 18.

1133 PAUTHIER, G., Description de la ville de Quinsay (Hang-tcheou-fou.) Paris, 1863, 8vo.

1134 VAUTÉ, de, et GRAS, A. le, Instructions nautiques sur les côtes Est de la Chine, la Mer jaune le golfe de Petchili et le Liau Tung, et la côte, Ouest de la Corée. Paris, 1863, 8vo.

1135 GRAS, A. le, Mer de Chine, 1863, 8vo.

1136 KIEPERT, H., Fahrweg durch die Gobi von Kiachta nach Peking. Leitschr. f. allg. Erdkunde, XIV, 1863, map.

1137 The Yeang-Tai mountains, Blackwood's Mag., April, 1863.

1138 ROSNY, L. de, Études asiatiques de géographie et d'histoire. Paris, 1864, 8vo.

1139 NOVELLA, F. J., Catalogus omnium civitatum in singulis imperii Sinarum provinciis existentium. Romae, 1864, fol.
   See L. de Rosny, Journ. As., 6. sér., VII, 1866, p. 556 ss.

1140 Topography of China and neighbouring states with degrees of longitude and latitude. Hongkong, 1864, 8vo.

1141 Etat actuel des provinces du Yang-tze-kiang, Rev. Mar. et Col., XI, 1864, p. 759-767.

1142 Chinese Topography, Kiangsu province, Chin. and Jap. Repos., II, p. 175

1143 BOURGEOIS, S., Notice sur la baie du Peiho, Revue marit. et colon., May, 1864, p. 43-61.

1144 — — , Notice sur le Peiho; ibid, 1866, p. 681-706; XVIII, p. 98-118, 6 maps.

1145 GRAD, C., La province de Pétchili et le Peiho, Nouv. Ann. d. Voy, February, 1865, p. 193-212.

1146 BLEKKING, J. II., Beschrijving der Chinesche en

Japansche zeeën en golf van Siam. Amsterdam, 1865, 8vo.

1147 Soochow, Hangchow and Ningpo, Chin. and Jap. Rep., III, 1865, p. 577-580.

1148 Names and Area of the Chinese provinces; ibid, III, p. 559.

1149 Statistics of the Tatsing Dynasty; ibid, IV, p. 548-559.

1150 SKATSCHKOFF, K., Ozaslugakh Venetsiantsa, M. Polo. (The merits of the Venetian, Marco Polo.) St. Petersbg., 1865, 8vo. (in Russian.)

1151 WILLIAMSON, A., Notes on the North of China, its productions and communications, J. N. Ch. Br. R. As. Soc., IV, p. 33-63.

1152 — — , Notes on the productions of Shantung; ibid, p. 64-73.

1153 YULE, H., Notice of Cathay, Proc. R. Geogr. Soc., X, 1866, p. 270.

1154 — — , Cathay and the way thither. Being a collection of mediæval notices of China. With a preliminary essay on the intercourse between China and the western nations previous to the discovery of the cape route. London, 1867, 2 vols., 8vo.

1155 — — , The great rivers of Yunan and the sources of the Irawaddi. "Ocean Highways," Nov., 1872, p. 249.

1156 — — , The Atlas sinensis and other Sinensia, Geogr. Mag., July, 1874, 3 maps.

1157 HOCKLY, J. M., Notes on the Yang-tze-kiang, together with corrections of the existing charts, Proc. R. Geogr. Soc., XI, 1867, p. 261.

1158 KINGSMILL, T. W., Notes on the topography of some of the localities in Manji or southern China mentioned by M. Polo, Not. and Quer., I, 1867, p. 52.

1159 MAYERS, W. F., Capitals of China; ibid, I, p. 60.

1160 — — , Sun wei in Kwangtung: ibid, II, p. 155.

1161 — — , Marco Polo's legend concerning Banyan; ibid, II, p. 162.

1162 — — , Advance of a Chinese general to the Caspian; ibid, II, p. 60.
1163 China Sea, Merc. Mar. Mag., Sept., 1868. p. 266.
1164 ELIAS, N., Notes on a portion of the old bed of the Yellow River, J. N. Ch. Br. R. As. Soc., IV, 1869, p. 80-86.
1165 — — , Report of an exploration of the new course of the Yellow River, J. N. Ch. Br. R. As. Soc., 1869, p. 259.
1166 — — , Appunti sul fiume Giallo della China, "Cosmos" di G. Cora, 1874, p. 233-243, map.
1167 REUSCHE, Städtebevölkerung in China, Krit, Misc. z. Geogr. Zeitschr. d. Ges. f. Erdk., IV, 1869.
1168 LOBSCHEID, W., The population of China, Chin. Rec., I, p. 89.
1169 KNOWLTON, M. J., The mountain tribes of Chekiang province; ibid, I, p. 241.
1170 — — , The population of the Chinese empire, Not. and Quer., II, p. 88, 103, 117.
1171 — — , The cities of China; ibid., III, p. 60.
1172 WYLIE, A., Advance of a Chinese general to the Caspian; ibid., II, p. 153.
1173 — — , Situation of Heen-too, Ch. Recorder, IV, p. 52.
1174 PHILIPS, G., The Tarsa; ibid, II, p. 292.
1175 — — , Marco Polo and Ibn Batutea in Fookien; ibid, III, p. 12, 44, 71, 87, 125.
1176 — — , On what sea was T'iao-chih situated and how was it reached from China? ibid., III, p. 137.
1177 — — , Where was Ansi? ibid., III, p. 164.
1178 — — , The roads to the western sea (Hsi 'hai) from China; ibid., III, p. 191, 258.
1179 — — , Notices of Southern Mangi with remarks by Col. H. Yule., J. R. Geogr. Soc., 1874. See Chin. Rec., V, 1874, p. 169-171.
1180 — — , Zaitun Researches, Chin. Rec., V, 1874, p. 327-339; VI, 1875, p. 31-42.

1181 BRETSCHNEIDER, E., Ta ts'in-kuo, Chin. Rec.,
      III, p. 29.

1182 — — , Notes on Chinese mediæval travellers to the
      West, Chin. Rec., V, p. 113-126, 173-199, 237-
      252, 305-327 ; also sep. Shanghai, 1875, 8vo.,
      130 pp. with Appendix : comparative chronology
      by A. Wylie, p. 125-130.

1183 FRITSCHE, H., Resultate aus astronomischen und
      magnetischen Beobachtungen auf einer Reise von
      St. Petersburg über Sibirien und die Mongolei nach
      Peking in den Jahren 1867 und 1868 angestellt. Re-
      pert. f. Meteorol., I. St. Petersbg., 1869, p. 151-174.

1184 — — , Geographische, Magnetische und hypso-
      metr. Bestimmungen an 22 in der Mongolei und
      dem nördlichen China gelegenen Orten, ausge
      führt in den Jahren, 1868 und 1869, Rep. f. Me-
      teorol, II ; also in "Iswestija" Sib. Sect. of Imp.
      Russ. Geogr. Soc., I, 1870-71, No. 3.   See Pe-
      termann's Mitth., 1872, p. 238.

1185 — — , Geographische, Magnetische und hypsom.
      Bestimmungen an 27 im nördlichen China gelege-
      nen Orten. Rep. f. Meteorol., III, 1873 ; Peter-
      mann's Mitth., 1874, p. 194.

1186 — — , Geographische etc. Bestimmungen an 59
      Orten angestellt auf einer Reise von Peking durch
      die östliche Mongolei. Rep. f. Meteorol., IV, 1874,
      map.

1187 .— — , Hypsometrical and geographical determi-
      nations of points based on the observations made
      in 1868-1872 by Arch. Palladius, Capt. Przewals-
      ki, Messrs. Lemonossow, Mosnin and Dr. Fritsche,
      " Sapiski" Imp. Russ. Geogr. Soc., V, 1875 (in
      Russian).

1188 LÉPISSIER, E., Positions géographiques de 12
      points de l'empire Chinois situés dans le Tcheuli,
      la terre des Herbes et le Chansi, Bull. Soc. géogr.
      Paris, July, Aug. 1870. See Peterm. Mitth., 1871,
      p. 390.

1189 MARKHAM, J., Notes on the Shantung province, J. N. Ch. Br. R. As. Soc., 1871, p. 1.

1190 EITEL, E. J., The fabulous source of the Hoangho; ibid, p. 45.

1191 SMITH, F. P., A vocabulary of proper names in Chinese and English of places, persons, tribes, etc. Shanghai, 1871, 8vo. See Chin. Recorder, III, 228.

1192 — — , The great rivers of China, Ocean Highways, April, 1873.

1193 RICHTHOFEN, F. von, Letters on different provinces of China, 6 Nos. Shanghai, 1871, fol.

1194 — — , Die geographische Lage von Si-ngan-fu und seine Weltstellung. Leitschr. K. K. geol. Reichsanst. Wien, 1872; also in Peterm. Mitth., XIX, 1873, No. 1.

1195 — — , Ueber die Bevölkerungszahl von China. Verh. Ges. f. Erdk. Berlin, 1875, p. 35-41.

1196 MARTIN, E., Sur la statistique relative au dénombrement de la population en Chine, Bull. Soc. Géo. Paris, July, 1872.

1197 — — , L'extrême orient; ibid, Jan., 1873.

1198 BRANDAT, P., Mers de Chine. Paris, 1872.

1199 HIRTH, F., The peninsula of Leichou, China Review, II, p. 149-160.

1200 — — , The Geographical distribution of commercial products in Kwangtung; ibid, p. 306-309, 376-382, map.

1201 — — , The West River or Sikiang; ibid, III, p. 46-49.

1202 WENUKOFF, Col., Essai d'une topographie stratégique de la frontière russe en Asie, 1873, 2 vols., 2 maps.
        German by Krahmer.

1203 GARNIER, F., Navigations du Yangtse-kiang, Bull. Soc. de Géogr. 6. sér., V, 1873, p. 187.

1204 Verfall des Kaisercanals in China, "Globus," XXV, 1874, No. 4.

1205 Der Busen von Petschili. Hydrogr. Mitth. Berlin,
II, 1874, No. 3.
1206 DOUGLAS, C., Notes on the identity of Zayton,
J. R. Geogr. Soc., 1874, p. 118, map.
1207 ALLEN, C. F. R., Chung-ling-ch'üan (Chinkiang),
China Rev., II, p. 351.
1208 STRITT MATTER, A., Around Lüsan (Kiukiang),
Chin. Rec., VI, p. 267-270.
1209 Lothungen im Chinesischen Meere. Annal. der Hydrogr. Berlin, 1875, No. 23-24.

b. The Open Ports.

1210 SMITH, G., A narrative of an exploratory visit to
each of the consular cities of China and to the
islands cf Hongkong and Chusan. London, 1847,
8vo., map, 12 copper engravings.
See S. W. Williams, Ch. Repos., XX, 436.
German in Mag. f. d. neueste Gesch. der
evang. Miss. ges. Basel, 1848, 8vo.
1211 BOWERS, A., The Yang-tzekiang and the new
Treaty Ports, Ch. and Jap. Repos., I, 1863,
p. 268-270.
1212 Canton, Kiung-cheu, Swatow, Tangcheu and New-
chwang; ibid III, 238.
1213 DENNYS, N. B., The Treaty Ports of China and
Japan, A complete guide to the open ports of
these countries, together with Peking, Yedo, Hongkong and Macao, With 29 maps and plans by
W. F. Mayers, N. B. Dennys and C. King. London and Hongkong, 1867, 8vo.

Canton.

1214 GAUBIL, P., Plan de Canton, Souciet, Observ.
math., 1729.
1215 HORSBURGH, J., Chart of the Canton river.
1216 BRIDGMAN, E. C., Fire in the city of Canton, Ch.
Repos., IV, p. 390.

1217 — — , Description of the city of Canton ; ibid,
II, p. 145, 193, 241, 289,; IV, p. 42, 101, 189,
244, 291, 341, 534, 569 ; XV, p. 47, 317 ; Short
essays, XII, p. 604 ; XIV, p. 335 ; XV, p. 157,
219, 364 ; XVI, p. 247, 331.

1218 — — , Proposition for promoting the public se-
curity in the Union of the Eight Streets at Canton,
Ch. Repos, XVII, p. 360.

1219 — — , Trip to Fushan near Canton, Ch. Rep.,
XVI, p. 142.

1220 Description of the city of Canton. Canton, 1839,
8vo.

1221 WILLIAMS, S. W., Pagodas in and near Canton,
Chin. Rep., XIX, p. 535.

1222 — — , Account of the Hiang-fan, a Mohammedan mosque and burying ground near Canton ;
ibid., XX, p. 77.

1223 RONDOT, N., Une promenade dans Canton, Journ.
as., 4. sér., XI, 1848.

1224 PARKES, H. S., An inscription on a tablet in the
Polo temple near Canton, Transact. Ch. Br. R.
As. Soc., III, 1853, p. 133.

1225 DIETERICI, Arabisches aus Kanton, Zeitschr. d.
d. morgenl. Ges., XIII, p. 475.

1226 YVAN, M., Inside Canton. London, 1858, 8vo.

1227 The new foreign settlement at Canton. Macao,
1858, 8vo.

1228 KROOMAN, D., Map of the city and entire suburbs
of Canton. Canton, 1860, 8vo.

1229 Three weeks on the West river of Canton, compiled
from the journals of Rev. Dr. Legge, Dr. Palmer
and Mr. Tsang-kweih-wan. Hongkong, 1866, 8vo.

1230 Fire brigades in Canton. Notes and Queries, II,
p. 1.

1231 KERR, J. G., Description of the great Examination
Hall at Canton, Journ. of N. C. B. of R. A. S.,
1866, p. 63-70, with plan.

1232 — — , The native benevolent institutions of Canton, China Review, II, p. 88-95; III, p. 108-114.

1233 — — , The prisons of Canton; ibid, IV, p. 115-122.

1234 Rivière de Canton ou Chou kiang. Paris, depôt de la Marine, 1867.

1235 TAINTOR, E. C., Mohammedan mosque at Canton, Notes and Quer., III, p. 12.

1236 The great bell at Canton; ibid, III, p. 22.

1237 Canton River, Bodham Cave, Com. Reed. London, hydrogr. office, 1868.

1238 Canton, China Mag., 1869, p. 13.

1239 GRAY, Walks about the city of Canton. Hongkong, 1874, 8vo.

1240 MUNDY, W. W., Canton and the Bogue. London, 1875. 8vo.

Shanghai.

1241 LOCKHART, W., Regulations of the Hall of United Benevolence at Shanghai, Ch. Repos., XV, p. 402.

1242 BRIDGMAN, E. C., Notices on Shanghai; ibid, XV, p. 466; XVIII, p. 384.

1243 — — , Description of Shanghai; ibid, XVI, p. 529.

1244 — — , Walks about Shanghai; ibid, XVII, p. 468, 530; XIX, p. 105, 227, 390.

1245 — — , Address from the people of Shanghai to the foreign residents of Shanghai against eating beef; ibid, XVII, p. 260.

1246 — — , Memoranda made on a trip to the hills; ibid, XVIII, p. 181.

1247 MORRISON, J. R., Reminiscences of Shanghai in 1842; ibid, XVII, p. 528.

1248 SHAW, C., Historical sketch of Shanghai; ibid, XVIII, p. 18.

1249 — — , Notice of the years of famine and distress which have occurred at Shanghai; ibid XIX, p. 113; also in Ch. and Jap. Rep., III, p. 33-37.

1250 FRANCE, Notice sur la ville de Shanghai, Rec. d. mém. de méd. mil., 3. sér., IV, 1860.
1251 CASTANO, Esquisse topographique de la ville de Shanghai et de ses environs, Rec. mém. de méd, mil., V, 1861.
1252 HENDERSON, J., Shanghai hygiene. Shanghai, 1863, 8vo.
1253 The district of Shanghai as described by native authors, and more especially in the Tai-tsing-yi-t'ung-chi, Ch. and J. Rep., II, 185; III, 331.
1254 Das Leben in Shanghai. Ausland (1864), No. 52, p. 836.
1255 Reminiscences of the opening of Shanghai to Foreign Trade, Ch. and Jap. Repos., II, p. 79-88.
1256 The foundling hospital at Shanghai; ibid, III, p. 37-40, 129-136.
1257 Shanghai harbour, London, hydrogr. office, 1866.
1258 Shanghai, Topogr. departm. of the War office, Southampton, 1867.
1259 LANGE, H., Shanghai considered socially. Shanghai, 1869, 8vo.
1260 ANDREE, R., Shanghai, "Der Welthandel," II, 1870, with plan.
1261 Der Welthafen Shanghai, Globus, XXI, p. 268, 1872.
1262 SCHMIDT, C., Aus der Geschichte von Shanghai, Zeitschr. d. Deutsch. Ges. f. Natur-und Völkerk. Ostasiens, No. 4, 5, 1874.
1263 GORDON, Map of the country around Shanghai. Shanghai.

Fuchou.

1264 SMITH, G., Notices of Fuchau, Ch. Repos., XV, p. 185.
1265 COLLINSON, R., Notices of the city of Fuchau; ibid, XV, 225; also in Ch. and Jap. Repos., III, p. 462. 1865.

1266   JOHNSON, S., Notices and description of Fuhchau ;
           ibid, XVI, p. 483, 613.
1267   ROSE, J., Medical notes and topography of Foochow,
           Pacif. Med. and Surg. Journ., 1862.

Ningpo.

1268   MILNE, W. C., Description of Ningpo, Chin. Rep.,
           XIII, p. 14, 77, 127, 337 ; XVII, p. 14, 57, 105.
1269   EDKINS, J., Persian street in Ningpo, Not. and
           Quer., III, p. 55.

Amoy.

1270   COLLINSON, R., Survey of the harbour of Amoy,
           Naut. Mag., 1842 ; also Chin. Rep., XII, p. 121.
1271   Kulangsu and Amoy, Chin. Rep., XI, p. 504.
1272   DOUGLAS, C., Missionary map of Amoy and the
           neighbouring country.   Edinburgh, 1873.

Chefoo.

1273   Renseignements sur la baie de Tchefou et sur Tien-
           tsin, Ann. Hydr., 1873, p. 214.
1274   Die Rhede von Tschifu und die Kungkung Inseln.
           Hydrogr. Mitth.   Berlin, 1875.

Tientsin.

1275   CONTENSON, G. DE, Les inondations dans la plai-
           ne de Tientsin, Recherches sur leur causes et les
           moyens d'y remédier., Bull. Soc. de Géogr.   Pa-
           ris, 1874, map).

Niuchwang.

1276   SCHUECK, A., Ein Ritt nach den Salzmarschen in
           Nicuchwang, Mag. für d. Lit. d. Ausl., 1865,
           No. 28, p. 389-391.

1277 Beschreibung des Hafens von Niuchuang, Hydrogr. Mitth. Berlin, II, 1874, No. 8, 9.

c. Peking.

1278 GERBILLON, Topography of Peking, 1705, Lettr. édif. nouv., éd., XXVIII (1832), p. 35-43.
1279 DELISLE, Plan de la ville de Pékin, et PINGRÉ, Description de la ville de Pékin, pour servir à l'intelligence du plan de cette ville gravé par Delisle. Paris, 1765, 4to.
1280 HYACINTH, Opissanie Pekina i yevo okrestnostei (Description of Peking and its environs). St. Petersburg, 1829, 8vo. with plan (in Russian).
   French by Ferry de Pigny; ibid, 1829, 8vo.
1281 EYRIES et KLAPROTH, Rapport sur le plan de Péking, publié à St. Pétersbourg en 1829, Nouv. Journ. As., IV, 1829, p. 356 ss.
   German in Krit. Wegweiser der Landkartenkunde, II, 1830.
1282 TRACY, J., Description of the city of Peking, Ch. Repos., II, p. 433, 481.
1283 JERVIS, T. B., Chinese plan of the Tartar or Inner city of Peking. London, 1843.
1284 RONDOT, N., Peking et la Chine. Paris, 4to.
1285 SKATCHKOFF, C., Description of the Russian observatory at Peking (in Russian).
1286 Grundplan und Beschreibung der Stadt Peking, Allgem. Bauzeitung. Wien, 1860, 4to.
1287 Ein Besuch in Peking. "Ausland," 1863, No. 49, p. 1157.
1288 MORACHE, G., La météréologie de Pékin, Rec. Mém. d. méd. mil., XII, 1864.
1289 — — , Pékin et ses habitants. Paris, 1869.
1290 The situation of Peking, Ch. and Jap. Repos., I (1864), p. 487-494.
1291 PAUTHIER, G., Une visite à Youen-ming-youen,

palais d'été de l'empereur Khien-loung, Le Tour du Monde, 1864, 2. sem., p. 97-112.

1292 RENNIE, D. F., Peking and the Pekingese. London, 1865, 2 vols., 8vo.

　　　　See Westm. Rev., XXIX, No. 67, p. 251; Reader, 1865, No. 152, p. 593; Athenaeum, Nov., 1865, p. 719.

1293 BEAUMONT, O. de, Huit jours à Pekin en 1865. Paris, 1866, 8vo.

1294 The tombs of the emperors of the Kin dynasty near Peking, "Iswestija" Imp. Russ. Geogr. Soc., II, 1866 (in Russian).

1295 LOCKHART, W., Notes on Peking, Journ. R. G. S., 1866, p. 128.

1296 LAMPREY, J., Notes of a journey in the N. W. neighbourhood of Peking; ibid, 1867, p. 239-269.

1297 EDKINS, J., The old roman catholic cemetery at Peking, Ch. Recorder, II, 73.

1298 — — , Description of Peking in A. Williamson's journeys in N. Ch., Vol. II. (No. 1601.)

1299 DUDGEON, J., The great medical college at Peking, Ch. Recorder, II, p. 237.

1300 The Kwo-tsze-kien (Peking); ibid, IV, p. 85.

1301 FRITSCHE, H., Ueber die geographischen Constanten Pekings, Bull. de l'acad. imp. des sc. St. Petersbg., XVI, 1871, No. 6, p. 465-485, plan.

1302 MARTIN, Pékin, sa météréologie, son édilité, sa population, Bull. Soc. Géogr., 6. sér., VI, 1873, p. 290 ss.

1303 Peking und seine Umgebung. "Ausland," 1873, p. 536.

1304 Peking, "Europa," 1874, No. 21.

1305 MEECH, S. E., A recent visit to the Yün-shui-tung (Peking), Chin. Rec., V, 1874, p. 339 ss.

1306 BRETSCHNEIDER, E., Archaeological researches on Peking and its environs, Chin. Rec., VI, 1875, p. 161-181, 307-322, 377-401, maps, plans; also separately Shanghai, 1876, 8vo., 63 pp.

1307   — — , The Po'huashan near Peking, "Iswesti-ja" Imp. Russ. Geo. Soc., XI, 1875, No. 2 (in Russian).

d. Chusan.

1308 OUCHTERLONY, J., Statistical notes on Chusan. Madras, 1840, 8vo.
1309 — — , A statistical sketch of the island of Chusan. London, 1841, 8vo.
1310 LOCKHART, W., Topographical account of Chusan. Canton, 1841, 8vo.
1311 — — , Geology and people of Chusan, Ch. Repos., X, 424.
1312 BRIDGMAN, E. C., Situation and advantages of Chusan; ibid, IX, 101.
1313 Dr. CUNNINGHAM'S account of Chusan from Harris' voyages; ibid, IX, 133.
1314 — , Voyage to Chusan. London, 8vo.
1315 THOM, R., Letters from Chusan after its capture, Ch. Repos., IX, p. 230, 232, 325.
1316 Chusan archipelago; ibid, X, p. 251.
1317 MORRISON, J. R., Topographical account of Chusan; ib., X, p. 328.
1318 GUEZLAFF, K., Reminiscences of Chusan during its occupation by the British in 1840-41; ibid, X, p. 481.
1319 LOOMIS, A. W., Scenes in Chusan. Philadelphia, 1857, 12mo.
1320 Beschreibung der Insel Chusan, Hydrogr. Mitth., 1873, No. 20.

e. Formosa.

1321 Verhaal van de verövering t'eyland Formosa door de Sinesen, op. den 5. Juli, 1664, 4to.
1322 SAKEN, E. A., Het verwaerloosde Formosa of waerachtig verhael. Amsterdam, 1675, 4to., met plaaten.

French by Candidius (Formosa negligée) in collection of Voyages. London, 1703, Vol. I; Recueil de Voyages, X, p. 202-387. German in Beschreibung dreier mächtigen königreiche Japan, Siam und Corea. Nüraberg, 1672, 8vo., p. 685-706.

See Gützlaff, Chin. Rep., VI, 1838, p. 583.

1323 PSALMANAZAR, An historical and geographical description of Formosa. London, 1704, 12mo.

French : Amsterdam, 1705, 8vo. See Pinkerton Travels, XVII, p. 154 : "known and acknowledged to have been an imposition." Gützlaff, Ch. Rep., VI, p. 583.

1324 MAILLA, DE, Description de l'isle de Formose (1715), Lettres édif., XIV, 1-70, map ; Nouv. Ed., 1781, XVIII, p. 413-467 ; 1832, XXIX, p. 65-114.

1325 VALENTYN, Fr., Beschryvinge van Tayouan of Formosa en onzen Handel aldaar. in Beschr. van den Handel en Vaart der Niederlanders of Tsjina. T., IV, p. 33-94. Amsterdam, 1726.

1326 AMIOT, Sur la submersion de l'isle de Formose, Mém. conc., X.

1327 KLAPROTH, J., Description de Formosa, extraite des livres chinois, Mém. relat. à l'Asie, I, 1826.

1328 MALTE-BRUN, Analyse de quelques mémoires Hollandais sur l'isle de Formose, Annales des Voy, VIII.

1329 STEVENS, E., Situation, divisions, etc. of Formosa with map, Ch. Repos., II, p. 408.

1330 BRIDGMAN, E. C., Luhchau's remarks on the dealings of the Chinese government in Formosa ; ibid, VI, p. 418.

1331 WILLIAMS, S. W., Visit of the U. S. brig "Dolphin" to the port of Kilung in Formosa ; ibid, XVIII, p. 392.

1332 SWINHOE, R., Narrative of a visit to the island of Formosa, Journ. of N. C. B. of R. A. S., II, p. 145, 1859.

1333 — — , Notes on the island of Formosa, 1863, 8vo.

1334 — — , Additional notes on Formosa, Proc. R. G. S., X, 1866.

1335 Expeditionen auf der Insel Formosa, Globus, XII, p. 365.

1336 COLLINGWOOD, C., A boat journey across the northern end of Formosa, Proc. R. G. S., XI, p. 167, 1867.

1337 Formosa island and strait. London, hydrog. office, 1867.

1338 Formosa, south and west coast, China pilot, I; in Naut. mag., March, 1867, p. 153.

1339 Notes of an overland journey from Takao to Tamsui, Notes and Queries, I, p. 71.

1340 Native description of Formosa; ibid, II, p. 22.

1341 KOPSCH, H., Jottings about Formosa; ibid, II, p. 149.

1342 — — , Notes on the rivers in northern Formosa, Proc. R. G. S., XIV, p. 79.

1343 Violent persecution in Formosa, Ch. Recorder, I, p. 65.

1344 MAXWELL, J. L., Present state of affairs in Formosa; ibid, I, p. 258.

1345 MARTIN, V. de St., Aperçu général de l'ile de Formose, Bull. de S. géo. Paris, June, 1868.

1346 BROOKER, E. W., Formosa and islands, Naut. mag., Sept. 1868.

1347 OBERLAENDER, B., Formosa, "Der Welthandel." Stuttgart, 1869, map.

1348 SCHETELIG, A., Bericht über eine Reise in Formosa, Ztschr. der Ges. f. Erdk. Berlin, III, p. 385.

1349 Ein Besuch auf der Insel Formosa. Weserzeitung, 25, 26 Juni, 1870.

1350 Die Haefen auf der Westküste von Formosa, Ztschr.
der Ges. f. Erdk., VI, p. 384.

1351 GREEY, E., Taiwanfu auf Formosa, Globus, XX,
1871, No. 15.

1352 BECHTINGER, J., Het eiland Formosa in de Chineesche zee. Batavia, 1871, 8vo.

1353 Die Insel Formosa. Ausland, 1872, No. 17, 18, 20.

1354 HUGHES, T. F., Visit to Tok-e-tok, chief of the
eighteen tribes of southern Formosa, Proc. R. G.
S., XVI, 1872, No. III, 265.

1355 — —, Formosa and its southern aborigines,
Ocean Highways, N. S., I, 1873, p. 44.

1356 CAROLL, C., Rambles among the Formosan sava-
ges, "The Phoenix," I, p. 133.

1357 Extrait d'un voyage du "Bourayne" sur la côte
ouest de Formose, Ann. Hydr., 1873, p. 226.

1358 A gossip about Formosa, China Review, II, p. 40-47.

1359 Formosa, "The Mail," Sept. 7th, 1874.

1360 Die Insel Formosa, Mitth. K. K. geogr. Ges. Wien,
1874, No. 11.

1361 RAVENSTEIN, Formosa, Geogr. mag., Oct., 1874.

1362 LEGENDRE, Remarques sur Formose et sur ces
produits, Revue marit. et Col., Oct. 1874.

1363 THOMSON, J., Notes on a journey in southern
Formosa, Journ. R. Geogr. Soc., XLIII, 1873, p.
97, map.
See Peterm. Mitth., 1874, p. 160.

1364 KNOBLAUCH, F., Einige Notizen über Formosa,
Mitth. d. deutsch. Ges. f. Nat. und. Völkerk. Ostasiens, No. 8, 1875.

1365 RITCHIE, H., Notes of a journey in east Formosa,
Chin. Rec., VI, p. 206-211.

f. Hainan.

1366 KLAPROTH, J., Description de l'isle de Hainan,
Nouv. Ann. de Voy, VI.

1367 — —, Carte de l'isle de Hainan. Paris, 1827.

1368   TAINTOR, E. C., Hainan, Custom's trade report, 1867, 4to.

1369   HIRTH, F., The port of 'Hai-k'ou (Hainan), China Review, I, 1872-73, p. 124-127.

1370   —   — , Topography of the department of Ch'iung-chou fu on the island of Hainan ; ibid, p. 266-269.

1371   SWINHOE, R., Narrative of an exploring visit to Hainan, J. N. Ch. Br. R. As. Soc., 1873, p. 41.

1372   MAYERS, W. F., A historical and statistical sketch of the island of Hainan ; ibid, VII, p. 1.

1373   Ueber die Insel Hainan, Hydr. Mitth., 1873, No. 20.

1374   Die Insel Hainan, Mitth. K. K. geogr. Ges. Wien N. F., VI, No. 11, 1873.

1375   BOWRA, E. C., Hainan, China Review, II, p. 332-335.

g. Maps.

1376   MARTIN, M., Atlas sinensis. Amstelodami, 1656, fol. (See General descript., No. 1998.)

1377   MONTANUS, A., Atlas Chinensis, being a second part of a relation of remarkable passages in two embassies. London, 1671, fol.

1378   D'ANVILLE, Nouvel Atlas de la Chine. La Haye, 1737, fol.

1379   —   — , Atlas général de la Chine pour servir à la Description générale de la Chine par Grosier. Paris, 1775, fol.
       See Stählin, Atlas von China in Büsching's Mag., III, 576.

1380   Memoir of a chart of the China sea, 1771.

1381   The Oriental navigation or new directions for sailing to and from the East Indies, China. London, 1802.

1382   HORSBURGH, New chart of the Chinese sea, 1806.

1383   BURNEY, J., Chart of the coast of China and of the sea eastwards of Canton to Japan with a memoir. London, 1810.

1384 ARROWSMITH, Map of Asia. London, 1818;
Addit. 1822.
1385 — — , Map of China.
1386 BERTHE, L. H., Nouv. carte de l'Asie. Paris, 1825.
1387 JOHNSTON, K., China and Japan. Edinburgh.
1388 REICHARD, C. G., China und Japan. Gotha, 1826.
1389 WALKER, Map of China, 1829.
1390 ABBOT, C., Map of the route of the British embassy upon the river Yangtsckiang from Kwa-chow
to Nanchang Fu.
1391 WEILAND, Charte von China, 1829.
1392 ALLEN, P., Map of China and the adjacent countries. London, 1833; new ed., 1840.
1393 RITTER, K., und ETZEL, F. A., Atlas von Asien
(zu Ritter's Erdkunde). Berlin, 1834-54.
1394 Admiralty charts of the Chinese sea, 1840-42.
1395 WYLD, J., Map of China. London, 1840.
1396 BERGHAUS, H., China und Japan. Potsdam,
1842 und Gotha, 1853.
1397 — — , Asia Atlas. Gotha, 1843.
1398 ENDLICHER, S., Atlas von China, nach den Aufnahmen der Jesuiten Missionnäre. Wien, 1843
(4 maps.)
1399 WILLIAMS, S. W., Map of the Chinese empire,
1847, s. l.
1400 SCHOTT, W., Noch etwas zur Kartographie der
Chinesen. Ausland, 1856, No. 45.
1401 KLAPROTH, J., Carte de la Chine. Paris, 1857.
1402 STUELPNAGEL, F. von, China und Japan. Gotha,
1858.
1403 DUFOUR, M. A., Carte de la Chine. Paris, s. a.
1404 BARTHOLOMEW, J., Chinese empire and Japan.
London and Liverpool.
1405 WYLD, J., Map of China. London.
1406 EDKINS, J., Road map from Peking to Kiachta.
Peking, 1864.
1407 WILDS, E., East Coast of China, Swatow port and
views. London hydrogr. off., 1865.

1408 PAUTHIER, G., Carte générale de l'Asie, dans la 2me. moitié du 13. siècle pour servir à l'intelligence du livre de Marco Polo. Paris, 1865.

1409 Leang-chu-chin, A complete map of the 18 provinces. Canton, 1866.

1410 Côte orientale de la Chine. Paris, depôt de la marine, 1866-74.

1411 Mer de Chine. Paris, depôt de la marine, 1866-74.

1412 China Sea. London, hydrogr. off., 1867-69.

1413 VOLUNTIERI, S., Map of the Sun-on district in Kwang-tung. Leipzig, 1868.

1414 Yangtsekiang, upper waters. London, hydrogr. off., 1870, 5 maps.

1415 Golfe de Leao-tong, plan de l'entrée de la rivière Liau et de ses approches d'après Wand. Paris, depôt de la marine, 1870.

1416 Atlas der Baseler Missionsgesellschaft, No. 10: das eigentliche China; No. 11 Der Si-non oder Sanonkreis.

1417 HIRTH, F., Sketch map of the province of Kwang-tung. Canton, 1872; also in Petersmann's Mitth., 1872.
See Ch. Review, I, p. 200.

1418 ELIAS, N., The Yellow river. London, 1872, 2 maps.
See Petermann's geogr. Mitth., 1872, p. 400.

1419 WAEBER, K., Map of the province of Chihli. St. Petersburg, 1872 (in Russian).

1420 FRITSCHE, H., Map of north China. St. Petersburg, 1874; also in Zeitschr. d. Ges. f. Erdkunde. Berlin, 1874.

1421 RAVENSTEIN, Map of Burmah and Western China, Geogr. Mag., April, 1875.

h. Travels.

1422 POLO, MARCHO, Hie hebt sich an das puch des edeln Ritters und Landfarers Marcho Polo. In dem er schreibt die grossen wunderlichen Ding dieser Welt. Sunderlichen von den grossen Künigen und

Keysern, die da herrschen in den selbigen Landen. Nünberg, 1477, fol.

Italian, Venice, 1496, fol., and a great number of French, German, Dutch, Spanish,
etc. editions. For the bibliography see
Charton's voyages, p. 438, and especially
Yule's edition, II, p. 465. See Mém.
conc., VI, p. 275.

English: Marsden, 1818, 4to.; T. Wright,
1854.

See Rémusat, Nouv. Mel. as., I, p. 381.

German: A. Bürk, mit Anmerkungen von
K. F. Neumann. Leipzig, 1855, 8vo.

French: G. Pauthier. Paris, 1865, 2 vols., 8vo.

See N. de Khanikoff. Paris, 1866, and P. Ca-
hier, Etudes littéraires et religieuses.
Paris, 1866-67; The Phoenix, I, p. 19.

The best edition is: H. Yule, The Book of
Ser Marco Polo. London, 1871, 2 vols.,
roy. 8vo.; 2nd ed., 1875.

1423 VEER, G. DE, Waeragtige Beschryving van William
Barents drie Sey lagien by Noorden, Noorveghen,
Mosvovia en de Tartaria na de konyngryken van
Cathay ande China. Amsterdam, 1599; also
1605, 4to.

Latin: Amsterdam, 1599, fol.; Italian: Venice, 1599; French: Paris 1610.

English by C. Beke. London, 1852, 8vo.;
Hackluyt Society, No. 13.

1424 HAKLUYT, R., The principal navigations, voyages,
etc. London, 1599, fol.

1425 PINTO, FERNAM MENDEZ, Peregrinaçam em
que da conta de muytas y muyto estranchas cho-
sas que vioe ouvio no regno da China, no da
Tartaria, no da Sornam que vulgarmente se chama
Siam, etc. Lisbon, 1614, fol.; Ibidem, 1829,
3 vols., 8vo.

Spanish: Madrid, 1627; Valencia, 1645, fol.

French: Paris, 1645, 4to.
Dutch: Amsterdam, 1653, 4to.
English by H. Cogan. London, 1663, fol.
German: Amsterdam, 1653, 4to., and by
T. H. Külb. Jena, 1868, 8vo.

1426 Indianische Raiss von dreyen ehrwürdigen Priestern der Soc. Iesu, welche im Jahr 1618 nach Goa geschifft, mit Bevelch von dannen in China zu raisen. Augsburg, 1620, 4to., 60 pp.

1427 Avis certain d'une plus ample découverte de la Chine et particularités sur la côte de la Cochinchine. Paris, 1628, 12mo.

1428 FEYNES, H. DE, Voyage fait par terre à la Chine et le retour par mer. Paris, 1630, 8vo.

1429 HERBERT, Travels in the East. London, 1634, 4to.

1430 MANDELSTO, J. A., Morgenlaendische Reisebeschreibung, etc. Schleswig, 1647; ibid, 1668, fol.
French by Wicquefort. Amsterdam, 1727, 2 vols., fol., maps, plans and views.

1431 RHODES, A. DE, Divers voyages en China et autres royaumes de l'Orient. Paris, 1653, 4to.; ibid, 1656, 1666, 1682.

1432 THEVENOT, M., Recueil des voyages du Nord. Paris, 1662-1673.

1433 — — , Relation de divers voyages curieux. Paris, 1666-1672, 4 vols., fol., maps and views; 2nd edit., ibid, 1696, 4 pts. in 2 vols., fol.
Contains: Voyage d'A. Jenkinson pour découvrir le chemin de Cathay par la Tartarie en 1558; also in Bernard's Recueil, Vol. IV (No. 1457). Voyage des P. P. Grueber et d'Orville à la Chine, etc.

1434 CRAMER, M., Voyagie van Baltasar Brots naar de Küste van China en Formosa. Amsterdam, 1670, 8vo.

1435 BOURGES, M. DE, Wahrhaftige und eigentliche Erzaehlung von der Reise des Bischofs von Beryte aus Frankreich nach China. Leipzig, 1671, 4to.

1436 Beskriffning uppä trenne Reesor och Peregrinationer
sampt Konungarijket Japan, etc., etc. (Travels of
Nils Matson and others to China and Japan, in
Swedish). Wijsindzborg, 1674, 4to.

1437 Zee an Land Reyzen. Amsterdam, 1675-1702
(Travels to the Levant, China, Formosa, etc. etc.)

1438 Reisen des Herrn Zachariae Wagners durch ein gross
Theil der Welt und unter anderm nach China; in
A. Müller's Abdallae Beidavi Hist. Sin., 1689.
See Dudgeon, Ch. Rec., 1874, p. 28.

1439 OLEARIUS, A., Colligirte und vermehrte Reisebe-
schreibung. Hamburg, 1690, fol.
English: 1692, fol.; Dutch: 1691, 4to.;
French: Amsterdam, 1726, fol.

1440 MALDONDE, J. B., Prodigieux événemens de notre
temps arrivés à des Portugais dans un voyage ex-
trément dangereux du côte de la Chine. Mons,
1693, 12mo.

1441 AVRIL, F., Voyages en divers Etats d'Europe et de
l'Asie. Paris, 1693, 8vo.
English: London, 1693, 12mo. See E. C.
Bridgman, Chin. Rep., X, p. 297.

1442 NEUVILLE, B. H. DE LA, Relation nouvelle et curieuse de la Moscovie contenant, etc., etc. et le
recit d'un voyage par terre à la Chine. Paris,
1698; Hague, 1699, 12mo.

1443 A collection of voyages and travels, some now first
printed from original MS., others now first published in English, with a general preface giving an
account of the progress of navigation from its
first beginning. London, 1704, 4 vols., fol.; 2nd.
ed., 1732, 6 vols., fol.; 3rd ed., 1744-46, 6 vols.,
fol.

1444 Voyage de van Bechteren aux Indes Orientales avec
le voyage de Langes à la Chine. Amsterdam,
1705, 12mo.

1445 RENAUDOT, E., Anciennes relations des Indes et
de la Chine de deux voyageurs mahométans* qui

y allèrent le 9mc. siècle, traduites de l'Arabe. Paris, 1718, 8vo.

> English: London, 1733, 8vo.; Italian: Bologna, 1749, 4to. See Chin. Rep., I, p. 6, 42.

1446 GEMELLI CARERI, Giro del Mondo. Venezia, 1719, 5 vols., 8vo.; 2nd ed., ibid, 1728.

> Vol. IV, China.

1447 Les trois navigations de Martin Frobisher pour chercher un passage à la Chine et au Japon par la mer glaciale en 1576-78, Bernard's Recueil de Voy. (No. 1457), Vol. I, 1725.

1448 Relation du voyage de Jean de Plan Carpin, cordelier, qui fut envoyé en Tartarie par le Pape Innocent IV, l'anée 1246; ibid, Vol. VII.

1449 De reizende Chinees. Amsterdam, 1727, 4 vols., 8vo.

> English: London, 1775, 2 vols., 12mo.

1450 PREMARE, Voyage de la France à la Chine (1699); Lettr. édif. (nouv. éd., 1831, XXVI, p. 62-91.)

1451 BOUVET, Voyage à la Chine, 1699; ibid, p.'92-109.

1452 TARTRE, Voyage à la Chine, 1701; ibid, p. 147-209.

1453 CHAVAGNAC, Voyage à la Chine, 1701; ibid, p. 210-221.

1454 — — , Voyage de Nantchang fou à Foutchéou; ibid, XXVII, p. 23-43.

1455 LE GENTIL de la BARBINAS, Nouveau voyage autour du monde. Paris, 1727, 3 vols., 8vo.

1456 GAUBIL, P., Extrait du journal de voyage de Canton à Peking in P. E. Souciet observ. Math., etc., 1729; also Mém. Conc., VIII, 291.

1457 Recueil de voyages au Nord contenant divers mémoires très utiles au commerce et à la navigation par Bernard. Amsterdam, 1725-1731, 8 vols., 12mo.

1458 BERGERON, P., Voyages en Asie. La Haye, 1735, 4to.

1459 HARRIS, J., Navigantium atque itinerantium bibliotheca or a complete collection of voyages and travels. London, 1744 and 1748, 2 vols., fol.

See J. R. Morrison, Chin. Rep., II, p. 282.

1460 LEIMBECKOVEN, G., Reisebeschreibung von Wien nach China. Wien, 1740, 8vo.

1461 A collection of voyages and travels consisting of authentic writers in our own tongue, which have not before been collected in English or have only been abridged in other collections and continued, compiled from the curious and valuable library of the late Earl of Oxford. London, 1745, 2 vols., fol.

1462 A new general collection of voyages and travels, consisting of the most esteemed relations which have been hitherto published in any language, comprehending everything remarkable in its kind in Europe, Asia, Africa, America. London, 1745-47, 4 vols., 4to.

1463 MAUNEVILLETTE, Routines des côtes des Indes Orientales et de Chine. Paris, 1745, 4to.

1464 Histoire générale des voyages ou Nouvelle collection de toutes les relations de voyages par mer et par terre, qui ont été publiées jusqu'à présent dans les différents langues de toutes les nations connues. Paris, 1746, 80 vols., 12mo.; also 1746-61, 16 vols., 4to.

> Suite, tome XVII, Amsterdam, 1761, 4to.; continuation, tome XVIII, formant le 1er. vol. de la continuation. Paris, 1768, 4to.; Tome XIX, formant le dernier vol. des voyages de mer. Paris, 1770, 4to.; Tome XX, Bruxelles, et Paris, an X.

> Also La Haye, 1747-80, 25 vols., 4to.

1465 REINIUS, J., Anmörkning saemlade under en resa til China. Abo, 1749, 8vo.

1466 KURZE, J. H. H., Beschreibung über des Schiffs Cronprinz Christian glücklich gethane Reise nach und von China. Copenhagen und Leipzig, 1750, 8vo.

1467 REICHARD, J. P., Reisen nach China. Onolzbach, 1755, 8vo.

1468 Avvisamento del viaggio di Cathai per il camino della Tanna ad andare e tornare con mercantaria. Lisbon and Lucca, 1755.

1469 MUELLER, Die ersten Reisen die von Russen nach China geschehen. in Samml. Russ Gesch., IV, 1760.

1470 Voyages to the East Indies and China in 1747-48. London, 1762, 8vo.

1471 OSBECK, P., Reise nach Ostindien und China. Rostock, 1765, 8vo., plates.
  English: London, 1771, 8vo. See E. C. Bridgman, Chin. Rep., XVI, p. 136; J. R. Morrison, ibid, I, p. 209.

1472 DE LA PORTE, Le voyageur français. Paris, 1767, 12mo.

1473 LINNAEUS, Voyage d'Olof Torèn à Surate, à la Chine, etc. Milan, 1771.

1474 SONNERAT, P., Voyages aux Indes Orientales et à la Chine. Paris, 1782, 2 vols., 4to.; ibid, 1806, 4 vols., 8vo., atlas.
  German: Zürich, 1783, 2 vols., 4to., maps, plates.
  Dutch: Leyden, 1785, 3 vols., 8vo.

1475 FORSTER, J. R., History of the voyages and discoveries made in the North. London, 1786, 4to.

1476 Memoir and travels of M. A. Count of Benyowsky. London, 1790, 2 vols., 4to.
  See Chin. Rep., III, p. 396.

1477 GILBERT, Th., A voyage from New South Wales to Canton in the year 1788. London, 1789, 8vo.

1478 MORTIMER, G., Observations and remarks during a voyage to the Isles of Teneriffa, etc., etc., and to Canton. London, 1791, 4to.

1479 MEARES, J., Voyages from China to the N. W. Coast of America. London, 1791, 2 vols., maps.

1480 LA PÉROUSE, Voyage autour du monde. Paris, 1797, 3 vols., 4to.

1481 COSSIGNY, le comte C., Voyage à Canton, suivi d'observations sur le voyage de Lord Macartney et du citoyen van Braam. Paris, 1799, 8vo.

1482 LINSCOLAMUS, J. H., Navigatio ac itinerarium in orientalem sive Lusitanorum Indiam. Hague, 1799, fol.

1483 BURNEY, J., Chronological history of the discoveries in the South Sea. London, 1803.

1484 JOHNSON, J., The Oriental voyager. London, 1807, 8vo.

1485 MALTEBRUN, Annales de Voyages. Paris, 1807-1818.

1486 — — et EYRIÈS; Annales nouvelles. Paris, 1819 ss.

1487 GUIGNES, DE (fils), Voyages à Péking. Paris, 1808, 3 vols., 8vo., maps.
       English: London, 1809, 4to. Compare Montucci No. 1488.

1488 (MONTUCCI, A.), Sinologus berolinensis, Rémarques philologiques sur les voyages en Chine de M. de Guignes. Berlin, 1809, 8vo. (See No. 1487.)

1489 SAINT-CROIX, F. R. DE, Voyage commercial et politique aux Indes orientales, aux iles Philippines, à la Chine. Paris 1810, 3 vols., 8vo., maps.

1490 PINKERTON, J., Voyages and travels. London, 1811 ss., 4to.

1491 KRUSENSTERN, A. J. von, Reise um die Welt in den Jahren, 1803-6. Berlin, 1811, 16mo.

1492 WATHEN, J., Journal of a voyage in 1812-13 to Madras and China. London, 1814, 4to., plates.

1493 WAKEFIELD, P., The traveller in Asia or a visit to the most celebrated parts of the Eastern Indies and China. London, 1817, 12mo.

1494 ABEL, C., Narrative of a journey in the interior of China. London, 1818, 4to.

1495 VERNEUR, J. T., Journal des voyages, découvertes, etc. Paris, 1819 ss.

1496 MARTINOFF, A., Voyage pittoresque de Moscou

aux frontières de la Chine. St. Petersburg, 1819, fol.

1497 LEIDENFROST, C. F., Tagebuch einer Landreise durch die Küstenprovinzen China's. Weimar, 1822, 8vo.
1498 DOBEL, P., Travels in Kamtschatka, Siberia with a narrative of a residence in China. London, 1823, 2 vols., 12mo.
> Russian : St. Petersburg, 1833, 2 vols., 8vo.
> French : Sept années en Chine, etc., trad. par le prince Galitzin. Paris, 1842, 8vo.
1499 WHITE, J., History of a voyage in the Chinese sea. Boston, 1823, 8vo.
1500 MURRAY, A., Historical account of discoveries and travels in Asia. Edinburgh, 1824, 3 vols., 8vo.
> See A. Rémusat, Nouv. Mél. As., I, p. 413.
1501 PUREFOY, J., Diary of a journey from Manchao on the coast of Hainan to Canton, 1824-5 ; As. Jour., XX, 1825.
1502 The modern traveller to Persia and China. London, 1827, 12mo.
1503 Travels of Ibn Batuta, translated from the Arabic Msc. by S. Lee. London, 1829, 4to.
> German extract : "Ausland," 1858, No. 46.
1504 Voyage from Nepal into China, As. Journ., XXIV.
> German in "Ausland," 1830, 137, 141.
1505 BRUGUIÈRE, Voyage en Chine et Tartarie Chinoise, Ann. Prop. Foi, L.
> See "Athenaeum," 25th Feb., 1837 ; Chin. Rep., VI, p. 287.
1506 BEECHEY, J. W., Narrative of a voyage to the Pacific. London, 1831.
1507 BRIDGMAN, E. C., Remarks on voyages to the north of China, Chin. Rep., I, p. 196.
1508 — — , Notices of a voyage from Canton to Shanghai ; ibid, XVI, p. 398.
1509 Experimental voyage to the N. E. coast of China, As. Journ., n. s., XII, 1833.

1510 Report of proceedings on a voyage to the northern ports of China in the ship "Lord Amherst," extracted from papers printed by order of the House of Commons. London, 1833, 8vo.

1511 GUETZLAFF, K., Report of proceedings on a voyage to the northern ports of China, Chin. Rep., I, p. 76, 81, 122, 180 ; II, p. 20, 99.

1512 — — , Journal of two voyages along the coast of China in 1831 and 1832. New York, 1833, 8vo.
    See Chin. Repos., I, p. 530.

1513 — — , Journal of three voyages along the coast of China. London, 1834, 8vo., map.
    Dutch : Rotterdam, 1835, 8vo.

1514 — — , Bericht seiner Reise von China nach England. Kassel, 1851, 8vo.
    Dutch : Rotterdam, 1835, 8vo.

1515 FUSS, M. G., Rapport préalable fait à l'academie de St. Petersbourgh sur un voyage en Chine. St. Petersburg, 1833.

1516 STEPHENS, E., Expedition to the Bohea hills, Chin. Rep., IV, p. 82.

1517 — — , Missionary voyage in the brig "Huron" along the coast of China ; ibid, IV, p. 308.

1518 MEDHURST, W. H., Notes of the voyage of the "Huron ;" ibid, IV, p. 406.

1519 — — , Glance at the interior of China (Trip to Fouliang in Anhui.) Shanghai, 1849, 8vo.

1520 MALCOLM, S. J., Travels in south eastern Asia, embracing Hindostan, Malaya, Siam and China. London, 1839, 2 vols., 12mo., map, woodcuts.

1521 TERNAUX-COMPANS, H., Archives des voyages ou collection d'anciennes relations, etc. relatives à la géographie et aux voyages. Paris, 1839 ss.

1522 FULTON, Travelling sketches in India and China. London, 1840, 12mo.

1523 KERR, Collection of voyages. London, 1840 ss., 26 vols.

1524 HOLMAN, J., Travels in China. London, 1840, 8vo.

1525 Reminiscences of a trip up the river of Canton on board the U. S. frigate "Constellation" in the spring of 1842, Chin. Rep., XI, p. 329.

1526 WENDT, E. und VOCKERODE, F., Jahrbuch der Reisen. Leipzig, 1843, 12mo.

1527 — — , Des Missionär Gützlaff's Reisen. Leipzig, 1848, 8vo., maps.

1528 BELCHER, Sir E., Narrative of a voyage around the world in H. M. S. "Sulphur." London, 1843, 2 vols., 8vo.
   See E. C. Bridgman, Chin. Repos., XII, p. 490.

1529 COHALLAYE, Une excursion à Whampoa. Paris, 1844, 8vo.

1530 BERNARD, W. D., Narrative of the voyage and services of the "Nemisis." London, 1844, 2 vols., 8vo.

1531 LOWRIE, W. M., Visit to the city of Chang-chau-fu, Chin. Rep., XII, 1844, p. 523.

1532 HEDDE, J., Excursion to the city of Suchau in 1845; ibid, XIV, p. 584.

1533 BERTRAND, M. D., The "Nemesis" in China. London, 1846, 8vo.

1534 HALL, H. H., "Nemesis" in China. London, 1846, 8vo.

1535 FORTUNE, R., Three years wanderings in the northern provinces of China. London, 1847, 8vo.
   German by Himly. Göttingen, 1853, 8vo.
   See E. C. Bridgman, Chin. Rep., XVI, p. 570.

1536 — — , A journey to the tea countries of China. London, 1852, 8vo.
   German by Zenker. Leipzig, 1854, 8vo.

1537 — — , Two visits to the tea countries of China and India. London, 1853, 2 vols., 8vo.

1538 — — , A residence among the Chinese. Lon-1857, 8vo.

1539 — — , Yedo and Peking, a narrative of a journey

to the capitals of Japan and China. London, 1863, 8vo.

See "Reader," 1863, No. 13; "Athenaeum," 1863, p. 420; Westm. Rev., July, 1863, p. 255; Quart. Rev., Oct., 1863, p. 449; Götting. Gel. Anz., 1863, p. 1975. Compare No. 1561.

1540 DUEBEN, G. W. von, Resa till Kap, Ostindien och Kina. Stockholm, 1847, 8vo.

1541 DAVIDSON, G. T., Trade and travels in the Far East or recollections of twenty-one years passed in Java, Singapore, Australia and China. London, 1847, 8vo,

1542 ROY, M., Campagnes dans les mers de l'Inde et de la Chine à bord de la frégate "l'Erigone." Paris, 1847-48, 2 vols., 8vo.

1543 HAUSSMANN, A., Voyage en Chine, Cochinchine, etc. Paris, 1847-48, 3 vols., 8vo.

English : Paris, 1848, 3 vols., 8vo.

1544 GRUBE, F. W., Reise nach China und Indien. Cassel, 1848, 8vo.

1545 DELESSERT, E., Voyages dans les deux océans atlantique et pacifique. Paris, 1849, 8vo., with maps.

1546 WILLIAMS, S. W., Journal of a trip overland from Hainan to Canton, Chin. Rep., XVIII, 1849, p. 392 ss.

1547 The midshipman in China. London, 1850, 12mo.

1548 ERMAN, A., Travels in Siberia, etc. Philadelphia, 1850, 2 vols., 8vo.

1549 BERNCASTLE, J., Voyage to China. London, 1850, 2 vols., 8vo.

1550 YVAN, M., La Chine et la presqu'île Malaise. Paris, 1850, 8vo.

1551 — — , Voyages et recits. Paris, 1853, 8vo.

1552 MACAULAY, W. H., Kathay, a cruise in the Chinese seas. New York, 1852, 16mo.

1553 HUC, Souvenirs d'un voyage dans la Tartarie et le

Thibet. Paris, 1852, 2 vols., 8vo.; 5th ed., Paris, 1868, 2 vols., 12mo.

> English by W. Hazlitt. London, 1854, 2 vols., 8vo.; 2nd ed., 2 vols., 12mo., s. a.

> German by K. Andree. Leipzig, 1855, 8vo.; 2nd ed., 1867; 3rd ed., 1874, 8vo., 360 pp.

1554 — — , L'empire Chinois. Paris, 1855, 2 vols., 8vo.; 4th ed., Paris, 1862, 2 vols., 8vo.

> English: London, 1855, 2 vols., 8vo. Condensed translations of the above two works: Recollections of a journey through Tartary, Thibet and China, by Mrs. Percy Sinnet. London, 1852, 8vo.; Life and travels in Tartary, Thibet and China, by M. Jones. London, 1868, 8vo.

> German, by Andree. Leipzig, 1856, 8vo.; 2nd ed., 1866; 3rd ed., 1874, 364 pp.

1555 LAVOLLÉ, C., Voyages en Chine. Paris, 1852, 8vo.

1556 STIER, J., Journal d'un voyage en Chine. Paris, 1853, 2 vols., 8vo.

1557 HERVEY, Mrs., The adventures of a lady in Tartary, Thibet, China and Kashmir. London, 1853, 3 vols., 8vo.

1558 KOVALEVSKY, Puteschestvic v Kitai (Travels in China.) St. Petersburg, 1853, 8vo. (in Russian).

1559 GOETZ, C. von, Reise um die Welt. Stuttgart und Tübingen, 1854, 3 vols., 8vo.

1560 GRAVIÈRE, J. DE LA, Voyage en Chine et dans les mers et archipels de cet empire pendant les années 1847-1850. Bruxelles, 1854, 3 vols., 12mo., 284, 289, 290 pp.

1561 Adventures de R. Fortune dans ses voyages en Chine. Paris, 1854, 8vo.

1562 MONTFORT, Voyage en Chine avec un appendice historique sur les derniers événements par G. Bell. Paris 1854, 8vo.

1563 BALL, R. L., Rambles in Eastern Asia, including China and Manilla. Boston, 1855, 12mo.

1564 TAYLOR, B., Travels. New York, 1855, 5 vols., 8vo., maps, plates.
      Vol. V: India, China and Japan; also A visit to India, China and Japan. London, 1859, 8vo.

1565 PFEIFFER, IDA, Meine zweite Weltreise. Wien, 1856, 4 vols., 8vo.

1566 — — , A woman's journey round the World. London, 1856, 8vo., 6th ed.

1567 TRAIN, G. F., Young America abroad. New York, 1857, 12mo.

1568 BRADSHAW, W. S., Voyages to India, China and America. London, 1857, 8vo.

1569 Travelling in China, Dublin Univ. Mag., Febr., 1857.

1570 HABERSHAN, A. W., The North pacific surveying and exploring expedition. Philadelphia and London, 1857, 8vo.

1571 VAIL, Rambles in Eastern Asia. Boston, 1857, 12mo.

1572 **BIERNATZKY, K. L., W. H. Medhurst's Reise von Shanghai nach dem Tienmuh Gebirge, Neumann's Zeitschr. f. allg. Erdk., II, 1857, No. 3.**

1573 LECOQ, J., Souvenirs d'un voyage en Chine in Gaz. d. Hôpit, 1857, 1858.

1574 HALLIWELL, The voyages and travels of Sir S. Maudeville. London, 1859, 8vo.

1575 TRONSON, J. M., Voyage to Japan, Kamtschatka, Siberia, Tartary and the coast of China in H. M. S. "Barracoute", London, 1859, 8vo.

1576 ELLIS, H. T., Hongkong to Manilla. London, 1859, 8vo.

1577 ANDRASSY, GRAF E., Reise nach Ostindien, Ceylon, China und Bengalen. Pesth, 1859, fol., plates.

1578 MICHIE, A., Siberien overland route from Peking to Petersburg. London, 1860, 8vo., map, plates.

1579 SCHMARDA, L. K., Reise um die Erde in den

Jahren 1853-57. Braunschweig, 1861, 3 vols., 8vo.

1580 DUNNE, From Calcutta to Peking. London, 1861, 8vo.

1581 KÉROULÉ, H. DE, Un voyage à Pekin. Paris, 1861, 8vo.

1582 BLAKISTON, F. W., Five months on the Yangtsze. London, 1862, 8vo.
See Peterm. Mitth., 1863, p. 194.

1583 SCHERZER, C. von, Reise der K. K. österreichischen Fregatte Novara um die Erde. Wein, 1862, 3 vols., 8vo.

1584 — — , Die ostasiatische Expedition, Oestr. Rev., IV, 10, p. 118-131. (Oct. 1866.)

1585 Eine Fahrt auf dem Ostfluss in der Provinz Canton, Peterm. Mitth., 1862, p. 161-164.

1586 CHARTON, Voyageurs anciens et modernes. Paris, 1863, 4to.

1587 GRANT, C. M., Journey from Peking to St. Petersburg across the desert of Gobi, J. R. Geo. Soc., XXXIII, 1863, p. 167-177.
German in Zeitschr. f. allg. Erdk. N. F., XIV, 1863, p. 272; notes by Koner, ibid, p. 351-356. See "Ausland," 1863, No. 12.

1588 TROLLOPE, H., Voyage of H. M. S. "Melville" from Singapore to Hongkong, Naut. Mag., XXXII (1863), p. 169.

1589 SOMRBEUIL, P. DE, Voyages en Chine et au Japon. Paris, 1863, 12mo.
(Biblioth. chrét. de l'adolesc.)

1590 WILLIAMS, Mrs. H. Dwight, A year in China and a narrative of capture and imprisonment when homeward bound on board the Rebel Pirate "Florida," with an introduction by W. C. Bryant. New York, 1864, 8vo.

1591 The route to China by way of Russia and Siberia, Chin. and Jap. Rep., II (1864), p. 127-137.

1592 Notices and reminiscences of a voyage from Canton to Shanghai in 1847; ibid, II, p. 62-69.

1593 BILLE, S., Min reise til China. Kopenhagen, 1865, 8vo., map.
1594 Report of a Chinese on his voyage to Jehol, "Iswestija" Imp. Russ. Geo. Soc., I, 1865 (in Russian.)
1595 DICKSON, W., Narrative of an overland trip through Hunan from Canton to Hankow, J. N. Ch. Br. R. As. Soc., 1865, p. 159-173.
1596 WYLIE, A., The overland journey from St. Petersburg to Peking; ibid, p. 1-20.
1597 — — , Itinerary of a journey through the provinces of Hoopih, Ssechuan and Shensi; ibid, 1869, p. 153 ss.
1598 — — , Notes of a journey from Chingtoo to Hankow, Proc. R. Geo. Soc., XIV, 2, p. 168-185.
1599 WILLIAMSON, A., From Peking to Chefoo by river and canal, Naut. Mag., May, 1866.
1600 — — , Notes of a journey from Peking to Chefoo viâ Grand Canal, J. N. Ch. Br. R. As. Soc., III, 1867, p. 1-25.
1601 — — , Journeys in North China, Manchuria and Eastern Mongolia. London, 1870, 2 vols., 8vo. illustr., map.
       See Chin. Rec., III, p. 194; The Phoenix, I, p. 49.
1602 ROY, J. J. E., Un Français en Chine pendant les années 1850-56. Tours, 1866, 8vo.
1603 FURTH, C. de, Un Parisien en Asie, voyage en Chine, au Japon, dans la Mandchourie russe et sur les bords de l'Amour. Paris, 1866, 8vo.
1604 POUSSIELGUE, A., Voyage en Chine et en Mongolie de M. de Bourboulon et de Mme. de B., 1860-61. Paris, 1866, 8vo., plates.
1605 KROLCZYK, A., The entrance to the Yin territory; Chin. Recorder, III, p. 62, 93, 126.
1606 WEPPNER, Miss M., Journey from Tientsin to Peking; ibid, III, p. 178.
1607 DUDGEON, J., Notes on a bible tour in S. E. Shansi; ibid, III, p. 212, 239.

1608 SIEGFRIED, S., Seize mois autour du monde et particulièrement aux Indes, en Chine et au Japon. Paris, 1869, 8vo., map.

1609 OLIVER, Excursions in the South of China, Murray's Journ. of Travels, I, p. 346; also Proc. R. Geo. S., XIV, p. 227.

1610 SWINHOE, R., A trip to Kalgan in the autumn 1868, Proc. R. Geo. S., XIV, 1869, No. 1.

1611 Reports of journeys in China and Japan performed by Messrs. Alabaster, Oxenham, Markham and Dr. Willis. Presented to parliament. London, 1869, 4to., map.
German in Petermann's Mitth., 1869, 1870.

1612 GARDNER, C. T., Notes on a journey from Ningpo to Shanghai, Proc. R. Geo. Soc., 1869, p. 170, 249.

1613 CARNÉ, L. DE, Exploration du Mékong, Rev. des deux Mond., 1869.
German: "Ausland," 1870.

1614 — — , Voyage dans l'Indo-Chine et l'empire Chinois. Paris, 1871, 8vo., map.
English: London, 1872, 8vo.

1615 GARNIER, Fr., Voyage d'exploration en Indo Chine, Rev. Mar. et Col., April, June, July, Aug., 1869, map.

1616 — — , Épisode du voyage d'exploration en Indo Chine, Bull. Soc. Géo. Paris, May, 1869.

1617 — — , Voyage dans l'Indo Chine et l'empire Chinois. Paris, 1873, 2 vols., 4to., maps, illustr.
German extracts in Globus, XXVIII, No. 22-24.

1618 RICHTHOFEN, F. von., Reisen in China, Petermann's Mitth., 1869, 1870, 1873.

1619 — — , Letters on different provinces of China. Shanghai, 1871, 6 Nos., fol.

1620 BICKMORE, A. S., Voyage dans l'intérieur de la Chine, Bull. de la Soc. géo. de Paris, Aug., 1867.

1621 — — , Sketch of a journey from Canton to Hankow, Journ. R. Geo. Soc., XXXVIII, 1868.

Also J. N. Ch. Br. R. As. Soc., IV, 1868, p. 1-20.

1622 KNOWLTON, M. J., Trip into the interior of Chekiang, Chin. Rec., I, 1867, p. 61 ss.

1623 — — , Notes of a tour from Ningpo to Kinghwa;
ibid, V, 1874, p. 204 ss.

1624 MARTIN, W. A. P., Account cf an overland journey
from Peking to Shanghai, made in Febr. and
March, 1866, J. N. Ch. Br. R. As. Soc., III,
1867, p. 26-39.

1625 LEES, J., Notes of a journey from Tientsin to Chi-
nanfu, Chin. Rec., I, p. 77, 97.

1626 MARCOU, J., Voyage dans l'intérieur de la Chine,
Bull. Soc. de Géogr., 5 sér., XIV, 1867, p. 173 ss.

1627 Between Peking and Kalgan, Chin. Rec., I, p. 162.

1628 WILLIAMS, Mrs. J. R., Travelling in North China;
ibid, II, p. 189.

1629 A trip to Kienning; ibid, II, p. 225, 246, 279, 298.

1630 COOPER, T. T., Expedition from the Yangtzekiang
to Tibet and India, Proc. R. Geo. S., XII, 1868.

1631 — — , Journal of an overland journey from
China to India. Calcutta, 1869, 8vo.

1632 — — , Travels of a pioneer of commerce or an
overland journey from China towards India. London, 1871, 8vo., illustr., map.
See The Phoenix, I, p. 202.

1633 COFFIN, C. C., Our new way round the World.
London, 1869, 8vo.

1634 PHILIPS, G., The cruize of the Netherland ship
"Groeningen" in the Chinese waters in 1662-64,
Chin. Mag., 1869, p. 49, 81, 97.

1635 Overland trip from Kiukiang to Foochow, Chin.
Rec., III, p. 15, 37, 64.

1636 ELIAS, N., Notes of a journey to the new course of
the Yellow River, 1868, Proc. R. Geo. S., XIV,
p. 20 ss.

1637 MARKHAM, J., Notes on a journey through Shantung, Proc. R. Geo. S., XIV, 137.
See Petermann's Mitth., 1869.

1638 BEAUVOIR, Marquis de, Voyage autour du monde. Paris, 1869 ss., 2 vols., 8vo.; 2nd edition, 1874. English: London, 1873, 8vo.

1639 PUMPELLY, R., Across America and Asia, Notes of 5 Years' journey around the world. London, 1870, 8vo., 4 maps.

1640 SIMON, G. E., Recits d'un voyage en Chine, Bull. Soc. Imp. d'Acclim., March, 1870; also Paris, 1870, 8vo.

1641 BUISSONET, E., De Pékin à Shanghai, Souvenirs de voyage. Paris, 1871, 8vo.

1642 BASTIAN, A., Die Völker des östlichen Asiens. Studien und Reisen. Jena, 1871, 6 vols., 8vo. Vol. VI: Reisen in China. Von Peking zur mongolischen Grenze und Rückkehr nach Europa.

1643 — — , Alte und neue Wege nach China, in: Geogr. und Ethnogr. Bilder. Jena, 1873, 8vo.

1644 SLADEN, E. B., Exploration via the Jrawaddi and Bhamo to Southwest China, Proc. R. Geo. S., XV, p. 343 ss.

1645 DAVID, A., Lettres sur ses voyages en Chine, Bull. Soc. de Géogr. Paris, 1871.

1646 — — , Voyage dans la Chine occidentale; ibid, Août, 1874.

1647 — — , Journal de mon troisième voyage d'exploration dans l'Empire Chinois. Paris, 1875, 2 vols., 12mo., 382, 391 pp., maps. See J. Gros, l'Explor. Geogr. et comm., 1875, 373-75, 392-94; Petermann's Mitth., 1876, No. 1.

1648 WHYTE, W. A., A land journey from Asia to Europe, being an account of a camel and sledge journey from Canton to St. Petersburg. London, 1871, 8vo.

1649 CARDWELL, J., Boat excursion in Central China, Inland Miss. News. London, Nov., 1871.

1650 — — , The boat mission on the Poyang lake; ibid, Nov., 1872.

1651 PRZEWALSKI, Journey from Kiachta to Peking, "Inwestija" Imp. Russ. Geo. Soc., VII, p. 139 (in Russian).
German: Petermann's Mitth., 1872, p. 10 ss.

1652 CARLISLE, A. D., Round the world in 1870, an account of a brief tour made through India, China, Japan, California and America. London, 1872, 8vo.

1653 GABRIAC, Cte. DE, Course humoristique autour du monde. Paris, 1872, 8vo. (Indes, Chine, Japon.)

1654 Hongkong to London or our new road home from China. London, 1872, 8vo.

1655 ANDERSON, J., Report on the expedition to Western Yünnan. Calcutta, 1872, 8vo., maps.

1656 — — , The exploring expeditons to Western Yünnan of 1868 and 1875, Macmill. Mag., Oct. 1875.

1657 — — , Mandalay and Momien: a narrative of the two expeditions to Western China of 1868 and 1875, under Col. E. B. Sladen and Col. H. Brown. London, 1876, 8vo. See Saturday Review, 1876, April, p. 465.

1658 Voyage de Canton à Sy-lin-hien, Ann. de la Prop. de la Foi, Jan., 1872.

1659 From Gotham to Cathay, via the Great West, China Review, I, p. 45, 105, 190, 256.

1660 (BRETSCHNEIDER, E.), Briefe eines Kurländers auf einer Reise nach Indien und China, Riga'sche Zeitung, 1872.

1661 BERHATH, G., Kelet-ázsiai utazás (Voyage to Eastern Asia) Buda-Pesth., 1872, 8vo. (in Hungarian).

1662 PRIME, E. D. G., Around the world, Sketches of travel through many lands and over many seas. New York, 1872, 8vo., XVI, 455 pp., illustr.

1663 LAFOND, G., Fragments de voyage autour du monde. Paris, 1873, 4to.

1664 BRYSON, T., A week in Nanking. Shanghai, 1873, 8vo.

See China Rev., II, p. 60.
1665 SEWARD, Miss O. R., William H. Seward's travels around the world. New York, 1873, 8vo. (China, p. 39-284.)
1666 HUEBNER, Baron A. DE, Promenade autour du monde. Paris, 1873, 2 vols., 8vo.
> German: Leipzig, 1874, 2 vols., 8vo. See Lit. Centralbl., 1874, p. 626-28.
1667 BUSHELL, S. W., Notes of a journey outside the Great Wall of China, Proc. R. Geo. Soc., 1874, p. 149-168, map; also separately.
> See Chin. Rec., V, p. 171.
1668 DURET, Th., Voyage en Asie, Le Japon, la Chine, la Mongolie, etc. Paris, 1874, 18mo.
1669 THOMSON, J., The straits of Malacca, Indo China and China or ten years' travels, adventures and residence abroad. London, 1874, 8vo.
1670 OHLINGER, F., An overland tour from Foochow to Kiukiang, Chin. Rec., V, p. 152.
1671 ING, J., Notes of a visit to Nanchangfoo; ibid, V, p. 266.
1672 LEGGE, J., Notes of a tour in North China, Orient. Mag., 1874.
1673 SMITH, A., Glimpses of travel in the middle Kingdom. Shanghai, 1875, 8vo.
1674 J. L. M., Notes of a trip to Soochow, Chin. Rec., VI, p. 362.
1675 Notes of a journey from Hankow to Talifoo by the late A. R. Margary. Shanghai, 1875, 8vo.
1676 HUTCHINSON, A. B., Three weeks in the interior, China Review, III, p. 242-248, 393-308; IV, p. 21-26.
1677 MOELLENDORFF, O. F. von, Ein Ausflug in Nordchina. Zeitschr. d. Deutsch. Ges. f. Natur-und Völkerkunde Ostasiens, VII, June, 1875, p. 17.
1678 Ein Besuch des Grabes des Confucius und des heiligen Berges Tai, "Globus," XXVIII, 1875, No. 15-17.

1679 Voyage of J. A. Sosnowski in China, 1874,-75, "Is-westija" Imp. Russ. Geo. S., XI, 1875, No. 2 (in Russian.)

1680 BAX, R. W., The eastern seas, being a narrative of the voyage of H. M. S. "Dwarf" in China, Japan and Formosa. London, 1875, 8vo.
See Saturd. Rev., 1875, p. 718.

1681 PRESTON, C. F., Trip to the city of Leenchau, China Rev., IV, p. 160-168.

1682 LAIRD, E. K., The Rambles of a globe trotter in Australia, Japan, China, India and Cashmere. London, 1876, 8vo.

XII.

Natural History.

a. General.

1683 FORSTER, A voyage to China by Peter Osbeck, to which is added a Faunula and Flora Sinensis. London, 1771, 8vo.
See No. 1471.

1684 WILLIAMS, S. W., Specimens of Natural History, collected in a voyage to Lewchew and Japan, Chin. Rep., VI, p. 406.

1685 CANTOR, Th., Collections made in Chusan, Calcutta, Journ. of Nat. Hist., V, 1841; also Chin. Rep., X, p. 434-438.

1686 — — , Flora and Fauna of Chusan, Ann. Mag. of Nat. Hist., X, 1842; Journ. As. Soc. of Bengal, XXIV, 1855.

1687 HEDDE, J., Description méthodique des produits divers recueillies dans un voyage en Chine. St. Etienne, 1848, 8vo.

1688 COLLINGWOOD, C., Rambles of a naturalist on the shores and waters of the Chinese Sea during 1866-1867. London, 1868, 8vo.

1689 DAVID, A., Histoire naturelle de Pékin et ses environs. Bull. Nouv. Arch. du Mus. d'Hist. Nat.,
III, 1867.

1690 — — , Quelques renseignements sur l'histoire
naturelle de la Chine septentrionale et occidentale,
Journ. N. Ch. Br. R. As. S., VII. Shanghai, 1873,
p. 205-234.

1691 — — , BLANCHARD, E., Les récentes explorations des naturalistes en Chine, Revue des deux
mondes, Febr., March, May, June, 1871 (compiled chiefly from P. David's travels.)

1692 — — , Natural History of North China with notices of that of the South, West and North East
and of Mongolia and Tibet, compiled from the
travels of P. A. David. Shanghai, 1873, 4to.,
45 pp.

1693 SWINHOE, R., The natural history of Hainan.
London, 1870, 8vo., 20 pp. Reprinted from the
"Field" of 1870.

1694 FAUVEL, The province of Shantung, China Review, III, 1874-75, p. 364-377.

b. Climatology, Geology, Mineralogy.

1695 Ueber den Borax in China, As. Mag., II, p. 256-261,
1803.

1696 SEWERGUINE, B., Sur la pierre chinoise, nom-
mée Yu. St. Petersburg, 1820.

1697 RÉMUSAT, A., Recherches sur la substance miné-
rale appelée par les Chinois pierre de Yu et le
Jaspe des anciens. Paris, 1820, 12mo.

1698 HUMBOLDT, A. von, Fragmens de géologie et de
climatologie asiatiques. Paris, 1831.
German by J. Löwenberg. Berlin, 1832.

1699 BRIDGEMAN, E. C., Climate at Canton and Macao,
Chin. Rep., I, p. 488.

1700 WILLIAMS, S. W., Notices of the geology of the
vicinity of Lintin and Canton; ibid, III, p. 87.

1701 MEYEN, Bemerkungen über die Klimatischen Verhältnisse des südlichen China's, 1835, 4to.
1702 BIOT, E., Mémoire sur divers mineraux chinois appartenant à la collection du jardin du Roi. Paris, 1839, 8vo.
1703 — — , Recherches sur la temperature ancienne de la Chine. Paris, 8vo.
1704 — — , Note sur un phénomène de mirage en Chine, Journ. Asiat., 4. sér., XII, 518.
1705 — — , Examen de diverses séries de faits relatifs au climat de la Chine. Paris, 1849, 8vo.
    See Journ. Asiat., 4. sér., XV, p. 338.
1706 Course of tyfoons in the Chinese and Japanese seas, Chin. Rep., VIII, 1839-40, p. 225.
1707 COLLINSON, R., Meteorological observations at Chusan, Chin. Rep., X, p. 352.
1708 OUCHTERLONY, Geological notices of Chusan, Calcutta journ. of nat. hist., 1841; also Chin. Rep., X, p. 425.
1709 MAHLMANN, Untersuchung über das Klima von Peking, Poggend. Ann., LX, 1843, p. 213 ss.
1710 GUETZLAFF, K., On the mines of the Chinese empire, Transact. Ch. Br. R. As. Soc., I, 1848, p. 51-70.
1711 BOWRING, J. C., A short account of a visit to the hot springs of Yong-mak; ibid, p. 17-22.
1712 — — , Visit to the hot springs of Yung-mak in Hiang shan hien near Macao, Chin. Rep., XVIII, p. 86.
1713 MACGOWAN, D. J., Remarks on showers of sand which fall in the Chinese plains; ibid, XIX, p. 328.
1714 — — , Notices of coal in China; ibid, XIX, p. 385.
1715 — — , Note on recent physical phenomena in Japan and China, Transact. Ch. Br. R. As. Soc., V, 1856, p. 143-150.
1716 — — , On the cosmical phenomena observed in the neighbourhood of Shanghai during the past

13 centuries, Journ. Ch. Br. R. As. Soc., II, 1860, p. 45-76.

1717 SHADWELL, Capt., On the present state of the magnetic elements in China and places adjacent, Journ. N. Ch. Br. R. As. S., I, p. 222; II, p. 95.

1718 Wind and weather at Chefoo; ibid, II, p. 97-104.

1719 LAMPREY, Dr., Notes on the geology of the great plain; ib., II, p. 1-20, map.

1720 KINGSMILL, F. W., A sketch of the geology of a portion of Quangtung; ib., II, p. 21-38, map. See Not. & Quer., I, p. 4, 12.

1721 — — , Notes on some outlying coal fields in the South eastern provinces of China, Journ. N. Ch. Br. R. As. Soc., III, p. 99-106, plan.

1722 — — , Coal in China, Not. & Quer., II, p. 74.

1723 — — , Jade stone; ibid, II, p. 173.

1724 FRIEDEL, C., Beiträge zur Kenntniss des Klimas und der Krankheiten Ostasiens. Berlin, 1863, 8vo.; Zeitschr. f. allg. Erdk., XV, 1863, p. 269 ss.

1725 PUMPELLY, R., Notice of an account of geological observations in China, Japan and Mongolia, Amer. Journ. of Scienc. and Arts, XLI, 1865.

1726 — — , Geological researches in China, Mongolia and Japan during the years 1862-1865, Smithson. Contr. to Knowl., XV, 1867.

1727 EDKINS, J., The bituminous coal mines West of Peking, J. N. Ch. B. R. As. S., IV, p. 240-250.

1728 BICKMORE, A. S., A few notes on the distribution of gold in China, Not. & Quer., I, p. 22, 33.

1729 — — , Some remarks on the recent geological changes in China and Japan, Silliman's Amer. Jour., March, 1868. See also his travels No. 1620 and 1621.

1730 Geology of Kulangsu, Amoy, Not. & Quer., I, p. 22.

1731 Devonian fossils in China; ibid, I, p. 50.

1732 SIBBAW, W. L., Chinese coal; ibid, II, p. 75.

1733 Jade stone; ibid, II, p. 173, 174, 187; III, p. 63.

1734 RICHTHOFEN, Fr. von, Schichtgebirge am Yang-

tsekiang Verh. K. K. geol. Reichsanst., 1869,
p. 131.

1735 — — , Geologische Untersuchungen in China;
ibid, p. 343.

1736 — — , Ueber den chinesischen Loess; ibid, 1872,
No. 8, 10.

1737 — — , Die Kohlenfelder China's. Mitth. d. K. K.
Geogr. Ges. Wien N. F., VII, 1874.
See also his letters on different provinces of
China, No. 1619.

1738 WOJEIKOFF, A. von, Das Klima von Ostasien,
Oestr. meteorol. Zeitschr., 1870; also Petermann's
Geogr. Mitth., 1870, p. 153.

1739 — — , Die Winde Nordasiens; ibid, 1872, p. 81-88.

1740 HANN, J., Das Klima des südlichen China; ibid,
1873, No. 5.

1741 SCHLAGINWEIT-SAKUENLUENSKI, H. von,
Ueber Nephrit und Jadeit, Math. Phys. Kl. K.
Bayr. Ac., 1873, p. 227 ss. See "Ausland," 1874,
No. 10.

1742 DAVID, A., Lettre sur la géologie de la Chine, Bull.
de la Soc. Géol. de France, 3. sér., II, 1874, No. 5,
p. 406 ss.

1743 A trip to the hot springs of Yungmak, China Rev.,
IV, p. 130-134.

1744 BLONDEL, G., Le jade, Étude historique, archéolo-
gique, et littéraire sur la pierre appelée Yü par les
Chinois. Paris, 1875, 8vo.

c. Botany.

1745 BOYM, M., Flora sinensis. Vienna, 1656, fol.

1746 RICCIOLI, B., Flora sinensis in geographia refor-
mata. Bononiae, 1661, fol.

1747 MENTZEL, K., Opusculum de radice Jin-seng ex
herbariis sinicis. Berolini, 1685.

1748 BUCHOZ, s. c., Herbier ou collection desplan tes me-
dicales de la Chine. Paris, 1781, fol., pl.

1749 — — , Collection precieuse et enluminée des fleurs qui se cultivent dans les jardins de la Chine. Paris, 178..., fol., 100 pl.

1750 JARTOUX, P., Lettre sur le Ginseng (1711.) Lettr. édif., XVIII, 1781, p. 127-143, illustr.; Nouv. Éd., XXVIII, 1832, p. 84-99.

1751 LOUREIRO, de, Flora Cochinchinensis, sistens plantas in regno Cochinchina nascentes, quibus accedunt aliae observatae in Sinensi imperio. Ulyssipolae, 1790, 2 vols., 4to.

1752 REHMANN, J., Sur le sol natal et le commerce de la Rhubarbe, Mém. Soc. Imp. de Moscou, 1812.

1753 BRAAM, Icones plantarum sponte in China nascentium. London, 1821, fol.

1754 DON, D., Rhubarb of commerce, Jameson Edinb. N. Phil. Journ., 1827, p. 304.

1755 BUNGE, A., Enumeratio plantarum quas in China boreali collegit, 1833, 4to.

1756 — — , Plantarum Mongolico-chinensium decas I. Casan, 1835, 8vo.

1757 DELÉCLUSE, E. J., Le lis d'eau de Yingli. Paris, 1839, 8vo.

1758 LAY, G. T., Remarks on some euphorbiaceous plants, Chin. Rep., V, p. 437.

1759 — — , On Blanco's Flora de Filippinas; ibid, VII, p. 422.
(Contains some notes on Chinese plants.)

1760 MEYEN, F. J. F., Observationes botanicae in itinere circum terram institutae. Breslau, 1843, 4to., 13 plates.

1761 MACGOWAN, D. J., Notice regarding the plants yielding the fibres from which grass cloth is made, Chin. Rep., XVIII, p. 554.

1762 — — , The tallow-tree and insect-wax of China; ibid. XX, p. 422.

1763 HOFFMANN et SCHULTES, Noms indigènes d'un choix de plantes du Japon et de la Chine. Paris, 1853, 8vo.

1764 MAXIMOWICZ, C. J., Primitiae florae Amurensis, Acad. St. Petersburg, 1858, 4to., 10 plates, map.

1765 — — , Rhamneae Asiae orientalis, Mém. Ac. des Sc. de St. Petersb., X, 1866, No. 11.

1766 — — , Revisio hydrangearum Asiae orientalis; ibid. X, No. 16.

1767 — — , Rhododendraceae Asiae orientalis; ibid. XVI, 1870, No. 9.

1768 — — , Ophiogonis species in herbariis Petropolitanis servatas exposuit; ibid. Bull., 1870.

1769 — — , Diagnoses plantarum novarum Japoniae et Mandschuiae; ibid. Bull., 1874.

1770 DEBEAUX, O., Sur la végétation de quelques localités du littoral de la Chine, Rec. des Mém. de méd. mil., 3. sér., VI, 1861.

1771 BENTHAM, M. G., Flora Hongkongensis. London, 1861, 8vo.

1772 Flora of Hongkong, summarized from the valuable Fl. Hongkongensis of M. G. Bentham.

1773 HOOKER, S., Florula of Hongkong, Kew Garden Misc., IX, p. 339.

1774 — — , List of ferns collected on the Yangtsekiang in the province of Sz'chuan by Lieut. Sarel. In Blakiston, Five months on the Yangtze, p. 361.

1775 REGEL, E., Tentamen Florae Ussuriensis oder Versuch einer Flora des Ussuri-Gebiets. Mém. Ac. Sc. St. Petersb., IV, 1861, No. 4.

1776 OLIVER, Notes upon a few of the plants collected chiefly near Nagasaki and in the islands of the Korean archipelago in the years 1862-63, by Mr. R. Oldham, J. Linn. Soc. Bot., IX, 1865, p. 163 ss.

1777 HANCE, H. F., On the genus Brainea, J. of Bot., III, 1865, p. 341-344.

1778 — — , Descriptions of four new plants from Southern China; ibid, III, p. 378-381.

1779 — — , A few critical, little known or otherwise interesting plants; ibid, IV, 1866, p. 51-57.

1780 — — , Description of a new species of Polygala

from Southern China; ib., IV, 1866, p. 117-120.

1781 — — , Adversaria in stirpes imprimis Asiae orientalis criticas minusve notas interjectis novarum plurimarum diagnosibus, Ann. d. Sc. Nat., 5. sér., Bot., V, p. 202-256; also separately Paris, 1866, 8vo.

1782 — — , Note sur deux espèces du genre Scolopia Schr., ibid.

1783 — — , Manipulus plantarum novarum Chinensium, ibid.

1784 — — , Stirpium novarum tetras, J. of Bot., IV, 1866, p. 171-173.

1785 — — , Symbolae ad floram Sinicam adjectis paucissimarum stirpium Japonicarum diagnosibus, Ann. d. Scienc. Nat., 4. sér., XIV, No. 4.

1786 — — , On the Fagus Castanea of Loureiro's Fl. Coch. with descriptions of two new Chinese Corylaceae, J. of Linn. Soc. Bot., X, 1868.

1787 — — , Notes of some plants from northern China, ibid.

1788 — — , On the silkworm oaks of northern China, ibid.

1789 — — , Chinese silkworm oaks, Not. & Quer., I, p. 88; II, p. 28.

1790 — — , Supplementary note on Chinese silkworm oaks, J. Linn. Soc. Bot., XIII.

1791 — — , The Kinkeo plum, Not. & Quer., II, p. 124.

1792 — — , The Okgue; ibid, II, p. 173.

1793 — — , The Fung tree; ib., III, p. 31.

1794 — — , Chinese sagopalm; ib., III, p. 95.

1795 — — , Florae Hongkongensis prostheke, a compendious supplement to Mr. Bentham's description of the plants of the island of Hongkong, J. Linn. Soc. Bot., XIII, 1871. See China Review, I, p. 134.

1796 — — , On the source of the Radix Galangae minoris of Pharmacologists, J. Linn. Soc. Bot., XIII.

1797 — — , On the so-called "olives" (Canarii sp.) of Southern China, J. of Bot., Febr., 1871.

1798 — — , On the Ch'ing muh hsiang or green Putchuk of the Chinese, J. Bot., 1873, p. 72.

1799 — — , On Pinus Bungeana; ibid, p. 91.

1800 — — , On a Chinese maple; ib., p. 168.

1801 — — , On the Fruit of Galangal; ib., p. 175.

1802 — — , Lysimachia nova Chinensis; ib., p. 187.

1803 — — , Erythrostaphyle, genus novum Verbanaceis affine adumbravit; ibid, Sept., 1873.

1804 — — , On Pterocarya stenoptera; ib., Dec., 1873.

1805 — — , Novam plectranthi speciem profert; ib., Febr., 1874.

1806 — — , De nova Asplenii specie; ib., May, 1874.

1807 — — , On a new Chinese Hydrangea (H. Möllendorffi); ib., June, 1874.

1808 — — , On Ginseng, China Review, II, p. 131.

1809 — — On some Asiatic Corylaceae, J. of Bot., Aug., 1874.

1810 — — , On three new Chinese calami; ib., Sept., 1874.

1811 — — , On a small collection of plants from Kiukiang (made by O. F. von Möllendorff); ib., Sept., 1874.

1812 — — , De Jride dichotoma Pall.; ib., April, 1875.

1813 — — , On some mountain plants from northern China (collected by E. Bretschneider); ib., May, 1875.

1814 FAVRE, E., Recherches sur la fleur femelle du Podocarpus Sinensis, Ann. d. Sc. Nat., 5. sér., Bot., III, 1865, p. 377 ss.

1815 RACZYNSKI, S., Notice sur le Ginseng, Bull. Soc. d. Nat. de Moscou, XXXIX, 1866, p. 70-76, 2 pls.

1816 FARRE, F. J., On the growth and preparations of Rhubarb in China, Pharm. Journ. and Transact.; 2nd ser., VII, No. 7.

1817 Reise der Fregatte Novara. Botanischer Theil, 1867 ss.

1818 Die preussische Expedition nach Ostasien. Botanischer Theil, I, Die Tange von G. von Martens. Berlin, 1867, 8vo.

1819 SAMPSON, T., The Chinese pine, Not. & Quer., II, p. 52.

1820 — — , The white nuts; ib., II, p. 141.

1821 — — , Chinese figs, ib., III, p. 18.

1822 — — , Grapes in China; ib., III, p. 50.

1823 — — , The Banyan or Yung tree; ib., III, p. 72.

1824 — — , The Puti tree; ib., III, p. 100.

1825 — — , Palm trees; ib., III, p. 115, 129, 147, 170.

1826 MAC CARTEE, D. B., The Chinese pine; ib., II, p. 95.

1827 KOPSCH, H., The Okgue; ib., II, p. 172.

1828 — — , Notes on the vegetable Kingdom of Formosa; ib., II, p. 134.

1829 — — , Reeds of the Yangtse; ib., IV, p. 97.

1830 TAINTOR, E. C., The tallowtree; ib., II, p. 76, 112.

1831 — — , The Chun tree; ib., III, p. 46.

1832 KNOWLTON, M. J., The Kinkeo plum; ib., II, p. 107.

1833 MAYERS, F. W., The Utampa flower; ib., III, p. 85.

1834 Paddy husks; ib., II, p. 31.

1835 The Beteltree; ib., II, p. 136.

1836 The Fung tree; ib., III, p. 4, 31, 47.

1837 The Kowpi plant; ib., III, p. 46.

1838 Chinese names of plants; ib., III, p. 62, 95, 175.

1839 The Chun tree; ib., III, p. 73.

1840 SMITH, F. P., The wax tree; ib., III, p. 88.

1841 CALDRONI, B., Star anise and fennel; ib., III, p. 258.

1842 PHILIPS, G., Palm growing countries; ib., III, p. 169.

1843 BRETSCHNEIDER. E., Les palmiers de la Chine; ib., III, p. 139, 150.

1844 — — , The sacred fig tree; ib., III, p. 361.

1845 — — , On the study and value of Chinese bota-

nical works with notes on the history of plants
and geographical botany from Chinese sources,
Chin. Rec., III, p. 157, 172, 218, 241, 264, 281,
290, 296; also separately Foochow, 1870, 8vo.
II, 51 pp.

1846 HANBURY, D., Notes on the Radix Galangae of
Pharmacy, J. of Bot., XIII, 1871.

1847 BOWRA, E. C., Index plantarum sinice et latine, in
Doolittle's Handbook, Vol. II.

1848 BAILLON, H., Sur l'origine et les caractères de la
rhubarbe officinelle, Rev. Scient., Sept., 1872;
English in Journ. of Bot., Dec., 1872.

1849 DECAISNE, J., Trois genres nouveaux découverts
par A. David en Chine, Bull. Soc. Bot. de France,
XVIII, 1873.

1850 KREMPELHUBER, A. von, Chinesische Flechten.
"Flora," LVI, 1873.

1851 BAKER, J. G., On a new species of Heleniopsis
from Formosa, J. of Bot., Sept., 1874.

1852 — — , Ferns from Kiukiang; ib., 1875.

1853 MOORE, S., Dr. Shearer's collection of plants from
Kiukiang; ibid, 1875.

On Tea.

1854 FRANC, J., Veronica théezans i. e. collatio Veroni-
cae europaeae cum Thé chinico. Lipsiae, 1710,
12mo.

1855 DESFONTAINES, Observations sur le Thé, Ann.
du Mus. d'Hist. Nat. Paris, 1804, IV.

1856 MARQUIS, F., Du Thé, ou nouveau traité sur sa
culture, sa recolte, sa préparation et ses usages.
Paris, 1820, 12mo.

1857 KLAPROTH, J., Liste des thés les plus célèbres de
la Chine, Journ. Asiat., 1827.

1858 REHMANN, J., Sur les briques du Thé des Mongo-
les, Mém. Soc. d. Nat. de Moscou, 1830.

1859 GORDON, G. T., Memorandum of an excursion to

the tea hills, Chin. Rep., IV, p. 72.

1860 WILLIAMS, S. W., Description of the tea plant; ib., VIII, p. 132.
1861 SIGMUND, Tea, its effect, medical and moral. London, 1839, 8vo.
1862 HOUSSAY, M. J., Monographie du Thé. Paris, 1843, 8vo.
1863 SHAW, C., An account of the tea plant, Ch. Rep., XVIII, p. 23.
1864 Remarks on the tea plant, Chin. & Jap. Rep., III, p. 177-181.
1865 GRANT, C. M., Brick tea, Friend of China, 26th July, 1866; Not. & Quer., II, p. 30.
1866 HANCE, H., Brick tea, Not. & Quer., I, p. 91.
1867 SAMPSON, T., Tea; ib., III, p. 110.

d. Zoology.

1868 ACKSELL, P. M., Fauna Chinensis. Upsala, 1823, 4to.
1869 FRAUENFELD, R. von, Notizen über die Fauna Hongkong's und Schanghais, Sitz. Ber. d. Math. Phys. Cl. K. K. Ac. Wiss. Wien, 1859, p. 241-272.
1870 — — , Zoologische Miscellen: Vogel und Säugethiere von Formosa. Verh. Zool. Bot. Ver. Wien, XII, 1866, p. 427-447.
1871 ANDREAE, Sinologisch Zoologische Notizen. Weinland's "Zool. Garten," II, 1861, p. 476.
1872 MARTENS, E. von, Die preussische Expedition nach Ostasien. Zoologische Abtheilung, I. Ueber die Thierwelt der besuchten Gegenden im Allgemeinen. Berlin, 1865, 8vo. (China, p. 155-185).
1873 Reise der Fregatte Novara um die Erde, Zoologischer Theil, 1865, 4to.
1874 SWINHOE, R., Papers on Chinese Zoology. London, 1870, 8vo. (reprinted from the Proc. Zool. Soc., London.)
1875 — — , Zoological notes of a journey from Can-

ton to Peking and Kalgan, Proc. Zool. Soc., 1870,
p. 427-451.

1876 MOELLENDORFF, O. F. von, Contributions to the
Natural History of North China, Mitth. der
Deutsch. Ges. f. Ostas. Heft, 9, p. 7-19, 1876.

Mammals.

1877 GRAY, Description of some new or little known
Mammalia, Charlesworth's Mag. of Nat. Hist.,
1837.

1878 MARTENS, E. von, Ueber chinesische Hausthiere.
Weinland's Zool. Garten, II, 1861, p. 222 ss.

1879 SWINHOE, R., Mammals observed in Formosa,
Proc. Zool. Soc., 1862, p. 347-365; 1864, p. 185.

1880 — — , On a new rat from Formosa; ib., 1864,
May.

1881 — — , On the Cervine animals of the island of
Hainan; ib., 1869.

1882 — — , On a new deer from China (Hydropotes
inermis); ib., 1870, p. 89-92, 2 plates.

1883 — — , On the mammals of Hainan; ib., 1870.

1884 — — , Catalogue of the mammals of China,
South of the river Yangtse; ib., 1870, p. 615-653.

1885 GRAY, J. C., Notice of a new Finner Whale from
Formosa, Ann. & Mag. of Nat. Hist., XVI, 1865,
p. 148.

1886 MILNE EDWARDS, A., Note sur le Milou or Sseu-
pou-siang, mammifère du nord de la Chine, qui
constitue une section nouvelle de la famille des
cerfs, Ann. d. Science. Nat., 5. sér., Zool., V, 1866,
p. 380 ss., pl.

1887 — — , Etudes pour servir à l'histoire de la Fau-
ne mammalogique de la Chine in Recherches pour
servir à l'histoire naturelle des Mammifères. Paris, 1870, fol., plates.

1888 BUSK, G., On the Tiger of northern China, Proc.
Zool. Soc., 1874. p. 146 ss.

Birds.

1889 SWINHOE, R., Notes on some new species of birds found in the island of Formosa, J. N. Ch. Br. R. As. Soc., I, 1859, p. 225-230.

1890 — — , The small Chinese lark; ib., III, p. 287.

1891 — — , Ornithology of Amoy, Dr. Sclater's "Ibis," II, 1860, p. 45, 130, 428, Journ. As. Soc. Bengal, 1860, p. 240-266.

1892 — — , Notes on the ornithology of Hongkong, Macao and Canton, Sclater's Ibis, III, 1861, Jan.

1893 — — , Ornithological ramble in Foochow; ib., IV, 1862, July.

1894 — — , Birds observed at Tientsin, Proc. Zool. Soc., 1862, p. 315-320.

1895 — — , New species of birds of Formosa, "Ibis," 1863, p. 196, 250, 377.

1896 — — , On the species of Zosterops inhabiting China and Japan, Proc. Zool. Soc., 1863, p. 203 ss.

1897 — — , Catalogue of the birds of China and its islands, Proc. Zool. Soc., 1863, p. 259-329; additional notes, ibid, 1864, p. 271.

1898 — — , A voice on ornithology from Formosa; ibid, p. 129-134, pl.

1899 — — , Ornithological notes from Formosa, "Ibis" 1866, p. 292-316, 392-406, 2 pls.

1900 — — , On a new species of Beech Martin of Formosa, Ann. & Mag. of Nat. Hist., XVIII, 1866, p. 286.

1901 — — , On the Pied Wagtails of China, Pr. Zool. Soc., 1870, p. 120-124, 129-130, illustr.

1902 — — , On a new species of Accentor from North China, Pr. Zool. S., 1870, p. 124 s., plate.

1903 — — , On the plovers of the genus Aegialites found in China; ibid, p. 137 s., plate.

1904 — — , Descriptions of seven new species of birds procured during a cruise up the river Yangtse, ib., 131-136, plate.

152

1905 — — , List of birds collected by Mr. Collingwood during a cruise in the Chinese and Japanese seas; ib., p. 600-604.

1906 — — , Descriptions of three new species of birds from China, Ann. & Mag. Nat. Hist., March, 1870.
> The six preceding articles also in "Papers on Chinese Zoology," No. 1874.

1907 — — , On the ornithology of Hainan, "Ibis," Jan., 1870.

1908 — — , A revised catalogue of the birds of China and its islands with descriptions of new species, reference to former notes and remarks, Proc. Zool. Soc., 1871, p. 337-423.

1909 GOULD, J., Description of 16 new species of birds from Formosa collected by Swinhoe, Pr. Zool. Soc., 1862, p. 280 ss.

1910 SCLATER, P. L., List of the species of Phasianidae with remarks on their geographical distribution; ibid, 1863, p. 113 ss.

1911 — — , Note on Kittacincla auricularis Swinh., "Ibis," 1866, p. 109, plate.

1912 ANDERSON, J., New species of birds collected in Yunnan, Proc. Zool. Soc., 1871.

1913 DAVID, A., Catalogue des oiseaux de Chine, observés dans la partie septentrionale de l'empire, au nord du fleuve bleu, de 1862-1870, Bull. Nouv. Archiv. du Mus., VII, 1872.

Reptiles.

1914 SWINHOE, R., List of reptiles and batrachians collected in the island of Hainan, Pr. Zool. Soc., 1870.
> Reptiles formerly collected by Swinhoe are described in Günther's Reptiles of India, 1864.

1915 — — , Notes on reptiles and batrachians collect-

ed in various parts of China, Proc. Zool. Soc.,
1870, p. 409-413, plate.
1916 HANCE, H., Serpents in China, Not. and Quer.,
III, p. 94.
1917 Snakes in Hongkong; ibid, III, p. 158.
1918a BUSHELL, S. W., Green haired tortoise; ibid,
III, p. 158.

Fishes.

1918b RICHARDSON, J., Report on the ichtyology of the
seas of China and Japan. London, 1846, 8vo.
1919 BASILEWSKY, S., Ichthyographia Chinae borea-
lis, Nouv. Mém. de la Soc. d. Nat. de Moscou, X,
1855; also separately, 4to., plates.
1920 MARTENS, E. von, Ueber den Schwertfisch des
Yangtzekiang (Polyodon gladius), Mon. Berlin
Acad., Mai, 1861, p. 476.
1921 BLEEKER, On fishes from Peking and Amoy, Nederl. Tijdschr. voor de Dierkunde, 1869, p. 18,
58 (in Dutch.)
1922 — , Mémoire sur les cyprinoides de la Chine,
Verh. K. Akad. van Wetensch. Amsterdam, XII,
1871, 14 plates; also separately.
1923 JOLY, N., Études sur les moeurs, le développement
et les métamorphoses d'un petit poisson chinois
du genre macropode. Toulouse, 1874, 8vo., 31
pp.

Insecta, Crustacea, Arachnidea.

1924 DONOVAN, E., Epitome of the insects of China.
London, 1798, 4to., plates.
Second edition with additions by J. O. West-
wood: Natural history of the insects of
China, containing upwards of 220 figures
and descriptions. London, 1842, 4to.
1925 FALDERMANN, Coleopterorum ab illustrissimo

Bungio in China boreali, Mongolia et montibus Altaicis collectorum descriptio, Mem. Acad. Imp. d. Scienc. St. Petersb., II, 1835.

1926 BERTHOLD, A., Ueber Crustaceen aus China. Göttingen, 1846, 4to.

1927 BREMER und GREY, Beiträge zur Schmetterlings-fauna des Nördlichen China's. St. Petersburg, 1853, 8vo., plates.

See Kollar, Verh. Zool. Bot. Ver. Wien, 1854.

1928 SNELLEN VAN VOLLENHOVEN, Die Ritter-schmetterlinge von China und Japan. Leyden, 1860.

1929 LUCAS, H., Quelques remarques sur les Lepidop-tères du genre Argynnis qui habitent les environs de Pékin et description d'une espèce nouvelle, Ann. Soc. Entom. de France, 4. sér., VI, 1866, p. 218-222.

1930 McCARTEE, D. B., On some wild silkworms of Chi-na, J. N. Ch. B. R. As. Soc., III, 1867, p. 75.

1931 PRYER, W. B., Entomology of Shanghai; ibid, IV, p. 71-79.

1932 The wax insect, Not. and Quer., II, p. 161, 183.

1933 Chinese spiders, China Review, III, p. 188.

Mollusca, Radiata, etc.

1934 CANTOR, Th. and BENSON, W. H., Chusan shells, J. As. Soc. Bengal, 1855.

1935 DEBEAUX, O., Note sur les mollusques vivants observés dans le nord de la Chine, Rec. de Mém. de méd. mil., VI, Dec., 1861, p. 481; Guerin, Rev. Zool., 1862, p. 214.

1936 — — , Notice sur la malacologie de quelques points du littoral Chinois, Journ. de Conch., July, 1863.

1937 — — et CROSSE, H., Note sur quelques espèces nouvelles ou peu connus du littoral de l'empire

chinois; ibid, XI, 1863, p. 239-252; XII, 1869,
p. 316-320.

1938 MARTENS, E. von, Ostasiatische Paludinaceen,
Malac. Bl., 1865.

1939 — — , Ostasiastische Echinodermen, Archiv. f.
Naturg., XXXI, 1865, p. 345-360; XXXII, 1866,
p. 57-81, 133-189.

1940 — — , Ostasiatische Limnaeaceen, Malac. Bl.,
1867, p. 211-227.

1941 — — , Die preussische Expedition nach Ostasien, Zoolog. Abtheilg., II, Die Landschnecken.
Berlin, 1868, 8vo. (p. 155-185 Chinese land shells),
plates.

1942 — — , Neue Helix arten aus China, Mal. Blätt.,
1873.

1943 LEA, J., Notes on some singular forms of Chinese
species of Unio., Proc. Ac. Nat. Sc. Philadelph.,
1868, p. 145.

1944 BLANFORD, Descriptions of new land and fresh
water molluscan species collected by Dr. J. Anderson in Upper Burmah and Yunnan, Proc. Zool.
Soc., 1869, p. 444 ss.

1945 ADAMS, H., List of species of land and freshwater
shells collected by R. Swinhoe in China and Formosa; ibid, 1870, p. 374 ss.

1946 HERKLOTS, J. A., Description de deux espèces
nouvelles de Pennatulides des mers de la Chine,
Verh. K. Ak. v. Wetensch. Amsterdam, 1870.

1947 HEUDE, R. P., Diagnoses molluscorum in flumini-
bus provinciae Nankingensis collectorum, Journ.
de Conch., 1874, p. 112 ss.

1948 — — , Conchyliologie fluviatile de la province
de Nanking. Paris, 1875, 4to., fasc. I, pl.

1949 MOELLENDORFF, O. F. von, Diagnosen neuer
Arten aus dem Binnenlande von China, Jahrb. der
Deutsch. Mal. Ges., 1874, p. 78 ss.

1950 — — , Die Landschnecken der Umgegend von
Peking; ibid, 1875.

APPENDIX.

Medical Observations in and on China.

1951 De la petite vérole en Chine, Mém. Conc., etc., IV, p. 392.

1952 MILNE, W. C., Asiatic cholera in Ningpo and in China, Chin. Rep., XII, p. 485.

1953 HOBSON, B., A brief account of the leprosy of China and the East, Transact. Ch. Br. R. As. Soc., III. Hongkong, 1853, p. 23-36.

1954 BARTHE, J., Observations médicales prises pendant la campagne de la Sibylle dans l'Inde, la Chine, etc., Compt. Rend. Ac. de Sc., XL, VI, 1858.

1955 DUMAY, Relation médico-chirurgicale de la campagne de la corvette le Catinat dans les mers de l'Inde, de la Chine et de l'Indochine. Montpellier, 1861.

1956 GAUTHIER, G., Deux années de pratique médicale à Canton. Paris, 1863, 8vo.

1957 FALOT, Relation médicale d'une campagne en Chine, années 1859, 1860, 1861 et 1862. Montpellier, 1863.

1958 NELSON, Medical results of the late war in China, Brit. & For. Med. Chir. Rev., 1863.

1959 MACKAY, A. E., Naval medical contributions in China. Edinburgh Med. Journ., 1863.

1960 ARMAND, A., Lettres de l'expedition de Chine. Paris, 1864.

1961 DUTEUIL, Quelques notes médicales recueillies pendant un séjour de cinq ans en Chine, Cochinchine et Japon. Paris, 1864.

1962 HUGUET, Relation médicale d'une campagne dans les mers de Chine à bord de la Dryade, 1859-1861. Paris, 1865.

1963 MORACHE, G., Notes sur une épidemie de Typhus avec cas de Relapsing Fever observée à Pékin, Rec. d. Mém. de méd. mil., 3. sér., XVI, 1866.

1964 — — , Chine, In Dictionn. encycl. des Scienc. méd. Paris, 1874, p. 127-223.

1965 LE ROY de MÉRICOURT, Contributions à la géographie médicale, Le littoral de la Chine, Arch. de Méd. Navale, VI, 1866.

1966 Concerning leprosy at Hankow, Not. & Quer., II, p. 314.

1967 DUDGEON, J., Hernia in China; ibid, III, p. 59.

1968 SMITH, F. P., Hernia in China; ibid, III, p. 59.

1969 CHEVAL, Relation médicale d'une campagne en Chine, au Japon et en Corée. Montpellier, 1868.

1970 DUBURQUOIS, Note sur les maladies des Européens en Chine et au Japon. Paris, 1872.

1971 ROCHEFORT,E., Contributions à la géographie médicale, Les ports de la Chine, Arch. de méd. navale, 1873.

XIII.

China and the Chinese.

a. General Descriptions of the Chinese Empire.

1972 Kanun nameh i Tschin u Hata (book on the principles of state of Tshin and Catai), ca. 1494 in Persian. For Turkish translation and analysis see J. Th. Zenker, Ztschr. d. D. M. G., XV, p. 785-805. New Turkish translation: Terdschümei newadird dschin madschin (transl. of the curiosities of China). Constantinople, 1854, 8vo., 70. pp. See Schlechta Wssehrd, Ak. d. Wiss. Wien, XVII, p. 157.

1973 NOVUS ORBIS Regionum et Insularum veteribus incognitarum. Basil., 1532, fol.; ibid, 1535. Paris, 1582, fol.

1974 BARROS, J. de, Asia. Lisboa, 1560; ibid, 1778-88, 24 vols., 12mo.

Dutch: Amst., 1668, fol.; French: 1670;
German: 1676, fol.

2000 FRANCISCI, E., Ost. und Westindischer wie auch
Sinesischer Lust u. Staatsgarten. Nürnberg,
1668, fol., 3 vols.

2001 DAPPER, O., Beschryving den keyserryks van Tainsing of Sina. Amsterdam, 1670, fol.

2002 ROGEMONT, Fr., Relação do estado politico e moral
do Imperio da China pelos annos de 1659 á 1666,
etc. Lisbon, 1672, 4to. Latin: Löwen, 1673, 8vo.

2003 OGILBY, J., Description of Asia. London, 1672,
fol.

2004 NAVARETTE, D. F., Tradados historicos politicos,
ethicos y religiosos della monarchia do China.
Madrid, 1676, fol.

2005 VRIES, S. DE, Curieuse Aanmerkingen der by zon-
derste Oost en West Indische verwonderings waar-
digen Dingen nevens die van China. Utrecht,
1684, 4to.

2006 MAGALHAENS, G. DE, A new history of China,
containing a description of the most considerable
particulars of that vast empire (In Portuguese).
French: Nouvelle relation de la Chine, trad.
du Portugais par l'abbé Bernon. Paris,
1688, 4to.; Latin and English: London,
1688, 12mo. See Bridgeman Chin.
Rep., X, p. 641.

2007 MUELLER, A., Abdallae Beidawei historia sinensis.
Jenae, 1689, 4to.

2008 — — , De rebus Sinensium epistola. Jenae,
1689, 12mo.

2009 WAGNER, J. C., Das mächtige kaiserthum Sina
und die asiatische Tartarei. Augsburg, 1689, fol.

2010 MEISTER, G., Orientalisch—Ostindianischer Kunst
und Lust gärtner wie auch Anmerkungen was bei
des Autoris zweimaliger Reise nach Japan, Java,
Küsten Sina, etc. observiret wurden. Dresden,
1692; Leipzig, 1713; ibid, 1730, 4to.

2011 LECOMTE, L., Nouveaux Mémoires sur l'état présent de la Chine avec figures. Amsterdam, 1693-1698, 3 vols., 12mo.; also Paris, 1696, 2 vols., 12mo. ; Dutch : Amsterdam, 1698. ; German : Frankfurt, 1699, 3 vols., 12mo. London, 1697, 8vo. Reprinted with Ch. le Gobien's Histoire de l'Edit de l'Empereur, etc. (See No. 3420.) Paris, 1701, 1702, 3 vols., 12mo.; English: London, 1733, 8vo. See Bridgeman Chin. Rep., I, p. 249.

2012 CARLIERI, Notizie varie dell'imperio della China e di quelche altri paësi adjacenti con la vita de Confucio. Firenze, 1697, 12mo.

2013 RELAND, E., De magno Sinarum imperio. Holmes, 1697, 8vo.

2014 BOUVET, J., État présent de la Chine en figures gravées, par P. Giffart sur les dessins apportés au Roi par le P. J. Bouvet. Paris, 1697, fol.
Dutch : Utrecht, 1710, 4to.

2015 COUPLET, P., Imperii Sinarum et rerum in eo notabilium synopsis.

2016 Regni Chinensis descriptio, intercalato Bened. Goësii itinerario ex India in Sinarum regnum. Lyons, 1700, 4to.

2017 Korte Beschryving van 't magtig keizerryk China door Dionysius Kao (Short description of the mighty empire of China by D. Kao) in E. Y. Ides, Driejaarige Reise, etc. (No. 3057), 2nd edition, p. 139-243.

2018 HALDE, DU, Description géographique, historique, chronologique, politique et physique de l'empire de la Chine. La Haye, 1735, 4 vols., fol.; 1736, 4 vols., 4to.
English: The general history of China. London, 1736, 4 vols., 4to.; A description of the empire of China. London, 1738, 2 vols., fol.; 1744, 4 vols., 8vo.; German: Rostock, 1747-49, 4 vols., 4to.; suppl.. 1756, 4to.

2019 ODERICO de PARTENON, De mirabilibus mundi. Venetia, 1761, 4to.

2020 Lettres chinoises. Hague, 1766, 8vo.

2021 D'ANVILLE, Mémoires sur le Chine. Paris, 1766, 4to.

2022 P. D. B., Description abrégée de l'empire de la Chine in Herbelot, Bibl. Or., 1776; Suppl., p. 191-260.

2023 GROSIER, l'abbé, Description générale de la Chine ou tableau de l'état actuel de cet empire. Paris, 1785, 4to.; ibid, 1787, 2 vols., 8vo.; 1818, 7 vols., 8vo.; 1821, 7 vols., 8vo.
    English: London, 1788, 2 vols., 8vo.
    See Rémusat, Nouv. Mél. As., I, p. 283.

2024 HEINZE, V. A., Beschreibung von China aus den besten Reisebeschreibungen gesammelt. Leipzig, 1785, 4 vols., 8vo.

2025 Beschreibung von China in einzelnen Schilderungen der vorzüglichsten Merkwürdigkeiten des Staats, der Literatur, Gelehrsamkeit und Kunst. Strassburg, 1789, 8vo.

2026 Beschreibung des chinesischen Reichs, seiner Einwohner und deren Sitten, Gebräuche und Religion. Weissenfels, 1790, 8vo.

2027 NORBERG, M., De regno Chataja ejusque re sacra, litteraria, militari, judiciaria, magnificentia imperiali et metropoli Kambalu. Lund., 1790-95, 5 pts., 4to.

2028 WINTERBOTHAM, W., A historical, geographical and philosophical view of the Chinese empire. London, 1795, 8vo.

2029 La Chine mieux connue ou les Chinois tels qu'il faut les voir. Paris, 1797, 2 vols., 12mo.

2030 A complete view of the Chinese empire. London, 1798, 8vo.; also 1842, 12mo.

2031 MORRISON, R., A view of China. Macao, 1817, 4to.

2032 —— —— , On the language, history, religion and government of China, Evang. Mag., 1825, 6 letters.

2033 China, dialogues between a father and his two children concerning the history and present state of that country. London, 1821, 12mo.

2034 DAVIS, Sir J. F., Memoir concerning the Chinese, Transact. of R. As. Soc., I, 1. London, 1824.

2035 — —, Notices of China by P. Serra; ibid, July, 1830.

2036 — —, The Chinese, a general description of the empire of China. London, 1836, 2 vols., 12mo.; 2nd ed., 1847, 2 vols., 8vo.
　　　French by A. Pichard. Paris, 1837, 2 vols., 12mo.; Dutch: Amsterdam, 1840, 2 vols., 8vo.; German by Wesenfeld, Magdeburg, 1843, 2 vols., 8vo. ; by Drugulin. Stuttgart ; 1847, 4 vols., 8vo.; 1852, 2 vols., 12mo. Italian: Venedig, 1845, 2 vols., 8vo.

2037 — —, Sketches of China. London, 1841, 12mo.; Dutch: Groeningen, 1843. See Chin Rep., XI, p. 81.

2038 MALPIÈRE, D. B. DE, La Chine, moeurs, usages, coutumes, arts et metiers, peines civiles et militaires, cérémonies religieuses, monumens et paysages d'après les dessins originaux du P. Castiglione du peintre chinois Pu-quà, de W. Alexandre de Chambres, Dadly etc. avec des notes explicatives et une introduction. Paris, 1825-39, 2 vols., 4to., 180 plates. See A. Rémusat, J. As., XI, p. 303 ss.

2039 RÉMUSAT, A., Coup d'oeil sur la Chine et sur ses habitants, Nouv. Mél. As., I, 1, 1829.

2040 WOOD, W. W., Sketches on China. Philadelphia, 1830, 12mo.

2041 SCHOTT, W., China in Encycl. von Ersch & Gruber, XXI, 1830.

2042 BORGET, A., La Chine et les Chinois. Paris, 1832, fol.
　　　English : London, 1842, fol.

2043 ABEEL, D., Journal of a residence in China. London, 1835, 12mo.

2044 MURRAY, H., Crawford, J.; Gordon, P.; Lyon, T.; Wallace, W.; and Burnett, G., An historical and descriptive account of China. Edinburgh, 1836, 3 vols., 12mo.

> See E. C. Bridgman, Ch. Repos., V, p. 193; VI, p. 59.

2045 PAUTHIER, G., La Chine ou description historique, géographique et littéraire. Paris, 1837, 8vo. avec 72 planches.

> German by C. A. Mebold. Stuttgart, 1839, 8vo., 529 pp., map, 72 plates.

2046 — — , et BAZIN, A., La Chine moderne. Paris, 1853, 8vo.

> See J. H. Plath, Münch. gel. Anz., I, No. 3-4; III, No. 4-6.

2047 DOWNING, C. T., The Fanqui in China. London, 1838, 3 vols., 12mo. See Chin. Rep., VII, p. 328.

> German by C. Richard. Aachen und Leipzig, 1841, 8vo.

2048 GUETZLAFF, K., China opened, or a display of the topography, history, customs, etc. of the Chinese empire, revised by the Rev. A. Reed. London, 1838, 2 vols., 12mo.

> See S. W. Williams, Ch. Repos., VIII, p. 84.

2049 — —, Chinesische Berichte. Kassel, 1850, 8vo.

2050 WINES, E. C., A peep at China in Mr. Dunn's collection with miscellaneous notices relating to the institutions of the Chinese. Philadelphia, 1839, 8vo., 403 pp.

> See Chin. Rep., VIII, p. 581 ss.

2051 URBAN, F. D', Description de la Chine et des états tributaires. Paris, 1840, 3 vols., 12mo. Extracts from Grosier's Description (No. 2023.)

2052 BRIDGEMAN, E. C., Letters on China. Boston, 1840, 12mo.

2053 Ancient and modern history of China, comprising an account of its government, law and religions, language and literature. London, 1840, 8vo.

2054 MUDIE, R., China and its resources and peculiar
ties. London, 1840, 8vo.

2055 HYACINTH, Bitschurin, Kitai, yevo jiteli, nrav
obytschai, prosvieschtschenie. (China, its pe
ple, its customs, costumes and instruction.) S
Petersburg, 1840, 8vo., 442 pp. (in Russian).

2056 — — , Kitai v grajdanskom i nravstvennom so
toyanii (Chinese manners, customs, social lif
etc.) St. Petersburg, 1848, 4 vols., 8vo. (
Russian.)
Pt. I: General administration; II, The Cl
nese penal code; III, Public instructic
and schools; IV, Manners and Custom

2057 KIDD, S., China or illustration of the symbols, pl
losophy, etc. of the Chinese. London, 184
8vo.

2058 LAY, G. T., The Chinese as they are, their mor
social and literary character. London, 1841, 8v
German by Wilfert. Crefeld, 1844, 12mo. a
by H. Schirges. Hamburg, 1843, 12n

2059 LANGDON, W. B., Ten thousand things relating
China. London, 1842, 8vo.; also New Yoı
1850, 8vo.
See Chin. Rep., XII, p. 561 ss.

2060 MEDHURST, W. H. (sen), China, its state a
prospects with special reference to the spread
the gospel. London, 1842, 8vo.
German: Stuttgart, 1843, 8vo.
See E. C. Bridgman, Ch. Repos., IX, p. 7

2061 China as it was and as it is. London, 1842, 8vo.

2062 CORNER, Miss, Descriptive history of China. Lc
don, 1842, 8vo.

2063 SQUIER, The Chinese as they are. Albany, 18
8vo.

2064 ALLOM, T., China in a series of views. Lond
1843, 2 vols., 4to.
German: China historisch romantisch ma
risch. Karlsruhe, 1844, 8vo., 36 Stahl

2065 PARLEY, Tales about China and the Chinese. London, 1843, 8vo.

2066 LA FARINA, G., La China considerata nella sua storia ne suoi riti et costumi, nella sua industria, nelle sue arti. Firenze, 1843-1850, 4 vols., 4to., engrav.

2067 PHILIPP, R., China, its creed and customs. London, 12mo.

2068 People of China, their history, court, religion. London, 1845, 12mo., map, plates.

2069 La Chine ouverte, aventures d'un Fan Kouei dans le pays de Tsin. Par old Nick. Paris, 1845, 8vo.

2070 BIOT, E., Chine et Indo chine. Paris, 1846, 8vo.

2071 PETERS, S. R., Miscellaneous remarks upon the government, history and customs of the Chinese. Boston, 1846, 8vo.

2072 KLEMM, G., China das Reich der Mitte. Leipzig, 1847, 8vo., plates.

2073 MARTIN, R. M., China political, commercial and moral. London, 1847, 2 vols., 8vo.

2074 BONACOSSI, A., La Chine et les chinois. Paris, 1847, 8vo., 376 pp.

2075 WILLIAMS, S. W., The Middle Kingdom or Survey of the Geography, Government, Education, Social Life, Arts, Language, Religion, etc. of the Chinese Empire and its Inhabitants with a map of the Empire and numerous illustrations. New York, 1848, 2 vols., 8vo.; 4th ed., ibid, 1857, reprinted 1871, 2 vols., 8vo., 590, 640 pp.
    German by L. L. Collmann, Kassel, 1852, 2 vols., 8vo.

2076— — , The present position of the Chinese empire, Transact. Am. Ethnol. Soc., II, 1849, No. 7.

2077 FORBES, F. E., Five years in China. London, 1848, 8vo., plates.

2078 GERSTAECKER, F., China, das Land und seine Bewohner. Aus dem Englischen. Leipzig, 1848, 8vo.

2079 SIRR, H. C., China and the Chinese. London, 1849, 2 vols., 8vo.

2080 RHIND, China, its past history and future hopes. London, 1850, 8vo.

2081 China, its population, trade and the prospects of a treaty, Journal Am. Os. Soc., I, p. 143-161.

2082 POWER, P. T., Recollections of three years' residence in China. London, 1853, 8vo.

2083 The celestial empire, or points and pickings of information about China and the Chinese. London, 1853, 12mo.

2084 BIERNATZKI, K. L., Beiträge zur Kunde Chinas und Ostasiens. Kassel, 1853, 8vo.

2085 China pictorial, descriptive and historical. London, 1853, 8vo.

2086 La Chine depuis le traité de Nankin. Paris, 1853, 8vo.

2087 CHAVANNES, Les Chinois pendant une période de 4458 années. Paris, 1854, 8vo.

2088 GILLESPIE, W., The land of Sinim. London, 1854, 8vo.

2089 PHILLIPS, T., The Chinese. London, 1854, 8vo.

2090 NEUMANN, K. F., Das chinesische Reich. "Unsre Zeit," 7. Heft, p. 417. Leipzig, 1857.

2091 — — , Der gegenwärtige Zustand des chinesischen Reiches; ibid, 11. Heft, p. 673, 1857.

2092 D'EWES, J., China, Australia and the Pacific Islands. London, 1857, 8vo.

2093 MILNE, W. C., Life in China. London, 1857, 8vo. French by A. Tasset. Paris, 1858, 12mo. See J. Mohl in Journ. As., 5. sér., XI, p. 107.

2094 China, Land und Volk. Stuttgart, 1858, 8vo.

2095 China und die Chinesen. Stuttgart, 1859, 8vo.

2096 St. DENYS, le Marquis H. DE, La Chine devant l'Europe. Paris, 1859, 8vo.

2097 LEGGE, J., The land of Sinim. London, 1859, 8vo.

2098 TAYLOR, C., Five years in China. New York, 1860, 12mo.

2099 SCARTH, J., Twelve years in China. Edinburgh, 1860, 8vo.

2100 The Englishman in China. London, 1860, 8vo., 272 pp., illustr.

2101 LECHLER, R., Acht Vorträge über China. Basel, 1861, 8vo.

2102 LAFITTE, P., Considérations générales sur l'ensemble de la civilisation chinoise et sur les relations de l'Occident avec la Chine. Paris, 1861, 8vo.

2103 MACLAY, B. S., Life among the Chinese. New York, 1861, 8vo.

2104 COLLINS, Mrs., China and its people, a book for young readers. London, 1862, 12mo.

2105 Das Interessanteste und Neueste aus China. Wien, 1863, 8vo.
      See Lit. Centralbl. (1864), No. 35, p. 822; Kath. allg. Lit. Ztg., 1864, No. 27, p. 237.

2106 SMITH, W. L. G., Observations on China and the Chinese. New York, 1863, 8vo.

2107 WOLFF, F., Album von Ost-Asien. Düsseldorf, 1864, fol.
      See Petermann's geogr. Mitth., 1865, p. 312; Köln. Ztg., 1865, p. 317.

2108 ESCAYRAC DE LAUTURE, Comte d', Mémoires sur la Chine. Paris, 1864-65, 4to., maps.
      See Lit. Centralbl., 1868, No. 7, p. 162; Ch. and Jap. Rep., I (1864), 441; Athenaeum, 1866, June 16, p. 793; The Reader, 1866, No. 172, p. 367; H. Passy Séances et travaux de l'Ac. des sc. mor. et pol., 1865, III, livr. 7, p. 143-148.

2109 BUSH, C. P., Five years in China. Philadelphia, 1865, 12mo.

2110 COURCY, Marquis de, L'empire du Milieu, description géographique, précis historique, institutions sociales, religieuses, politiques, notions sur les sciences, les arts, l'industrie et le commerce. Paris, 1866, 8vo.

> See Journ. d. Sav., 1867, p. 324 ss.; Lit. Centralbl., 1868, No. 7, p. 164.

2111 SCHLIEMANN, H., La Chine et le Japon au temps présent. Paris, 1867.

2112 FERRARI, J., La Chine et l'Orient, leur histoire et leurs traditions comparées. Paris, 1867, 8vo.; 2nd ed., 1868, 12mo.

> See Journ. des Sav., 1868, fév., p. 126; Le Courier français, 1868, 24 févr.; L'opinion nationale, 19 Oct., 1867; Siècle 7. Oct., 1867.

2113 MOSSMANN, S., China, a brief account of the country, its inhabitants and their institutions. London, 1867, map, 12mo.

2114 NEVIUS, J. L., China and the Chinese. New York, 1869, 8vo.

2115 — — , Mrs. H. S. C., Our life in China. New York, 1869, 8vo.

2116 MOULE, A. E., Four hundred millions, chapters on China and the Chinese with maps and illustrations. London, 1870, 8vo.

> See "Phoenix," I, p. 64.

2117 PESCHEL, O., China und seine Cultur. "Ausland," 1872, p. 313 ss.

2118 FORBES, A. G., The Empires and cities of Asia. London, 1873, 8vo., map.

2119 THOMSON, T., Illustrations of China and its people, a series of 200 photographs with letterpress descriptive of the places and people represented. London, 1873-74, 4 vols., fol.

> See Chin. Rec., V, p. 109-110.

2120 MARTIN, L'extrême Orient, Bull. Soc. Géo. Paris, Jan., 1873.

2121 STRAUSS, L., La Chine, son histoire, ses ressources. Paris, 1874, 8vo.

2122 SACHOT, O., Pays d'extrême Orient, Siam, Indo-
chine, Chine, Corée. Paris, 1874, 8vo.

2123 DUFOREST, J., Dix ans en Chine, 1860-1870, Souvenirs d'un militaire français. Lausanne, 1874,
8vo.

b. Government, Law, Army.

2124 BAUDIER, M., Histoire de la cour du roi de la Chine. Paris, 1662, 12mo.
English: London, 1664, 4to.

2125 L'empereur de la Chine avec toute sa cour en habits
ordinaire et de cérémonie. Paris, fol., s. a.

2126 LOLOOZ, DE, Les militaires audelà de Gange. Paris, 1770, 2 vols., 8vo.

2127 ST. MAURICE, DE, St. Leu, de, Puységur, de, État
actuel de l'art et de la science militaire de la Chine, tiré de livres militaires des Chinois. Paris,
1773, 12mo.

2128 AMIOT, Revenue de l'empire de la Chine, Mém.
Conc., VI, p. 297-304.

2129 — — , Remarques critiques sur l'art militaire des
Chinois; ibid, VII, p. 1.
See No. 188.

2130 — — , Du Kong-pou ou du tribunal des ouvrages publics; ibid, VIII, p. 278.

2131 — — , Sur la sévérité avec laquelle l'empereur
réprime les vexations des mandarins; ibid, X,
p. 132.

2132 Requête à l'empereur pour la cérémonie du labou-
rage; ibid, III, p. 499.

2133 SCHILLER, C. H., Neueste Nachrichten über China und dessen innere Verfassung. Leipzig, 1799,
8vo.

2134 MASON, H., Punishments of China, illustrated by
22 engravings. London, 1801, 4to.

2135 CRUKSHANK, P., The capital punishments of the
Chinese, drawn on stone. London, 4., s. a.

2136 LEONTIEFF, A., Laws of the Chinese Empire. St. Petersburg, 1801, 3 vols., 8vo. (in Russian).

2137 HUTTMANN, On the public revenue of the Chinese Empire, As. Journ., III, 1817, p. 333 ss.

2138 THOMS, P. P., On the revenue of China, Appendix to his edition of the Hwa-chien. Macao, 1824 (No. 155), p. 283-324.

2139 RÉMUSAT, A., Lettres sur le régime des lettrés de la Chine et sur l'influence qu'ils ont dans le gouvernment de l'état, Mél. posth., p. 322-372.

2140 KLAPROTH, J., Occupations journalières de l'empereur de la Chine, Ann. de Voy, XXXIX, 1828, p. 225-229.

2141 — — , Sur le papier monay de la Chine, J. As., I, p. 358; English: London, 1823, 8vo., and in J. Am. O. S., I, p. 136.

2142 — — , Etats des populations et des revenues Chinoises in Timkovsky's Travels, No. 3083.

2143 MORRISON, R., Retirement of statesmen from the service of the government and honors conferred on them, Ch. Repos., I, p. 32; II, p. 144.

2144 — — , Taukwang's prayer for rain; ibid, I, p. 234.

2145 — — , Mode of arresting an outlaw; ibid, I, p. 247.

2146 — — , Official patronage, rascality, etc.; ibid, I, p. 422.

2147 — — , Governor Li, accusations, etc.; ibid, I, p. 469.

2148 — — , Provisions made by government for the poor; ibid, I, p. 503.

2149 — — , Movements of officers, military schools, etc.; ibid, I, p. 511.

2150 — — , Examinations, executions, etc.; ibid, II, p. 47, 95.

2151 — — , Edict relating to monopolizing grain; ibid, II, p. 90.

2152 — — , Governor Lu's instructions to the troops; ibid, II, p. 129.

2153 — —, On the execution of the laws in China; ibid, II, p. 131.

2154 — —, Proceedings on the death of the empress; ibid, II, p. 144, 212.

2155 — —, Rewards to the military; ibid, II, p. 179.

2156 — —, Proportion of Manchu and Chinese officers in the high posts of government; ibid, II, p. 312.

2157 — —, Crimes and punishments thereof; ibid; II, p. 335.

2158 — —, Emperor reprimands his naval officers; ibid, II, p. 421.

2159 — —, Trait of the imperial clan; ibid, II, p. 378, 512.

2160 — —, Sale of office to supply revenue; ibid, II, p. 430.

2161 — —, Danger of advising the emperor; ibid, II, p. 567.

2162 — —, Provincial officers and atrocities in Shantung; ibid, II, p. 286.

2163 — —, Benefactions to the poor by provincial officers; ibid, II, p. 425.

2164 — —, Laws respecting homicides and the kinds recognized in the laws of China; ibid, III, p. 38.

2165 — —, Visit of Li to ports of Kiangsu; ibid., III, p. 144.

2166 — —, Reminiscences of Chinese government and politics, in extracts from the gazettes; ibid, XIV, p. 156.

2167 STEVENS, E., Farewell address of the fuyuen Chu; ibid, II, p. 325.

2168 MORRISON, J. R., Efforts to prevent sycee being exported; ibid, II, p. 383.

2169 — —, Structure of the Chinese government and various classes of the people; ibid, IV, p. 11, 49, 135, 276, 181.

2170 — —, Ordnance issued on occasion of the empress-dowager reaching the age of sixty; ibid, IV, p. 576.

2171 — — , Movements and disgraces of high officers; ibid, XII, p. 275, 327.

2172 BRIDGMAN, E. C., Government tries to assist the sufferers by the inundations at Canton; ibid, II, p. 238.

2173 — — , Capture of smugglers, Ch. Re., III, p. 487.

2174 — — , War between Burmah and China; ibid, VIII, p, 134, 169, 437.

2175 — — , Defects in Chinese strategy and army by Wang; ibid, XI, p. 389.

2176 — — , Present condition of the Chinese government; ibid, XII, p. 1.

2177 — — , Peking gazettes form a good index of the feelings of the goverment; ibid, XIII, p. 107.

2178 — — , Mode of appointing Kiying to be commissioner; ibid, XIII, p. 386.

2179 — — , Account of the Tsung-jin fu or board controlling the imperial family; ibid, XIV, p. 130.

2180 — — , Movement of Kiying and other officers as given in the Peking gazette for 1846; ibid, XV, p. 273, 321, 374, 473.

2181 — — , Stability and durability of the Chinese monarchy; ibid, XVI, p. 50.

2182 — — , Proverbs illustrating the character of Chinese officers as regarded by the people; ibid, XVII, p. 355.

2183 — — , Notice of a complete map of the military stations in Kiangsu; ibid, XVII, p. 523.

2184 — — , Reading the sacred edict by Chinese officers to benefit the common people; ibid, XVII, p. 586.

2185 — — , Taxes remitted and delayed in Kiangsu on account of famine; ibid, XVIII, p. 90.

2186 — — , Sale of rank adopted by the Chinese government to increase its revenue; ibid, XVIII, p. 207.

2187 AUBER, P., China, an outline of its government, laws and policy. London, 1834, 8vo.

2188 INGLIS, R., Characteristics, policy and laws of the Chinese government, Chin. Rep., IV, p. 17.

2189 — — , Character and power of the officers who compose the superior and inferior magistracy in China; ibid, IV, p. 160, 214.

2190 — — , Modes and results of appeals in Chinese courts and abuses in justice; ibid, IV, p. 262.

2191 — — , Manner in which the literary examinations are conducted; ib., IV, p. 118.

2192 — — , Courts of justice among the Chinese and detail of their proceedings; ibid, IV, p. 335.

2193 — — , Means and various modes of punishment in Chinese courts of justice; ibid, IV, p. 361.

2194 JOHNSTON, A. R., Characteristics and real power of the Chinese government; ibid, IX, p. 9.

2195 GUETZLAFF, K., Sacred instruction of the Manchu emperors; ibid, X, p. 593.

2196 KEATING, A. S., Military skill and power of the Chinese; ibid, X, p. 165.

2197 LAY, G. T., Account of the Manchus and the arrangements of their garrison at Chapu; ibid, XI, p. 425.

2198 — — , Soldiers manual guide to the art of war; ibid, XI, p. 489.

2199 BIOT, E., Mémoire sur la constitution politique de la Chine au XII siècle avant notre ère. Paris, 1844, 4to.

2200 — — , Histoire de l'istruction publique en Chine. Paris, 1846, 8vo.
    See Journ. As., 4. sér., IX, p. 1.

2201 — — , Mémoire sur la condition de la propriété territoriale en Chine depuis les temps anciens. Paris, 8vo.

2202 — — , Mémoire sur les colonies militaires et agricoles des Chinois, Jour. As., 4. sér., XV, p. 338 ss., 529 ss.; also separately. Paris, 1850, 8vo.

2203 DEAN, W., Yü Puyun's important instructions to soldiers, Chin. Repos., XII, p. 69.

2204 DAVIS, Sir J. F., Notices of the Chinese court and politics by Padre Serra; ibid, XIV, p. 519.

2205 MEADOWS, T. T., Desultory notes on the Government and People of China and on the Chinese language, illustrated with a sketch of the Province of Kwangtung, showing its division into Departments and districts. London, 1847, 8vo.

2206 — — , Remarks on the acquisition, common tenure and alienation of real property in China, accompanied by a facsimile and translation of a deed of sale, Transact. Ch. Br. R. As. Soc. Hongkong, I, 1848, p. 1-16.

2207 WADE, T. F., Chinese currency and revenue, Chin. Rep., XVI, p. 273, 293.

2208 — — , Note on the condition and government of the Chinese empire in 1849. Hongkong, 1850, 8vo.

2209 — — , Account of the Army of the Chinese Empire, Chin. Repos., XX, p. 250, 300, 363.

2210 Proclamation from the commissioner of finances of Suchau against the circulation of base cash; ibid, XVII, p. 482.

2211 WILLIAMS, S. W., Paper money among the Chinese; ibid, XX, p. 289.

2212 — — , Tenure of mines, Notes & Queries, II, p. 97.

2213 — — , Memorial of Yiyung, Chin. Recorder, II, p. 9.

2214 SACHAROFF, J., The landed property of China, Russ. Eccl. Miss., II, No. 1, 1853 (in Russian). German by Abel and Mecklenburg in No. 882.

2215 PARKES, H. S., Description of proceedings in the criminal court of Canton with an account of an execution at Canton, Transact. Ch. Br. R. As. S., III, 1853, p. 55-71.

2216 BOWRING, J. B., Life and writings of Commissioner Lin; ibid, p. 73-115.

2217 HARLAND, W. A., Notice of a Chinese work on medical jurisprudence; ibid, IV, 1855, p. 87-92.

2218 BAZIN, A. (sen.), Recherches sur les institutions administratives et municipales de la Chine, Journ. As., 5. sér., III, 5; IV, 249, 445; also separately Paris, 1856, 8vo.

2219 — — , Notice sur le collège médical de Peking; ibid, 5. sér., VIII, p. 394.

2220 — — , Recherches sur l'academie impériale de Peking; ibid, VIII, p. 356.

2221 Das älteste Staatshandbuch der Chinesen. Ausland, 1856, No. 60.

2222 DABRY, P., Organisation militaire des Chinois. Paris, 1859, 8vo.

2223 MACGOWAN, D. J., On the banishment of criminals in China, Journ. of N. C. B. of R. A. S., I, 1859, p. 293-301.

2224 BEAL, S., Account of the Shui-lui or infernal machine, Tr. Ch. Br. R. As. S. Hongkong, VI, 1859, p. 53-62, plates.

2225 FUZIER, Notes sur les armes chinoises et les blessures qu'ils déterminent, Rec. de Mém. de Méd. Mil., V, 1861.

2226 MARON, H., Bevölkerung und Grundeigenthum in China, Viertelj. f. Volkswirthsch., 1863, I, p. 28.

2227 GABELENTZ, H. A. v. d, Chinesische Justiz, Nach einer Schilderung in dem Roman Gin-ping-mei. Globus, 1864, V, lief., 11-12.

2228 PLATH, J. H., Gesetz und Recht im alten China nach chinesischen Quellen, Abh. d. K. bay. Ak. der Wiss. München, 1865, 4to.
See Ausland, 1867, No. 26, p. 609-612.

2229 STRONACH, W. T., Traces of the judicium dei or ordeal in Chinese law, Journ. N. C. B. of R. A. S., II, Dec., 1865, p. 176.

2230 MAYERS, W. F., Laws against infanticide, Notes and Queries, I, p. 4.

2231 — — , Tabular view of Chinese hereditary ranks and titles of distinction; ibid, II, p. 113.

2232 — — , The buddhist rosary and its place in Chinese official costume; ibid, III, p. 26.

2233 — — , The "button" in Chinese official uniform; ibid, III, p. 44.

2234 — — , Institution of provincial offices in China; ibid, III, p. 124.

2235 — — , Inquests in China; ibid, III, p. 127.

2236 — — , Chinese oaths; ibid, III, p. 142.

2237 — — , Hwang-ti and other sovereign titles; ibid, III, p. 164.

2238 — — , Titles of literary graduates; ibid, III, p. 177.

2239 — — , On the introduction and use of gunpowder and firearms among the Chinese, with Notes on some ancient engines of warfare and illustr., J. N. C. B. of R. A. S., VI, 1871, p. 73.

2240 SAMPSON, T., Law prohibiting emigration, Notes and Queries, II, p. 31.

2241 KNIGHT, S., The eight banners; ibid, II, p. 35.

2242 Punishment by impalement; ibid, II, p. 108.

2243 Chinese official ranks; ibid, II, p. 184; III, p. 29.

2244 EWER, F. H., The triennial examination; ibid, III, p. 330.

2245 TAINTOR, E. C., The censorate in China; ibid, III, p. 12.

2246 Judicial oaths for Chinese; ibid, III, p. 17, 120.

2247 KOPSCH, H., Execution of women in China; ibid, III, p. 47.

2248 Employment of Chinese Criminals; ibid, III, p. 47.

2249 HARTWELL, C., Chinese law on divorce, Chin. Rec., I, p. 187.

2250 DUDGEON, J., Chinese inquests, Notes and Queries, III, p. 127.

2251 LAY, W. T., The Governor-generals and governors of the 18 provinces, Ch. Recorder, II, p. 198.

2252 The Foochow Arsenal; ibid, II, p. 216.

2253 The Peking gazettes; ibid, III, p. 10.
2254 Caged to death; ibid, III, p. 77.
2255 MINCHIN, G., Adam Schaal as chief minister of state of China, Not. & Quer., IV, p. 247.
2256 Proclamation forbidding idol procession issued by Wen, acting governor-general of Fookien and Wang, Lieutenant-governor; ibid, IV, p. 267.
2257 Ting Futai's Memorial to the throne, Ch. Mag., 1869, p. 173.
2258 PRESTON, C. F., Notice of Lok Ping Cheung, late Gov.-Gen. of Sze-chuan, Journ. N. C. B. of R. A. S., V, 1869, p. 67.
2259 MOULE, G. E., Notes on the provincial examination of Chekiang, J. N. Ch. Br. R. As. Soc., VI, 1871.
2260 ALCOCK, Sir Rutherford, On Peking Gazettes, Fraser's Mag., 1873.
2261 The Peking gazette, China Review, III, 1874-75, p. 13-18.
2262 GILES, H. A., The Hsi-yuan-lu or instruction to coroners; ibid, III, p. 30-38, 92-99, 159-172.
2263 PLAYFAIR, G. M. H., The grain transport system of China; ibid, III, p. 354-364.
2264 EITEL, E. J., Chinese official ranks; ibid, III, p. 377-379; IV, pp. 125-130.
2265 GIQUEL, P., L'Arsenal de Fou-tchéou. Shanghai, 1874, 8vo.
2266 Note on Chinese commercial law, China Review, II, p. 144-148.
2267 LAY, L. M., On the execution of state criminals; ibid, II, p. 173-175.
2268 Administration of Chinese law; ibid, II, p. 230-244.

On Coinage and Coins.

2269 HAGER, J., Numismatique chinoise. Paris, 1803, fol.
2270 — — , Description des médailles chinoises du

cabinet impérial de France. Paris, 1805, 4to.
2271 Chinese coins described in Grote, Blätter für Münz-
kunde. Hannover, 1835 ss.; Akerman, numismatic
journal. London, 1837 ss.; numismatic chronicle.
London, 1838 ss.
2272 BIOT, E., Mémoire sur le système monétaire des
Chinois, Journ. As., 3. sér., III, p. 422; IV,
p. 97, 209, 441.
2273 ENDLICHER, S., Verzeichniss der chinesischen
und japanesischen Münzen des Münz Kabinets in
Wien. Wien, 1837, 4to.
2274 — — , Die chinesische Numismatik. Blätter f.
Münz Kunde, III, p. 161, 1837.
2275 CHAUDOIR, le Baron de, Recueil de monnaies de
la Chine, du Japon, de la Corée, d'Anam et de Java. St. Pétersbourg, 1842, fol.
2276 HILLIER, C. B., Notes on the Tsien or copper cash
of the Chinese, Transact. Ch. Br. R. As. Soc., I.
Hongkong, 1843, p. 47-50.
2277 — — , Chinese coinage: a brief notice of the
Chinese work 錢 志 新 編 (chronicles of Tsien, a
new arrangement) and a Key to its 329 wood cuts
of the coins of China and neighbouring nations;
ibid, II, 1852, p. 1-162, wood cuts.
Reprinted (without the wood cuts) in Doolittle's Hand book, II, p. 603-615.
2278 MONTIGNY, de, Monnaies, pois et mesures Chinois, Revue Orient., IX, p. 324, 1846.
2279 WILLIAMS, J., Chinese numismatics. London,
1853, 8vo.
2280 WYLIE, A., Coins of the Tats'ing or present dynasty of China, Journ. Shangh. Lit. & Scient. S., I,
1858, p. 44-106, wood cuts.
Reprinted without the wood cuts in Doolittle's Hand book, II, p. 615-617.
2281 PFIZMAIER, A., Bericht über einige eingesandte
chinesische und japanische Münzen. Sitz. Ber.

Phil. Hist. Cl. K. K. Ac. d. Wiss. Wien, 1861, p. 45 ss.

2282 HOLT, On a collection of Chinese coins, Numism. chron., XXI, 1866, p. 68-90.

2283 Dots on cash, Notes and Queries, I, p. 61, 75; II, p. 47.

2284 Characters on Chinese coins; ibid, II, p. 63.

2285 BUSHELL, S. W., Chinese authors on numismatics, Chin. Rec., IV, p. 62.

2286 — — , Roman and Chinese coinage, China Rev., I, p. 117, illustr.

2287 — — , Note on some Chinese cash; ibid, I, p. 397.

c. Customs and Manners.

2288 HYDE, T., Historia nerdiludii, h. e. dicere trunculorum, cum quibusdam aliis Arabum, Persarum, Indorum, Chinensium et aliarum gentium ludis. Oxoniae, 1694, 8vo.

2289 GEISLER, A. F., Karakter, Sitten und Meinungen der Chinesen. Halle, 1782, 8vo.

2290 MASON, H., The costume of China, illustrated by 60 engravings. London, 1800, fol.

2291 Ueber die Magie bei den Chinesen, As. Mag., II, p. 224-228.

2292 Notizen aus China, As. Mag., I, 1802, p. 64-68.

2293 BRETON, La Chine en miniature. Paris, 1811, 6 vols., 12mo.

2294 WILKINSON, G., Sketches of Chinese Customs and Manners. Bath, 1814, 8vo.

2295 MONTUCCI, A., Della divisione de tempo fra Cinesi ed delle loro feste, Giorn. Acad., XLII, 1829, p. 199; XLIII, p. 86, 381.

2296 MORRISON, R., Suicides, betrothments, etc., Ch. Repos., I, p. 291; II, p. 189.

2297 — — , Instance of insecurity of property in China; ibid, I, p. 332.

2298 — — , Account of a fashionable Dr. Chin in Canton; ibid, I, p. 343.

2299 — — , Themes at the examinations; ibid, I, p. 459.

2300 — — , Proclamation by Chu to exhort to morality; ibid, I, p. 460.

2301 — — , Humanity of a Chinese female; ibid, II, p. 161.

2302 — — , Chinese chitchat and news; ibid, II, p. 163.

2303 — — , Cruelties to Chinese emigrants in the Straits; ibid, II, p. 180, 230.

2304 — — , Native charitable institutions in Canton; ibid, II, p. 165.

2305 — — Ideas of a native respecting calamities; ibid II, p. 232.

2306 — — , Characters and forms of the Kotau; ibid, II, p. 374.

2307 — — , Fortunes of an unsuccessful scholar; ibid, III, p. 118.

2308 MILNE, W. C., National character of the Chinese; ibid, I, p. 326.

2309 The Chinese Kotow; ib., II, p. 374.

2310 BRIDGMAN, E. C., Kidnapping children and suicide; ibid, II, p. 527.

2311 — — , Beggars and autumnal assizes; ibid, III, p. 45.

2312 — — , Origin and effects of the custom of compressing the feet of females; ibid, III, p. 537.

2313 — — , Education among the Chinese; ibid, IV, p. 1.

2314 — — , Intellectual character of the Chinese; ibid, VII, p. 1.

2315 — — , Exhortation against infanticide by Kikung; ibid, VII, p. 54.

2316 — — , Likenesses of distinguished men by Ting qua; ibid, IX, p. 516.

2317 — — , Discourse to the simple people to appreciate life by H. E. Hwang Ngantung; ibid, XIV, p. 436.

2318 — — , Translation of an essay by a graduate against drowning female children; ibid, XVII, p. 11.

2319 — — , Statement regarding the murder of a woman by her grandson and of him by the neighbouring villagers; ibid, XVII, p. 480.

2320 TRACY, J., Condition of females among the Chinese; ibid, II, p. 313.

2321 — — , Description of a Chinese wedding; ibid, IV, p. 568.

2322 SCHOTT, W., Zur Etymologie des Schachspiels, Mag. des Auslands, Dec. 1835, No. 154.

2323 Diet of the Chinese, Chin. Rep., III, p. 457 ss.

2324 WILLIAMS, S. W., Example of 24 filial children; ibid, VI, p. 130.

2325 — — , Three examples of female constancy; ibid, VI, p. 568.

2326 — — , Example of revenging a father's death; ibid, VIII, p. 345.

2327 — — , Festivals given by the emperors Kanghi and Kienlong to old men; ibid, IX, p. 258.

2328 — — , Illustrations of men and things in China; ibid, IX, p. 366, 506, 635; X, p. 99, 104, 172, 472, 519, 613, 666; XI, p. 325, 434; XVII, p. 591.

2329 — — , Description and translation of a Shau Ting or Longevity Screen; ibid, XIII, p. 535.

2330 — — , Anecdotes from Chinese authors to illustrate human conduct; ibid, XVII, p. 646; XVIII, p. 159.

2331 — — , Revenge of Miss Shang Sankwan; ibid, XVIII, p. 400.

2332 STEVENS, E., Clanships and feuds among the Chinese; ibid, IV, p. 411.

2333 MORRISON, J. R., Charms, talismans and felicitous appendages worn about the person or hung up in houses, etc. used by the Chinese, Transact. R. As. Soc., III, p. 2; Chin. Rep., XIV, 1845, p. 229-234.

2334 BROWN, S. R., Character, customs and condition of the Chinese, Chin. Rep., IX, p. 284, 399, 483, 617; X, p. 65.

2335 — —, Chinese culture and remarks on the causes of the peculiarities of the Chinese, Journ. of Am. Or. Soc., II, p. 167, 1851.

2336 ALEXANDER, Picturesque representations of the dress and manners of the Chinese. London, 4to.

2337 GUETZLAFF, K., Traits of Chinese character, Ch. Repos., XI, p. 480.

2338 ABEEL, D., Notices of infanticide in Fuhkien, Ch. Repos., XII, p. 340.

2339 LAY, G. T., Remarks on Chinese character and customs; ibid, XII, p. 135.

2340 RÉMUSAT, A., Discours sur le génie et les moeurs des peuples orientaux, Mél. posth., p. 221-252.

2341 BIOT, E., Recherches sur les moeurs des anciens Chinois d'après le Chiking, Journ. As., 4. sér., II, 1843, p. 307 ss., 430 ss.; also separately, Paris, 1844, 8vo.
English in Legge's Shiking, introd. (No. 176.)

2342 — —, Memoir on the condition of slaves and hired servants in China, Ch. Repos., XVIII, p. 347.

2343 Anecdotes of the Chinese, illustrative of their character, etc. London, 1845, 12mo.

2344 FAIVRE, Observations sur les Chinois et sur quelques-uns de leurs pratiques populaires. Annales de Voy. Mai, 1847, p. 177-184.

2345 Notice soliciting subscriptions for the purpose of preventing the desecration of printed papers, Ch. Repos., XVII, p. 417.

2346 MOLLER, J. H., Ethnographische Uebersicht des chinesischen Reiches. Gotha, 1850, 8vo.

2347 Findelhäuser in China. "Ausland," 1856, No. 40.

2348 MEDHURST, W. H., Marriage, affinity and inheritance in China, Transact. Ch. Br. R. As. Soc., IV, p. 1-32.

2349 ZWETKOFF, P., Customs of the Chinese, Russ. Eccl. Miss., III, No. 9 (in Russian.) German in No. 882.

2350 CULBERSTON, M. S., Darkness in the flowery land. New York, 1857, 12mo.

2351 Zustand der Armen im chinesischen Reich. "Ausland," 1857, No. 38.

2352 ZACCONE, P., Le fils du ciel. Paris, 1857, 8vo.

2353 MACGOWAN, D. J., Contribution to the Ethnology of Eastern Asia, Journ. Shangh. Lit. and Sc. Soc., I, 1858, p. 103 ss.

2354 COBBOLD, R. H., Pictures of the Chinese, drawn by themselves. London, 1860, 8vo.

2355 RICHOMME, C., Contes Chinois, précédés d'une histoire pittoresque de la Chine. Paris, 8vo.

2356 SHUCK, Mrs. H. H., Brief sketches of some of the scenes and characteristics of China.

2357 MUTEL, Notices sur les crânes chinois, Rec. d. Mém. de Méd. Mil., 3. sér., VII, 1862.

2358 LIBERMANN, Recherches sur l'usage de la fumée d'opium; ibid, 1862.

2359 FUZIER, De l'usage de la déformation du pied chez les femmes chinoises; ibid.

2360 PLATH, J. H., Ueber die häuslichen Verhältnisse der alten Chinesen. München, 1862, 8vo.
See Lit. Centralbl., 1864, No. 5, p. 101.

2361 BIRCH, Fairy Foxes, Chin. and Jap. Repos., 1863, No. 3.

2362 STOBBS, W., Chinese scenes and people. London, 1863, 8vo.

2363 BOUROT, Notes sur le moule d'un pied de femme chinoise, Rec. de Mém. de Méd. Mil., 3. sér., IX, 1863.

2364 EDKINS, Mrs. J. R., Chinese scenes and people, with narrative of a visit to Nanking by her hus-

band the Rev. J. Edkins; also a memoir by her
father, the Rev. W. Stobbs. London, 1863, 8vo.

2365 SMITH, W. L. G., Observations on China and the
Chinese. New York, 1863, 12mo.

2366 KEITH, Mrs. C. P., Memoirs edited by her brother
W. C. Tenney. New York, 1864, 12mo.

2367 Die Flussböte Cantons, Westermann's illustr. Monatsh., XV (1864), p. 518-524, 616-622.

2368 Der Sampan der Chinesen; ibid, XVI (1864), p.
423-427.

2369 MARTIN, E., De l'usage de la déformation du pied
chez les femmes chinoises, Rec. d. mém. de méd.
mil., 3. sér., XII, 1864.

2370 — — , Considérations sur la valeur ethnique de
la Mutilation des pieds de la femme chinoise,
Bull. Soc. d'Anthrop., Nov. 1871.

2371 — — , Quelques généralités sur l'alimentation
en Chine, Bull. Soc. d'Accl., Oct., 1872.

2372 — — , De l'infanticide dans l'empire Chinois,
Gaz. Hebdom., 1872.

2373 — — , L'avortement dans l'empire Chinois, ibid.

2374 — — , Etude sur la prostitution en Chine, ibid.

2375 DOOLITTLE, J., Social life of the Chinese with
some account of their religious, governmental,
educational and business customs and opinions,
with special but not exclusive reference to Fuh-
chou. New York, 1865, 2 vols. 8vo., illust. See
Athenaeum, 1866, March 3, p. 293; Lit. Centralbl., 1868, No. 7, p. 166; also Skizzen aus China.
Ausland, 1866, No. 36, p. 841-847; A new revised edition by Paxton Hood. London, 1868, 8vo.

2376 — — , Jottings about the Chinese, Ch. Recorder, I, p. 49.

2377 The Chinese Clans and their customs, Ch. and Jap.
Repos., III (1865), p. 281-284.

2378 Chinese chess; ibid, III, p. 580-586.

2379 BUTCHER, C. H., Notes on the funeral rites performed at the obsequies of Takee, Journ. N. C. B.

of R. A. S., n. s., No. II (1866), p. 173-176.

2380 JAMIESON, R. A., Remarks made upon exhibiting a To-la Pall; ibid, p. 178-181.

2381 BOWRING, Sir J., Education in China, Shilling Magazine, No. 2 (1865), June, art. 8, No. 4; (Aug.), art. 6, No. 5; (Sept.), art. 5.

2382 Aus dem Haus und Volksleben in China, Globus, X (1866), No. 2, p. 33-41; No. 5, p. 144-147, illustr.

2383 HOLLINGWORTH, H. G., A short sketch of the Chinese game of Chess, Journ. N. C. B. of R. A. S., III, Dec., 1866, p. 107-112.

2384 SCHLEGEL, G., Jets over de Prostitutie in China, Verhand. van het Batav. Genootsch. van K. en W., XXXII (1766).

German in Ausland, 1866.

2385 — — , Punch and Judy shows in China, Notes and Queries, I, p. 139.

2386 — — , Easter-eggs in China; ibid, II, p. 21.

2387 — — , Monkeys in horse stables; ibid, II, p. 49.

2388 — — , Preference for fox-flesh and prejudice against horse-flesh amongst antediluvian nations; ibid, II, p. 68.

2389 — — , A Chinese proverb; ibid, III, p. 181.

2390 — — , Chinesische Bräuche und Spiele in Europa. Breslau, 1869, 8vo.

2391 — — , Die Prostitution bei den Chinesen. "Ausland," 1869.

2392 PFIZMAIER, A., Beiträge zur Geschichte der Perlen. Sitzungsber. der Wiener Ak., Philos.-hist. Cl., LVII (1867), p. 617-654.

2393 BREWSTER, Sir D., Chinese magic mirors, Scientific Review, No. 2, art. I.

2394 A legend of Shiu-hing, Notes and Queries, I, p. 9.

2395 Tanka Boatmen; ibid, I, p. 28, 107.

2396 CHAMPS, E. de, Yellow as an imperial color; ibid, I, p. 52.

2397 — — , Apropos des bottes; ibid, I, 85.

2398 Dress of Chinese ladies; ibid, I, p. 76, 107, 143; Ch. Magaz., 1869, p. 84.
2399 Presentation of boots to outgoing officials, Notes and Queries, I, p. 77.
2400 Circulating libraries in China; ibid, I, p. 100, 118.
2401 Albinos in China; ibid, I, p. 92, 93, 106.
2402 Infanticide in China; ibid, I, p. 109; II, p. 81; III, p. 45; Ch. Review, II, p. 55.
2403 MAYERS, W. F., Yellow as the imperial colour, Notes and Queries, I, p. 142.
2404 — — , Small feet and prohibition of the practice; ibid, II, p. 27.
2405 — — , Chinese actors; ibid, II, p. 56.
2406 — — , Hereditary Genius; ibid, II, p. 154.
2407 — — , Mermaids and mermen in the Chinese seas; ibid, III, p. 99.
2408 — — , Black slaves in China; ibid, III, p. 105.
2409 — — , The legend of the moon and Changnoo; ibid, III, p. 123.
2410 The Lo-fau shan; ibid, I, p. 148.
2411 EITEL, E. J., Spirit rapping in China; ibid, I, p. 164.
2412 — — , Somnambulism in China; ibid, II, p. 19.
2413 Self immolation in China; ibid, II, p. 3.
2414 Cost of living among the Chinese; ibid, II, p. 11, 26.
2415 MINCHIN, G., Small feet and prohibition of the practice; ibid, II, p. 43.
2416 — — , Origin of Dragon boats; ibid, II, p. 157.
2417 — — , The legend of Hung Cheng-chou; ibid, II, p. 177.
2418 — — , Presentation of umbrellas; ibid, II, p. 180.
2419 — — , The tomb of Kung Ming; ibid, III, p. 36.
2420 — — , The legend concerning Chang Tien-she; ibid, III, p. 89.
2421 — — , Prediction concerning the Tatsing dynasty, Chin. Recorder, III, p. 257.
2422 — — , Divorces among the Chinese; ibid, IV, p. 135.

2423 — — , Curious Chinese superstition, Notes and Queries, II, p. 96.

2424 SAMPSON, T., Chinese pawntickets; ibid, II, p. 108.

2425 — — , Urn-burial in China; ibid, II, p. 109.

2426 — — , Antimarriage associations; ibid, II, p. 142.

2427 KNOWLTON, M. J., Burial in China; ibid, II, p. 125.

2428 — — , A Chinese lottery; ibid, II, p. 131.

2429 — — , Parental authority in China; ibid, III, p. 54.

2430 — — , Early marriages in China; ibid, III, p. 54.

2431 Chinese belief in the power of Foreigners to discover precious metals or stones ; ibid, II, p. 130.

2432 A King of the dogs; ibid, II, p. 132.

2433 Chinese conjurors and Ventriloquists; ibid, II, p. 147.

2434 The feast of lanterns; ibid, II, p. 147.

2435 Chinese benefit societies; ibid, II, p. 148; III, p. 105.

2436 Cremation in China; ibid, II, p. 152; III, p. 47.

2437 WYLIE, A., Steaks from living cattle; ibid, II, p. 155.

2438 Intermarriages between Tartars and Chinese; ibid, II, p. 156.

2439 The Dragon boat feast; ibid, II, p. 158.

2440 The Chinese method of computation; ibid, II, p. 177.

2441 Chinese salutation dance and amateur actors; ibid, II, 178.

2442 Taming of wild cattle in Formosa; ibid, II, p. 179; III, p. 49.

2443 KOPSCH, H., Life boats in China; ibid, II, p. 190.

2444 — — , The Yang tsze life boats, Ch. Review, I, p. 381.

2445 Respect paid to written paper, Notes and Queries, II, p. 191.

2446 Die Chinesen, Petermann's geogr. Mitth., 1869.
2447 SIMON, E., Note sur les petites sociétés d'argent en Chine, Journ. N. C. B. of R. A. S., V (1869), p. 1.
2448 — — , Sur les institutions de crédit en Chine; ibid, VI (1871), p. 53.
2449 Compression of women's feet, Chin. Recorder, I, p. 232, 259; II, p. 230; III, p. 21, 24.
2450 DUDGEON, J., The small feet of Chinese women; ibid, II, p. 93, 130.
2451 — — , Solitaire with woodcuts; ibid, III, p. 259, 334.
2452 KERR, J. G., Small feet; ibid, II, p. 169; III, p. 22.
2453 — — , Drinking habits of Chinese; ibid, III, p. 85.
2454 An enigma; ibid, III, p. 77.
2455 On Chinese oaths and swearing; ibid, III, p. 103.
2456 ARENDT, K., On Chinese riddles; ibid, III, p. 184.
2457 Quail fighting in Canton, Notes and Queries, III, p. 22.
2458 PHILLIPS, G., Tea first used as an article of drink in China; ibid, III, p. 79.
2459 SMITH, F. P., The art of selfdefence in China; ibid, III, p. 88.
2460 — — , Chinese abstaining from animal food; ibid, III, p. 94.
2461 — — , Burying straw effigies with the dead, Ch. Recorder, III, p. 190.
2462 — — , Games and sports of Chinese children, The Phoenix, II, p. 33.
2463 Kissing among the Chinese, Notes and Queries, III, p. 108.
2464 ALABASTER, C., Fairs in China; ibid, III, p. 109.
2465 — — , Catalogue of Chinese objects in the S. Kensington Museum. London, 1872, 8vo., 80 pp.
2466 In the highlands of the Chinese, Chin. Magaz., 1869, p. 177.
2467 On the mode of raising and administering public

subscriptions, Notes and Queries, III, p. 134.
2468 Chinese Cannibalism, Chin. Recorder, III, p. 205.
2469 Tsaou-ngo temple (near Wuch'ang fu, Hupei); ibid, III, p. 206.
2470 THOMSON, J., A visit to Yuan-foo monastery; ibid, III, p. 296.
2471 The literati of China; ibid, III, p. 327.
2472 The first of the white month; ibid, IV, p. 197.
2473 HIMLY, K., Das Schachspiel der Chinesen, Zeitschr. d. Deutsch. Morg. Ges., XXIV, p. 172.
2474 — — , The Chinese game of chess as compared with that practised by Western nations, J. N. Ch. Br. R. As. Soc., 1871, p. 105 ss.
2475 Woman in China, her rights and her wrongs, Ch. Magaz., 1869, p. 51.
2476 Sketches in China; ibid, p. 55, 88.
2477 BOWRA, E. C., The national monuments at Yaishan with map, China Review, I, p. 127.
2478 Some very desultory remarks on China; ibid, I, p. 301.
2479 NACKEN, J., Chinese street cries in Hongkong; ibid, II, p. 51-55.
2480 A Chinese Tichborne; ibid, I, p. 388.
2481 PRESTON, J., Charms and spells in use amongst the Chinese; ibid, II, p. 164-169.
2482 MAY, J. J. S., Die chinesischen Frauen. Ausland, 1873, No. 44.
2483 STENT, G. C., Chinese legends, J. N. Ch. Br. R. As. S., 1873, p. 183-195.
2484 — — , Legend of the building of Peking, China Review, IV, pp. 168-173.
2485 PITON, CH., Chinese charity, China Rev., II, p. 307.
2486 Fortschritt und Barbarei in China. "Globus," XXIII, 1873, p. 105.
2487 Chinesisch-Arische Beziehungen; ibid, p. 44 ss.
2488 JUNKER, F., Kin-lien die goldne Lilie. Eine Beschreibung der Zergliederung eines verkrüppelten Chinesen-fusses. Archiv. f. Anthrop., VI, 1873.

2489 Female infanticide, China Rev., II, p. 55-58.
2490 Chinese proverbs, "All the year round," Octob., 1874.
2491 Chinese proper names; ibid, Dec., 1874.
2492 Unter den Chinesen. "Ausland," 1874, No. 30.
2493 Der häusliche Herd im himmlischen Reich. "Europa," 1874, No. 1.
2494 Feudal China, Cornhill Mag., Nov., 1874.
2495 A Chinese love history, Fraser's Mag., Oct., Nov., Dec., 1874.
2496 BISMARCK, K., Brautschau und Hochzeit des Kaisers von China. Zeitschr. Ges. f. Erdk. Berlin, IX, 1874, No. 2.
2497 CROSSETTE, J. F., The Chinese daughter-in-law, Chin. Rec., V, p. 207-214.
2498 GALPIN, T., Notes concerning the Chinese belief of evil and evil spirits; ib., V, p. 42-50.
2499 Die Tortur in China. "Ausland," 1875, No. 7.
2500 T. H., Chinese pauperism, China Review, III, p. 51-57.
2501 L. C. P., The noble art of selfdefence in China; ib., p. 84-92.
2502 DENNYS, N. B., The folklore of China; ibid, III, p. 269-284, 331-342; IV, p. 1-9, 67-84, 139-152, 213-227, 278-293.
2503 GILES, H. A., Chinese sketches. London, 1876, 8vo., IV, 204 pp.

d. Arts, Industry, Agriculture.

2504 ECKEBERG, Notes on the agriculture of the Chinese (in Swedish.)
German by Georgi. Rostock, 1765, 8vo., plates.
French by Blackford. Milan, 1771, 8vo.
2505 D'ENTRECOLLES, Lettre sur la fabrication de la porcellaine à King-te-tching, 1712, Lettr. Édif. nouv. ed.; XXVIII, 174; XXIX, 281.

2506 CHAMBERS, Sir W., A dissertation on oriental gardening. London, 1773, 4to.

2507 — — , Traité des édifices, meubles, etc. des Chinois. London, 1775, fol., 21 plates; Paris, 1776, 4to.

2508 Mémoire sur l'intérêt de l'argent en Chine, Mém. Conc., IV, p. 299.

2509 Vin, eau de vie, vinaigre de Chine; ibid, V, p. 467.

2510 Teinture Chinoise; ibid, V, p. 495.

2511 Abricotier; ibid, V, p. 505.

2512 Armoise; ibid, V, p. 514.

2513 AMIOT, De la musique des Chinois tant anciens que modernes; ibid, VI, p. 1-254.

2514 Essai sur les pierres sonores en Chine; ibid, VI, p. 255.

2515 Notice sur la poterie de Chine; ibid, VIII, p. 275.

2516 Essai sur les jardins de plaisance des Chinois; ibid, VIII, p. 301.

2517 Notice du frêne de Chine; ibid, II, p. 598.

2518 Sur les colonniers; ibid, II, p. 602.

2519 Sur le bambou; ibid, II, p. 623.

2520 Ueber die Musik der Chinesen, Asiat. Mag., I, p. 64-68.

2521 DELATUR, Essai sur l'architecture des Chinois, sur leurs jardins, leurs principes de médicine et leurs moeurs et usages. Paris, 1803, 2 vols., 8vo.

2522 BRETON, Coup d'oeil sur la Chine ou nouveau choix de costumes, arts et metiers de cet empire. Paris, 1812, 2 vols., 8vo.
English: London, 1812, 2 vols., 12mo.

2523 FINK, G. W., Ueber die chinesische Musik, Encycl. von Ersch und Grub., 16. Theil, 1827.

2524 WILLIAMS, S. W., Chinese weights and measures, Chin. Rep., II, p. 444.

2525 — — , Agriculture of the Chinese; ibid, III, p. 121.

2526 — — , Mode of Raising rice; ibid, III, p. 231.

2527 — — , Description of Chinese bellows; ibid, IV, p. 37.
2528 — — , Description of common agricultural implements used by the Chinese; ibid, V, p. 485.
2529 BOONE, W. J., Inquiries respecting Chinese long measure; ibid, X, p. 649.
2530 SEALEY, The porcelain tower. London, 1841, 8vo.
2531 BRIDGMAN, E. C., Description of the Porcelain tower at Nanking; ibid, XIII, p. 261.
2532 — — Manufacture of Chinese grass cloth; ibid, XVI, p. 209.
2533 — — , Memoir and account of the cultivation of hemp and the manufacture of grass cloth by Roudot; ibid, XVIII, p. 216.
2534 LAY, G. T., Music and description and drawings of Musical instruments of the Chinese; ibid, VIII, p. 38.
2535 HYACINTH, Bitschurin, On agriculture in China. St. Petersburg, 1842 (in Russian).
2536 Sur le commerce des livres en Chine. Paris, 1843, 8vo.
2537 Agriculture in China, illustrated by 72 agricultural implements. St. Petersburg, 1844, 8vo., 100 plates (in Russian).
2538 LANGDON, W. B., Descriptive catalogue of the Chinese collection at St. George's Place. London, 1844, 8vo.
2539 BIOT, E., Note sur la direction de l'aiguille aimantée en Chine. Paris, 1844, 8vo.
2540 JULIEN, St., Notice sur l'art d'imprimer en Chine, Journ. As., 4. sér., IX, 1846, p. 505 ss.
2541 — — , Histoire et fabrication de la procellaine chinoise. Paris, 1856, 8vo. See No. 251.
See Journ. As., 5. sér., VII, p. 443 ss.
2542 — — , Notice sur les miroirs magiques des Chinois, Compt. Rend., XXIV, 1847.
2543 HEDDE, J., Description de l'agriculture et du tissage en Chine. Paris, 1850, 8vo., 142 pp.

2544 St. DENYS, Marquis Hervey de, Recherches sur l'agriculture et l'horticulture des Chinois. Paris, 1850, 8vo.
See Journ. As., 4. sér., XVIII, 183.

2545 SKATCHKOFF, K., O rastitelnom vosko w Kitaye (On vegetable wax in China), Journ. of Rural Economy. Moskow (in Russian), 1851.

2546 — — , O rastitelnom salo w Kitaye (On vegetable tallow in China); ibid, 1851 (in Russian).

2547 — — , O Kitaiskoi batate (On the Chinese batate, ipomoea batatas); ibid, 1857 (in Russian).

2548 — — , O morskom diclie w Kitaye (On the nautical art of the Chinese), Russian Maritime Journal, 1858 (in Russian).

2549 RONDOT, N., Lettre sur la composition de la poudre chez les Chinois, Journ. As., 4. sér., XVI, p. 100 ss.

2550 — — , Notice du vert de Chine et de la teinture en vert chez les Chinois. Paris, 1858, 8vo., 205 pp.
See "Ausland," 1858, p. 936, p. 1102.

2551 MACGOWAN, D. J., Account of the modes of keeping time known among the Chinese, Chin. Rep., XX, p. 426.

2552 PERSOZ, J., On a green colouring material produced in China, Compt. Rend., Oct., 1852.

2553 HARLAND, W. A., Manufacture of magnetic needles and vermilion, Transact. Ch. Br. R. As. S., II. Hongkong, 1852, p. 163 ss.

2554 BOWRING, J. C., The rice-paper plant and its uses; ibid, III. p. 37-43.

2555 MEDHURST, W. H., Inscriptions on Chinese porcelain bottles, alleged to have been found in ancient Egyptian tombs; ibid, p. 45-54.

2556 PARKES, H., Chinese porcelain bottles found in the Egyptian tombs, their antiquity and uses; ibid, IV, p. 93-102.

2557 GOSCHKEWICZ, Concerning the manufacture of

ink and rouge among the Chinese, Russ. Eccl. Miss., I, No. 4 (in Russian.)

2558 — — , The imperial rice; ib., II, p. 475 (in Russian.)

2559 — — , The culture of the Schaujao (Dioscoraca alata); ib., II, p. 505 (in Russian.)

2560 — — , The Chinese abacus; ibid, II, No. 3 (in Russian.)

2561 ZWETKOFF, P., On the manufacture of salt in China; ibid, III, No. 2 (in Russian.)

Nos. 2557-61; German in No. 882.

2562 MILNE, W. C., A general description of the pagodas in China, Transact. Ch. Br. R. As. Soc., V, 1856, p. 17-63.

2563 SYLE, E. W., On the musical notation of the Chinese, Journ. N. Ch. Br. R. As. S., I, 1859, p. 176-179, plates.

2564 ROBERTSON, D. B., Cotton in China; ibid, p. 302-308.

2565 LOEFFLER, K., Das chinesische Zuckerrohr (Kaolien) Braunschweig, 1859, 8vo.

2566 COLLINS, V. D., Sorgo or northern Chinese sugar cane, J. N. Ch. Br. R. As. Soc., II, p. 85-98.

2567 JACQUEMAR, A. et C. LE BLANC, Histoire artistique de la porcellaine. Paris, 1861, 2 vols., fol.

2568 SIMON, G. E., Carte agricole générale de l'empire Chinois, J. N. Ch. Br. R. As. Soc., IV, p. 209-224, map.

2569 — — , L'agriculture de la Chine, Bull. Soc. de Géo. Paris, Dec., 1871, map.

2570 SKATSCHKOFF et PAUTHIER, Agriculture chinoise, Notice sur la plante Mou-sou ou Luzerne Chinoise. Paris, 1864, 8vo.; also in Revue de l'Or. et de l'Alg.

2571 — — , Discours sur l'agriculture en Chine, 1866.

2572 Suttee in China, Chin. & Jap. Rep., I, p. 457-461.

2573 Directions for the cultivation of cotton, especially in the district of Shanghai; ib., II, p. 199-209 ; III, p. 17-24.

2574 The cultivation of Chinese hemp and the manufacture of grass cloth ; ib., III, p. 41-45.

2575 THIBAULT, H., Le China grass. Nimes, 1866, 8vo.

2576 EDKINS, J., On the origin of paper making, Notes and Queries, I, p. 67.

2577 HANCE, H. F., Grass cloth ; ibid, I, p. 125.

2578 — — , and W. F. MAYERS, Introduction of maize into China, Pharm. Journ., Dec., 1870, p. 522 ss.

2579 MAYERS, W. F., Chinese junk building; ibid, I, p. 170.

2580 TAINTOR, E. C., Architecture in China; ibid, II, p. 16, 45.

2581 SAMPSON, T., Architecture in China; ibid, II, p. 29.

2582 The use of iron cylinders in bridge building ; ib., II, p. 180.

2583 OWEN JONES, Examples of Chinese ornament. London, 1867, 4to.

2584 CHAMPION, P., Industries anciennes et modernes de l'empire chinois. Paris, 1869, 8vo.

2585 BRACKENBURG, H., Invention of gunpowder, Notes and Queries, III, p. 121.

2586 JENKINS, B., Notions of the ancient Chinese respecting music, J. N. Ch. Br. R. As. Soc., V, 1869, p. 30.

2587 LIPPMANN, F., Eine Studie über chinesische Emailvasen, Mitth. des K. K. Oestr. Mus., 1870; also separately, 1870, 8vo., plates.

2588 MacPHERSON, J., Note on the manufacture of Brick-tea, "The Phoenix," I, p. 46.

2589 PFIZMAIER, A., Die Kunstfertigkeiten der alten Chinesen.

2590 Early inventions of the Chinese, Chin. Rec., II, p. 311.

2591 DABRY de THIERSANT, P., La pisciculture et la pêche en Chine. Paris, 1872, 8vo., 51 plates.

2592 — — , Ostriculture in China, Chin. Rev., IV, p. 38-42.

2593 HIRTH, F., The manufacture of Canton matting, China Review, I, p. 254.

2594 FABER, E., The Chinese theory of music; ib., I, p. 324-329, 384-888; II, p. 47-50.

2595 MORIN, H., Sur quelques bronces chinoises, Compt. Rend., LXVIII, 1874, p. 811.
See "Naturforscher," 1874, p. 224.

2596 PLATH, H., Die Landwirthschaft der Chinesen und Japanesen im Vergleich mit der europäischen. Sitz. Ber. Phil. hist. Cl. K. Bayr. Ac. d. Wiss. München, 1873, No. 6; also separately München, 1874, 8vo.

2597 RENARD, E., La pisciculture en Chine et au Japon, "L'explorateur géogr. et comm.," 1875, p. 227.

Silk Manufacture, Rearing of Silkworms.

2598 Sur les vers à soie, Mém. Conc., II, p. 575.

2599 REICHENBACH, E., Ueber Seidenraupenzucht und Cultur des Maulbeerbaum's in China. München, 1807, 8vo.

2600 KLAPROTH, J., Conjecture sur l'origine du nom de la Soie, Journ. As., 1823, II, p. 243; additional remarks by Rémusat; ibid, p. 245.

2601 JULIEN, St., Résumé des principaux traités chinois sur la culture des muriers et l'éducation des vers à soie. Paris, 1837, 8vo.
See No. 246.

2602 On rearing of silkworms in China. St. Petersburg, 1840, 8vo. (in Russian).

2603 SKATCHKOFF, K., O domaschnich scholkevitsch-nych tscherwiach w Kitaye (On domesticated silkworms in China), Journal of Rural Economy. Moskow, 1855 (in Russian).

2604 GOSCHKEWICZ, On silk manufacture, Russ. Eccl. Miss., II, p. 509 (in Russian.)
German in No. 882.
2605 CASTELLANI, C. B., De l'éducation des vers à soie en Chine faite et observée sur les lieux. Paris, 1861, 8vo., 182 pp.
2606 On cultivating the mulberry and rearing the silkworm, Chin. & Jap. Rep., III, p. 73-85.
2607 DELL'ORO, L'educazione dei bachida seta. Studisni piu distinte autore giapponesi e chinesi. Milano, 1870, 16mo.

e. Sciences.

2608 TERENTIUS, Epistolium ex regno Sinarum ad mathematicos Europaeos missum cum commentario J. Kepleri. Sagani, 1630, 4to.
2609 ACOSTA, S., Sapientia sinica. Kiuchan (Kiangsi), 1662, fol.
2610 VERBIEST, F., Liber organicus astronomiae europaeae apud Sinas restitutae sub imp. Camhi. Peking, 1668, fol.
2611 — — , Astronomia europaea sub imp. Camhy ex umbra in lucem revocata. Dilingae, 1688, fol.
2612 Secret de la médecine des Chinois. Grenoble, 1671, 12mo.
2613 INTORCETTA, P., La science des Chinois.
La vie de Confucius.
Viaggio del P. Grueber da China in Europa.
Grueberi Tartarica et Sinica. Paris, 1672, fol.
2614 BOYM, M., Clavis medica ad Chinarum doctrinam de pulsibus. Francofurti, 1680, 4to.
French in Du Halde's descr., III, p. 384.
See Wylie's notes, p. 79.
2615 CLEYER, A., Specimen medicinae sinicae. Francofurti, 1682, 4to.
This also contains the preceding treatise by Boym.

2616 VOSS, J., Observationum variarum liber. Londini, 1685, 4to. (contains a diss. de urbibus et scientiis Sinensium).

2617 La morale de Confucius. Amsterdam, 1688, 12mo. English : London, 1783, 12mo.

2618 Observations physiques et mathématiques envoyées des Indes et de la Chine par les P. P. Jésuites. Paris, 1692, 8vo.

2619 SCHOEPFER, M. J., Dissertatio de natalibus philosophiae Sinensis. Rostochii, 1698.

2620 ALGOEWER, M. D. et HAAS, J. M., Disputatio de mathesi sinica. Aug. Vindelicorum, 1702, 4to.

2621 PURGSTALL, A., Synopsis vitae et doctrinae Confucii. Viennae, 1708.

2622 NOEL, E., Observationes mathematicae et physicae in India et China factae ab anno, 1684-1708. Pragae, 1710, 4to.

2623 — — , Philosophia sinica, tribus tractibus, primo cognitionem primi entis, secundo ceremonias erga defunctos, tertio ethicam juxta Sinarum mentem complectens. Pragae, 1711, 3 vols., 4to.

2624 BUELFINGER, G. B., Specimen doctrinae veterum Sinarum moralis et politica, libellis Sinicae gentis classicis, Confucii sive dicta sive facta complexis. Francofurti, 1724, 8vo.

2625 SOUCIET, E., Observations mathématiques, astronomiques, etc. tirées des anciens livres chinois par les P. P. de la Cie. de Jésus. Paris, 1729, 3 vols., 4to.

2626 WOLLFF, Chr., De sapientia Sinensium. Trevolt., 1725, 4to.

2627 — — , Oratio de philosophia Sinarum practica. Francofurti, 1726, 4to.

2628 LAGERLOEF, N., De Wolffii sententia de philosophia Sinarum. Lund., 1737, 4to.

2629 REIMANNUS, J. F., Historia philosophiae sinensis. Brunswigae et Hildesiae, 1741, 8vo.

2630 COLLINA, H., L'origine della bussola nautica nell'

Europa e nell' Asia. Firenza, 1748, 4to.

2631 GUIGNES, J. DE (père), Essai historique sus l'étude de la philosophie chez les anciens Chinois, Rec. de l'ac. des inscr., tom. 38, 1777.

2632 — — , Observations sur le dégré de certitude des éclipses du soleil rapportées par Confucius ; ibid, tom. 45, 1793.

2633 Confucius' Lebensbeschreibung und hinterlassene Lehren der Weisheit. Nürnberg, 1779, 12mo.

2634 Observations de physique et d'histoire naturelle de l'empereur Kanghi, Mém. conc., IV, p. 452.

2635 GAUBIL, A., Histoire de l'astronomie chinoise, Lettres édif. et cur., XXVI, 1781.
See Wylie's Notes, p. 86.

2636 Remédes Chinois, Mém. Conc., V, p. 492 ; VIII, p. 271.

2637 LÉVESQUE, Pensées morales de Confucius, recueillies et traduites du latin. Paris, 1782, 12mo.

2638 GUIGNES, de (file), Réflexions sur les anciennes observations astronomiques des Chinois, Annales des voy., II.

2639 — — , Mémoire sur le planisphère céleste chinois, Rec. des savans étr. de l'ac. des sc., X, 1785.

2640 RAUX, P., Sur la chirurgie chez les Chinois, Journ. de Méd., An. IX, Vend.

2641 RÉMUSAT, A., Tableau des 119 constellations de la sphère tartare comparée avec celles des planisphères chinois et grecs. Mines de l'Orient.

2642 — — , Recherches historiques sur la médecine des Chinois. Paris, 1813, 8vo. ; also in Mél. as., I, p. 240-252.

2643 — — , De l'étude des langues étrangères chez les Ch. Mél. as., II, p. 242-66.

2644 — — , Sur l'acupuncture, Nouv. mél. as., I, p. 358.

2645 — — , Dissertatio de glossosemeiotice sive de signis morborum quae e lingua sumuntur praesertim apud Sinenses. Paris, 1813, 4to.

2646 — — , Discours sur l'état des sciences naturelles chez les peuples de l'Asie orientale, Ac. des Inscr., X, p. 116-167; and Mél. posth., p. 206-220.

2647 REHMANN, J., Beschreibung einer tibetan. Handapotheke. Ein Beitrag zur Kenntniss der Arzneikunde des Orients. St. Petersburg, 1811.

2648 LEPAGE, Recherches sur la médecine des chinois. Paris, 1813, 4to.

2649 KLAPROTH, J., Notice d'une mappemonde et d'une cosmographie chinoises, avec une planisphère chinoise. Paris, 1833, 8vo.

2650 WINDISCHMANN, Die Philosophie im Fortgange der Weltgeschichte. Bonn, 1827, 8vo.

2651 STUHR, P. F., Untersuchungen über die Ursprünglichkeit und Alterthümlichkeit der Sternkunde unter den Chinesen. Berlin, 1831.

2652 BRIDGMAN, E. C., Introduction of vaccination among the Chinese, Chin. Rep., II, p. 35.

2653 — — , Notice of the golden mirror of medical authors; ibid, IX, p. 486.

2654 — — , On the Philosophy of the Chinese and desirableness of translating their standard authors; ibid, XVIII, p. 43.

2655 — — , Memoir of Chu Hi, the Chinese philosopher; ibid, XVIII, p. 187.

2656 — — , Cosmogony of the Chinese, as given by Chu Hi; ibid, XVIII, p. 342.

2657 WILLIAMS, S. W., Diet of the Chinese; ibid, III, p. 457.

2658 — — , Notices of Chinese Natural History; ibid, VII, p. 44, 90, 136, 212, 250, 321, 394, 485, 541, 595.

2659 — — , Popular ideas of the Chinese relating to the powers and operations of nature; ibid, X, p. 49; XI, p. 434.

2660 MOHNIKE, Zur Moralphilosophie der Chinesen, 1834, 8vo.

2661 NEUMANN, K. F., Die Natur-und Religionsphilosophie der Chinesen nach Tschu-hi, Jllgen's Ztschr. f. hist. Theologie, 1837, 1.

2662 BIOT, J., Recherches sur l'ancienne astronomie chinoise. Paris, 1839-40, 4to.

2663 — — , Études sur l'astronomie Indienne et Chinoise. Paris, 1862, 8vo.

2664 LOCKHART, W., Description of a Chinese anatomical plate, Ch. Repos, IX, p. 194.

2665 BOONE, W. J., Astronomy of the Shuking; ibid, IX, p. 573.

2666 COOLIDGE, Mrs., Biographical notice of Mang-tsze or Mencius, the Chinese philosopher, Chin. Rep., X, 1841-42, p. 320.

2667 BIOT, E., Note sur une grande carte chinoise, Journ. As., 3. sér., No. 3, 1843, p. 279.

2668 — — , Notice sur deux cartes chinoises; ibid, V, p. 506.

2669 — — , Catalogue général des étoiles filantes et des autres météores observés en Chine. Paris, 1846, 8vo.

2670 — — , Catalogue des comètes observées en Chine. Paris, 1846, 8vo.; Précis de l'histoire de l'astronomie chinoise. Paris, 1861, 4to.

2671 SCHOTT, W., Chinesische Nachrichten über den Kangar und das Osmanische Reich. Berlin, 1844, 8vo.

2672 CAZIN, La morale de Confucius. Paris, 1844, 8vo.

2673 PAUTHIER, G., Esquisse d'une histoire de la philosophie Chinoise. Revue indépend, 1844.

2674 — — , La médecine, la chirurgie et les établissements d'assistance publique en Chine. Paris, 1860, 8vo.

2675 Lettre sur la morale de Confucius. Amsterdam, 8vo., s. a.

2676 GLADISCH, A., Einleitung in das Verhältniss der Weltgeschichte, 1ste Abtheilung: Die Pythagoräer und die alten Schinesen. Posen, 1844, 8vo.

2677 MEDHURST, W. H., (sen.), Philosophical opinions

of Chufutze on primary matter, Chin. Rep., XIII,
p. 552, 609.

2678 DAVIES, E., China and her spiritual claims. London, 1845, 12mo.

2679 HARLAND, W. A., A treatise on the Chinese system
of anatomy and physiology, Transact. Ch. Br. R.
As. Soc., I, 1848, p. 23-46.

2680 GAUGER, G., Ueber chinesische Roharzneiwaaren.
Repert. f. Pharm. und pract. Chemie in Russl.,
VII, 1848.

2681 Pensées morales de Confucius et de divers auteurs
chinois. Paris, 1851, 12mo.

2682 WYLIE, A., Jottings on the science of the Chinese,
North China Herald, 1852; republ. in Shanghai
Almanac, 1853 and in Ch. and Jap. Repos. (1864),
p. 411, 498.
German by K. L. Biernatzky, Die Arithmetik
der Chinesen. Berlin, 1856, 4to.
Contains a translation of the Tshou pei suan
tshing. See Wylie's notes, p. 86.

2683 — — , Notes on the opinion of the Chinese with
regard to eclipses, J. N. Ch. Br. R. As. S., III,
p. 71-74.

2684 — — , Eclipses recorded in Chinese works; ibid,
IV, p. 67-158.

2685 — — , A Chinese Theorem, Notes and Queries,
III, p. 73.

2686 TATARINOF, A., On Chinese medicine, Russ. Eccl.
Miss., II, p. 421 (in Russian).

2687 — — , The Chinese art of healing; ibid, II,
No. 5 (in Russian).
German in No. 882.

2688 — — , On the employment of anaesthetic means
in operations by the Chinese and the hydropathy;
ibid, III, No. 5 (in Russian).

2689 — — , Catalogus medicamentorum Sinensium
quae Pekini comparanda et determinanda curavit.
Petropoli, 1856, 8vo.

2690 JULIEN, S., Notices sur les pays et les peuples étrangers tirées des géographes et des annales chinoises, J. as., 4. sér., VIII, IX; also in Mél. de géogr. (No 485.)
    See W. A. Macy, Chin. Repos., XVII, p. 575.

2691 SKATSCHKOFF, C., History of Chinese philosophy, 1856 (in Russian).

2692 — — , Geographitscheskiya posnania Kitaïtsev. (Geographical Knowledge of the Chinese). St. Petersburg, 1866, 8vo. (in Russian).

2693 — — , Sudba Kitaïskoi astronomii. in J. of the Min. of Nat. Educ., 1874 (in Russian); also separately, 1874, 8vo.
    See Chin. Rec., V, p. 304.

2694 BAZIN, A., Notice historique sur le collège médical de Pékin d'après le Tai-thsing hoei-tien. Paris, 1857, 8vo.

2695 JOHN, GRIFFITH, The ethics of the Chinese, with special reference to the doctrine of human nature and sin, Journ. N. C. Br. R. As. S., Nov., 1859, pp. 20-44; also separately, 8vo.

2696 MARTIN, R. M., Histoire de la morale chez les Chinois. Paris, 1859.

2697 CASTANO, Note sur l'état des sciences médico-chirurgicales en Chine, Rec. d. mém. de méd. mil., V, 1861.

2698 HANBURY, D., Notes on Chinese materia medica. London, 1862, 8vo.
    German by Martens. Speyer, 1863, 8vo.

2699 MARTIN, W. A. P., On the ethical philosophy of the Chinese. Princeton Review, April, 1862.

2700 LARIVIÈRE, A., Etude sur la médecine chinoise, Journ. de méd. de Bordeaux, 1863; also separately Bord., 1863, 8vo.

2701 DABRY DE THIERSANT, La médecine chez les Chinois. Paris, 1863, 8vo.

2702 CANTOR, M., Mathematische Beiträge zum Cultur-leben der Völker, 1863, III, Die Chinesen, 4 plates.

2703 BACMEISTER, A., Zur Völkerkunde der alten Chinesen. Ausland, 1864, No. 25.

2704 EDKINS, J., On the present state of science, literature and literary criticism in China, Ch. and Jap. Repos., I, p. 29-63.

2705 — — , Feng-shui, China Recorder, IV, p. 274, 291, 316.

2706 MORACHE, G., L'exercice de la médecine chez les Chinois, Rec. de mém. de méd. mil., 3. ser., XII, 1864.

2707 TOYE, Notes sur l'art medico-chirurgical chez les Chinois. Montpellier, 1864.

2708 Chinese cosmogony and sententious sayings, Ch. and Jap. Rep., II (1864), p. 210-212.

2709 DEBEAUX, O., Essay sur la pharmacie et la matière médicale en Chine. Paris, 1865.

2710 HENDERSON, J., The medicine and medical practice of the Chinese, Journ. of N. C. B. of R. A. S., I, art. 5, 1865.

2711 Chinese dentistry, Not. & Quer., I, p. 158.

2712 SMITH, F. P., A new work on Chinese medicine; ibid, I, p. 166.

2713 — — , Homoeopathy in Chinese medical practice, Notes and Queries, II, p. 179.

2714 — — , Chü ling (medicine); ibid, III, p. 89.

2715 — — , Chinese medicines; ibid, III, 117.

2716 — — , A handbook of Chinese Materia medica. Shanghai, 1871, 4to.
See The Phoenix, II, p. 30.

2717 — — , Chinese chemical manufacture, Journ. of N. C. B. of R. A. S., VI (1871), p. 139.

2718 HAAS, J., Das System der Pakua, Notes and Queries, III, p. 7, 23, 37.

2719 KERR, J. G., Medicine in China. Canton, 1869, 8vo.

2720 — — , Pure water, Chin. Rec., III, p. 322.

2721 — — , Chinese medicine, Chin. Rev., I, p. 176.

2722 MAYERS, W. F., Anglo-chinese Calendar Manual. Hongkong, 1869, 8vo., 2nd edit., 1875.

2723 GUMPACH, J. von, A Chinese theorem, Notes and Queries, III, p. 153.

2724 McGREGOR, W., A Chinese theorem; ibid, III, p. 167, 179.

2725 PFIZMAIER, A., Die chinesische Lehre von den Kreisläufen und Luftarten, Sitz. Ber. Phil. Hist. Cl. K. Ak. d. Wiss. Wien, 1869.

2726 — — , Denkwürdigkeiten von den Früchten China's, ibid.

2727 — — , Denkwürdigkeiten von den Insecten China's, ibid.

2728 — — , Abhandlung von den Bäumen China's; ibid, 1875.

2729 The history of medicine in China, The Phoenix, I, p. 41.

2730 DUDGEON, J., Chinese arts of healing, Ch. Recorder, II, p. 163, 183, 267, 293, 332; III, p. 40, 99, 120, 334; IV, p. 282.

2731 — — , On the disgusting nature of Chinese medicine; ibid, II, p. 285.

2732 PLATH, J. H., Die beiden ältesten Geographien China's von 4000 und 3000 Jahren, Zeitschr. Ges. f. Erdk, VI, 1871, p. 162-174.

2733 WILLIAMS, J., Observations of comets from B. C. 611—A.D. 1640, extracted from the Chinese Annals, translated with introductory remarks and an appendix comprising the tables necessary for reducing Chinese time to European reckoning and a Chinese celestial atlas. London, 1871, 8vo. See Chin. Rec., V, p. 98-108.

2734 MARTIN, E., Etude historique et critique sur l'art médical en Chine, Gaz. hebdom., 1872.

2735 McCLATCHIE, C., The symbols of the Yih-King, China Rev., I, p. 151.

2736 LISTER, A., Chinese almanacs, China Rev., I, p. 237-244.

2737   — — , Chinese proverbs and their lessons; ib., III, p. 129-138.

2738 MACGOWAN, D. J., Chinese use of shad in consumption and jodine plants in scrofula, J. N. Ch. Br. R. As. Soc., VII, p. 235.

2739 — — , On the mutton wine of the Mongols and anologous preparations of the Chinese; ibid, p. 237.

2740 Chinese medicine, China Review, I, 1872-73, p. 176 ss.

2741 EITEL, E. F., Feng-shui or the rudiments of natural sciences in China. Hongkong, 1873, 8vo. See Chin. Rec., II, p. 34-40.

2742 TURNER, F. S., On Fengshui, Cornhill Magaz., March, 1874.

2743 SOUBEIRAN, L. et DABRY DE THIERSANT, La matière médicale chez les Chinois. Paris, 1874.

2744 Zur Naturanschauung der Chinesen. "Ausland," 1874, No. 44.

2745 GARDNER, C., Hereditary genius in China, China Review, II, p. 206-214.

2746 MOULE, A. E., Chinese proverbial philosophy, Chin. Rec., V, p. 72 ss.

2747 Report of M. Gubler upon the Materia medica of the Chinese, China Rev., III, p. 119-124.

2748 Chinese calendars, Chin. Rec., V, p. 98-108.

2749 SCHLEGEL, G., Sing-chin-khao-youen, Uranographie chinoise ou preuves directes que l'astronomie primitive est originaire de la Chine et qu'elle a été emprunté par les anciens peuples occidentaux à la sphère Chinoise. Leyden, 1875, 2 vols., 4to., Atlas fol. See Chin. Rec., VI, p. 442-447.

f. Religions.
1. General. Confucianism. Taoism.

2750 PICART, B., The ceremonies and religious customs of the idolatrous nations. London, 1733. fol.

2751 DE GUIGNES, J., Observations sur quelques points

cencernant la religion et la philosophie des Egyptiens et des Chinois, Rec. de Mém. de l'Ac. des
Inscr., XL, 1780.

2752 Doctrine ancienne et nouvelle des Chinois sur la
piété filiale, Mém. conc., IV, p. 1-298.

2753 Notice du Kong-fou des Bonzes Tao-sée; ibid, IV,
p. 441-451.

2754 AMIOT, Abrégé historique des principaux traits de
la vie de Confucius, Mém. conc., XII.

2755 — — , Abrégé de la vie des principaux d'entre
les disciples de Koung-tsée; ibid, XIII, p. 1-38.

2756 — — , Sur la secte de Lao-tsée; ibid, XV,
p. 208-259.

2757 HAGER, J., Panthéon chinois ou parallèle entre le
culte religieux des Grecs et celui des Chinois.
Paris, 1806, 4to.

2758 On religious opinions in China, Indo-Chin. Glean.,
No. 18, 1821.

2759 RÉMUSAT, A., Mémoire sur la vie et les ouvrages
de Lao-tseu. Paris, 1823; Mél. As., I, p. 88-99.

2760 CREUZER, D., Die Religionen des Alterthums.
French by Guigniaut. Paris, 1825, 53 plates.

2761 MORRISON, R., Idolatry, Chin. Repos., I, p. 68.

2762 — — , Metempsychosis; ibid, I, p. 102.

2763 — — , Heterodoxy defined; ibid, I, p. 103.

2764 — — , Worship of Ancestors and at the tombs;
ibid, I, p. 201, 499.

2765 — — , Public opinion in China favors paganism;
ibid, I, p. 330.

2766 — — , Chinese ideas of the happiness of a future state; ibid, I, p. 373.

2767 — — , Worship of Confucius and the cost of it;
ibid, I, p. 502.

2768 — — , Instances of superstition and idolatry;
ibid, II, p. 327.

2769 — — , State religion of China; ibid, III, p. 49.

2770 On the three principal religions in China, As. journ.
and monthly reg., N. S., IX, 1832.

2771 KLAPROTH, J., De la religion des Taoszu en Chine, Nouv. ann. d. Voy., II, p. 129, 1833.

2772 STEVENS, E., Idolatry hopelessly depraves man,
Ch. Rep., II, p. 165.

2773 — — , Extracts from the writings of Chinese
moralists on human nature ; ibid, II, p. 310.

2774 MORRISON, J. R., Notice of the sacrificial ritual of
the sages ; ibid, II, p. 236.

2775 STUHR, P. F., Die chinesische Reichsreligion und
die Systeme der indischen Philosophie in ihrem
Verhältnisse zur Offenbarungslehre. Berlin, 1835,
8vo.

2776 — — , Allgemeine Geschichte der Religionsfor-
men der heidnischen Völker. Berlin, 1836-38,
2 vols., 8vo.

2777 GUETZLAFF, K., Indifference of Chinese to their
religion, Chin. Rep., IV, p. 271.

2778 — — , Extraordinary legends of Tauists ; ibid,
XI, p. 202.

2779 TRACY, J., Religious condition of China ; ibid, IV,
p. 572.

2780 BRIDGMAN, E. C., Surperstitions connected with
pagodas ; ibid, VI, p. 189.

2781 — — , Lessons in sacrificial rites ; ibid, VI, p.
253.

2782 — — , Chinese sacrifices illustrated by extracts
from the Shuking or book of records ; ibid, XVII,
p. 97.

2783 — — , Remarks on confounding the true god
with Shang-ti ; ibid, XVII, p. 262.

2784 PAUTHIER, G., Mémoire sur l'origine et la propagation de la doctrine du Tao. Paris, 1831, 8vo.
See No. 264.

2785 — — , Lettre inédite du P. Prémare sur le mo-
nothéisme des Chinois. Paris, 1861, 8vo.

2786 Analecta Sinensia : I. Chinese judges of the dead,
As. Journ. and Mthly. Reg., N. S., XXXI. London, 1840.

2787 KROEGER, J. C., Abriss einer vergleich. Darstellung der indisch-persischen und chinesischen Religionssysteme. Eisleben, 1842, 8vo.

2788 SHUCK, J. L., Sketch of Matsupu or Queen of Heaven, Ch. Repos., X, p. 84.

2789 — — , Sketch of Kwanyin or Goddess of Mercy; ibid, X, p. 185.

2790 — — , Sketch of Yuh-hwang Shangti; ibid, X, p. 305.

2791 PAVIE, T., Les trois religions de la Chine, Journ. Asiat., 5. sér., IX, 1845.

2792 Translation of a Confucian tract, exhorting mankind to preserve their principles and good hearts, Chin. Repos., XV, p. 377.

2793 Superstition of the people of Ningpo; ibid, XV, p. 477.

2794 YEATES, T., Religion of the Chinese, without altars, temples, priests or any term to denote the true God, Ch. Repos., XVI, p. 203.

2795 MOELLER, N., De la métaphysique de Lao-tseu, Revue cath., IV, 1849.

2796 Perspicuous form of prayer returning thanks to heaven in fulfilment of vows, Ch. Repos., XVII, p. 365.

2797 WILLIAMS, S. W., Sketch of life and character of Confucius; ibid, XI, p. 411.

2798 — — , Mythological account of Hiuen-tien Shang-ti, with notices of his worship; ibid, XVIII, p. 102.

2799 — — , Worship of Ancestors among the Chinese; ibid, XVIII, p. 363.

2800 BBIDGMAN, J. G., Deities connected with the elements; ibid, XIX, p. 312.

2801 WUTTKE, A., Geschichte des Heidenthums in Beziehung auf Religion, Wissen, Kunst, Sittlichkeit und Staatsleben. Bredau, 1852-53, 2 vols., 8vo.

2802 — — , China's religiöse, sittliche und gesellschaftliche Zustände. Berlin, 1855, 8vo.

2803 ZWETKOFF, The sect of the Tauists, Works of

Russ. Eccles. Miss., III, No. 13 (in Russian);
German in No. 882.

2804 PARAVEY, C. DE, Mémoire sur la trinité Assyrien-
ne et sur la trinité Chinoise. Paris, 1853, 8vo.

2805 EDKINS, J., Phases in the development of Tauism,
Transact. Ch. Br. R. As. Soc., V, 1856, p. 83-99.

2806 — — , A sketch of the Tauist Mythology in its
modern form, J. N. Ch. Br. R. As. Soc., I, 1859,
p. 309-315.

2807 — — , Notices of the character and writings of
Confucius; ibid, I, p. 165-169.

2808 — — , A sketch of the life of Confucius; ibid,
II, p. 1-19.

2809 — — , The religious condition of the Chinese
with observations on the prospects of christian
conversion amongst that people. London, 1859,
12mo., 288 pp.
　　　Partly republished from the "Beacon" news-
　　　paper.

2810 — — , Worship of Kwanti among the Lamas,
Not. & Quer., I, p. 35.

2811 MACCLATCHIE, T. M., The Chinese on the plain
of Shinar, or a connexion established between the
Chinese and all other nations by means of their
theology, J. of R. A. S., XVI. London, 1856.

2812 — — , Chinese mythology, Ch. Recorder, III,
p. 197, 234, 299, 310, 347; IV, p. 19, 46, 93,
130, 192, 217.

2813 BAZIN, A., Recherches sur l'origine, l'histoire et la
constitution des ordres religieux dans l'empire
Chinois. Paris, 1856; Journ. as., 5. s., VIII.

2814 DIECKHOFF, D., Das chinesische Heidenthum.
Göttingen, 1859, 8vo.

2815 GILLIOT, A., Études sur les religions comparées
de l'Orient. Colmar, 1862.

2816 PLATH, J. H., Die Religion und der Cultus der alten
Chinesen. München, 1862, 4.
　　　See Lit. Centralbl. (1864), No. 5, p. 100.

2817 — — , Die Unsterblichkeitslehre der alten Chinesen, Zt. Dm. Ges., XX (1866), p. 471-484.
2818 — — , Confucius und seiner Schüler Leben und Lehren. (Abh. der Bay. Ak. d. Wiss). München, 1867-1874, 4 Hefte., 4to.
See Lit. Centralbl., 1868, No. 8, p. 188.
2819 FRANCKEN, J. J. C., Gotsdienst en Bijgeloof der Chinezen. Tijdschr. voor ind. Taal-Land-, Volkenk., XIV. Batavia, 1863.
2820 BOWRING, J., Confucius and the religions of the East, Naut. Mag., 1864, No. 514.
2821 (FAY, Miss L. M.), Memoir of Kiuh-Yuen, Ch. and Jap. Repos., III (1865), p. 503-508.
2822 YATES, M. T., Ancestral worship and Fungshui, Notes and Queries, I, p. 23, 37, 39; also Shanghai, 1867, 8vo.
2823 SEVERINI, A., Tre religioni giudicate da un Cinese, Revista orient., I (Firenze, 1867-8,) p. 130-147.
2824 WATTERS, T., Laotzu, a study in Chinese philosophy, Chin. Rec., I, p. 31, 57, 82, 106, 128, 154, 209; and Foochow, 1870, 8vo.
2825 ASHMORE, W., A moral problem solved by Confucianism; ibid, II, p. 282.
2826 — — , The moral uses of heathenism; ibid, II, p. 126.
2827 — — , The ideal man of Confucius; ibid, III, p. 89, 129.
2828 MAYERS, W. F., On the legend relating to Nü-Kwa, Notes & Quer., II, p. 99.
2829 — — , The eight gods; ib., II, p. 189.
2830 — — , Who was Lupan; ibid, III, p. 174.
2831 — — , On Wen-ch'ang, the god of literature, J. N. Ch. Br. R. A. S., 1871, p. 31.
2832 SAMPSON, T., A-tseung and the dragon, Not. & Quer., II, p. 122.
2833 The Polo temple near Whampoa; ibid, III, p. 14.
2834 Pagan idolatry and revelation; ibid, III, p. 57.
2835 Canonization of a well; ibid, III, p. 155.

2836 EWER, F. H., Some account of festivals in Canton; ibid, III, p. 185.

2837 CHALMERS, J., Tauism, China Rev., I, p. 209-220.

2838 FABER, E., Lehrbegriff des Confucius. Hongkong, 1872, 8vo.

> See E. J. Eitel, China Rev., I, p. 260; Trübner's Rec., March, 1873, p. 34; Liter. Centralbl., 1875, No. 43.

2839 — — , Quellen zu Confucius und dem Confucianismus als Einleitung zum Lehrbegriff. Hongkong, 1873, 8vo.

> Nos. 2838 and 2839 translated into English by P. G. von Möllendorff. Hongkong, 1875, 8vo., XIII, 131 pp.

2840 WASSILYEFF, W., O religiakh v Kitaye (The religions in China). St. Petersburg, 1873.

2841 KINGSMILL, T. W., Chinese and Hindoo mythology, China Rev., II, p. 191.

2842 KOPSCH, H., The master of Heaven (天師); ibid, II, p. 226.

2843 STRAUSS, V. von, Der chinesische Philosoph Laotse ein Prophet aus den Heiden, Allgem. Missionszeitschr., 1874, p. 329.

2844 GALPIN, F., Notes concerning the Chinese belief of Evil and Evil spirits, Chin. Rec., V, 1874, p. 42.

2845 SCARBOROUGH, W., Notes of a visit to the famous Wutangshan (Taoism); ibid, V, p. 77-82.

2846 JONES, E. D., The Chinese, their religion and social condition, Sunday Mag., Octob., 1875.

2847 PFIZMAIER, A., Ueber einige Gegenstände des Taoglaubens Sitz. Ber. K. K. Ac. d. Wiss. Wien, Phil. Hist. Cl. 1875.

2. Buddhism.

Exclusively works on Chinese, Tibetan and Mongolian Buddhism. For a complete bibliography of Buddhism see Kistner No. 10.

214

2848 GUIGNES, J., DE (père), Recherches sur les philosophes appelés Samanéens, Mém. de litt. tirés des M. S. de l'acad. des inscr., XXVI, 1759.

2849 — — , Recherches sur la religion Indienne et sur les livres fondamentaux de cette religion, qui ont été traduits en Chinois ; ibid, XL, 1773.

2850 PALLAS, P. S., Beschreibung der feierlichen Verbrennung eines Kalmückischen Lamas, Neue nord. Beitr., III, 1782.

2851 AMIOT, Letter of the emperor of China (Kienlong) to the Dalai Lama, Mém. Conc., IX ; English in Dalrymple's Oriental Report., II, 1808.

2852 Das Buch des Fo. Sammlung asiat. Originalschr., I, Zürich, 1791.

2853 HUELLMANN, K. D., Historisch-kritischer Versuch über die lamaische Religion. Berlin, 1796, 8vo.
See Schleusner und Stäudlin, Gött. Bibl., II, 1796.

2854 Ueber die Foreligion in China, As. Mag., I, p. 148-169 ; II, p. 76-78, 1802.

2855 STAEUDLIN, C. F., Ueber die lamaische Religion, Mag. f. Rel., Moral und Kirchengesch, I, Hannover, 1801.

2856 — — , De religionis Lamaicae cum christiana cognatione. Göttingae, 1808, 8vo.

2857 — — , Ueber die Verwandtschaft der Lama Religion mit der christlichen. Archiv f. alte und neuere Kirchengesch., I. Leipzig, 1814.

2858 L'ETONDAC, Account of the Lamas and Bonzes, French and English, Dalrymple's or. Repos., II, 1808.

2859 The systems of Fo and Confucius compared, Indo-Chin. Gleaner, No. 5 ; also Ch. Repos., II, p. 265.

2860 The paradise of Fuh, an exhortation to worship Fuh and seek to live in the land of joy; ibid, No. 6, 1818.

2861 A bone of Fuh ; ibid, No. 12, 1820.

2862 The ecclesiastical language of the Buddhists and Mohammedans; ibid, No. 17, 1821.

2863 MORIS, Exposé des principaux dogmes tibétains-mongols. Extrait de l'ouvrage de D. Bergmann et traduit, Journ. As., III, 1823.

2864 RÉMUSAT, A., Aperçu d'un mémoire intitulé Recherches chronologiques sur l'origine de la hiérarchie Lamaïque, Journ. as., IV; Mél. as., I, p. 129-145.

2865 — — , Sur l'étendu de quelques-uns des livres sacrés de Bouddha, Mél. As., I, p. 146-152.

2866 — — , Observations sur quelques points de la doctrine samanéenne. Paris, 1831, 8vo.

2867 — — , Essai sur la cosmographie et la cosmogonie des bouddhistes d'après les auteurs chinois, Journ. des Sav., Oct., 1831.

2868 — — , Observations sur la religion samanéenne, Mél. Posth., 1843, p. 1-64.

2869 — — , Essai sur la cosmographie et la cosmogonie des bouddhistes d'après les auteurs chinois; ibid. p. 65-131.

2870 KLAPROTH, J., Vie de Bouddha d'après les livres mongols, Mém. relat. à l'Asie, II, 1825; also in No. 440.

2871 DES HAUTERAYES, Mémoire sur la religion de Fo, confessée par les bonzes Hochang dans la Chine, Journ. Asiat., VII, p. 150-174, 228-243, 311-316; VIII, p. 40-49, 74-88, 179-188, 219-224.

2872 Chinese Buddhism, As. Journ. and Monthly Reg., N. S., VI, 1831.

2873 Introduction of Buddhism in China, ibid.

2874 Sketch of the Buddhistic mythology amongst the Tibetans and Mongols; ibid, VIII, 1832.

2875 SCHMIDT, J. J., Ueber einige Grundlehren des Buddhismus, Mém. de l'Acad. de St. Pétersb., 6. sér., I, 1832.

3876 — — , Ueber Lamaismus und die Bedeutungslosigkeit dieser Benennung, Bull. Sc. de l'Ac. de St. Pétersb., I, 1836.

2877 — — , Kritischer Versuch zur Feststellung der Aera und der ersten geschichtlichen Momente des Buddhismus; ibid, VI, 1840.

2878 MORRISON, R., Remarks on Buddhism, Chin. Rep., I, p. 155.

2879 GUETZLAFF, K., Remarks on Buddhism together with brief notices of the island of Gou-to and of the numerous priests who inhabit it; ibid, II, p. 214.

2880 — — , Buddhistic temple at Meichau; ibid, II, p. 563.

2881 — — , Remarks on the present state of Buddhism in China, Journ. R. As. S., XVI, 1856.

2882 SEYFFARTH, Die Kabiren der Schamanen und die acht Kuas der Chinesen, 1833, 8vo., 1 plate.

2883 Miao-fa-lien-hoa-king, Le livre sacré du Lotus de la bonne loi, trad. du sanscrit en Chinois, l'an 403 de l'ère chrétien par Koumaradjiva. Paris, 2 vols., 8vo.

2884 NEUMANN, K. F., Buddhism and Shamanism, As. Journ. and monthly reg., N. S., XVI, 1835.

2885 LANDRESSE, C., Aperçu des travaux de M. Rémusat sur le bouddhisme, ou introduction à son commentaire sur le Foe Koue Ki. Paris, 1836, 4to. See No. 220.

2886 KOWALEWSKI, Buddhist Chronology, Transact. Kazan Univers., I, 1837 (in Russian).

2887 Buddhism in China, taken from Gützlaff's China opened and Medhurst's China, The Friend, III. Colombo, 1838.

2888 Reise eines chinesischen Buddhisten am Ende des 4ten Jahrhunderts. Ausland, 1838.

2889 PARKER, P., A buddhistic stratagem, Ch. Repos., VIII, p. 263.

2890 WILSON, H. H., Travels of Fa Hian in India, Ch. Repos., IX, p. 334.

2891 — — , Notes of a correspondence with Sir J. Bowring on buddhist literature in China, Journ. of R. A. S., XVI, p. 316, 1856.

2892 ABEEL, D., Temple of Amakok of Macao, Ch. Repos., IX, p. 402.

2893 SCHOTT, W., Ueber den Doppelsinn des Wortes Schamane und über den tungusischen Schamanenkultus am Hofe der Mandjukaiser. Abh. der Ak. der Wiss. Berlin, 1842, p. 463 ss.

2894 — — , Ueber den Buddhaismus in Hochasien und China. Berlin, 1846, 8vo.
See Journ. As., 1847; Amer. Or. Soc., I, p. 332.

2895 SALISBURY, E. E., Memoir on the history of Buddhism, Americ. Orient. Soc., I, 1844, p. 79-135. See Chin. Rep., XIV, 1845, p. 423-435.

2896 BANZAROFF, D., On the Black Religion i. e. Shamanism, 1846 (in Russian.)

2897 Die Insel der Bonzen. Ausland, 1846.

2898 MACGOWAN, D. J., An inscription from a tablet in a buddhist monastery at Ningpo in China, Journ. R. A. S. of Beng., XIII, 1844.

2899 POHLMANN, W. J., Translation of a buddhist print descriptive of Toloni or the Goddess of Mercy, Ch. Repos., XV, p. 357.

2900 JULIEN, S., Renseignements bibliographiques sur les relations des voyages dans l'Inde et des descriptions du Si-yu, qui ont été composées en Chinois entre le 5. et le 18. siècle, Nouv. journ. as., X, 1847; also in Mél. de géogr., No. 485.

2901 — —, Listes diverses des noms des 18 écoles schismatiques qui sont sorties du bouddhisme, Journ. as., 5. s., XIV, 1859; also in No. 485.

2902 SYKES, H. W., On a catalogue of Chinese buddhistic works, Journ. of R. A. S., IX, 1848.

2903 Buddhistischer Gottesdienst in China. "Ausland," 1850.

2904 JONES, J. T., Tenets of the buddhists and laws

respecting reverence to their idols in Siam, Chin.
Rep., XIX, p. 548.

2905 SCHIEFNER, A., Ueber die Verschlechterungspe-
rioden der Menschheit nach buddhistischer An-
schauungsweise, Mél. Asiat., I, 1852.

2906 PALLADIUS, O., Historical sketch of ancient Buddhism, Russ. Eccl. Miss., I, No. 2 (in Russian).
German in Abel & Meklenburg's Arbeiten der
Russ. Mission, I (No. 882); also in Erman's Archiv. f. Kunde Russlands.

2907 — — , The life of Buddha; ibid, I, No. 5 (in
Russian).
German in Erman's Archiv. and in No. 882.

2908 GURIUS, O., On Buddhism; ibid, 1853, Vol. II
(in Russian).
German in No. 882.

2909 — — , Vows of the Buddhists; ibid, II, No. 4
(in Russian).
German in No. 882.

2910 STEVENSON, J.. Buddhist antiquities in China,
Journ. of Bombay B. of R. A. S., V, 1855.

2911 EDKINS, J., Notices of Chinese Buddhism. Shanghae, 1855, 8vo.

2912 — — , Notice of the Wu-wei-kiau, a reformed
Buddhist sect, Transact. Ch. Br. R. As. Soc., VI,
1859, p. 63-69.

2913 WASSILYEFF, W., Buddhism, its dogmas. histo-
ry and literature. St. Petersburg, 1857-73, 2
vols., 8vo. (in Russian).
Treats of Northern Buddhism.
Vol. I, 1857: Aperçu of the Himayana and
Mahayana.
French by Le Comte. Paris, 1865, 8vo.
See St. Hilaire, Journ. des Savants,
Sept., 1865.
(Vol. II: not yet published, will contain the
buddhistic dogmas exhibited in a com-
mentary to the terminological dictionary

Maharinpatti, which is found in the 2nd
part of the Tandjur.)
Vol. III, 1873 : History of Buddhism in India,
translated from the Tibetan of Taranatha.
German by Schiefner. St. Petersburg, 1873.
See No. 4240 and No. 4254.
See A. Schiefner, Mél. As., II, 1857; Revue
germ., Dec. 31, 1860; Benfey, Götting.
Gel. Anz., Febr., 1859; St. Hilaire
Journ. des Sav., Févr., 1861.

2914 — — , Buddhist lexicon. St. Petersburg (in
Rusian).

2915 BENFEY, T., Nachweisung einer buddhistischen
Rezension und Mongolischen Bearbeitung der indischen Sammlung von Erzählungen, die unter
dem Namen Vetalapança-vinçati bekannt ist, Mél.
as., III, 1857-59.

2916 Buddhism in India and China, Bibl. Repert., XXXI.
Philadelphia, 1859.

2917 NICOLAS, M., Le Lamaïsme, Revue germ., XII,
1860.

2918 SCHLAGINTWEIT, E., Buddhism in Tibet, illustrated by literary documents and objects of religious worship, with an account of the Buddhist
systems preceding it in India and a folio Atlas
of 20 plates and 20 tables of native print in the
text. Leipzig, 1863, Royal 8vo.
See Journ. d. Savans, May, 1865.

2919 — — , On the bodily proportions of Buddhistic
idols in Tibet, Journ. R. As. Soc., XX, 1863.

2920 — — Ueber die Bon-pa Sekte in Tibet, Sitz.
Ber. Bayer. Akad., I, 1866.

2921 BEAL, S., Text and commentary of the memorials
of Sakya Buddha Tathagata, Journ. of R. A. S.,
XX, 1863.

2922 — — , An attempt to translate from the Chinese
a work known as the confessional services of the
great compassionate Kwan Yin ; ibid, II, 1866.

2923 — — and GOGERLY, D. J., Comparative arrangement of two translations of the Buddhist Ritual for the Priesthood. From the Chinese and from the Pali; ibid, XIX, 1862.

2924 FOUCEAUX, P. E., Le bouddhisme au Tibet. Paris, 1864, 8vo.

2925 The term Omitofu, Notes and Queries, II, p. 14.

2926 MAYERS, W. F., Chinese views respecting the date of introduction of Buddhism; ibid, II, p. 51.

2927 — — , Derivation of the word bonze; ibid, II, p. 79.

2928 — — , The characters San kiai (three words); ibid, III, p. 75.

2929 EITEL, E. J., Amita and the paradise of the West; ibid, II, p. 35.

2930 — — , A buddhist purgatory for woman; ibid, II, p. 66, 82.

2931 — — , The trinity of the buddhists in China; ibid, II, p. 115.

2932 — — , The characters San kai (three words); ibid, III, p. 175.

2933 — — , On dragon workship; ibid, III, p. 34.

2934 — — , Derivation of the terms Su and Mo; ibid, III, p. 45.

2935 — — , A buddhist tract; ibid, III, p. 86.

2936 — — , The svastika of the buddhists v. Thor's hammer; ibid, III, p. 98.

2937 — — , Notes on metempsychosis as taught by Chinese buddhists; ibid, III, p. 113.

2938 — — , The title Ta na; ibid, III, p. 144.

2939 — — , The nirvana of Chinese buddhists, Ch. Recorder, III, p. 1.

2940 — — , Buddhism versus Romanism; ibid, III, p. 142, 181.

2941 — — , Handbook for the student of Chinese Buddhism. Hongkong, 1871, 8vo.
      See Notes and Queries, III, p. 159; J. Edkins, Ch. Recorder, III, p. 215; The Phoenix, I, p. 155.

2942 — — , Three lectures on buddhism. Hongkong, 1871, 8vo.; 2nd ed., 1875, 8vo.
    See S. Beal, The Phoenix, II, p. 34; T. Watters, Ch. Recorder, IV, p. 64.
2943 — — , Buddhismus. "Ausland," 1874, No. 22, 23.
2944 ROSNY, LÉON DE, La parabole bouddhique de l'enfant égaré, Variétés Oriental, 1868.
2945 SAMPSON, T., Buddhist priests in America, Not. & Que., III, p. 78.
2946 WATTERS, T., Buddhism in China, Chin. Rec., II, p. 1, 38, 64, 81, 117, 145.
2947 SUMMERS, J., The buddhistic literature of Tibet. The Phoenix, I, p. 9, 223.
2948 SELBY, T. G., Yau-kwo, Yuk-lik or the purgatories of popular buddhism, China Rev., I, p. 301.
2949 HORNE, CH., On the methods of disposing of the dead at Llasse, Tibet, etc., J. R. As. Soc., new ser., VI, p. 2, 1873.
2950 YULE, H., Northern Buddhism, Oriental Magazine.
2951 HOINOS (GILMOUR, J.), For and against Mongolian Buddhism, Chin. Rec., V, p. 3-17.

3. Mohammedanism. Jews.

2952 GOZANI, Lettre sur les juifs à Kai-fong-fou, 1701; Lettr. Édif. (nouv. éd., XXVII, 1832, p. 266-287).
2953 KOEGLER, P. J., De bibliis Judaeorum Sinensibus, in von Murr's Journal, VII, p. 240 ss.
2954 — — , Versuch einer Geschichte der Juden in Sina. Halle, 1806, 8vo.
2955 GUIGNES, DE (fils), Observations sur plusieurs familles juives établies anciennement à la Chine, Rec. de l'acad. des inscr., XLVIII, 1808.
2956 BRIDGMAN, E. C., Jews in China, Ch. Repos., III, p. 172.
2957 SIONNET, l'Abbé, Essai sur les juifs de la Chine. Paris, 1837.

2958 WRIGHT, T., Israel in China. London, 1842, 12mo.
2959 LOWRIE, W. M., Land of Sinim, or an exposition of Jes., 49, 12, with a brief account of the Jews and Christians in China, Ch. Repos., XIII; also Philadelphia, 1846, 12mo.
2960 A narrative of a mission of inquiry to the jewish synagogue at K'ai fung fu. Shanghai, 1851, with hebrew facsimile.
  See China Repos., XX, p. 436.
2961 FINN, J., The Jews in China. London, 1853, 8vo.
  See Ch. Repos., XIV, p. 305, 388.
2962 — — , The Orphan Colony of Jews in China. London, 1872, 12mo.
2963 Juden in China. Ausland, 1858, No. 8.
2964 Muhammedaner in China; ibid, No. 17.
2965 WYLIE, A., Israelites in China, Ch. and Jap. Repos., I, (1864), p. 13-43.
2966 — — , The jewish roll from K'ai-fung-foo, Notes and Queries, II, p. 159.
2967 Hebrew MS. from K'ai-fung fu; ibid, II, p. 57.
2968 PALLADIUS, O., The Mahometans in China, with a plan of a mosque at Peking, Russ. Eccl. Miss., IV, No. 3, 1866 (in Russian).
2969 WASSILYEFF, W., The movements of mohammedanism in China, 1867 (in Russian).
2970 MORGAN, E. D., On Mohammedanism in China, The Phoenix, II, p. 133, 154.
2971 EDKINS, J., Notes on Mohammedanism in Peking, Ch. Recorder, I, p. 176.
2972 WATTERS, T., Notes on Chinese Mahometan literature, Ch. Review, I, p. 195.
2973 MAYERS, W. F., The Panthays of Yunnan, Fraser's Mag., Oct. 1872.
2974 Das neue Reich der Muhammedaner in Yunnan. "Ausland," 1873, No. 13.

g. Rebellions, Pirates and Secret Societies.

2975 MILNE, W. C., Account of the Triad Society, Journ. of R. A. S., 1826, p. 240; also in Chin. Repos., XII, p. 59. See J. R. A. S., I, p. 93.

2976 MORRISON, J. R., Rise and quelling of the rebellion in Lienchau in 1832, Chin. Repos., I, p. 29-78; III, p. 206, 246.

2977 — — , Secret associations; ibid, I, p. 207.

2978 — R., Pirates, murders, etc.; ibid, I, p. 380.

2979 STEVENS, E., Chinese pirates; ibid, III, p. 62.; IV, p. 518.

2980 — — , Clanships and feuds among the Chinese; ibid, IV, p. 411.

2981 INGLIS, R., Banditti pirates and plots among the Chinese in recent years; ibid, IV, p. 415, 557.

2982 — — , Rebellions of Mohammedans in Turkestan, of the Miautz and other mountaineers; ibid, IV, p. 489.

2983 — — , Rebellion of Jehangir in Turkestan and details of its suppression; ibid, V, p. 316, 351.

2984 BRIDGMAN, E. C., Assistance of government to the distressed and edicts against secret associations; ibid, V, p. 92.

2985a — — , Laws and essays against secret associations; ibid, XIV, p. 69.

2985b NEWBOLD, Lieut. and WILSON, The Chinese Triad Society or the Tien-ti-huih, J. R. A. S., Vol. VI, p. 120.

2986 Proceedings of secret societies at Singapore, Ch. Repos., XV, p. 400.

2987 WILLIAMS, S. W., Translation of the oath of the Triad Society; ibid, XVIII, p. 281.

2988 — — , Insurgents in Kwangsi; ibid, XX, p. 53, 111, 224, 286, 492.

2989 Correspondence relating to pirates; ib., XVIII, p. 558.

2990 SCOTT, B., An account of the destruction of the fleets of the celebrated pirate chieftains Chu-apoo and Shap-ng-tsai on the.coast of China. London, 1851, 8vo.

2991 ROETTGER, E. H., Tien-ti-hoih, Geschichte der
Brüderschaft des Himmels und der Erde. Berlin,
1852, 8vo.
> See Hoffmann, Period. of R. Institute f. Ne-
> therl. India, 1853, No. 3; and II, p. 292.

2992 MACFARLANE, C., The Chinese revolution. London, 1853, 8vo.

2993 MEDHURST, W. H. (sen.), Pamphlets issued by
insurgents at Nanking. Shanghai, 1853, 8vo.
(from the N. C. Herald).

2994 CALLERY et YVAN, L'insurrection en Chine depuis
son origine jusqu'à la prise de Nankin. Paris,
1853, 8vo.
> German by R. Otto. Braunschweig, 1854,
> 12mo.
> English by J. Oxenford. London, 1854, 8vo.

2995 Observations on the cause of the rebellion, Overland Register, 1853; China Mail, 1853.

2996 Papers respecting the civil war in China, Pres. to
the House of Lords, 1853, fol.

2997 The book of the Taiping wang dynasty. Shanghai,
1853, 8vo.

2998 The Chinese revolution, the causes which led to it,
its rapid progress and anticipated result. London, 1853, 8vo.

2999 BIERNATZKI, K. L., Die gegenwärtige politisch-
religiöse Bewegung in China. Berlin, 1854,
8vo.

3000 A history of China to the present time, including an
account of the rise and progress of the present
religious insurrection. London, 1854, 8vo.

3001 Religion of the Chinese rebels, Quat. Review, No. 187.
German in Ausland, 1854, No. 11.

3002 HAMBERG, T., The visions of Hung-siu-tsuen,
and the origin of the Kwang-see insurrection.
Hongkong, 1854, 8vo.; reprinted in Chin. and
Jap. Repos., I.

3003 — — , The Chinese rebel chief and the origin of

the insurrection in China, with an introduction by G. Pearse. London, 1855, 8vo.

3004 FISHBOURNE, Capt., Impressions of China and the present revolution. London, 1855, 8vo.

3005 KRONE, R., Gegenwärtiger Stand der Revolution in China, Petersmann's geogr. Mitth., XI, XII, 1856.

3006 MEADOWS, T. T., The Chinese and their rebellions. London, 1856, 8vo.

3007 NEUMARK, S., Die Revolution in China und ihre Entstehung nach Meadows. Berlin, 1857, 8vo.
See the preceding work.

3008 Die geheimen Gesellschaften der Chinesen in und ausser China. Ausland, 1857, No. 34.

3009 MACKIE, J. M., Life of Tai-ping-wang, chief of the Chinese insurrection. New York, 1857, 8vo.
See Gött. gel. Anz., 1858, No. 38-40, p. 383-387.

3010 LOVIOT, E., Les pirates Chinois. Paris, 1860, 8vo.

3011 JOHN, G., The Chinese rebellion. Canton, 1861, 8vo.

3012 BRINE, L., The Taiping rebellion in China. London, 1862, 8vo.
See Petermann's geogr. Mitth., 1863, V, p. 196.

3013 WOLSELEY, G. J., Narrative of the war with China in 1860, to which is added the account of a short residence with the Taiping rebels at Nankin. London, 1862, 8vo.
See Biernatzki in Gött. gel. Anz., 1863, p. 1401-16.

3014 SYKES, W. H., The Taiping rebellion in China, its origin, progress and present condition. London, 1863, 8vo.
See Petermann's geogr. Mitth., 1863, p. 196.

3015 HAUSSMANN, A., La Chine, Résumé de l'insurrection et des événements qui ont eu lieu dans ce pays depuis le commencement de la guerre de l'opium jusqu'en 1857. Paris, 1864, 8vo.

3016 OLIPHANT, L., A visit to the Taipings, "Good Words," 1863, March.

3017 CLAVELIN, Un missionnaire au milieu des Taipings, Études rel., hist. et litt., T. II (1863), p. 136.

3018 RENARD, L'insurrection chinoise, Le Correspondant, N. S., 1863, T. 23, p. 247-279.

3019 L'insurrection des Taë-pings en Chine, Revue mar. et col., 1862, Sept., p. 37-51.

3020 Der Charakter des Taiping Aufstandes in China. Ausland, 1863, No. 4.

3021 Ein deutscher Missionär und Arzt über die Taiping-insurgenten. Ausland, 1863, No. 10.

3022 LAY, W. T., The autobiography of the Chung Wang. Shanghai, 1865, 8vo., 104 pp.

3023 Political associations, feuds, etc., in China, Ch. and Jap. Repos., III (1865), p. 272-280.

3024 The fall of the city of Chinkiang-fu; ibid, p. 449-452.

3025 Lin-Le, Ti-Ping Tien-Kwoh, the history of the Ti-Ping revolution, including a narrative of the author's personal adventures. London, 1866, 2 vols., 8vo.
See Athenaeum, 1866, Sept. 8, p. 295; Lit. Centralbl., 1868, No. 7, p. 160.

3026 SCHLEGEL, G., The Hung-league or Heaven and Earth League. Batavia, 1866, 4to.
See W. Schott. Ausland, 1868, No. 1, p. 11; Notes and Queries, II, p. 79.

3027 MARTHE, F., Der Aufstand der Muhammedaner im westlichen China, Ztschr. Der Ges. f. Erdk. Berlin, 1867, p. 142.

3028 JAMIESON, Note on the coinage of the Tai-ping or Great-Peace Dynasty, Numism. Chron., No. XXI (1866, I,) p. 66.

3029 PFIZMAIER, A., Bericht über zwei Taiping-Münzen, Sitz. ber. der Wiener Ak. der Wiss, Philos.-hist. LII (1866), p. 424-426; also 1866, 8vo.

3030 FORREST, R. T., The christianity of Hung-tsin-

tsuen, Journ. N. C. B. R. A. S., IV, p. 187-208.
3031 MINCHIN, G., The origin of the Tien-ti hwui, Notes and Queries, III, p. 55.
3032 WILSON, A., The ever victorious army, A history of the Chinese campaign under Gordon. London, 1868, 8vo., with 6 maps.
3033 Die innern Wirren in China. Ausland, 1872, No. 9, p. 202.
3034 MAYERS, W. F., The Panthays in Yunnan, Fraser's Magaz., Oct., 1872.
3035 HUGHES, G., The small Knife rebels, Ch. Review, I, p. 244.
3036 — — , The capture of Chang-Chou Fu by rebels; ibid, I, p. 348.
3037a WENYUKOFF, The Muhammedan rebellion on the Russian-chinese frontier, 'Iswestija' imp. russ. geogr. soc., IX, 1873 (in Russian).
3037b YATES, M. T., The Taiping Rebellion. Shanghai, 1876, 8vo.

h. Emigrants and Chinese Colonies.

3038 Chinese emigrants, Ch. Rep., II, p. 230 ss.
3039 BOACHI, A., Notizen über die Chinesen auf der Insel Java. Zeitschr. d. Deutsch. Morg. Ges., IX, p. 808 ss.
3040 LOOMIS, A., Remarks of the Chinese merchants of San Francisco upon Brigler's message. San Francisco, 1855, 8vo.
3041 Die Auswanderung der Chinesen zur See. "Ausland," 1857, No. 35.
3042 BENJAMIN, J. J., Drei Jahre in Amerika. Leipzig, 1859, 8vo. (p. 310 ss., On Chinese in America.)
3043 MINCHIN, G., The population of Chinese residents in the Straits, Not. & Quer., II, p. 93.
3044 LOBSCHEID, W., Chinese emigration to the West Indies. Hongkong, 1870, 8vo.
3045 THIERSAULT, P. D. DE, De l'émigration chi-

noise, Rev. Mar. et Col., Déc. 1871, p. 877.

3046 MADIER DE MONTJAU, E., De l'émigration des Chinois au point de vue des intérêts européens. Paris, 1873, 8vo.

3047 The emigration convention of 1866, China Review, I, p. 63-70, 141-144.

3048a MARKHAM, C. R., On the condition of Chinese coolies in Peru.
See Anti-slavery Reporter, Sept., 1875.

3048b RATZEL, F., Die Chinesische Auswanderung, ein Beitrag zur Cultur-und Handels geographie. Breslau, 1876, 8vo., 272 pp.

XIV. Intercourse with Foreigners.
a. Political.
1. Foreign Embassies to the Court of Peking.

1. *Russian:* BAIKOFF, 1654.

3049 Voyage d'un ambassadeur Russe à la Chine, Rec. de Voy. Paris, 1681, 8vo.; also in Bernard's Recueil (No. 1457), Vol. IV.

3050 Reise eines moscowitischen Gesandten nach China in Müller, Abd. Beidaw. Hist. sin., 1689. See Dudgeon, Chin. Rec., 1874, p. 28 ss.

3051 Relatio ablegationis quam Czarea Majestas ad Catayensem Chamum Bogdi destinavit anno 1653 in Thevenot Rec. de Voy. Paris, 1696, I.

2. *Dutch:* P. DE GOYER and J. KAYSER, 1655-56.

3052 NIEWHOF, J., Gesandschap der Nederl. Oost-Indische Compagnie aen den grooten Tatarischen Cham, den Keyzer van China. Amsterdam, 1665, fol.
French by J. le Charpentier Leyden, 1665. Paris, 1666, fol.
German: Amsterdam, 1666, 4to.; English by

J. Ogilby. London, 1669, fol.; 2nd ed.,
1673, fol., 431 pp., maps, illustr.; Latin :
1670, fol.

3053 Voyages des ambassadeurs de la compagnie hollandaise des Ind. Orient., envoyés l'an 1656 en la
Chine, Thevenot's Coll., Pt. III.

3054 ADAMS, J., Letter on the Dutch Embassy to China,
1655, in Ogilby's Edition of Niewhof, p. 299-317
(No. 3052.)

3. *Dutch :* P. van HOORN, 1664.

3055 DAPPER, O., Gedenkwärdig Bedryf der nederländ.
Oost. Indische Mötschapye of de Kuste en in het
Keyserriyk van Tainsing of Sina. Amsterdam,
1670, 2 vols., fol.
English by Ogilby. London, 1671, 2 vols.,
fol.
German : Amsterdam, 1674, 2 vols., fol.

4. *Russian :* EVERT YSBRANTS IDES, 1692-1694.

3056 BRAND, A., Beschreibung seiner chinesischen Reise,
welche er anno, 1692-1694 in der Suite des
Herrn Ev. Ys. Ides von Moscow über Sibirien
nach China gethan. Frankfurt, 1697 ; Berlin,
1712 ; Lübeck, 1723 ; ibid, 1734.
French : Amsterdam, 1699, 12mo.; Dutch,
Tiel, 1699. Amsterdam, 1704 ; English : 1706, 8vo.

3057 IDES, E. Y., Driejaarige Reize naar China, etc.
Amsterdam, 1704, 4to. ; ibid, 1710, 4to., 243 pp.,
map, illustr.
English: London, 1706, 4to., Three years' Travels from Moscow overland to China
through Great Ustiga, etc. to Peking,
containing an exact and particular description of the extent and limits of those
countries and the customs, etc. of the
barbarous inhabitants. Written by H.

E. Ev. Ys. Ides, ambassador from the
Czar of Moscovy to the emperor of China.
Printed in Dutch and now faithfully done
into English. See William's Chin. Rep.,
VIII, p. 520.
German : Frankfurt, 1707, 8vo.; French in
Rec. de voy. au Nord. Amsterdam, VIII,
1727 (No. 1457).
    5. *French :* 1698-1699.
3058 GHIRARDINI, G., Relation du voyage fait à la
Chine en 1698 sur le vaisseau l'Amphitrite. Pa-
ris, 1700, 12mo.
3059 BANNISTER, S., A journal of the first French embassy to China, 1698-1700. London, 1859, 8vo.
    6. *Russian :* L. LANGE, 1715.
3060 LANGE, L., Tagebuch zweier Reisen nach China.
In "Ietziger Staat von Russland," II, 1780 ; also
separately Leipzig, 1781, 8vo ; also in Pallas'
Neue Nord. Beitr., II, 1781.
English by Dudgeon. Chin. Rec., III, p. 12.
    7. *Russian :* Count WASSILJEFF ISMAILOFF, 1719.
3061 LANGE, L., Voyage in 1719, etc. (in German),
"Ietziger Staat von Russland," II, 1780.
3062 — — , Journal du Sieur Lange contenant ses
negotiations à la cour de Chine. Leyden, 1726 ;
also in Rec. de Voy. au Nord, Vols. V and VIII,
1727 (No. 1457).
3063 UNVERZAGT, J. G., Die Gesandtschaft Ihro Kais.
Maj. von Gross Russland an den Sinensischen
Kaiser, 1719, von St. Petersburg nach Peking.
Lübeck, 1721 ; ibid, 1727, 8vo.
3064 BELL, J., Travels from St. Petersburg in Asia.
Glasgow, 1763, 2 vols., 4to., map.
    8. *Russian :* L. LANGE, 1727-1728.
3065 LANGE, L., Tagebuch einer Karavanenreise von
Kiachta nach Peking, 1727, Pallas' Neue Nord.
Beitr., II, 1781.
English by Dudgeon in Hist. Sketch of the

Rel. of Russia with China. Shanghai,
1872, Append.

9. *Russian:* L. LANGE, 1736-1737.

3066 LANGE, L., Tagebuch einer Reise von Zuruchaitu
durch die Mongolei nach Peking, 1736-37, Pallas'
Neue Nord. Beitr., II, 1781.

10. *English:* Lord MACARTNEY, 1792-1794.

3067 ANDERSON, A., A narrative of the British embassy
to China. London, 1795, 4to.
German: Hamburg, 1796, 8vo.

3068 STAUNTON, Sir G., Authentic account of Lord
Marcartney's Embassy to the emperor of China.
London, 1797, 2 vols., 4to., Atlas fol.; also 3 vols.,
8vo.
See Chin. Rep., II, 1833, p. 337-350.
German: Berlin, 1798, 3 vols., 16mo.
French: Paris, 1804, 5 vols., 8vo., Atlas.
Russian: St. Petesburg, 1804, 4 vols.

3069 — —, An historical account of the embassy to
the emperor of China. London, 1797, 8vo.
French by Castera. Paris, 1798, 8vo.

3070 — —, An abridged account of the Embassy to
the Emperor of China. London, 1797, 8vo.

3071 HUETTNER, J. G., Nachrichten von der britischen
Gesandtschaftsreise nach China. Berlin, 1797,
8vo.
French: Paris, 1800, 18mo.

3072 HOLMES, S., The journal of, during his attendance
on Lord Macartney's embassy to China. London,
1798, 12mo.

3073 — —, Travels in China and in Tartary in the
suite of L. Macartney. London, 1803, 2 vols., 8vo.
French: Paris, 1805, 2 vols., 8vo., 25 engr.
German in Sprengel & Ehrmann's Bibl. d.
Reisen, XXVIII.

3074 BARROW, J., Travels in China. London, 1804,
4to., Atlas.
French: Paris, 1805, 3 vols., 8vo.

See C. L. J. de Guignes, Observations sur le voyage de Barrow à la Chine. Paris, 1809.

German : Weimar, 1804, 2 vols., 8vo., maps, illustr.; Dutch : Haarlem, 1807-9, 3 vols., 8vo.

11. *Dutch:* J. TITZING, 1794-1795.

3075 BRAAM, A. E. van, Voyage de la Compagnie des Indes Orientales Hollandaise vers l'empereur de la Chine dans les années 1794 et 1795, tiré du journal d'André Everard van Braam Houkjest. Publié en français par M. de Saint Méry. Philadelphia, 1797, 4to.; also 2 vols., 8vo.

English : London, 1798, 2 vols., 8vo.; German: Leipzig, 1799, 2 vols., 8vo.; Dutch : Harlem, 1804, 8vo.

12. *Russian:* 1805-1806, Count GOLOVKIN.

3076 Authentische Nachrichten von der Russischen Gerandtschaft nach China im Jahre 1805 und 1806 ; Allgem. Geogr. Ephemerid., XX. Weimar, 1806.

3077 Die russische Gesandtschaft nach China im Jahre 1805. St. Petersburg und Leipzig, 1809, 8vo.

13. *English:* Lord AMHERST, 1816.

3078 ELLIS, H., Journal of L. Amherst's embassy to China, with observations on the policy of the Chinese. London, 1817, 4to.

French : Paris, 1818, 2 vols., 8vo. See A. Rémusat, Mél. As., I, p. 431-451.

3079 — — , Journal of the proceedings of the late embassy to China. London, 1818, 2 vols., 8vo. ; 2nd ed., 1840, 8vo.

3080 CLARK, A., Narrative of a journey in the interior of China and of a voyage to and from that country in the year 1816 and 1817, containing an account of the most interesting transactions of L. Amherst's embassy. London, 1818, 8vo.

3081 MORRISON, R., A memoir of the principal occurrences during an embassy from the British govern-

ment to the court of China. London, 1819, 8vo.
See also "The Pamphleteer," XXIX, c. f.;
As. Journ., VIII, p. 561-582.

3082 STAUNTON, Sir G., Notes on proceedings and
occurrences during the British embassy to Peking
in 1816. London, 1824, 8vo.

14. *Russian:* TIMKOVSKY, 1820-1821.

3083 TIMKOVSKY, Puteschvestvie v Kitaï perez Mon-
goliu 1820-21 (Voyage to China via Mongolia).
St. Petersburg, 1824, 3 vols., 8vo., map (in Russian).
German by J. A. E. Schmidt. Leipzig,
1825-26, 3 vols., 8vo.
French by Eyriès and Klaproth. Paris,
1827, 2 vols., 8vo., atlas.

15. *American:* CUSHING, 1844.

3084 BRIDGMAN, E. C., Message from the President
of the U. S. America transmitting treaty and
detail of Cushing's proceedings, Chin. Rep., XIV,
p. 353, 410, 487, 525.

16. *French:* M. DE LAGRENÉ, 1843-44.

3085 FERRIÈRE LE VAYER, T. DE, Une ambassade
française en Chine, Journal de voyage. Paris,
1854, 8vo.

17. *Russian:* Count PUTIATIN, 1857-58.

3086 Gesandtschaftsreise nach China und Japan. "Ausland," 1858, No. 43.

18. *English:* Lord ELGIN'S First Mission, 1857-58.

3087 OLIPHANT, L., Narrative of the Earl of Elgin's
mission to China and Japan. Edinburgh, 1859,
2 vols., 8vo.
French by Guizot. Paris, 1860, 2 vols.,
8vo. See Journ. As., 5. sér., XV, p. 278.

19. *French:* Baron GROS, 1857-58.

3088 CHASSIRON, BARON C. DE, Notes sur le Japon,
la Chine et l'Inde. Paris, 1861, 8vo.

3089 MOGES, DE, Souvenirs d'une ambassade en Chine.
Paris, 1859, 12mo.

3090 Negotiations entre la France et la Chine en 1860,
Livre jaune du baron Gros. Paris, 1864, 4to.
See Journ. des Sav., Dec., 1864, p. 793.
20. *English*: Lord ELGIN'S Second Mission, 1860.

3091 LOCH, H. B., Personal narrative of occurrences during L. Elgin's second embassy to China. London, 1870, 8vo.
See "The Phoenix," I, p. 103.

3092 Letters and journals of James, 8th Earl of Elgin,
edited by Walrood. London, 1872, 8vo.
21. *American*: J. E. WARD, 1859.

3093 WILLIAMS, S. W., Narrative of the American
embassy to Peking, J. N. Ch. Br. R. As. Soc., I,
p. 315-349.
22. *Prussian*: Count EULENBURG, 1861-62.

3094 SPIESS, G., Die preussische Expedition nach Ostasien. Leipzig, 1863, 8vo. See Lit. Centralbl.,
1864, No. 27; 1865, No. 12, p. 317.

3095 WERNER, R., Reisebriefe, Die preussische Expedition nach Ostasien, 1860-62. Leipzig, 1863, 2
vols., 8vo.; 2nd ed., 1873. See Lit. Centralbl.,
1863, No. 28, p. 655; J. G. Kohl in Gött. Gel.
Anz., 1863, No. 34, p. 1821-41.

3096 MARON, H., Japan und China. Berlin, 1863, 2
vols., 8vo. See Quart. Rev., 1864, Oct., p. 449;
China Mail, 1864, May 5; Augsb. Allg. Z., 1864,
No. 266. .

3097 KREYHER, J., Die preussische Expedition nach
Ostasien, Reisebilder aus Japan, China und Siam.
Hamburg, 1863, 8vo., 428 pp.

3098 WICHURA, M., Aus vier Welttheilen. Breslau,
1866, 8vo.

3099 BIRG, A., Ansichten aus Japan, China und Siam.
Berlin.

3100 SCHOBER, G., Erinnerung an Preussens ostasiatische Expedition. Danzig, 1863, 8vo.

3101 Amtlicher Bericht des dei Kgl. preussische Expedition nach Ostasien begleitenden Kgl. sächs. Com-

missars. Wissensch. Beilage d. Leipz. Zeitg.,
1862, No. 5-10, 14.

3102 Die preussische Expedition nach Ostasien, nach amt-
lichen Quellen. Berlin, 1864-1873, 4 vols., 8vo.,
maps, 48 illustr.

> Sec Lit. Centralbl., 1866, p. 108; Kohl in
> Gött. Gel. Anz., 1867, p. 1161-73; L.
> de Rosny, Journ. As., 1867, IX, p. 421;
> Westm. and For. Quart. Rev., No. 164,
> April, 1865.

2. Political Relations, Treaties.

3103 Idée générale de la Chine et de ses premières relations avec l'Europe, Mém. Conc., V, p. 1.

3104 Honneurs rendus par l'empereur de Chine aux Européens; ibid, VIII, p. 283.

3105 LANGLÈS, L. M., Observations sur les relations
politiques et commerciales de l'Angleterre et de la
France avec la China. Paris, 1805, 8vo.

3106 DUHANCILLY, Massacre de l'équipage du vaisseau
français le Navigateur, Exécution des assassins à
Canton, Journ. des Voyag., 1829, p. 109-117.

3107 KING, C. W., Intercourse with China, Chin. Rep.,
I, p. 141.

3108 — — , British intercourse with China. London,
1836, 8vo.

3109 — — , Outline of a consular establishment in
Eastern Asia for the U. S., Chin. Rep., VI, p. 69,
497.

3110 — — , Desirableness of a treaty with China;
ibid, IV, p. 441.

3111 — — , Queries to be asked respecting American
intercourse in Eastern Asia; ibid, VII, p. 206.

3112 — — , Review of the differences between the
English and Chinese authorities; ibid, VIII, p.
446, 529.

> See R. B. Forbes, ibid, VIII, p. 532.

3132 — — , Outrages committed on Americans in 1841; ibid, X, p. 415.

3133 — — , Notes of a trip up the river to Canton in U. S. S. "Constellation"; ibid, XI, p. 329.

3134 — — , Causes which may lead to a second war with China; ibid, XIV, p. 545.

3135 — — , Treaty at Wanghia; ibid, XIV, p. 30.

3136 — — , Annual provision made for the support of the widow and mother of Sü-Amun by the person who killed him; ibid, XV, p. 307.

3137 — — , Notices of the Danish man-of-war "Galathea" on a cruise around the world; ibid, XV, p. 461.

3138 — — , Prohibitions forbidding other foreigners than merchants to reside at Canton; ib., XV, p. 561.

3139 — — , Particulars of Sir J. F. Davis's 'Demonstration' on China; ibid, XVI, p. 182, 252, 366, 415.

3140 — — , Particulars of an attack on 3 missionaries near Shanghai; ibid, XVII, p. 151, 340, 461.

3141 MORRISON, R., Edict disallowing sedans to foreigners; ibid, II, p. 233.

3142 — — , Thoughts on the conduct of the Chinese government towards the E. I. Co.; ibid, VIII, p. 615.

3143 GODDART, J., Free trade with the Chinese; ibid, II, p. 355, 473.

3144 Correspondence between the E. I. Co.'s select committee and the government of Canton; ibid, II, p. 513.

3145 British relation with the Chinese empire. London, 1832, 8vo.

3146 NEUMANN, K. F., Die Chinesen und die Engländer. Allg. Preuss. Staatsz., 1832, No. 35.

3147 — — , Das Chinesische Reich, die gegenwärtigen Zustände desselben und seine Stellung zu den Vertragsmächten. "Unsere Zeit," I, 1857, p. 673.

3148 MORRISON, J. R., Early foreign intercourse with China, Chin. Rep., III, p. 107.

3149 — — , Relation of England towards China and the duty of the former to learn her history; ibid, VI, p. 244, 249.

3150 — — , Edict requiring foreigners to leave Canton; ibid, VI, p. 296.

3151 Communications respecting intercourse with China by merchants in Canton; ibid, III, p. 393.

3152 MARJORIBANKS, C., Letter to the R. H. Ch. Grant on the present state of British intercourse with China. London, 1833, 8vo.

3153 Remarks on British relation and intercourse with China, by an American merchant. London, 1834, 8vo.

3154 ABBOT, J., China and the English. Boston, 1835, 12mo.

3155 Capt. Elliot at Canton, Chin. Rep., V, p. 422, 527; VI, p. 352; VIII, p. 321.

3156 STAUNTON, Sir G., Remarks on the British relations with China. London, 1836, 8vo.
See E. C. Bridgman, Chin. Rep., V, p. 241.

3157 LINDSAY, H. H., Letter to the R. H. Visc. Palmerston on British relations with China. London, 1836, 8vo.
See E. C. Bridgman, Chin. Rep., V, p. 241.

3158 WILLIAMS, S. W., Jargon spoken in foreign intercourse at Canton, Chin. Rep., IV, p. 428.

3159 — — , Emperor's rescript on peace and a manifest against the English at Canton; ibid, XI, p. 627.

3160 — — , Riot and burning of the English Consulate; ibid, XI, p. 687.

3161 — — , Disturbances at Canton and death of Sü-Amun caused by an American; ibid, XIII, p. 333.

3162 — — , Interview between Gov. Gen. Sü and H. E. J. W. Davis in 1848; ibid, XVII, p. 540.

3163 — — , Combinations and preparations to prevent entrance of English into Canton and question of entry into the city considered; ibid, XVIII, p. 162, 216, 335.

3164 KEATING, A. S., Former English embassies to China; ibid, V, p. 518; VI, p. 17.

3165 Correspondence between the E. I. and China Association and the government of Great Britain; ibid, VI, p. 301.

3166 LAY, G. T., Remarks on diplomatic agency in China; ibid, VII, p. 141.

3167 SLADE, J., Narrative of the late proceedings and events in China. London, 1839, 8vo.

3168 Debates in parliament and blue book, Chin. Rep., VIII, p. 107, 241, 321; IX, p. 414.

3169 Memorial to Lord Palmerston from British merchants; ibid, VIII, p. 266.

3170 Petition of American merchants in Canton; ibid, IX, p. 53.

3171 CHEVALIER, L'Europe et la Chine. Paris, 1840, 8vo.

3172 YOUNG, The English in China. London, 1840, 8vo.
See Chin. Rep., XII, p. 8.

3173 Review of the management of our affairs in China, and the government despatches from 1836-39. London, 1840, 8vo.

3174 URBAN, F. D', La Chine et l'Angleterre. Paris, 1840-43, 3 pts., 12mo.

3175 PHILIPP, R., Peace with China. London, 1840, 8vo.

3176 — — , The Star of China. London, 1845, 8vo.

3177 Retrospection or a review of public occurrences in China from Jan. 1832 to Dec. 1841, Chin. Rep., X, p. 1, 65, 121, 185, 241, 297, 345, 401, 457, 521, 577, 672.

3178 SHUCK, J. L., Two propositions on the best mode of exterminating the English; ibid, X, p. 531.

3179 Gough's despatches; ibid, X, p. 535; XI, p. 148, 496; XII, p. 248, 341, 464.

3180 VOCKERODE, T., China mit besondrer Rücksicht auf die Verhältnisse der Europäer zu diesem Reich. Leipzig, 1842, 8vo.

3181 LOBÉ, La Chine et l'Europe. Amsterdam, 1843, 8vo.

3182 DILLON, Conquest of Siberia and the history of the transactions, wars, commerce, etc. carried on between Russia and China. London, 1843, 8vo.

3183 RÉMUSAT, A., Mémoire sur les avantages d'un établissement consulaire à Canton, Mél. Posth., 1843, p. 459 ss.

3184 Present condition of the Chinese empire, Chin. Rep., XII, p. 1.

3185 Items of the supplementary treaty, Chin. Rep., XII, p. 556; XIII, p. 449.

3186 Items of the American treaty of Wanghia; ibid, XIII, p. 500.

3187 MEDHURST, W. H. (sen.), Translation of the supplementary treaty; ibid, XIII, p. 143.

3188 — — , Translation of the treaty of Nanking; ibid, XIV, p. 26.

3189 CUSHING, C., Considerations on the language of communication between the Chinese and European governments; ibid, XIII, p. 181.

3190 Treaty of Nanking in English and Chinese; ibid, XIII, p. 438.

3191 Treaty of Whampoa; ibid, XIV, p. 41; XV, p. 10.

3192 Chinese account in the Ta-thsing Hwei-tien of foreign embassies to the court of Peking; ibid, XIV, p. 152.

3193 Letter from Pres. Tyler to the emperor of China; ibid, XIV, 542.

3194 The treaty of the U. S. with China; ibid, XIV, p. 353-377, 410-423, 487-493, 525-539, 555-583.

3195 Regulations agreed on for securing the safety of foreigners in Canton; ibid, XV, p. 104.

3196 Correspondence regarding the riot of July 1846; ibid, XV, p. 572, 534, 554; XVI, p. 382, 425.
3197 Interview between Kiying and A. H. Everett; ibid, XV, p. 624.
3198 LAVOLLÉ, C., Situation actuelle des Européens en Chine. Paris, 1846, 8vo.
3199 — — , Traités de Pékin, Revue des deux mondes, 1. Août, 1865, p. 697-731.
3200 Representation of the elders and gentry of Honan to the British consul at Canton, Chin. Rep., XVI, p. 366, 415.
3201 Official correspondence respecting seizure of the murderers of W. M. Lowrie; ibid, XVI, p. 607; XVII, p. 484.
3202 Murder of British subjects at Hwang-chuh-ki and papers relating thereto; ibid, XVI, p. 611; XVII, p. 54, 152.
3203 URMSTON, J. B., Chusan and Hongkong, with remarks on the treaty of peace at Nanking in 1842, and on our present position and relations with China. London, 1847, 8vo.
3204 Act of congress conferring powers on the American commissioners and consuls to China, Chin. Rep., XVII, p. 540.
3205 SPEER, W., Notices of the ancient intercourse with China through Central Asia and Chinese account of Jesus Christ; ibid, XVIII, p. 485.
3206 Letters from the imper. commissioner Ho and other Chinese authorities relating to the foreign Customs establishment. Shanghai, 8vo.
3207 Correspondence between the government of China and the legation of the U. S. relative to smuggling, Chin. Rep., XX, p. 468.
3208 DAVIS, Sir J. F., China during the war and since the peace. London, 1852, 2 vols., 8vo.
3209 MÉRY, Anglais et Chinois. Paris, 1853, 12mo.
3210 KELLY, F., A letter to Lord Lyndhurst on the late debate upon China. London, 1857, 8vo.

3211 MARS, V. DE, La question chinoise, Rev. d. deux Mond., 1857, IX, p. 481-534.

3212 QUINCY, T. DE, China. "Titan," XXIV, 1857; Complete works, XVI, p. 227-254.

3213 The rational of the Chinese question, by an American. Macao, 1857, 4to.

3214 AUBE, La Chine à la veille de la guerre. Paris, 1857, 8vo.

3215 Six Letters of an outside barbarian. Edinburgh, 1857, 8vo.

3216 HAUSSMANN, A., La Chine, résumé historique de l'insurrection et des événements depuis le commencement de la guerre de l'opium jusq' en 1857. Paris, 1858, 4to.

3217 MAS, Don S. DE, L'Angleterre, la Chine et l'Inde. Paris, 1858, 8vo.

3218 — — , La Chine et les puissances Chrétiennes. Paris, 1861, 8vo.

3219 OSBORN, S., The past and future of British relations in China. Edinburgh, 1860, 8vo.

3220 The Englishman in China. London, 1860, 12mo.

3221 LAVALLÉ, La Chine contemporaine. Paris, 1860, 8vo.

3222 BEAUVERGER, E. DE, Considération sur le passé et l'avenir de la Chine, Séanc. et Trav. de l'Ac. des Sc. Mor. et Pol., 1862.

3223 VARANNES, A. DE, La Chine depuis le traité de Pékin, Rev. d. deux mond., 1863, XLIV, p. 857-895.

3224 LAING, S., India and China, England's mission in the East. London, 1863, 8vo.

3225 ESCAYRAC DE LAUTURE, Thoughts on the past and the future of China, Chin. and Jap. Rep., I, 1863, p. 33-36, 70-77.

3226 Der Englische Finanzbeamte des Prinz-Regenten von China. "Ausland," 1863, No. 5.

3227 SUMMERS, J., Notices of the political aspect of

affairs in China and Japan, Chin. & Jap. Rep., I, 1863, p. 94-96, 132-138.

3228 The Lay-Osborne expedition to China; ibid, Jan. & Febr., 1864.

3229 LAY, H. N., Our interests in China. London, 1864, 8vo.
    See Westm. Rev., vol. 83, April, 1865, p. 594.

3230 GIQUEL, P., La France en Chine, le commerce français dans le Céleste Empire, le corps franco-chinois et les missions catholiques à la fin de 1863, Rev. d. deux mond., 15 Juin 1864, p. 962-993.

3231 — — , La politique française en Chine; ibid, March, 1872.

3232 JAMIESON, R. A., Retrospect of events in the north of China during the years 1861-1864, J. N. Ch. Br. R. As. S., 1865, p. 109-132.

3233 HART, R., Notes on Chinese matter.

3234 Du rôle de la France dans les mers de la Chine et du Japon du Thée-Ta-Iin, mandarin militaire européen, Revue d'Orient., 1865; also separately. Paris, 1865, 8vo.

3235 BRIDGES, J. H., England and China. London, 1866, 8vo.
    See "Reader," 1866, No. 190, p. 726.

3236 IVISSON, M., Études sur la Chine contemporaine. Paris, 1866, 8vo.
    See Westm. Rev., XXX, No. 169, July 1866, p. 255; G. Claudin in "Moniteur," 24. Jan., 1867.

3237 FRIEDEL, E., Die Gründung preussisch-deutscher Colonien im indischen und grossen Ocean. Berlin, 1867, 8vo.

3238 Reception and entertainment of the Chinese embassy by the city of Boston. Boston, 1868, 8vo., 77 pp.

3239 Memorials addressed to H. E. the British Minister on the approach of the revision of the Treaty of Tientsin and Sir Rutherford Alcock's Reply. Shanghai, 1868, 8vo.

3240 The new treaty between the U. S. and China, Chin. Rec., II, p. 228.

3241 Addresses presented by the American and British communities of Shanghai to the Hon. J. Ross Browne, U. S. Minister and H. E.'s reply, together with a letter addressed by Mr. Browne to Prince Kung regarding material progress in China. Shanghai, 1869, 8vo.

3242 GIRARD, O., France et Chine. Paris, 1869, 2 vols., 8vo.

3243 ROBERTSON, J. B., Three letters addressed to the "Daily News" on the political situation in China. Shanghai, 1869, 8vo.

3244 — — , The Chinese embassy to England, "Daily News," 28th Febr., 1868.

3245 — — , Our policy in China. Westm. Rev., Jan., 1870, p. 182.

3246 BUTCHER, C. H., Our countrymen in China, Chin. Rec., II, p. 13.

3247 The reception of Chinese envoys in Europe, Not. & Quer., III, p. 49.

3248 Zur Colonisation Formosa's, Globus, XVII, 1870, p. 217.

3249 MACDONALD, J., The China question. London, 1870, 8vo.

3250 BUTIN, Historical sketch of the relation of the Russians to China, "Iswestija" Sib. Imp. Russ. Geo. Soc., 1870, No. 5 (in Russian).

3251 Lin-tse-Sin, ein chinesischer Staatsmann, der Urheber des englisch-chinesischen Krieges 1840, Petermann's Mitth., 1870, p. 460. See "Iswestija" Russ. Imp. Geo. Soc., VI, p. 143.

3252 Foreign influence in China, Chin. Rec., IV, p. 126.

3253 British policy in China, by a Shanghai merchant. London 1871, 8vo., 51 pp.

3254 CANNY, J. M., Retrospect of events in China and Japan during the years 1869 and 1870, J. N. Ch. Br. R. As. Soc., 1871, p. 179-200.

3255 GUMPACH, J. von, The Burlingame mission, a political disclosure. Shanghai, 1872, 8vo.

3256 — , The tonnage dues fund, the harbour of Shanghai and the Wusung bar, reprinted from the Shanghai Evening Courier. Shanghai, 1873, 8vo., 46 pp.

3257 — — , The treaty rights of the foreign merchant and the transit system in China, etc., etc. Shanghai, 1875, 8vo., XVIII, 421 pp.

3258 MEDHURST, W. H. (jun.), The foreigner in Far Cathay. London, 1872, 8vo.
See "The Phoenix," II, p. 129; China Rev., I, p. 201.

3259 DUDGEON, J., Historical sketch of the ecclesiastical, political and commercial relations of Russia with China, Chin. Rec., III, p. 143, 273, 319, 337; IV, p. 10, 35, 68, 96, 186, 206, 227; also separately.

3260 ANDREE, R., Chinesische Politik, "Grenzboten," XXXII, 1873, p. 15.

3261 NYE, G., The morning of my life in China. Canton, 1873, 8vo.
See China Rev., II, p. 128.

3262 — — , Peking, the gaol, the sole hope of peace. Canton, 1837, 8vo,

3263a — — , An introduction to a retrospect of forty years of foreign intercourse with China and a review of her relations with Japan, China Review, IV, p. 191-199, 233-243.

3263b — — , The Opium Question and the northern campaigns. Canton, 1875, 8vo.

3264 Retrospect of events in China during the years 1871 and 1872, J. N. Ch. Br. R. As. Soc., 1873, p. 241-250.

3265 HUGHES, G., The Japanese and China, China Review, II, p. 369-375.

3266 ALCOCK, Sir Rutherford, The future of Eastern Asia, Macmillan's Mag., Sept., 1874.

3267 — — , Western powers and the East, Fortnightly Review, Jan., 1876.

3268 FERGUSSON, TH., Aperçu de la situation en Chine, 1861-1873. Shanghai, 1874, 8vo., 52 pp.

3269 Die Verträge China's mit den fremden Mächten. Deutsche Monatshefte, 1874.

3270 PLANCHET, E., Formose et l'expédition japonaise, Revue des deux mond., Nov., 1874.

3271 Die Indobritische Expedition nach Yünnan. "Ausland," 1875, No. 9.

3. Wars.

3272 GODDART, J., Remarks on Sir Napier's mission to China. London, 1836, 8vo.

3273 Commission to Lord Napier, Chin. Rep., III, p. 143, 186, 235, 285, 327; IX, p. 514.

3274 Lin's proclamations and battle at Chuenpi; ibid, VIII, p. 167, 212, 378, 426, 489.

3275 MORRISON, J. R., War with China; ibid, VIII, p. 216, 264, 619; IX, p. 408; X, 108, 235, 675; XI, p. 61, 289, 470; XII, p. 103.

3276 BRIDGMAN, E. C., War with China; ibid, VIII, p. 180, 221, 269, 441, 589; IX, p. 219, 234, 419, 639; X, p. 37, 116, 176, 292, 340, 475, 522, 587, 635, 682; XI, p. 341, 397, 646; XIV, p. 298.

3277 — — , Hostilities between Russia and China and the treaty made at Nipchu; ibid, VIII, p. 417.

3278 LINDSAY, H. H., Is the war with China a just one? London, 1840, 8vo.

3279 Rupture with China and its causes. London, 1840, 8vo.

3280 Remarks on occurrences in China since the opium seizure. London, 1840, 8vo.

3281 SCOTT, B., Narrative of a recent imprisonment in China. London, 1841, 8vo.

3282 JOCELYN, Six months with the Chinese expedition. London, 1841, 8vo.

German by Olfermann. Braunschweig, 1843, 8vo.

See Chin. Rep., X, p. 510.

3283 Mrs. Noble's account of her captivity, Chin. Rep., X, p. 191.

3284 THOM, R., War with China; ibid, X, p. 402, 438.

3285 Capture of Capt. P. Anstruther; ibid, X, p. 506.

3286 MACPHERSON, J., Capture of the heights above Canton; ib., X, p. 390.

3287 — — , Progress of the expedition and second attack and capture of Chusan; ibid, X, p. 618.

3288 — — , Two years in China, Narrative of the Chinese expedition from its formation in April 1840 till April 1842. London, 1843, 8vo.

3289 War with China, Chin. Rep., XI, p. 114, 179, 233, 274, 510, 569.

3290 MILNE, W. C., Narrative of serg. Campbell's capture; ibid, XI, p. 395.

3291 — — , Party of Chinese Kidnappers taken; ibid, XI, p. 614.

3292 MACKENZIE, K. L., Narrative of the 2nd campaign in China. London, 1842, 8vo.

See E. C. Bridgman, Chin. Rep., XI, p. 843.

German by Olfermann. Braunschweig, 1844, 8vo.

3293 BINGHAM, J. E., Narrative of the expedition to China. London, 1842, 2 vols., 12mo.

German by F. L. Petrie. Braunschweig, 1843, 2 vols., 8vo.

See E. C. Bridgman, Chin. Rep., XII, p. 353.

3294 LOCH, G. G., The closing events of the campaign in China, the operations in the Yangtsekiang and the peace of Nanking. London, 1843, 12mo.

See Chin. Rep., XIII, p. 57.

3295 MURRAY, A., Doings in China, being the personal narrative of an officer engaged in the late Chinese expedition from the recapture of Chusan to the peace of Nanking. London, 1843, 8vo., map.

3296 RICHARD, C., Der Krieg in China. Aachen und Leipzig, 1843, 8vo.

3297 The last year in China to the peace of Nanking. London, 1843, 8vo.

3298 Sir W. Parker's despatch on the capture of Wusung, Chin. Rep., XII, p. 287.

3299 Memorial respecting prisoners on Formosa and reply; ibid, XII, p. 501.

3300 ADAMS, J. Q., Lecture on the war with China; ibid, XI, p. 274-289.

3301 BERNARD, W. D., Narrative of the voyages and services of the "Nemesis" from 1840 to 1843 and of the combined naval and military operations in China. London, 1844, 2 vols., 8vo., maps, illustr.

3302 OUCHTERLONY, J., The Chinese war. London, 1844, 8vo.

3303 CUNYNGHAME, A., An Aide-de-camp's recollections of service in China. London, 1844, 2 vols., 12mo.

3304 Journal kept by Mr. Gully and Capt. Denham during a captivity in China in the year 1842, edited by a barrister. London, 1844, 8vo.
See Chin. Rep., XIV, p. 298.

3305 NEUMANN, K. F., Geschichte des englisch-chinesischen Krieges. Leipzig, 1855, 8vo.

3306 BAZANCOURT, DE, Les expéditions de Chine et de Cochinchine d'après les documens officiels. Paris, 1857-62, 2 vols., 8vo.

3307 COOKE, G. W., China, being "The Times" special correspondence from China in the years 1857-58. London, 1858, 8vo., XXXII, 457 pp.; 5th ed., 1861.

3308 BOELSCHER, K., Das Bombardement von Canton. Brandis Minerva, Jan., 1857.

3309 — — , Die chinesischen Wirren; ib., March 1857.

3310 LABBÉ, L'expédition des mers de Chine. Paris, 1858, 4to.

3311 SKARTH, J., Is our war with the Tartars or with the Chinese? London, 1860, 8vo.

3312 — — , Italy for the Italians and China for the Chinese. London, 1860, 8vo.

3313 — — , Neutral war and warlike peace. Edinburgh, 1861, 8vo.

3314 — — , Supplement; ibid, 1861, 8vo.

3315 SWINHOE, R., Narrative of the North China campaign of 1860. London, 1861, 8vo.

3316 LUCY, A., Souvenirs de voyage, Letters intimes sur la campagne de Chine en 1860. Marseille, 1861, 8vo., 204 pp., maps, illustr.

3317 MUTRECY, CH. DE, Journal de la campagne de Chine. Paris, 1861, 2 vols., 8vo.

3318 VARIN, P., Expédition de Chine. Paris, 1862, 8vo.

3319 M'GHEE, R. J. L., How we got to Peking. London, 1862, 8vo.

3320 Relation de l'expédition de Chine en 1860, rédigée au dépôt de la guerre. Paris, 1862, 4to., map.
German : Leipzig, 1865, 8vo. See von Sibel's Hist. Zeitschr., XV, 1866, p. 386.

3321 WOLSELEY, G. J., Narrative of the war with China in 1860 to which is added the account of a short residence with the Taiping rebels at Nankin. London, 1862, 8vo.
See Biernatzki, Gött. Gel. Anz., 1863, p. 1401-16.

3322 FISHER, Lieut.-Col., Personal narrative of three years' service in China. London, 1863, 8vo.
See "Athenaeum," May 1863, p. 578; "Reader," May 1863, p. 425.

3323 PALLU, Relation de l'expédition de Chine en 1860. Paris, 1863, 4to.

3324 CHANOINE, J., Examen critique et réfutation d'une relation de l'expédition de Chine. Paris, 1864, 18mo.

3325 CASTANO, F., L'expédition de Chine, Relation
physique topographique et médicale de la campagne de 1860 et 1861. Paris, 1864, 8vo.
See Lit. Centralbl., 1866, No. 38, p. 989.
3326 ARMAND, A., Lettres de l'expédition de Chine et
de Cochinchine. Paris, 1864, 8vo.
3327 NEGRONI, J. L. DE, Souvenirs de la campagne de
Chine. Paris, 1864, 8vo.
3328 LAVOLLÉE, C., L'expédition de Chine en 1860,
La prise des forts de Takou, Rev. des deux mond.,
15 Juill., 1865, p. 443-472.
3329 ENDURAN, C., La Chine et les Français en 1860.
Limoges, 1865, 8vo.
3330 RENNIE, D. F., The British arms in North China
and Japan. London, 1865, 8vo.
See Wesminst. Rev., XXVIII, July, 1865,
p. 247; Athenaeum, Dec., 1864, p. 886;
Reader, Aug., 1865, p. 195.
3331 ZILL, K., Erinnerungen eines Friedfertigen aus
dem letzten chinesischen Feldzug. "Ausland,"
1866, No. 3, 4. 8, 9, 25, 26.
3332 HAILLY, E. DU, Souvenirs d'une campagne dans
l'extrême Orient, Rev. de l'Orient., t. LXIV
(1866,) p. 957-983; LXV, p. 893-924; LXVI,
p. 396-420; LXVII, p. 441-469.

4. Hongkong.

3333 Proclamation taking possession of Hongkong, Ch.
Repos., X, p. 63.
3334 Official notices and places in the island; ibid, X,
p. 268; XV, p. 278.
3335 Sales of land and ordinances; ibid, X, p. 350; XIII,
p. 48, 164, 217, 327, 604; XIV, p. 57.
3336 History of Hongkong; ibid, XII, p. 362.
3337 Charter of the colony of Hongkong and rules of
court; ibid, XII, p. 380.

3338 BRIDGMAN, E. C., Shape of island and places in Hongkong; ibid, XII, p. 435.

3339 — — , Charitable institutions in Hongkong; ibid, XII, p. 438.

3340 — — , Record of criminals in Hongkong jail; ibid, XII, p. 534; XIII, p. 651.

3341 — — , Map and general account of Hongkong; ibid, XIV, p. 291.

3342 Tenure of land; ibid, XII, p. 445; XIV, p. 397.

3343 Commission of J. F. Davis as governor of Hongkong, ibid, XIII, p. 266.

3344 TUCKER and DILL, Drs., Review of diseases at Hongkong; ibid, XV, p. 124.

3345 Houses and revenue of Hongkong; ibid, XV, p. 135.

3346 Brief description of the town of Victoria. Hongkong, 1848, 8vo.

3347 MORRISON, W., Colonial surgeon's report on sickness and deaths at Hongkong in 1847; ibid, XVII, p. 313.

3348 BRUCE, M., Hongkong illustrated in a series of views. London, 1840.

3349 The Hongkong Almanac. Hongkong, 1840, 8vo.

3350 TARRANT, W., A digest and index of all the ordinances of the Hongkong government. Hongkong, 1850, 8vo.

3351 GOSHKEWICZ, Hongkong, Russ. Eccl. Miss., III, No. 11, 1857 (in Russian).

3352 LOBSCHEID, W., A few notices on the extent of Chinese education and the government schools of Hongkong. Hongkong, 1859, 8vo.

3353 — — , The evils of Hongkong and their cure. Hongkong, 1871, 12mo.

3354 SMART, R. E., Observations on the Climatology, Topography and Diseases of Hongkong, Transact. Epidemiolog. Soc. London, 1861.

3355 OBERLAENDER, B., Die Chinesen in Victoria, Zeitschr. f. Erd. Berlin, 1866, p. 499-503.

3356 European life in Hongkong, Ch. Magaz., 1868, p. 1, 24, 43, 83, 112.
3357 The happy valley ; ibid, 1868, p. 1.
3358 Round Hongkong in "the Daisy ;" ib., 1868, p. 68,89.
3359 Statute law of Hongkong, Notes and Queries, I, p. 30, 59.
3360 LISTER, A., The Hongkong Dragon feast ; ibid, II, p. 156.
3361 Execution in Hongkong ; ibid, II, p. 160.
3362 Statement of the circumstances which led to the resignation of R. Young and S. Edin, superintendent of the Hongkong Civil Hospital, on the 28th Aug., 1872. Hongkong, 1872, 8vo.
3363 The name "Hongkong," Ch. Review, I, p. 51, 271.
3364 MERCER, W. T., Under the Peak, or Jottings in verse, written during a lengthened residence in the colony of Hongkong. London, 1869, 8vo.
  See The Phœnix, I, p. 80.
3365 LEGGE, J., The Colony of Hongkong, From a lecture on reminiscences of a long residence in the East, Ch. Review, I, p. 163-176.

5. Macao.

3366 BRIDGMAN, E. C., Portuguese settlements and missions in China, Ch. Repos., I, p. 308, 425; III, p. 289, 533.
3367 — — , British burial ground at Macao ; ibid, XI, p. 48.
3368 LJUNSTEDT, Sir A., Portuguese in China. Canton, 1834, 8vo.
  See E. C. Bridgman, Ch. Repos., III, p. 289.
3369 — — , Contribution to an Historical sketch of the Portuguese settlements, principally at Macao. Macao, 1832, 8vo. ; Boston, 1836, 8vo.
  See E. C. Bridgman, Ch. Repos., I, p. 398.
3370 MORRISON, J. R., Memorial about an Intendant of circuit at Macao, Ch. Repos., VIII, p. 503.

3371 Edict reopening the Portuguese trade at Macao; ibid, VIII, p. 509.
3372 Correspondence relating to H. B. M. sloop "Hyacinth" entering the Inner harbour of Macao; ibid, VIII, p. 543.
3373 New regulations respecting Macao and harbour rules making it a free port; ibid, XIV, p. 151; XV, p. 325.
3374 WILLIAMS, S. W., Assassination of H. E. Governor Amaral of Macao; ibid, XVIII, 448, 532; XIX, p. 50.
3375 Die Portugiesen in Macao. Ausland, 1857, No. 38.
3376 SAMPAIO, M. DE C., Os Chins de Macao. Hongkong, 1867, 12mo.
       See Notes and Queries, II, p. 67.
3377 Governor Amaral, By a member of the portuguese community of Macao, Ch. Magaz., 1868, p. 82.
3378 Macao; ibid, p. 122.
3379 MAYERS, W. F., First arrival of the Portuguese in China, Notes and Queries, III, p. 129.
3380 MINCHIN, G., The possession of Macao by the Portuguese, Ch. Recorder, III, p. 22.
3381 Macao and its Slave trade, Ch. Review, II, p. 9-20.
       Reply by P. G. Mesnier, ib., II, p. 112.

XIV. b. Religions.
1. Romish Missions.

3382 CRUS, G. DA, Tratado em que se contem muito por extenso as causas da China. Evora, 1570, 4to; also 1829, 8vo.
3383 MAFFEI, J. P., Res a soc. Jesu in Oriente gestae. Coloniae, 1574, 8vo.
3384 Lettere del Giapone e della Cina degl' anni 1589 e 1590. Venetia, 1592.
3385 Recentissima de regno Chinae et morte Taicosima, Japonicorum monarcha relatio per miss. Jesuitas. Moguntiae, 1601, 8vo.

German : Dillingen, 1601, 8vo.

3386 MARCELLO, DE RIBADENEYRA, Historia de las Islas del Archipelago y Reynos de la gran China, Tartaria, Cochinchina, etc., de lo sucedido en ellos a los Religios del calzos de la orden de S. Francisco. Barcelona, 1601, 4to.

3387 GUZMAN, L. DE, Historia de las missiones en los Reynos de la China y Japon. Alcala, 1601, fol.

3388 — P. DE, Historia de la entrada de la christianidad en el Japon y China, traducida dal latin de P. H. Turselino. Valladolid, 1603, 4to.

3389 CARVAGLIO, V., Lettere della Cina dell' anno 1601. Roma, 1603, 8vo.

3390 Advis et lettres de la Chine, du Japon et de l'état du Roi de Mogor. Paris, 1604, 12mo.

3391 TRIGANTIUS, N., De Christiana expeditione apud Sinas suscepta a Soc. Jesu ex P. M. Ricci commentariis libri V. Augustae Vindil., 1615, 4to.
French : Lille, 1617, 8vo. ; Paris, 1617, 8vo.

3392 ANDRADA, A. DE, Novo descubrimento de grao Catayo dos Reynos de Tibet. Lisboa, 1626 ; also Madrid, 1627.
German : Augsburg, 1627, 12mo.

3393 CEVALLOS, O. DE, Relationes verdaderas de los Reynos de la China, Cochinchina y Camboja. Jaen, 1628, 4to.

3394 Histoire de de qui s'est passé aux royaumes d'Ethiopie, de Tibet et de la Chine. Paris, 1628, 8vo.

3395 Lettere dell'Ethiopia et della Cina. Roma, 1629, 12mo.

3396 SCHALL, J. A., Historica narratio de initio et progressu missionis soc. Jesu apud Sinensis. Viennae Austriae, 1635, 8vo.

3397 SEMEDO, A., Imperio de la China, i cultura evangelica en él. Madrid, 1642, 4to.
English : London, 1655, 4to.

3398 Relaçam da conversam da rainha e princesa da China a nossa santa fé. Lisboa, 1650, 4to.

3399 RHODES, P. A. DE, Divers voyages en la Chine et autres royaumes de l'Orient. Paris, 1653, 4to.; also 1666.
German: Missionsreisen in China. Freiburg, 1858, 8vo.

3400 MARTINIUS, M., Brevis relatio de numero et qualitate christianorum apud Sinas. Romae, 1654, 4to.

3401 BOYM, M., Briefve relation de la convertion notable des personnes royales et de la religion chrétienne en la Chine. Paris, 1654, 8vo.

3402 BARTOLI, Historia della comp. de Gesu dell'Asia, della Cina et de Giappone. Roma, 1667, fol.

3403 LEIBNITZ, G., Novissima sinica historiam nostri temporis illustrantia. Hannover, 1669, 8vo.

3404 INTORCETTA, P., Compendiosa narratione del stato della missione Cinese. Roma, 1671, 8vo.

3405 — — , Testimonium de cultu sinensi. Parisiis, 1700, 8vo.

3406 GOUVEA, A. DE, Innocentia victrix s. sententia comitiorum Sin. imp. pro innocentia christ. religionis. Quamcheu, 1671, fol.

3407 GARCIA, F., Relacion de la persecucion de los predicadores de Christo en la China. Sevilla, 1671, 4to.

3408 Historica relatio de ortu et progressu fidei orthodoxae in regno Chinensi ab a. c. 1581 usque ad a. c. 1669 ex literis R. P. J. A. Schall. Ratisbonae, 1672, 8vo.

3409 VERBIEST, P. F., Lettre écrite de Peking à tous les jésuites de l'Europe le 15. août, 1678. Paris, 1682, 12mo.

3410 — — , Lettac écrite de la Chine, où l'on voit l'état présent du christianisme dans cet empire et le bien qu'en y peut faire pour le salut des âmes. Paris, 1682, 4to.

3411 PHILIPUCCI, F. X., Praeludium ad plenam disquisitionem de cultu Confucii, 1682.

3412 TELLIER, P. DE, Défense des noureaux chrétiens et des missionnaires de la China, du Japon et des Indes. Paris, 1687, 12mo.

3413 ARNAUD, Lettre d'un théologien contre la défense des nouveaux chrétiens. Paris, 1687, 12mo. See No. 3412.

3414 Apologia dei padri Dominicani missionarii della China o pure risposta al libro del padre Letellier (No. 3412), intit. difesa de nuovi christiani. Colon, 1688, 8vo.

3415 Histoire d'une dame chrétienne de la Chine, où sont expliquez les usages, l'établissement de la religion, les manières des missionnaires, etc. Paris, 1688, 12mo.

3416 PARAGA, Defensa de los nuevos christianos. Madrid, 1690, 8vo.

3417 Histoire de D. J. de Palafox et des différences qu'il a sues avec les Jésuites, 1690, 12mo.

3418 Histoire des différences entre les missionaires Jésuites et ceux des ordres de S. Dominique et de S. François, touchant le culte que les Chinois rendent à leur maître Confucius, etc., 1692, 12mo.

3419 Relation de ce qui s'est passé à la Chine en 1697-99. Liège, 1700, 8vo.

3420 GOBIEN, C., Histoire de l'édit de l'empereur de la Chine en faveur de la religion chrétienne. Paris, 1698, 8vo.; also in Le Comte, Nouv. Mém. sur l'état, III, 1702 (No. 2011).
　　　　German: Frankfurt, 1699, 8vo.
　　　　On this edict see Suarez in Leibnitz, Novissima Sin., 2nd ed., 1699, p. 1-149 (No. 3403).

3421 — — , Dissertatio apologetica de Sinensium ritibus. Leodii, 1700, 8vo.

3422 — — , Eclaircissement sur les honneurs que les Chinois rendent à Confucius et aux morts, in his Histoire de l'édit, p. 217-322.

3423 Apologie des Dominicains missionaires de la Chine

ou reponse aux livres de Tellier (No. 3412) et de
Gobien (No. 3421). Cologne, 1699, 12mo.

3424 De Sinensium ritibus politicis acta. Parisiis, 1700,
8vo.

3425 Apologia pro decreto Alexandri VII et praxi Jesuita-
rum ex P. P. Dominicarum et Franciscanorum
scriptis concinnata. Lovanii, 1700, 8vo.

3426 BRACATI, De Sinensium ritibus. Parisiis, 1700,
12mo.

3427 Brevis relatio eorum quae spectant ad declarationem
Sinarum imperatoris Kamhi circa Coeli, Cumfucii
et Avorum cultu. Pekini, 8vo.

3428 De cultu Confucii philosophi et progenitorum apud
Sinas. Dillingiae, 1700.

3429 LEFABRE, J., De Sinensium ritibus politicis sive
de avita Sinarum pietate. Lugduni Bat., 1700,
5 vols., 8vo.

3430 — — , Dissertatio de avita Sinarum pietate praesertim erga defunctos et eximia erga Confucium
magistrum suum observantia.
Written against Navarette.

3431 BUDDEUS, J. F., Dissertatio de superstitioso mor-
tuorum apud Sinenses cultu. Halis, 1700.

3432 Historia cultus Sinensium. Coloniae, 1700, 2 vols.,
12mo.

3433 CICÉ, L., Lettre aux Jésuites sur les idolâtries de
la Chine. Cologne, 1700, 8vo.

3434 VARO, F., Estratto del trattato circa il culto, offerte,
rite che praticano i Chinesi. In Colonia, 1700, 8vo.

3435 LE COMTE, Les cérémonies de la Chine. Liège,
1700, 8vo.

3436 F. Xaverii acta de Sinensium ritibus politicis. Parisiis, 1700, 8vo.

3437 FURTADO, F., Informatio antiquissima de praxi
missionariorum sinensium soc. Jesu circa ritus
sinenses. Parisiis, 1700, 8vo.

3438 Conformité des cérémonies Chinoises avec l'idolâtries
grecque et romaine pour servir de comfirmation à

l'Apologie des missionnaires dominicains. Cologne (1700).

3439 Lettre à Monsgr. le Duc du Maine sur les cérémonies de la Chine, 1700, 12mo.

3440 Lettre d'un docteur de l'ordre de S. Dominique sur les cérémonies de la Chine au P. Le Comte, Jésuite. Cologne, 1701, 8vo.

3441 Six lettres d'un docteur, ou relation des assemblées de la Faculté de Théologie de P. sur les opinions des Jésuites touchant la religion, les cultes et la morale des Chinois. Cologne, 1701, 8vo.

3442 LONGOBARDI, Traité sur quelques points de la religion des Chinois. Paris, 1701.

Also in Vol. II of Leibnitz's letters (No. 406); in Navarette (No. 2004); and in Cicé (No. 3433).

3443 Lettre de Mr. Maigrot à M. Charmot au sujet de la religion des Chinois, 1701.

3444 Lettres de quelques membres de la Compagnie de Jésus, écrites de la Chine et des Indes Orientales. Paris, 1702, 12mo.

3445 Diffesa del giudizio formato della S. Sede Apostolica nel di 20 Nov. 1704 intorno ai riti e ceremonie Cinesi. Torino, 1709, 4to.

3446 Considerazioni sulla scrittura intitulata : riflessioni sopra la causa della Cina. Roma, 1709, 4to.

3447 Mémoires pour Rome sur l'état de la religion chrétienne dans la Chine, 1709, 4to. Suite, 1710, 8vo.

3448 FAQUINELLI, Réflexions sur le culte de la Chine, avec la réponse, 4to.

3449 Apologia delle risposte date del procuratore del Cardinale di Tournon alli 5 memoriali del P. Provana intorno il sacrificio cinese. Roma, 1710, 4to.

3450 Risposta dei signori delle missione stranieri alla protesta ed alle riflessioni dei P. P. Jesuiti intorno il sacrificio Cinese. Roma, 1710, 4to.

3451 MAURITIUS, Afgodendienst der Jesuiten in China. Amsterdam, 1711, 8vo.

3452 CASTORANI, C., Notae et observationes in bullam Benedicti XIV supra ceremonias et Ritus Sinicos.

3453 JOUVENCI, P., Examen des faussetez sur les cultes Chinois. Cologne, 1714, 8vo.

3454 Travels of several miss. of the soc. of Jesu into divers parts of the Archipelago, India, China and America. London, 1714.

3455 ST. PIERRE, F. G. DE, Relation de la nouvelle persecution de la Chine, 1714, 12mo.

3456 ASSEMANNUS, J. G., Syrus Maronita, Bibliotheca orientalis Clementino-Vaticana in qua M. S., etc. Romae, 1728, 4 vols., fol.
Contains notices on the Nestorian Christians and Missions in China.

3457 Esame e diffesa del decreto dal cardinale di Tournon sopra le cose dell'imperio della Cina. Roma, 1728, 4to.

3458 VISDELOU, C., Monument de la religion chrétienne, trouvé au Chensi en Chine, Bibl. or. Leyde, 1730 (No. 837.)

3459 VILLERS, Anecdotes sur l'état de la religion dans la Chine. Paris, 1733, 4 vols., 12mo.

3460 Chronicas de la apostolica provincia de S. Gregoria de religiozos descalzos de N. S. P. St. Francisco en China. Manilla, 1738, 3 vols., fol.

3461 VIANI, P., Istoria delle cose operate nella Cina de Mre. G. A. Mezzabarba, Legato apostolico, in quell' Imperio et di presente Vascovo de Sodi. Parigi (Turin), 1739, 8vo.; Venezia, 1760, 8vo.
Prohibited: French extracts in Hist. gén. des Voy., V; English in Coll. of voy., III, p. 584 ss.; German, V, p. 541 ss.

3462 MOSHEIM, J. L. von, Historia tartarorum ecclesiastica. Helstadii, 1741, 4to.

3463 — — , Erzaehlung der neuesten chinesischen Kirchengeschichte. Rostock, 1748, 8vo.; and German edition of Du Halde, II (No. 2018.)
English: London, 1750, 8vo.

3464 BAHR, F., Allerneueste chinesische Merkwürdigkeiten und gründliche Widerlegung vieler Irrungen von J. L. von Mosheim. Augsburg, 1758, 8vo.

3465 Memorie storiche dell' eminentissimo Mr. Card. di Tournon, exposte con monumenti rari ed autentici. Venezia, 1761, 8vo.

3466 LOCKMAN, J., Travels of the Jesuits into various parts of the world, particularly China and the East Indies, Transl. from the Lettres édif. London, 1762, 2 vols., 8vo.

3467 GUIGNES, J. DE (père), Recherches sur les Chrétiens établis à la Chine dans le VII siècle, Rec. de l'ac. des inscr., XXX, 1764.

3468 Geschichte der Streitigkeiten über die chinesischen Gebräuche. Augsburg, 1791, 3 vols., 8vo.

3469 ANIOT ET RAUX, Traduction d'un décret de l'empereur de la Chine du 9 Nov. 1785, qui rend la liberté à 12 missionaires, Mém. conc., XV, p. 373-383.

3470 Nouvelles des missions orientales. Liège, 1794, 12mo.

3471 LABOUDERIE, Lettres de Mr. de St. Martin, vicaire de Su-tchuen. Paris, 1822, 8vo.

3472 CAILLOT, A., Morceaux choisis des lettres édif. et cur. Paris, 1823, 2 vols., 8vo.

3473 RIPA, Storia delle fondazione della congregatione e del collegio de Cinesi. Naples, 1832, 3 vols., 8vo.

3474 NOEL, P., Mémoire sur l'état des missions de la Chine, trad. du latin, Lett. éd., VI, p. 68 ss.; Nouv. édition, XVIII, p. 160 ss; XXVII, p. 1-22.

3475 PARENNIN, Lettre de 1715, Mission à Peking; ibid, XXIX.

3476 MORRISON, R., Remarks on Dufresses death and on Timkowsky, Chin. Repos., I, p. 377.

3477 — — , Memorial of the catholic bishop Mouley to the emperor of China. Shanghae, 1855, 8vo.

3478 BRIDGMAN, E. C., Christian books published by the Romanists, Chin. Repos., I, p. 504.

3479 — — , Proclamation from the magistrate of Shanghae securing Romish missionaries a residence at Sukia hwei; ibid, XVIII, p. 477.

3480 — — , Missions of the Romish church in China and Mongolia; ibid, XVIII, p. 574, 617.

3481 — — , Translation of Paul Sü's apology for the Jesuits, addressed to the emperor Wanlih in 1617; ibid, XIX, p. 118.

3482 LJUNSTEDT, Sir A., Contributions to an historical sketch of the Roman Catholic church at Macao. Canton, 1834, 12mo.
See Chin. Repos., III, p. 289.

3483 Brugière's travels in China and Chinese Tartarie, Chin. Repos., VI, p. 287.

3484 Roman catholic missions to Corea; ibid, VIII, p. 567.

3485 MEDHURST, W. H. (sen.), Toleration of Roman catholicism in a proclamation at Shanghae by the intendant; ibid, XIV, p. 532.

3486 Toleration of Roman catholicism in a communication from Kiying to P. S. Forbes; ibid, XIV, p. 587.

3487 Rizzolati's letter on Roman catholic missions in China; ibid, XV, p. 39.

3488 HAPPER, A. P., Roman catholic missions in China; ibid, XV, p. 298, 400, 453, 507.

3489 — — , Letter of Bishop Besi respecting Romish missions in Shantung; ibid, XV, p. 250.

3490 NÈVE, Établissement et destruction de la première chrétienté dans la Chine. Loewen, 1846, 8vo.

3491 MILNE, W. C., An all important proclamation of Count de Besi against receiving scriptures from heretics, Ch. Repos., XVI, p. 246, 506.

3492 Geschichte der Katholischen Missionen im Kaiserreiche China. Wien, 1845, 2 vols., 8vo.

3493 DAMMANN, A., China und seine Bewohner mit Rücksicht auf ältere und neuere Missions-versuche unter diesem Volke. Düsselthal, 1847.

3494 ZWETKOFF, P., On christianity in China, Russ. Eccl. Miss., I (1853), 55 (in Russian).

3495 THOMS, P. P., Prohibitions addressed to Chinese converts of the Romish faith, Ch. Rep., XX, p. 85.

3496 BROULLION, R., Missions de Chine: mémoire sur l'état actuel de la mission de Kiangnan. Paris, 1855, 8vo.

3497 HUC, Le christianisme en Chine, en Tartarie, etc. Paris, 1857, 8vo.

3498 HEYD, W., Studien über die Kolonien der römischen Kirche, welche die Dominikaner und Franziskaner im 13. und 14. Jahrh. in den von den Tartaren beherrschten Ländern Europas und Asiens gegründet haben. Niedner's Ztschr. f. hist. Theol. 1858, Vol. III, p. 260.

3499 Die Leiden der römischen Christen in Anam und Korea. Neue Ev. K. Ztg., 1863, No. 32-33.

3500 ANDRÉ-MARIE, F., Missions dominicaines dans l'extrême Orient. Paris, 1865, 18mo.

3501 MEYNARD, P., Missions dominicaines dans l'extrême Orient, Revue cathol. de Louvain, VIII série, T. III (1865), p. 711.

3502 LENFANT, C., Missions de l'extrême orient, ou coup d'oeil sur les persécutions de la Chine, de la Cochinchine, du Tong-king et de la Corée. Paris, 1865, 12mo.

3503 Romish missions, Ch. Recorder, I, p. 70, 90, 141, 184, 220, 166, 216; Notes and Queries, II, p. 70, 132, 163, 107, 171.

3504 Souvenirs de Chine par un missionaire. Paris, 12mo.

3505 The massacre at Tientsin, Notes and Queries, III, p. 150.

3506 STANLEY, C. A., The Tientsin massacre; ibid, III, p. 207.

3507 The Tientsin massacre. Shanghai, 1870, 8vo.

3508 PALLADIUS, O., Traces of Christianity in Mongolia and China in the 13th century, drawn from

Chinese sources, Oriental Magazine, 1872, I, No. 1 (in Russian.)
> English: in Chin. Recorder, 1875, p. 104-113; French by R. R. Prémare in Annales de Philos. chrét.

2. Protestant Missions.

3509 An abridged account of the state of religion in China and Cochinchina during the years 1806-7. London, 1809-11, 2 parts, 12mo.
3510 Opinion of a Chinese priest respecting Christ, Indochin. Gleaner, No. 1, 1817.
3511 YATES, T., Indian church history or an account of the planting of the gospel in Syria, India and China. London, 1818, 8vo.
> See E. C. Bridgman, Chin. Repos., XVI, p. 153.
3512 MILNE, W. C., A retrospect of the Protestant Mission to China. Malacca, 1820, 8vo., 376 pp.
> See A. Rémusat, Mél. as., I, p. 31-50.
3513 — — 's Remarks on Chinese terms to express the Deity, Indo-Chin. Gleaner, III, 1821, p. 97; also in Chin. Repos., VII, p. 314.
3514 MORRISON, R., J. Barrow's remarks on Missions, Chin. Repos., I, p. 76.
3515 — — , Synopsis of 2 Christian tracts; ibid, I, p. 77.
3516 — — , Quarterly review on missions; ibid, I, p. 108.
3517 — — , Reasons for hostility to missions; ibid, I, p. 497,
3518 — — , England and America for the world; ibid, II, p. 507.
3519 Fuhkien people well disposed and ready to be instructed; ibid, I, p. 151.
3520 BRIDGMAN, E. C., Missionary journals of Tomlin and Medhurst; ibid, I, p. 224.

3521 — — , Wide field for missions in China; ibid, I, p. 333.
3522 — — , Early introduction of Christianity in China; ibid, I, p. 447.
3523 — — , Synopsis of a tract called " Two friends"; ibid, II, p. 283.
3524 — — , Account of the Chinese version of the Bible and the proper style for a version of the Bible in Chinese; ibid, IV, p. 249, 297.
3525 — — , Disposition of the Chinese government towards Christianity and laws in the code relating to it; ibid, VI, p. 49.
3526 — — , Brief memoir of the Chinese evangelist Leang Afah. London, 1840, 12mo.
3527 — — , Warranty for Christian missions; ibid, VIII, p. 44.
3528 — — , Comparative view of 6 versions of John i, 1; ibid, XIV, p. 54.
3529 — — , Queries respecting the translation of the words God, Spirit and Angel ; ibid, XIV, p. 101.
3530 — — , Increase of missionaries among the Chinese; ibid, XIV, p. 148.
3531 — — , Toleration of Christianity given in the emperor's reply to a memorial from Kiying; ibid, XIV, p. 195; XV, p. 154.
3532 — — , Words demanding attention in revising the Bible; ibid, XV, p. 108.
3533 — — , Revision of the Chinese version of the Bible and remarks on the words Spirit and God; ibid, XV, p. 161.
3534 — — , Views of Drs. Morrison, Milne, Marshman and others respecting the word for Deity; ibid, XVI, p. 99, 122.
3535 — — , Proceedings of the committee of Delegates on the revision of the New Testament and vote on word for God; ibid, XVII, p. 53.
3536 — — , Remarks on the notes of Z. Z. by Rev. W. H. Medhurst, and reply to these remarks in

explanation; ibid, XVII, p. 459.

3537 — — , Notice regarding Chinese tracts published with the funds of the Am. Tract Soc.; ibid, XVII, p. 649.

3538 — — , Protestant missions in Shanghai and their present operations, 1849; ibid, XVIII, p. 515; XIX, p. 330.

3539 KEATING, A. S., Parallel drawn between Romish and protestant missionaries; ibid, I, p. 268.
    See E. C. Bridgman, Chin. Repos., I, p. 270.

3540 GUETZLAFF, K., Diffusion of Knowledge in China; ibid, II, p. 508.

3541 — — , Remarks on the conversion of the Chinese; ibid, II, p. 565.

3542 — — , Slow progress of propagating the gospel in China; ibid, III, p. 244.

3543 — — , Measures for extending missions by preaching; ibid, III, p. 559.

3544 — — , Need of a new version of the Bible in Chinese; ibid, IV, p. 393.

3545 — — , State and prospects of Chinese viewed in connection with the late war and missions; ibid, XII, p. 294.

3546 — — , Remarks regarding the translation of the terms for Deity in the Chinese translation of the Scriptures; ibid, XV, p. 464.

3547 — — , Two notes against the use of Shin for God; ibid, XVI, p. 37, 121.

3548 — — , Die Mission in China. Berlin, 1860, 8vo.

3549 MORRISON, J. R., Lectures on the sayings of Jesus. Malacca, 1832, 8vo.

3550 TRACY, J., Extent of modern benevolence, Chin. Repos., II, p. 428.

3551 — — , New mode of teaching the Chinese; ibid, V, p. 41, 109.

3552 STEVENS, E., Promulgation of the gospel in China; ibid, III, p. 428.

3553 SCHMIDT, H. J., Uroffenbarung oder die grosse Lehre des Christenthums, nachgewiesen in den Sagen und Urkunden der ältesten Völker, vorzüglich in den canonischen Büchern der Chinesen. Landshut, 1834, 8vo.

3554 EVANS, J., Report of Anglo-Chinese College for 1834. Malacca, 1835.

3555 KIDD, S., Remarks on a new version of the S. S. in Chinese. London, 1836, 8vo.

3556 MEDHURST, W. H. (sen.), Memorial on a new version of the Chinese scriptures. London, 1836, 8vo.

3557 — — , A dissertation on the theology of the Chinese with a view to the elucidation of the most appropriate term for expressing the Deity in the Chinese language, Shanghai, 1847, 8vo.
See E. C. Bridgman, Chin. Repos., XVII, p. 414.

3558 — — , Reply to the few plain questions of a brother missionary. Shanghai, 1848, 8vo.

3559 — — , An inquiry into the proper mode of rendering the word God in translating the S. S. into the Chinese language. Shanghai, 1848, 8vo.; also Chin. Repos., XVI, p. 34; XVII, p. 105, 161, 209, 265, 321.

3560 — — , Reply to the essay of Dr. Boone on the proper rendering of the word elohim and theos into the Chinese language. Canton, 1848, 8vo.; also Chin. Repos., XVII, p. 489, 545, 601.

3561 — — , On the true meaning of the word Shin. Shanghai, 1849, 8vo.
See S. W. Williams, Chin. Repos., XVIII, p. 607.

3562 — — , Letter to the editor of the Ch. Repos., with a translation of a tract on nourishing the spirit, Chin. Repos., XIX, p. 445.

3563 — — , An inquiry into the proper mode of translating ruach and pneuma in the Chinese version. Shanghai, 1850, 8vo.

See E. C. Bridgman, Chi. Rep., XIX, p. 478.

3564 — — , To the protestant missionaries at Hongkong and the five ports of China. Shanghai, 1850, 8vo.

3565 — — , On the Chinese version of the scriptures. Shanghai, 1851, 8vo.

3566 — — , Reply to the Bishop of Victoria's ten reasons in favors of téenshin. Shanghai, 1851, 4to.

3567 — — , Reply to Dr. Boone's vindication of comments on the translation of Eph. I in the delegates' version, 1852, 8vo.

3568 — — , MILNE, W. C. and STRONACH, J., Strictures on the remarks contained in papers relating to the Shanghai revision of the Chinese scriptures. Shanghai, 1852, 8vo.

See S. W. Williams, Chin. Repos., XX, p. 485.

3569 WILLIAMS, S. W., Illustrations of Scripture, Chin. Repos., VIII, p. 640; XVII, p. 537.

3570 — — , Position and operations of the protestant missions at the 5 ports and Hongkong in 1849; ibid, XVIII, p. 48.

3571 — — , Church at Amoy and trip up the Min; ibid, XVIII, p. 444.

3572 — — , Proceedings of missionaries at the several ports and of the delegates upon the version of the testaments; ibid, XIX, p. 544

3573 — — , Testimony of the truth of Christianity given by Kiying and remarks by Bishop Boone; ibid, XX, p. 41.

3574 — — , Proceedings relating to the Chinese version, report of a committee of the Am. Bible Society; ibid, XX, p. 216.

2575 — — , List of protestant missionaries sent to the Chinese up to Jan. 1852 and present position of their missions; ibid, XX, p. 513.

3576 LEGGE, J., Letters on the rendering of the name of God in the Chinese language. Hongkong, 1840, 8vo.

See E. R. Moncrieff, Chi. Repos., XIX, p. 524.

3577 — — , An argument for Shang Te as the proper rendering of the words elohim and theos. Hongkong, 1850, 8vo.

3578 ABEEL, D., Mission at Amoy and Kulangsu, Chin. Repos., XI, p. 50; XII, p. 266.

3579 — — , Journal kept at Kulangsu and Amoy; ibid, XIII, p. 74, 233.

3580 Meeting in Hongkong for revising the Bible in Chinese; ibid, XII, p. 549.

3581 MILNE, R. G., Sinim, a plea for China. London, 1843, 8vo.

3582 ELLIS, W., The history of the London Missionary Society. London, 1844, 8vo.

3583 DAVIES, E., China and her spiritual claims. London, 1844, 8vo.

3584 TOMLIN, J., Missionary journals during 11 years' residence. London, 1844, 8vo.

3585 LOWRIE, W. M., The land of Sinim or a survey of Christian missions to the Chinese, Chin. Repos., XIII, p. 113, 466, 537, 578, 644.

3586 — — , Remarks on the words God and spirit, and the transference of proper names into Chinese; ibid, XIV, p. 101.

3587 — — , The words Shin, Shangti and T'ien examined with reference to the version of the Bible; ibid, XV, p. 311.

3588 — — , Remarks on the words and phrases best suited to express the names of God in Chinese; ibid, XV, p. 568, 577; XVI, p. 30.

3589 SMITH, G., Address on the subject of Christian missions; ibid, XV, p. 234.

3590 — — , The natural religion of China as illustrative of the proper word for translating God into the Chinese language. Shanghai, 1853, 8vo.

3591 — — , A visit to some of the Outstations of the church mission in the prefecture of Foochow, Chin. Recorder, I, p. 17.

3592 ANDERSON, R., Theory of missions to the heathens, Chin. Repos., XV, p. 481.

3593 POLLMANN, W. J., Missions at Amoy up to 1846; ibid, XV, p. 355.

3594 — — , List of tracts printed in Chinese; ibid, XVI, p. 379.

3595 Ordination of Tsin-shen as a minister of the gospel; ibid, XV, p. 527.

3596 YVAN, M., Les missions protestantes en Chine. Paris, 1846, 8vo.

3597 PEET, L. B., Plea in behalf of China, Chin. Repos., XVI, p. 321.

3598 — — , Remarks for the best terms for God in Chinese. Canton, 1852, 8vo.

3599 — — , Letter to the friends of protestant missionaries to the Chinese. Fuchow, 1853, 8vo.

3600 — — , On Mission schools, Chin. Recorder, I, p. 132, 150.

3601 — — , Observances of Sabbath by our teachers; ibid, I, p. 231.

3602 GODDART, J., Inquiry respecting the mode of designating the third person of the Godhead in Chinese, Chin. Repos., XVI, p. 391.

3603 WATTEVILLE, B. von, China und das Evangelium. Drei Vorträge über die evangelische Mission. Karlsruhe, 1845, 8vo.

3604 HAMILTON, J., China and the China Mission. London, 1847, 8vo.

3605 DAMMANN, A., China und seine Bewohner mit Rücksicht auf ältere und neuere Missionsversuche. Berlin, 1847, 8vo.

3606 Position of protestant missionaries in China, 1848, Chin. Repos., XVII, p. 101.

3607 BOONE, W. J., A few plain questions addressed to those missionaries who teach the Chinese to worship Shangti; ibid, XVII, p. 357; XVIII, p. 97.

3608 — — , An essay on the proper rendering of the

words elohim and theos. Canton, 1848, 8vo.; also Chin. Repos., XVII, p. 17, 57.

3609 — — , Defence of an essay, etc. Canton, 1850, 8vo.; Chin. Repos., XIX, p. 345, 409, 465, 569, 625.

3610 — — , A vindication of comments on the translation of Ephes. I in the delegates' version. Canton, 1852, 8vo.

3611 — — and LEGGE, J., The notions of the Chinese concerning God and spirits. Hongkong, 1852, 8vo.

3612 Letter upon the use of the terms Shin and Shangti and that ti is not a generic term, Chin. Repos., XVIII, p. 100.

3613 BOWRING, J., Thoughts on the manner of expressing the word for God in the Chinese language ; ibid, XVIII, p. 600.

3614 STAUNTON, G., An inquiry into the proper mode of rendering the word God in translating the S. S. into the Chinese language. London, 1849, 8vo. See S. W. Williams, Chin. Repos., XVIII, p. 607.

3615 Edict against Christianity by the prefect of Kiaying chou, Chin. Repos., XIX, p. 566.

3616 MONCRIEFF, E. T. R., On using two terms for God; ibid, XIX, p. 280.

3617 DOTY, E., Thoughts on the proper term to be employed to translate Elohim and Theos into Chinese. Shanghai 1850, 8vo. (Ch. Repos., XIX, p. 185.)

3618 Native Evangelization in China. London, 1850, 8vo.

3619 Notes of an interview between H. E. Sü Kiyii and the Bishop of Victoria at Fuhchau, Dec., 1850, Chin. Repos., XX, p. 247.

3620 RADLEY, J., Chinese Version. London, 1851, fol.

3621 CULBERSTON, M. S., Reply to the strictures on the remarks made on the translation of Genesis and Exodus in the revision of the Chinese Scriptures. Canton, 1852, 8vo.

3622 — — , Essay on the bearing of the publications of the Taiping Dynasty insurgents in the controversy respecting the words Elohim and Theos. Shanghai, 1853, 8vo. (Chin. Repos., XIX, p. 90).

3623 BRIDGMAN, J. G., Daughters of China. Glasgow, 1852, 8vo.

3624 BETTELHEIM, B. J., The mission of Loo-chew. Canton, 1852, 8vo.

3625 BIERNATZKI, K. L., Beiträge zur Kunde China's in Beziehung auf die Missionssache. Kassel, 1853, 8vo.

3626 Christianity in China, the history of Christian missions. London, 1854, 8vo.

3627 KESSON, J., The cross and the dragon or the fortunes of Christianity in China. London, 1854, 8vo.

3628 MALAN, S. C., Who is God in China, Shin or Shang-ti? London, 1855, 8vo.

3629 — — , A letter on the pantheistic and on the buddhistic tendency of the Chinese and Mongol version of the Bible published by the British and foreign Bible Society. London, 1856, 8vo.

3630 NEUMANN, K. F., Das Christenthum, die Jesuiten und die evangelischen Sendboten. Zeitschr. der d. morg. Ges., VII, p. 141.

3631 MARSHAL, T. W. M., Christianity in China. London, 1858, 8vo.
French: L. DE Wazier, Les missions chrétiennes. P. 1865, 2 vls., 8vo.; Vol. I, 62-191, Missions en Chine.

3632 WILEY, J. W., The mission cemetery and the fallen missionaries of Fuchau, China. New York, 1858, 8vo.

3633 DEAN, W., The christian missions. New York, 1859, 8vo.

3634 SMITH, R., A charge delivered to the Anglican Clergy at Shanghai. Shanghai, 1860, 8vo.

3635 BURKHARDT, G. E., Kleine Missionsbibliothek. Bielefeld, 1861, 8vo.

3636 HARTWELL, C., A few thoughts on the question: what term can be christianized for God in China. Shanghai, 1864, 8vo.

3637 — —, The relation of Christians to the examinations, Ch. Recorder, I, p. 217.

3638 — —, The American board of commissioners for foreign missions on Polygamy; ibid, II, p. 187.

3639 — —, Ordination in Tungchau; ibid, III, p. 257.

3640 — —, Selecting and training of native helpers; ibid, IV, p. 116.

3641 BALDWIN, S., Directory of protestant missionaries in China. Fuchow, 1865, 16mo.; also 1866.

3642 — —, On the purchasing of slave girls by christians, Ch. Recorder, II, p. 244.

3643 HANSPACH, Report of the Chinese vernacular schools in Kuangtung. Hongkong, 1865, 8vo.

3644 MATHESON, D., Narrative of the Mission to China of the Eng. Presbyt. Church, with remarks on the social life and religious ideas of the Chinese by the Rev. J. Macgowan. London, 1866, 8vo.

3645 WHATELY, Miss, Mission to the women of China. London, 8vo.

3646 HAMILTON, J., China and the Chinese Mission. London.

3647 GAMBLE, W., Statistics of protestant missions in China. Shanghai, 1865.

3648 HUDSON, T. H., Important considerations relative to English translation in reply to the proposal for a new version of the S. S. Shanghai, 1865, 8vo.

3649 CRAWFORD, F. P., A few thoughts in reply to a short essay on the question: what term can be christianized for God in China. Shanghai, 1866, 8vo.

3650 WYLIE, A., Memorial of protestant missionaries to the Chinese, giving a list of their publications and obituary notices of the deceased. Shanghai, 1867, 8vo.

Contains short notices on 338 protestant missionaries up to 1867.

3651 — — , Bible in China, Ch. Recorder, I, p. 121, 145; also, 1869, 8vo.

3652 — — , On the Knowledge of a weekly sabbath in China; ibid, IV, p. 4, 40.

3653 TUCKER, H. C., Thoughts on missions; ibid, I, p. 1.

3654 THOBURN, J. M., Tracts and Tract societies; ibid, I, p. 5.

3655 Divorce and remarriage; ibid, p. 14, 36, 54, 55, 56, 90.

3656 BUTCHER, C. H., Missionary labor, trials and consolation of; ibid, I, p. 43.

3657 WOLFE, J., Persecution in Lo-yuen; ibid, I, p. 48.

3658 KNOWLTON, M. J., Work of Christian missionaries in China; ibid, I, p. 63.

3659 — — , The relation of protestantism to romanism in China; ibid, I, p. 110.

3660 — — , Bible distribution in China as means of civilisation; ibid, II, p. 209.

3661 — — , Modern Christian missions in China; ibid, II, p. 312, 340.

3662 — — , Hon. J. Ross Brown on Missions; ibid, II, p. 109.

3663 — — , Positivism; ibid, II, p. 222.

3664 — — , The Yangchow Riot; ibid, II, p. 69.

3665 — — , China as a Mission field, A premium tract. New York, 1873, 8vo.

See Chin. Recorder, V, 1875, p. 108.

3666 Attack on Missionaries at Yangchow, Ch. Recorder, I, p. 88.

3667 MOULE, A. E., On the sale of books and tracts to the Chinese; ibid, I, p. 104.

3668 — — , Some remarks on a recent gossip in the North China Herald (China Missions from a Chinese point of view); ibid, VI, p. 130-137.

3669   NELSON, R., Relation of Christianity to polygamy; ibid, I, p. 169.

3670   On preaching to the Chinese public; ibid, I, p. 173.

3671   STANLEY, C. A., Chihli and Shantung, Notes on a missionary tour; ibid, I, p. 177.

3672   — — , Will missionaries be permitted to reside in the interior of China ? Ibid, II, p. 323.

3673   SYLE, E. W., Present aspect of missionary work in China; ibid, I, p. 193.

3674   — — , Female education at Shanghai; ibid, I, p. 214.

3675   NOYES, H. V., On teaching to Chinese assistants, English; ibid, I, p. 217.

3676   — — , Letter from Canton; ibid, II, p. 258.

3677   — — , Persecution at Tung kun in the province of Canton; ibid, II, p. 316.

3678   — — , Out-break at Fat-shan; ibid, III, p. 193.

3679   TURNER, F. S., Best method of presenting the Gospel to the Chinese; ibid, I, p. 225, 255; II, p. 29, 88, 123, 150, 241, 272, 301.
         See Ch. Recorder, III, p. 169.

3680   — — , Christianity versus polygamy; ibid, I, p. 233.

3681   LOBSCHEID, W., Christianity versus polygamy; ibid, p. 234.

3682   LOERCHER, J., Christianity versus polygamy; ibid, I, p. 235.

3683   KERR, J. G., Protestant missions in Kuangtung; ibid, I, p. 237.

3684   DOUGLAS, C., Mission building in the country; ibid, I, p. 260.

3685   — — , A reply to the charges brought against protestant missionaries in China, 1869, 8vo. See Ch. Recorder, II, p. 111.

3686   — — , The Delegates' version, Ch. Recorder, III, p. 18.

3687   Missionaries and their consuls; ibid, II, p. 11, 51, 53, 77, 110, 171.

3688 DODD, S., Missionary celibacy; ibid, II, p. 19.
3689 — —, The relation of christianity to Polygamy; ibid, II, p. 31, 253.
3690 — —, The Synod of China; ibid, III, p. 332.
3691 ASHMORE, W., Preparatory work in missions; ibid, II, p. 35.
3692 The protestant missionaries in China; ibid, II, p. 57, 63, 95, 141, 142; III, p. 255; V, p. 72 and p. I-VII, 1874.
3693 WHEELER, L. W., A missionary conference in Peking; ibid, II, p. 75.
3694 — —, Polygamy or concubinage; ibid, II, p. 136.
3695 BLODGET, H., Eight years in North-China; ibid, II, p. 76.
3696 — —, Address on missionary work in China; ibid, II, p. 250.
3697 — —, Distribution of the Bible; ibid, IV, p. 312.
3698 Schools in Kuangtung province; ibid, II, p. 79.
3699 TALMAGE, J. V. N., The relation of Chirstianity to Polygamy; ibid, II, p. 89.
3700 The Chinese government and missionaries; ibid, II, p. 105.
3701 DUDGEON, J., Notes of a Bible tour in Shansi; ibid, II, p. 134.
3702 The polygamy question; ibid, II, p. 162, 194.
3703 On native contribution; ibid, II, p. 211.
3704 A plea for Christian polyandry; ibid, II, p. 220.
3705 The Rival missions; ibid, II, p. 254.
3706 The Lord's day; ibid, II, p. 275.
3707 DOOLITTLE, J., Salaries of native helpers; ibid, II, p. 308.
3708 McGREGOR, W., The Lord's day; ibid, II, p. 320.
3709 — —, Amoy missionary statistics; ibid, IV, p. 234.
3710 CRIBB, A. W., WOODIN, S. F., Printing books in Foochow Colloquial; ibid, II, p. 324, 329.
3711 SWANSON, W. S., Ten Years of missionary life in Amoy; ibid, III, p. 8. 31.

3712 NEVIUS, J. L., Religious interest in Ping-tu; ibid, III, p. 140.
3713 RITCHIE, H., Missionary work among the Formosan aborigines; ibid, III, p. 167.
3714 MACLAY, R. S., Tenth annual methodist meeting at Foochow; ibid, III, p. 233.
3715 — — , Speeches of Chinese Christians on self support; ibid, IV, p. 284.
3716 HALL, W. N., Protestant missionaries in Lao-liang, Shantung; ibid, III, p. 359.
3717 BALDWIN, C. C., Self-supporting churches; ibid, III, p. 346.
3718 MAHOOD, J. E., Study of the Scriptures among Chinese Christians; ibid, III, p. 315.
3719 Duty of self Support; ibid, III, p. 309.
3720 EWER, F. H., Anti-polygamy; ibid, III, p. 353.
3721 Proposed regulations respecting missionaries in China; ibid, IV, p. 29.
3722 BOOMERANG, The missionary question; ibid, IV, p. 57.
3723 — — , The proposed missionary regulations; ibid, IV, p. 165.
3724 — — , The revision controversy; ibid, IV, p. 175.
3725 — — , The origin of the missionary troubles; ibid, IV, p. 200.
3726 — — , Discussion about missionaries in 1869; ibid, IV, p. 238.
3727 — — , Indiscretions of diplomatists; ibid, IV, p. 269.
3728 LECHELER, R., German missionaries in Canton province; ibid, IV, p. 137.
3729 Circular of the Chinese Government; ibid, IV, p. 141.
3730 JOHN, G., The Chinese Circular on foreign missions; ibid, IV, p. 149.
3731 — — , The Chinese Government and christian missions; ibid, IV, p. 151.
3732 CHALMERS, J., The missionary question; ibid, IV, p. 155.

3733 The Tsungli yamen mission circular; ibid, IV, p. 158.
3734 Second meeting of the Synod of China; ibid, IV, p. 235.
3735 BURDEN, J. S., Causes of hostility to missionaries; ibid, IV, p. 263.
3736 MUIRHEAD, W., China and the Gospel. London, 1871, 8vo., 305 pp.
3737 WILLIAMSON, A., The claims of China on Christian men. Edinburgh, 1871, 8vo.
See The Phoenix, II, p. 52.
3738 THOMSON, E., Our oriental missions. New York, 2 vols., 16mo. Vol. I: India and China; II: China and Bulgaria.
3739 MUELLER, C., Ueber Religion und Mission in China. Aus allen Welttheilen, Mai, 1872, p. 249.
3740 BOWRA, E. C., Christian missions in Kwangtung, China Review, II, p. 244-254, 1874.
3741 HUBRIG, F., Report for the year 1873-74 of the mission schools connected with the Rhenish mission in China. Hongkong, 1874, 8vo.
3742 Ein Chinesisches Urtheil über die Missionare, Deutsch. Protest. Blatt 1874, No. 28.
3743 Translation of a letter from R. Li Yumi, presiding elder of the Hok ch'iang district, in connection with the methodist mission at Foochow, 1874.
3744 BUTLER, J., The use of money as an aid and a hindrance to mission work in China, Chin. Recorder, V, p. 18-28.
See A. E. Moule; ibid, p. 91-98.
3745 PIERCY, G., The extension of missionary effort in the Canton province; ibid, p. 132-137.
3746 Opening of a new mission church; ibid, p. 214-216.
3747 GORDON, A., The late emeute at Chi-mi; ibid, p. 270-273.
3748 The proposed general conference of all the missionaries in China; ibid, p. 355-359.
3749 The terms for God and spirit, Chin. Recorder, VI, correspondence.

3750 GRAVES, R. H., What are the best means of developing the Christian character of our native converts? Ibid, VI, p. 197-205.
3751 DAVIS, J. W., The number of missionaries in China; ibid, VI, p. 340-344.
3752 Colportage in China; ibid, VI, p. 409-413.
3753 Minutes of the 3 meeting of the Synod of China, convened at Chefoo, Aug. 6th, 1874. Shanghai, 1875, 8vo.
　　　　See Chin. Recorder, VI, p. 237.
3754 TAYLOR, J. H., China's Millions and our work amongst them. London, 1875 ss. (monthly magazine).

3. Medical Missions.

3755 BRIDGMAN, E. C., Account of Hospitals at Macao and Canton, Chin. Repos., II, p. 270, 276; III, p. 364; VII, p. 551.
3756 COLLEDGE, T. R., Suggestions with regard to employing medical practitioners as missionaries to China; ibid, IV, p. 386.
3757 PARKER, P., Quarterly Reports of the Hospital at Canton; ibid, IV, p. 461; V, p. 32, 185, 323, 456; VI, p. 34, 433; VII, p. 92, 569; XIII, p. 239, 301; XIV, p. 449; XVII, p. 133; XIX, p. 253.
3758 — — , Reports of the Hospital at Macao; ibid, VII, p. 411.
3759 The medical missionary society; ibid, IV, p. 575; V, p. 370; VI, p. 32; VII, p. 419, 457; VIII, p. 624; X, p. 448, 465; XI, p. 659, 335, 520; XII, p. 189; XIII, p. 369; XV, p. 281.
3760 LOCKHART, W., Report of the hospital at Chusan, 1840; ibid, X, p. 453.
3761 — — , Reports of the hospital at Shanghai; ibid, XIII, p. 408; XVII, p. 188; XIX, p. 307; XX, p. 152.

3762 — — , Report of the Foundling hospital at Shanghai; ibid, XIV, p. 177.

3763 — — , 11 annual reports.

3764 — — , The medical missionary in China. Lon-
don, 1861, 8vo.
German by H. Bauer. Würzburg, 1863, 8vo.
See Ausland, 1863, p. 475 ss.

3765 — — , Medical missionary practice in Peking in
1861-1862, Chin. and Jap. Repos., I, May, June,
1864.

3766 MACGOWAN, D. J., Claim of the missionary enter-
prise on the medical profession. New York, 1842,
8vo.

3767 — — , Report of the hospitals at Ningpo and
Hongkong and of the dispensary at Amoy, 1847,
Chin. Repos., XVII, p. 242.

3768 HOBSON, B., Report of the Hospital at Hongkong,
1844; ibid, XIII, p. 377.

3769 — — , General report of the Hospital at Kam-li-
fau in Canton, 1848-49; ibid XIX, p. 300.

3770 — — , 9 annual reports. Canton 1848-57.

3771 — — , Forensic medicine in China, Med. Times
& gazette, 18 Nov., 1860.

3772 HEPBURN, J. C., Reports of the dispensary at
Amoy, 1844-45, Ch. Repos., XV, p. 181.

3773 WILLIAMS, S. W., Report of Lockhart's Hospital
at Shanghai and Macgowan's at Ningpo, 1848;
ibid, XVIII, p. 505.

3774 HEGEWALD, L., Chinese medical review. Paris,
1852, 8vo.

3775 KERR, J. G., 8 reports of the Medical Mission Hospital at Canton. Macao, 1857-60; Canton, 1861-
62; Hongkong, 1863-66 ss.

3776 COLLINS, W. H., The 13th annual report of the
Chinese Hospital at Shanghai. Shanghai, 1860,
8vo.

3777 HENDERSON, J., 5 annual reports of the Chinese
Hospital. Shanghai, 1861-65, 8vo.

3778 — — , Shanghai Hygiene or hints for the preservation of the health in China. Shanghai, 1863, 8vo.

3779 — — , Notes on some of the physical causes which modify climate. Shanghai.

3780 CARNEGIE, J., 4 annual reports of the Medical mission Hospital at Amoy. Hongkong, 1862-65, 8vo.

3781 CARMICHAEL, J. R., Report of the mission hospital at Kum-li fau. Canton, 1863, 8vo.

3782 GORDON, C. A., China from a medical point of view. London, 1863, 8vo.
> See Reader, 1863, No. 3, p. 62; Quart. Review, 1864, Jan., 1-42.

3783 SMITH, F. P., 2 annual reports of the Hankow medical mission hospital. Shanghai, 1865, 8vo.; Hankow, 1866, 8vo.
> See Chin. Recorder, III, p. 156.

2784 — — , The five annual reports of the Hankow medical mission hospital. Shanghai, 1870, 8vo.
> See J. Dudgeon, Physiology in the Hankow hospital report, Chin. Recorder, II, 232 ss.

3785 GENTLE, J., The annual reports of the Chinese dispensary. Shanghai, 1865, 8vo.

3786 Diet and regimen for Europeans in China, China Magazine, 1868, p. 146 ss.

3787 Medical mission at Peking, Chin. Recorder, I, p. 51; at Swatow; ibid, I, p. 74; at Hankow; ibid, I, p. 262.

3788 SYLE, E. W., Shanghai Asylum for the blind; ibid, I, p. 138.

3789 MORRISON, W. T., The medical missionary in China; ibid, I, p. 178.

3790 DUDGEON, J., The annual reports of the Peking hospital, 1865 ss., 1-12.
> See Chin. and Jap. Repos., III, p. 508, 561.

3791 MAXWELL, J. L., The medical missionary work in Formosa. Birmingham, 1869, 8vo.

See Chin. Recorder, I, p. 112.

3792 SHEARER, G., Annual report of the Hankow medical hospital. Shanghai, 1871, 8vo.
See Chin. Recorder III, p. 305.

3793 Medical Reports of the Foreign Maritime Customs. Shanghai, 1871, 4to., ss.
Medical statistics from the Treaty ports.

3794 Medical mission work in China, The Phoenix, II, p. 37.

3795 HARDEY, E. P., Annual report of the Hankow hospital. Hankow, 1873, 8vo.
See China Review, I, p. 330.

3796 JOHNSTON, J., Annual report of the Chinese hospital at Shanghai. Shanghai, 1874, 8vo.

3797 OSGOOD, D. W., Report of the Foochow medical mission hospital. Foochow, 1874, 8vo.

3798 GAULD, W., Report of the medical mission hospital at Swatow. Hongkong, 1874, 8vo.

3799 — — , Medical missions, Chin. Recorder, VI, p. 47-57.

3800 Report of the medical mission society in China. Hongkong, 1874, 8vo.

3801 SCARBOROUGH, W., Medical missions, Chin. Recorder, V, p. 137-152.

3802 MOULE, S. E., The opium refuge and general hospital at Hangchow; ibid, p. 256-262.

c. Commercial.
1. General.

3803 VALENTYN, F., Beschryvinge van den Handel en Vaart der Nederlanders of Tjsina. Amsterdam, 1726.

3804 COXE, S. W., history of the transactions and commerce between Russia and China, an Account of the Russian discoveries between Asia and America. London, 1780, p. 197 ss.

3805 GUIGNES, J. DE (père), Idée générale du commerce et des liaisons que les Chinois ont eues avec les nations occidentales, Rec. de l'Ac. des Inscr., XLVI, 1793.

3806 Notice sur les objets de commerce à importer en Chine, Mém. concern., VIII, p. 267.

3807 MILBURN, W., Oriental commerce. London, 1813, 2 vols., 4to.

3808 SLADE, J., Notices on the British trade to the port of Canton. London, 1820, 8vo.

3809 STAUNTON, Sir G., Miscellaneous notices relating to China and our commercial intercourse with the country. London, 1822, 8vo.
   See Rémusat, Nouv. Mél. as., I, p. 309.

3810 — — , Observations on our Chinese commerce, including remarks on the proposed reduction of tea duties, 1822 and 1850, 8vo.

3811 KLAPROTH, J., Commerce de la Russie avec la Chine en 1823, Annales des voy., XL, p. 273-299.

3812 Gedachten over den Chinahandel en de Theehandel. Rotterdam, 1824, 12mo.

3813 DAVIS, F., Two edicts from the Hoppo of Canton to the Hong merchants, 20th Oct., 1825, Transact. R. A. S., I, p. 541.

3814 A letter to Lord Althorp on the China trade. London, 1833, 8vo.

3815 MORRISON, R., Notices concerning the Chinese and the port of Canton. Malacca, 1833, 8vo.

3816 URMSTON, J. B., Observations on the China trade. London, 1833, 8vo.

3817 — — , A Pamphlet. London, 1834, 8vo.
   See As. Journ., N. S., VIII, 1834, p. 120.

3818 BRIDGMAN, E. C., Early nations who visited China to trade, Ch. Repos., I, p. 364.

3819 — — , Visit of the government and high officers to the E. I. Co.'s factory in Canton; ibid, III, p. 46.

3820 — — , Letters from foreign merchants to the governor and hoppo; ibid, V, p. 178.

3821 — — , Suspension of trade at Canton, Dec. 1838; ibid, VII, p. 137.

3822 — — , Passageboats allowed to run with passports; ibid, VII, p. 500.

3823 — — , Trade at Canton resumed in 1841; ibid, X, p. 233.

3824 — — , Notices of Curling Young's proposal to remove British Trade to an island; ibid, XII, p. 8.

3825 — — , Commerce a liberal pursuit; ibid, XV, p. 345.

3826 GODDART, J., Free trade with China; ibid, II, p. 355.

3827 — — , Fire insurance in Canton; ibid, IV, p. 30.

3828 MORRISON, J. R., Efforts to prevent sycee being exported; ibid, II, p. 383.

3829 — — , A Chinese commercial guide. Canton, 1834, 8vo.
This useful work has gone through several subsequent editions.

3830 — — , Regulations of the foreign trade at Canton, Ch. Repos., III, p. 579.

3831 — — , Report in reference to the circulation of Dollars; ibid, V, p. 419.

3832 — — , Edict stopping the passageboats for smuggling; ibid, VI, p. 103.

3833 — — , Proposal of Tsang Wang yen to stop all the foreign trade at Canton; ibid, VIII, p. 560.

3834 WILLIAMS, S. W., Chinese weights and measures; ibid, II, p. 444.

3835 — — , Imports and exports of Canton; ibid, II, p. 447.

3836 — — , Extent of the fur trade; ibid, III, p. 548.

3837 — — , A Chinese commercial guide. Canton, 1856, 8vo.

3838 THOMPSON, Considerations respecting the trade with China. London, 1835, 12mo.
See No. 3840.

3839 PHILIPPS, J., A practical treatise on the China and eastern trade. Calcutta, 1835, 8vo.

3840 KEATING, A. S., Review of Thompson's trade with

China, Ch. Repos., IV, p. 537.   See No. 3838.
3841 MATHESON, J., The present position and prospects
of the British Trade with China. London, 1836, 8vo.
See E. C. Bridgman, Ch. Repos., V, p. 241.
3842 Address to the people of Great Britain explanatory
of our commercial relations with China.   London,
1836, 8vo.
3843 INGLIS, R., Influence of foreign commerce and the
political relations of the Chinese empire, Ch. Repos., V, p. 202.
3844 Canton General Chamber of Commerce; ibid, VI,
p. 44, 327; VII, p. 386; XVI, p. 87.
3845 British and American Trade for 1836-37; ibid, VI,
p. 280.
3846 Dutch Trade; ibid, VI, p. 351; XVII, p. 208;
French trade; ibid, VI, p. 606; Russian trade;
ibid, XIV, p. 280; Foreign trade, ibid XV, p. 150,
291; XVIII, p. 295; XIX, p. 513; XII, p. 513.
3847 LAY, G. T., Probable advantages to British trade
from occupying the Bonin islands; ibid, VI, p. 381.
3848 — — , Notice of the Wusung custom-house register; ibid, XII, p. 144.
3849 Memorial to Lord Palmerston respecting the re-
covery of the Hong merchants' debts; ibid, VI,
p. 540.
3850 Address of foreign merchants respecting Hingtai
debts; ibid; VI, p. 543, 589.
3851 WINES, E, C., A peep at China and our commercial
intercourse with the Chinese.   Philadelphia, 1839,
8vo.
See D. Abeel, Ch. Repos., VIII, p. 581.
3852 Correspondence between Capt. Elliot and the British merchants on demurrage, Ch. Repos., VIII,
p. 122.
3853 Tea and Silk exports; ibid, IX, p. 191; XIV,
p. 401; XV, p. 386, 396.
3854 MARTIN, R. M., The Colonial magazine and com-
mercial-maritime journal.   London, 1840 ss.

3855 Commercial intercourse with China. London, 1842, 12mo.

3856 SCHOTT, W., Skizze zu einer Topographie der Produkte des Chinesischen Reiches. Berlin, 1842, 4to.

3857 On duties, Ch. Repos., XII, p. 33, 94, 393, 631; XIII, p. 655; XV, p. 262.

3858 Prospects and character of the British trade with China, Hunt's Merch. Mag., March, 1843; also Chin. Rep., XII, p. 513.

3859 FORBES, R. B., Remarks on China and the China trade. Boston, 1844, 8vo.

3860 DAVIDSON, Trade and travel in the far east. London, 1846, 8vo.

3861 Documents sur le commerce avec la Chine et l'Inde. Paris, 1846.

3862 Assay of sundry foreign coins and their value in sycee, Ch. Repos., XIV, p. 245.

3863 Cotton trade; ibid, XVI, p. 47, 134; XVII, p. 374.

3864 RONDOT, N., Etude pratique du commerce d'exportation de la Chine. Paris, 1848, 8vo.

3865 — — , Commerce de la France avec la Chine. Lyon, 1860, 8vo.

3866 LILJEWALCK, C. F., China's Handel, Industrie och Staatsförfattning, etc. Stockholm, 1848, 8vo.

3867 NYE, G. (jun.), Tea and the Tea trade. New York, 1850, 8vo.

3868 GUETZLAFF, K., Ueber die Handelsverhältnisse im östlichen Asien. Berlin, 1850, 8vo.

3869 Review of the trade of Shanghai in 1850. Shanghai, 1851, 8vo.

3870 Comparison between Opium and Tea in a commercial view, Ch. Repos., XX, p. 554.

3871 Commercial and political relations with China. Washington, 1855, 8vo.

3872 LOUREIRO, P., New tea tables. Shanghai, 1857, 8vo.

3873 — — , Tables showing the approximate cost of

tea laid down in New York. Shanghai, 1858, 4to.

3874 — — , Tables showing the approximate cost of tea laid down in England. Shanghai, 8vo.

3875 — — , Hongkong and Shanghai Bank share quotations. Shanghai, 1870, 8vo.

3876 PALLADIUS, O., Navigation between Tientsin and Shanghai, Russ. Eccl. Miss., III, No. 10, 1857 (in Russian).

3877 EULAMPADIUS, On Chinese paper money; ibid, No. 11 (in Russian).

3878 Remarks on the gales which occurred on the coast of China. Shanghai, 1857, 8vo.

3879 KORSAK, A., Historico-statistical sketch of the commercial relations of Russia with China. St. Petersburg, 1858 (in Russ.)

3880 DUCKWORTH, H., New route to Western China. Liverpool, 1860, 8vo; also London, 1861, 4to., map.

3881 ESCAYRAC DE LAUTURE, COMTE D', On the telegraphic transmission of Chinese characters, May, 1862.

3882 Papers relating to the rebellion in China and trade on the Yangtze Kiang River. London, 1862, fol.

3883 LAURENS, C., Navigation et commerce du Yang-tse-kiang en Chine, Revue marit. et col., 1863, Oct., p. 197-214.

3884 Customs Quarterly Gazettes and Annual Returns. Shanghai, 1863, 4to., ss.
   Besides carefully compiled statistics of the foreign trade with China, they contain a number of essays on native produce and trade in general.

3885 SKATSCHKOFF, C. A., Our commerce with China. St. Petersburg, 1863, 8vo. (in Russ.)

3886 STEPHENSON, Sir MACD. Railways in China, Report upon the feasibility and most effectual means of introducing railway communication into the empire of China. London, 1864, 8vo., with map.

Athenaeum, 1864, Sept. 3., p. 297; Westermann's illustr. Monatsh., 1865, No. 102,
p. 668.

3887 MEADOWS, T. T., Report on the consular district
of New Chwang, with reference to its commercial
capabilities, Naut. Mag., 1864, p. 505-514.

3888 SUMMERS, J., On Railways in China, Ch. and Jap.
Repos., I (1864), p. 443-448.
See Westermann's ill. Monatsh., 1865, No.
109, p. 111.

3889 WILLIAMS, C., Memorandum on the question of
British Trade with Western China via Burmah,
Journ. R. A. S. of Beng., 1864, No. IV, p. 407-
433 with map.

3890 — — , Through Burmah to Western China, being notes of a journey in 1863 to establish the
practicability of a trade route between the Irawaddi and the Yang-tse-kiang. Edinburgh, 1868,
8vo., 2 maps.

3891 GIBSON, The Trade of Tien-tsin, Naut. Mag., 1865,
Jan., p. 18-24.

3892 Renseignements sur les ports de Tchin-kiang et Han-
kao, Mouvement commercial de ce dernier port en
1862, etc., Annales du commerce extérieur, 1865,
Nov.

3893 KRIT, The ways of the overland commerce between
Russia and China, "Iswestija" Russ. Geo. Soc.,
1865 (in Russian).
German by F. Marthe, Ztschr. der Ges. f.
Erdk., 1867.

3894 PRINZ, G., The commerce of the Russians with the
Chinese; ibid, I, 1865 (in Russ.)

3895 Metallgeld in China, Augsb. Allg. Ztg., 1865, No.
257, Beilage.

3896 SCHLAGINWEIT, E., Der Nordrand von Berma und
der neue Handelsweg nach dem Innern von China, Globus, X (1866), No. 4, p. 118-122.

3897 China's auswärtiger Handel in den Jahren 1863 und

1864, Preuss. Handels-Archiv, 1866, 23. März, p. 330-335; 20. Apr., p. 439.

3898 LACROIX, Le papier monnaie en France et en Chine, Revue de l'économie chrétienne, 1867, Mai, No. 69, p. 787-818.

3899 DUCHESNE de BELLECOUR, P., La Chine, et le Japon à l'exposition universelle, Revue des deux mondes, T. LXX, livr. 3 (1. Aug. 1867), p. 710-742.

3900 ANDREE, R., Geographie des Welthandels. Stuttgart, 1867, 2 vols., 8vo.; 2nd edition, 1872.

3901 China and Rangoon, Further correspondence on the proposed communication between Rangoon and western China, Parliam. papers. London, 1867, fol.

3902 MAYERS, W. F., Salt monopoly in China, Notes and Queries, I, p. 126.

3903 COTTON, Sir A., On a communication between India and China by the line of the Burhampooter and Yangtsze, Journ. R. Geo. Soc., XXXVII, 1867, p. 231-239, map.

3904 LUEHDORF, F. A., Das Amurland, seine Verhältnisse und Bedürfnisse. Petermann's geogr. Mitth., 1868.
Remarks on the trade with Manchuria.

3905 CATTANEO, C., Le vie per l'Asia orientale, Bollet. d. soc. geogr. ital., Aug. 1868, p. 251.

3906 GOODENOUGH, F. A., Routes between upper Assam and western China, Proc. R. Geogr. Soc., XII, 1868, p. 334.

3907 Brick Tea, Notes and Queries, II, p. 30.
3908 The East India Company; ibid, II, p. 125-126.
3909 Rate of interest in China; ibid, II, p. 160.
3910 Life insurance in China; ibid, III, p. 51.
3911 BECCARI, G. B., Il commercio Chinese nel 1865. Righi, 1869, 8vo.
3912 BOWERS, A., Bhamo expedition, report on the practicability of reopening the trade route between

Burma and western China. Rangoon, 1869, 8vo.

3913 Papers relating to railway communication between British Burmah and western China, presented to Parliament. London, 1869, 4to.

3914 MICHIE, A., Reports on the trade of the upper Yang-tse. Shanghai, 1869.

3915 — — and FRANCIS, R., Reports of the delegates of the Shanghai general chamber of commerce on the trade of the upper Yangtse River, pres. to Parliament. London, 1870, 4to., 2 maps.

3916 MOSS, M., Narrative and commercial report of an exploration of the West River to Nan-ning fu. Hongkong, 1870, 8vo.

3917 VIGUIER, S. A., Code for transmitting Chinese despatches by Telegraph. Shanghai, 1870, 8vo.

3918 — — , A Chinese edition of the Code, containing a translation of his system of secret cyphering Chinese despatches. •Shanghai 1870, 8vo.

3919 The manufacture of Tea, Ch. Recorder, IV, p. 114.

3920 MACY, W. A., On the mode of applying the electric telegraph in connection with the Chinese language, Am. Or. Soc., Vol. III.

3921 SCHERZER, K. von, Die wirthschaftlichen Zustände im Süden und Osten Asiens. Berichte der fachmänn. Begleiter der K. K. Expedition nach Siam, China und Japan. Stuttgart, 1871, 8vo., 2 maps.
See Petermann's geogr. Mitth., 1872, p. 39.

3922 GARNIER, L. F., Des nouvelles routes de commerce avec la Chine, Bull. Soc. geogr. de Paris, Févr. 1872, p. 147-160.

3923 CRÉMAZY, F. L., Le commerce de la France dans l'extrême Orient, Revue marit. et col., Mai, 1872, p. 221-252.

3924 Trade routes to Western China. Liverpool, 1872, 8vo., map.

3925 POLTORATZKY, Report on the commerce with

western China, "Istwestija" Imp. Russ. Geogr. Soc., 1873, Vol. IX (in Russian).

3926 MARTIN, W. A. P., The metric system for China, Ch. Rec., V, p. 57-66, 1874.

3927 HANBURY, D., On a peculiar Camphor from China, Pharm. Journ., March, 1874.

3928 PLOWMAN, S., The chemistry of Ngai Camphor; ibid.

3929 Chinese Railways, China Review, II, p. 286-293.

3930 M'MAHON, A. P., On our prospects of opening a route to South Western China, Proc. R. Geo. S., XVIII, 1874, p. 463 ss.

3931 RICHTHOFEN, F. von, Ueber den natürlichsten Weg für eine Eisenbahnverbindung zwischen China und Europa. Verh. d. Ges. f. Erdk. Berlin, 1874, No. 4, p. 115-126.

  See F. Hirth, China Review, III, p. 49-51.

3932 LISTER, A., The shroff's mystery, China Rev., III, p. 1-13.

3933 YULE, H., Trade routes to Western China, Geo. Mag., 1875, p. 96-101, map.

3934 CORYTON, J., Trade routes between British Burmah and Western China, Proc. R. Geo. Soc., XIX, 1875, p. 264-291.

3935 JONES, C. T., Shanghai Exchange Tables. Shanghai.

3936 RUSSELL, H. V., China Coast Signal Book.

3937 BERGMAN, Captain, The China and Japan Pocket Diary, Almanac and Navigating directory for 1875-76. Shanghai, 1875, 8vo.

3938 MAERTENS, Shanghai Silk Tables. Shanghai, 1871, 8vo.; new ed., 1875.

3939 HOLLINGWORTH, H. G., List of the principal Tea districts in China and Notes on the names applied to the various black and green teas. Shanghai, 1876, 8vo.; also J. N. C. B. of R. A. S., Vol. X.

2. Opium.

3940 MORRISON, J. R., On Opium, Ch. Repos., III,
p. 487; V, p. 138, 259, 390, 398, 405, 462; VI,
341, 473; VII, 271, 599, 602.

3941 BRIDGMAN, E. C., On Opium; ibid, V, p. 470,
495, 546, 571; VI, p. 197; VII, p. 107, 173, 391,
605, 609; VIII, p. 1, 12, 57, 310, 425, 506; IX,
p. 311, 404.

3942 STEWARD, J. C., Remarks on the Opium trade;
ibid, V, p. 297.
Replies by J. Innes and A. S. Keating, Ch.
Repos., V, p. 367, 407, 524, 560; VI,
p. 40, 92.

3943 OLYPHANT, D. W. C., Premium for an essay on
the opium trade, showing its effects; ibid, V,
p. 413.

3944 Conditions of the award of £ 100 for an essay on
opium; ibid, V, p. 573.

3945 Revenue derived by the Indian government from
opium; ibid, VI, p. 193.

3946 Annual consumption of opium in China for 18 years;
ibid, VI, p. 302,

3947 WILLIAMS, S. W., On Opium; ibid, VI, p. 607;
XX, p. 479.

3948 Crisis of the Opium traffic. Canton, 1839, 8vo.

3949 THELWALL, A. S., The iniquities of the opium
trade with China. London, 1839, 8vo.

3950 THOM, R., Proclamation to the people of Kwangtung to refrain from opium; ibid, VII, p. 498.

3951 Question of indemnity for the opium seized by Lin;
ibid, VIII, p. 113.

3652 ACHANG, Letter of a Chinese youth respecting the
conduct of the English; ibid, VIII, p. 318.

3953 Opium crisis, a letter to Capt. Elliot by an American
merchant. London, 1839, 8vo.

3954 HOBSON, B., Opium and alkohol compared, Ch.
Repos., IX, p. 147.

3955 — — , Confessions of an English opium-eater and the effects of opium; ibid, IX, p. 425.

3956 SAURIN, La Chine, l'Opium et les Anglais. Paris, 1840, 8vo.

3957 WARREN, S., The Opium question. London, 1840, 8vo., 2nd edition.

3958 BULLOCK, T. H., The Chinese vindicated, or another view of the Opium question, A reply to S. Warren. London 1840, 8vo.

3959 ABEEL, D., Instances of the effects of opium smoking; Ch. Repos., IX, p. 289.

3960 SHUCK, J. L., Lin's ten regulations to remove opium evils; ibid, IX, p. 560.

3961 Memorial to Sir R. Peel on the opium trade; XII, p. 168.

3962 Export of Opium from Calcutta in 1834-45; ibid, XIV, p. 544.

3963 Proposition to legalize opium and Sir H. Pottinger's opinion; ibid, XVI, p. 39, 97.

6964 Remarks on the increased production of opium and character of the traffic; ibid, XVI, p. 179.

3965 PEGGE, J., A voice from China and India, relative to evils of the cultivation and smuggling of Opium. London, 1846, 8vo.

3966 Protection and extension of Opium cultivation in India, Ch. Rep., XVII, p. 655.

3967 ALLEN, N., The opium trade. Boston, 1850, 4to.

3968 MEDHURST, W. H., Remarks on the Opium trade. Shanghai, 1855, 8vo.

3969 MACGOWAN, D. J., Note on Chinese opium, Transact. Ch. Br. R. As. Soc., VI, 1859, p. 41-52.

3970 MATTEI, Quelques reflexions sur l'abus de la fumée d'opium. Montpellier, 1862.

3971 LIEBERMANN, Les fumeurs d'opium en Chine, Étude médicale, Rec. de Mém. de méd. mil., VIII; also separately. Paris, 1862, 8vo.

3972 Native opium. Shanghai, 1864, 8vo.

3973 SAMPSON, T., The Chinese word for Opium, Notes
and Queries, II, p. 158.
3974 MINCHIN, G., The Chinese word for Opium; ibid,
II, p. 159.
3975 SMITH, F. P., The Chinese word for Opium; ibid,
II, p. 171.
3976 DUDGEON, J., On the extent and some of the evils
of opium smoking, Ch. Recorder, I, p. 203; II,
p. 46.
3977 KERR, J. G., Opium and other narcotics; ibid, II,
p. 50, 170.
3978 MARTIN, E., L'opium en Chine. Paris, 1871, 8vo.
3979 The Friend of China, published by the Antiopium
Society. London.
3980 FRY, E., China, England and Opium, Contemp.
Review, 1876, Febr., p. 447-459.

d. Biographies of Europeans.

3981 COUPLET, P., Catalogus patrum societatis Jesu.
Paris, 1686, 8vo.; also in Verbiest's Astronomia
Europea, p. 100-123 (No. 2611).
3982 D'ENTRECOLLES, Mort du P. Ch. de Broissia,
Lettre de 1704, Lettr. édif., nouv. éd., XXVIII,
1832, p. 25-34.
3983 GUIGNES, J. DE, (père), Abrégé de la vie d'E.
Fourmont. Paris, 1747, 4to.
3984 XUARES, Vida iconologica del apostol F. Xavier.
Roma, 1798.
3985 BOUHOURS, La vie de S. François Xavier. Avi-
gnon, 1819, 2 vols., 12mo.
English by J. Dryden. London, 12mo.
See E. C. Bridgman, Ch. Repos., XII, p.
258; Ch. Magaz., 1869, p. 117.
3986 Memoir of the life and family of the late G. T.
Staunton, Brt., 1823, 8vo.
3987 MORRISON, R., Memoir of the Rev. W. Milne.
Malacca, 1824, 8vo.

3988 — — , Faithfulness of Dr. Milne, Ch. Repos., I, p. 410.

3989 Memoir of the Rev. W. Milne, D. D. Dublin, 1825, 24mo.

3990 STEVENS, E., Life and labors of W. Milne, Ch. Repos., I, p. 316.

3991 — — , Life and writings of Rev. R. Morrison; ibid, III, p. 177.

3992 BRIDGMAN, E. C., Sermon on the life and character of Lord Napier; ibid, III, p. 271.

3993 — — , Obituary of Rev. E. Stevens; ibid, V,p. 513.

3994 — — , Review of the life of G. Magaillans; ibid, X, p. 605.

3995 — — , Biographical notice of Robert Thom; ibid, XVI, p. 236.

3996 MORRISON, Mrs. E., Memoirs of the life and labours of R. Morrison, D. D. London, 1839, 2 vols., 8vo.

3997 JONES, Mrs. E. G., Obituary of the Rev. A. Reed, Ch. Repos., VI, p. 548.

3998 CARTON, Notice biographique sur le père F. Verbiest. Bruges, 1839, 8vo.

3999 PHILLIP, R., The life and opinions of the Rev. W. Milne. London, 1840, 8vo.

4000 CASWELL, J., Obituary notice of the Rev. N. S. Benham, Ch. Repos., IX, p. 84.

4001 STRONACH, J., A sermon, occasioned by the death of the Rev. S. Dyer. Singapore, 1843, 8vo.

4002 WOODWARK, J., A sermon, occasioned by the death of the Rev. S. Kidd. London, 1843, 8vo.

4003 MORRISON, J. R., Memoir of the life and labors of Dr. Morrison, Ch. Repos., X, p. 25.

4004 BROWN, S. R., Remusat's biographical notice of Prémare; ibid; X, p. 668.

4005 — — , A sermon preached on the occasion of the death of the Hon. J. R. Morrison. London, 1844, 8vo.
See Ch. Repos., XII, p. 456.

4006 P. RIPA, Memoirs during thirteen years' residence at the court of Peking, selected and translated from the Italian by F. Prandi. London, 1844, 8vo. ; ibid, 1861.

4007 DAVIES, E., Memoirs of the Rev. S. Dyer. London, 1846, 12mo.

4008 DEAN, W., Biographical notice of Mrs. Dean, Ch. Repos., XII, p. 207.

4009 JETER, J. B., A memoir of Mrs. H. Shuck. Boston, 1846, 12mo.

4010 SHUCK, J. L., Obituary notice of Mrs. H. Shuck, Ch. Repos., XIV, p. 19.

4011 PARKER, P., Funeral sermon on Mrs. Sword ; ibid, XIV, p. 377.

4012 GRUBE, Mrs. E., F. W. Grube und seine Reise nach China. Crefeld, 1848, 8vo.

4013 Obituary notices of Mrs. Pohlman, Mrs. Fairbrother and Mrs. Hobson, Ch. Repos., XVI, p. 168.

4014 Notices of Mrs. Marshman and Mrs. Moor ; ibid, XVI, p. 297.

4015 POHLMAN, W. J., Obituary of the Rev. J. Lloyd ; ibid, XVII, p. 651.

4016 WILLIAMS, S. W., Williamson's memoir of Rev. D. Abeel ; ibid, XVIII, p. 260.

4017 — — , Obituary of D. W. C. Olyphant and of the Rev. C. Gützlaff ; ibid, XX, p. 509.

4018 En kort Beretning om C. Gützlaff og den Chinesiske mission. Copenhagen, 1850, 8vo.

4019 ERDBRINK, G. R., Gützlaff, der Apostel der Chinesen. Rotterdam, 1850, 8vo.

4020 Memoir of the Rev. W. M. Lowrie. Philadelphia, 8vo.

4021 CULBERSTON, M. S., Memoir of the life of the Rev. W. M. Lowrie, Ch. Repos., XIX, p. 491.

4022 K. Gützlaff's Leben und Heimgang. Berlin, 1851, 12mo.

4023 MILLIES, Levensberigt van Dr. K. F. A. Gützlaff. Amsterdam, 1852, 8vo.

4024 MUIRHEAD, W., A sermon preached in comme-
moration of the death of the Rev. W. H. Medhurst,
D. D. Shanghae, 1857, 8vo.

4025 SACY, S. DE, Notice historique sur la vie et les ouvrages de M. A. Remusat. Paris, 1859, 4to.

4026 Notice nécrologique sur Biot, Journ. Asiat., 4. sér.,
XVI, p. 116.

4027 BONAR, Memoir of the life of the Rev. D. Sande-
mann. London, 1861, 8vo.

4028 Memoir of A. Rémusat, translated from the "Biographie universelle," Ch. & Ja. Rep., Aug., 1863.

4029 Memoir of J. Klaproth; ibid, Nov. 1863.

4030 NEUMANN, K. F., Der Sinologe A. Gonçalves,
Ztschr. der d. m. Ges., XVIII (1864), p. 294-96.

4031 BRIDGMAN, J. G., The life and labours of E. C.
Bridgman. New York, 1864, 8vo.

4032 MAYERS, W. F., Chinese names of Roman Catholic missionaries, Notes and Queries, I, p. 108.

4033 Chinese names of Roman catholic priests at Peking;
ibid, I, p. 125.

4034 LAPRIE, F., Panégyrique de l'abbé Beaulieu, missionnaire en Corée, martyrisé le 8 mars 1866.
Bordeaux, 1867, 8vo.

4035 PERRAND, A., Notice biographique sur l'abbé Cam-
bier, mort en Chine le 12 juin 1866. Lille et Paris, 1867, 8vo.

4036 GABORIT, P., Vie de François Mabileau, miss.
apostolique et provicaire au Su-Tchuen oriental,
mis à mort en haine de la rel. cath. dans la ville
de Yeou-Yang-Tchéou. Nantes, 1867, 12mo.

4037 BURNS, J., A memoir of the late Rev. W. C. Burns,
missionary to China. London, 8vo.

4038 Memorials of J. Henderson, medical missionary to
China. London, 8vo.

4039 BUSH, C. B., Five years in China or the factory
boy made a missionary, The life and observations
of Rev. W. Aitchison, late miss. to China. Philadelphia, 1866, 16mo.

4040 SWANSON, W. S., Death of Rev. W. C. Burns, Ch. Recorder, I, p. 28.

4041 Tribute to the memory of Rev. J. Cardwell; ibid, I, p. 97.

4042 KNOWLTON, M. J., David Brainard; ibid, I, p. 196.

4043 The late Rev. J. Williamson; ibid, II, p. 200.

4044 The late Rev. W. T. Morrison; ibid, II, p. 304.

4045 MacILVANE, J. S., Obituary notice of W. T. Morrison; ibid, II, p. 259.

4046 NEVIUS, J. L., The late Mrs. J. B. Hartwell; ibid, III, p. 82.

4047 The late Rev. R. F. Laughton; ibid, III, p. 83.

4048 BLODGET, H., The late Mrs. E. C. Bridgman; ibid, IV, p. 261, 298.

4049 Obituary notice of S. Julien; Trübner's lit. Record, 1873, March, p. 49.

4050 YULE, H., Francis Garnier, In Memoriam, Ocean Highways. March, 1874.

4051 Rev. M. J. Knowlton, Chin. Rec., V, p. 360-363.

4052 Memoir of the late Mrs. Mill; ibid, V, p. 274.

4053 HARTLAUB, G., Père A. David, Petermann's Mitth., 1876, p. 29-33.

XV. Aborigines, Miaotsze, Hakkas, etc.

4054 GROVIUS, van, Le Formulier des Christendoms met de Verklaringen van dien in de Sideis-Formosansche tale. Amsterdam, 1662, 4to.

4055 KLAPROTH, J., Sur la langue des indigènes de l'isle de Formosa, Journ. As., I, 1822.

4056 — — , Sur les indigènes de la province de Yunnan, Mag. As., II, 1826.

4057 — — Formosan vocabulary in Asia polyglotta, p. 380 (No. 440).

4058 Dialect of the people of the island of Hainan, Chin. Rep., I, p. 151.

4059 MEDHURST, W. H. et RITTER, dictionnaire de la langue Favorlangique (Formosa), Tijdschr. voor Nederl. Indie.

4060 — — , Dictionary of the Favorlang dialect of the Formosan language. Batavia, 1842, 12mo.

4061 WILLIAMS, S. W., Account of the Miaotzü, Ch. Rep., XIV, p. 106, 113; Reprinted in Ch. and Jap. Repos., I, Oct. 1863, p. 139-149.

4062 BRIDGMAN, E. C., Sketches of the Miau Tsze, J. N. Ch. Br. R. As. Soc., I, 1859, p. 257-292.

4063 LOBSCHEID, W., On the natives of the west coast of Formosa. Hongkong, 1860, 8vo.
Translated from the Dutch.

4064 SWINHOE, R., Notes on the ethnology of Formosa. London, 1863, 8vo.

4065 — — , The aborigines of Hainan, Journ. of N. C. B. of R. A. S., 1873, p. 25.

4066 HAPPART, G., Favorlang vocabulary. Verhandelingen van het Batav. Genotsch., XVII.

4067 EITEL, E. J., Hakka literature, Not. & Quer., I, p. 37.

4068 — — , Ethnographical sketches of the Hakka Chinese; ibid, I, p. 48, 65, 81, 97, 113, 129, 145, 161; II, p. 145, 167; III, p. 1.

4069 — — , An outline history of the Hakkas, China Review, p. 160-164.

4070 Formosan vocabularies, Not. & Quer., I, p. 70.

4071 BOWRA, E. C., The aborigines of Hainan; ibid, I, p. 83.

4072 Common origin of Formosans and Malays; ibid, I, p. 122.

4073 Spoken language of the Miautze and other aborigines; ibid, I, p. 131.

4074 TAINTOR, E. C., The aborigines of Hainan; ibid, II, p. 17.

4075 — — , The aborigines of Northern Formosa. Shanghai, 1874. See "Globus," 1874, No. 15, 16.

4076 Curious Hakka customs at burials of women who die in childbed; ibid, II, p. 96.

4077 Hakkas, Ch. Mag., 1868, p. 134.

4078 GUÉRIN et BERNARD, Les aborigènes de l'île de Formose, Bull. de la Soc. de géo. de Paris, Juin, 1868, map.

4079 — , Vocabulaire du dialecte Tayal ou aborigène de l'île de Formose, Note sur la langue des aborigènes et remarques sur le précédent vocabulaire par M. l'abbé Favre; ibid, 1869, Nov. et Déc., 1868, p. 466.

4080 SCHETELIG, A., Ueber formosanische Sprachreste, Zeitschr. f. Völkerpsychologie, 1869.

4081 Dialects of the Miautze and Chongtze, their affinity to that of the Siamese, Not. & Quer., III, p. 61.

4082 GRAVES, R. H., The Miautze, Chin. Rec., II, p. 264.

4083 PITTON, C., The Hia-k'ah in the Chekiang province; ibid, II, p. 218.

4084 — — , On the original history of the Hakkas, China Rev., I, p. 222-226.

4085 EDKINS, J., The Miautzï tribes, their history, Chin. Rec., III, p. 33, 74; also separately.

4086 — — , A vocabulary of the Miaudialects; ibid, III, p. 96, 134, 147, 149.

4087 MACGOWAN, D. J., Note on the Chehkiang Miautsz, Journ. N. C. B. of R. A. S., 1871, p. 123.

4088 HAMY, C. T., Les negritos à Formose et dans l'archipel japonais, Bull. Soc. d'Anthrop, 1873.

4089 DESGODINS, Mots principaux des langues de certains tribus, qui habitent les bords du Lan-tsang-Kiang, du Sou-tze-Kiang et Irawaddy, Bull. Soc. de Géogr. de Paris, Febr., 1873.

4090 PLATH, H., Die fremden barbarischen Stämme im alten China, Sitz. Ber. Phil. Hist. Cl. Acad. München, 1874, IV; also separately. München, 1874, 8vo.

4091 BULLOCK, T. L., Formosan dialects and their connection with the Malay, China Rev., III, p. 38 ss.

4092 STEERE, J. B., The aborigines of Formosa; ibid, 171 ss.

c. Extraprovincial China.

XVI. Languages and Literature.

a. Mandshu Language and Literature.

4093 GERBILLON, P., Elementa linguae tartarico-man-tchuricae, Thévenot, Rel. de div. voy., 2nd ed. Paris, 1696, Vol. II, 34 pp.
> The Catalogue of the Jesuits and Hyde in his syntagma diss. state, that this Grammar was written by Verbiest.
> French by Amiot, Grammaire Tartare-mant-chou. Paris, 1787, 4to; also Mém. conc.,XIII, p. 39-73 ("with the omission of the last 42 paragr. on the peculiarities of the Mandchu," Wylie).
> English: Shanghae, 1855.

4094 DESHAUTERAYS, Alphabet Mandchou, in Petity's Encyclopaedie élémentaire ou bibliothèque des arts et des amateurs. Paris, 1766, II, No. 2, p. 546 ss.

4095 HYDE, Syntagma dissertationum ed. G. Sharpe. Oxonii, 1767, 2 vols., 4to.
> Contains remarks on Mandshu characters.

4096 LA CROZE, Thesauri epistolici, contains notes on Mandshu.

4097 AMIOT, Eloge de la ville de Moukden de ses environs, poëme composé par Kienlong accompagné des notes curieuses et publié par M. de Guignes. Paris, 1770, 8vo.
> See Mém. conc., IX, p. 2; Klaproth, Mém. rcl. à l'Asie, III, p. 48 ss.

4098 — — , Art militaire des Chinois. Paris, 1772, 4to.; and Mém. conc., VII, p. 161-224.
> Translation of the tshauha baita be gisurengge.

4099 — — , Dictionnaire Tartare-Mandchou-Français, composé d'après un dictionnaire Mandchou-Chinois, redigé et publié avec des additions et l'alphabet de cette langue par M. Langlés. Paris, 1789, 2 vols., 4to.

Translations of the 清文彙書 t'shing-wen hui-shu, manju isabuha bithe, 1750.

4100 — — , Hymne Tartare-Mandchou, chanté à l'occasion de la conquête du Kin-tchhouan, traduit en Français et accompagné de notes pour l'intelligence du texte par M. Amiot et publié par M. Langlés. Paris 1792, 4to., 26 pp.

4101 — — , Rituel des Tartare-Mandchoux, Notes et Extraits, VII, p. 241-308; also Paris, 1804, 4to.

Published under the name of Langlés, but written by Amiot. See J. des Savans, ed. Amsterdame, 1773, LXV, p. 112-127; German in Murr's Journal z. Kunstgesch. und Litt., IV, p. 249 ss. For corrections see Klaproth, Mém. rel. à l'Asie, III, p. 66-80.

4102 LEONTIEFF, A., Kitaiskaya mysli (Chinese thoughts), translated from the Mandshu. St. Petersburg, 1772, 8vo. (in Russian).

4103 — — , Complete customs of the Taitsing dynasty. St. Petersburg, 1781, 8vo. (in Russian).

Mandshu original: Dai tsing gurun i uheri kauli.

4104 — — , Chinese embassy to Ayuka, Khan of the Kalmucs with a description of the country and customs of the Russians, translated from the Mandshu. St. Petersburg, 1782, 8vo.

Compare Staunton's translation of the same work, No. 203.

4105 — — , Translation of the history of the 8 banners from the Mandshu. St. Petersburg, 1784 (in Russian).

4106 BAYER, T. S., De litteratura Mangiurica, Comment. Acad. Petropol., VI, p. 330.
4107 — — , Dissertatio de lingua Mangiurica. Ibidem.
4108 Notices et Extraits des M. S. de la bibliothèque du Roi. Paris, 1787-1831, 12 vols., 4to.
"This work notices upwards of 200 MS. relating to Manchu Literature and gives extended descriptions of some of the works," Wylie.
4109 LANGLÉS, M., Alphabet Tartare-Mandchou. Paris, 1787, 8vo. ; 2nd ed., 1789 as introduction to Amiot's dictionary (No. 4099); 3rd. ed., 1807, 8vo.
4110 — — , Sur deux MS. Mantchoux de la bibliothèque nationale (Rituel avec 2 planches, dictionnaire), Notices et Extraits, 1792-97, 70 pp.
On Langlés works and editions see Klaproth, Lettres No. 4115, and Mél. rel. à l'Asie, III, 1828.
4111 AGAFONOFF, A., The sacred edict, translated from the Mandshu. St. Petersburg, 1788 (in Russian).
4112 Adelung's Mithridates (No. 846.) Mandschurische Sprache, I, p. 514-527, 1806.
4113 VLADYKIN, A., Familiar conversations in Chinese and Mandshu, translated from the second book of the T'shing wen t'shi meng bithe (in Russian).
4114 ORLOFF, A., Grammar of the Mandshu language (in Russian).
4115 KLAPROTH, J., Lettres sur la littérature mandchoue, traduites du Russe de M. A. L. Leontiew. Paris, 1815, 8vo.; also Mél. rel. à l'Asie, III, p. 7 ss., 1828.
Severe critique of Langlés' publications.
4116 — — , Verzeichniss No. 668, contains many extracts from Mandshu works.
4117 — — , Asia polyglotta No. 440, contains list of Mandshu words.
4118 — — , Chrestomathie Mandchou ou Recueil de

textes Mandchou destiné aux personnes qui veulent s' occuper de l'étude de cette langue. Paris, 1828, 8vo.

4119 Catalogue des livres composant la bibliothèque de feu M. Klaproth par Landresse.

4120 RÉMUSAT, A., L'invariable milieu, ouvrage moral de Tseu-sse, en Chinois et en Mandchou avec une version ltitérale latine, une traduction françoise et des notes. Précédé d'une notice sur les quatre livres moraux communément attribués à Confucius, Notices et Extraits, X; also Paris, 1817, 4to.

4121 — — , Recherches sur les langues Tartares ou Mémoires sur différents points de la grammaire et de la littérature des Mandchous, des Ouigours et des Tibétains. Paris, 1820, 4to.

4122 JULIEN, S., Latin translation of Meng-tseu, No. 156.

4123 — — , Les deux frères (with Mandshu text), Revue Orientale et Américaine, 1862.
   Also as appendix to Adam's grammar, No. 4141.

4124 LIPOFTSOFF, E., Institutions of the Li-fan-yüan or board of foreign relations, translated from the Mandshu. St. Petersburg, 1828, 4to. (in Russian).

4125 GABELENTZ, H. C. von der (sen.), Elémens de la grammaire Mandchoue. Altenbourg, 1832, 8vo.

4126 — — , Mandschu-Mongolische Grammatik aus dem San-ho-pian-lan übersetzt. Ztschr. f. d. Kunde d. Morgenl., I, p. 255-286; Göttingen, 1837, 8vo.

4127 — — , Mandschuische Grammatik nach dem San-ho-pian-lan; ibid, III, p. 88-104, 1840.

4128 — — , Singli-tschin-thsiouan die wahrhafte Darstellung der chinesischen Naturphilosophie, aus dem Mandschu übersetzt; ibid, III, p. 150 ss.

4129 — — , Beiträge zur mandschuischen Conjugationslehre, Ztschr. d. D. M. G., XVIII, p. 202 ss.

4130 — — , Sseschu, Schuking, Schiking in mandschuischer Uebersetzung mit einem Mandschu-deutschen Wörterbuche. Ztschr. f. d. K. d. M. Leipzig, 1864, 2 vols., 8vo.

4131 SCHMIDT, I. J., Neue Erläuterungen über den Ursprung des Namens Mandschu, Bull. sc. de l'Acad. de St. Petersbourg, VIII, 1841.

4132 CUSHING, C., Considerations on the language of communication between the Chinese and European government, Chin. Repos., June 1844.

4133 MEADOWS, T. T., Translations from the Manchu. Canton, 1949, 8vo.
> See S. W. Williams, Chin. Repos., XVIII, p. 607-617.

4134 WYLIE, A., Translation of the T'sing wen k'emung, a Chinese grammar of the Manchu Tartar language, with introductory notes on Manchu literature. Shanghai, 1855, 8vo., LXXX, 310 pp.

4135 KAULEN, F., Linguae Mandschuricae institutiones quas conscripsit, indicibus ornavit, chrestomathia et vocabulario auxit. Ratisbonae, 1856, 8vo.

4136 WASSILYEFF, W., Mandshu chrestomathy. St. Petersburg, 1857, 8vo. (in Russian).

4137 — — , Kratki mandjursko-russki slovar (Abbridged Mandshu-Russian dictionary). St. Petersburg, 1866, 8vo. (in Russian).

4138 GABELENTZ, H. C. von der (jun.), Mandschu Bücher angezeigt. Ztschr. d. D. M. G., XVI, p. 538. 1862.

3139 — — , Ueber die Ausdrücke für sterben im Mandschnischen, Mitth. d. Vereins f. Erdk. Leipzig, 1873.

4140 TAINTOR, E. C., Thesaurus of the Manchu language, Notes and Queries, III, p. 47.

4141 ADAM, L., Grammaire de la langue mandchou. Paris, 1873, 8vo.
> See Chin. Recorder, V, p. 228, 1874.

4142a SACHAROFF, J., Polnui mantschursko-russki slovar (Complete Mandshu Russian dictionary). St.

Petersburg, 1875, XXX, 1129 pp., gr. 8vo.

4142b GABELENTZ, G. von der, 太極圖 Thaï kih-thu des Tscheu-tsï Tafel des Urprincipes mit Tschu-Hi's Commentare nach dem Ho- pih-sing-li Chinesisch mit Mandschuischer und Deutscher Uebersetzung, Einleitung und Anmerkungen herausg. Dresden, 1876, 8vo.
　　　See Chin. Rec., VII, p. 307.

b. Mongolian Language and Literature.

4143 WHITE, Institutes political and military, written originally in the Mogul language by the great Timur. Oxford, 1783, 4to.

4144 MAJER, F., Kalmückische Lieder, As. Magaz., I, p. 547-554, 1802.

4145 RÉMUSAT, A., Recherches sur les langues Tartares. Paris, 1820, 4to.
　　　See No. 4121.

4146 SCHMIDT, J. J., Text und Uebersetzung zweier Briefe von den Königen von Persien, Argun und Adschaitu an Philipp den Schönen. St. Petersburg, 1824, 8vo.

4147 — — , Zugabe zu den von A. Rémusat bekannt gemachten zwei mongolischen Originalbriefen. St. Petersburg, 1824.

4148 — — , Geschichte der Ostmongolen, aus dem Mongolischen des Ssenang Ssetsen übersetzt, mit dem Originaltexte. St. Petersburg, 1829, 4to.
　　　See A. Rémusat, Analyse de l'histoire des Mongols de Sanang-Setsen. Mél. posthumes, p. 373-458; K. F. Neumann, Jahrb. f. wiss. Kritik, 1829.

4149 — — , Grammatik der Mongolischen Sprache. St. Petersburg, 1831, 4to.
　　　In Russian: 1832, 8vo.; In French by A. M. Hamelin. Rennes, 1870, 8vo.

4150 — — , Bericht über eine Inschrift aus der ältesten Zeit der Mongolenherrschaft. St. Petersburg, 1833, 4to.

4151 — — , Mongolisch-Deutsch-Russisches Wörterbuch. St. Petersburg, 1835, 4to.

4152 — — , Ueber eine mongolische Grabinschrift. St. Petersburg, 1847.

4153 KLAPROTH, J., Table chronologique des plus célèbres patriarches et des événements remarquables de la religion bouddhique, red. en 1678, trad. du mongol, J. as., 2. sér., VII, 1831.

4154 KOVALEVSKY, Mongol Grammar. Kazan, 1835, 8vo. (in Russian).

4155 — — , Mongol Chrestomathy. Kazan, 1837, 2 vols., 8vo. (in Russian).

4156 — — , Dictionnaire Mongol-Russe-Français. Kazan, 1844-49, 3 vols., 4to.

4157 BOBRONEKOV, A., Mongol Grammar. St. Petersburg, 1835, 4to. (in Russian).

4158 — — , Mongol-Kalmück grammar. Kazan, 1849, 8vo.

4159 SCHOTT, W., Versuch über die tatarischen Sprachen. Berlin, 1836, 4to.

4160 — — , Das Zahlwort in der tschudischen Sprachklasse, wie auch im Türkischen, Tungusischen und Mongolischen. Berlin, 1854, 4to.

4161 POPOV, Mongol Chrestomathy. Kazan, 1837, 2 vols., 8vo. (in Russian).

4162 YULE, Primer in the Mongol language, 1837, 4to.

4163 GABELENTZ, C. von der, Versuch über eine alte Mongolische Inschrift. Göttingen, 1839, 8vo.

4164 HUC, M. et GABET, Les 42 points d'enseignement professés par Bouddha, traduits du Mongol, J. as., 4. sér., XI, 1848.

4165 ZWICK, H. A., Grammatik der westmongolischen Sprache. Donaueschingen, 1853, 4to.

4166 — — , Handbuch der westmongolischen Sprache. Donaueschingen, 1853, 4to.

4167 EDKINS, J., An account of Sanscrit and Mongolian

characters found in Chinese books, Transact. C. B. of R. A. S., V, 1856, p. 101-108.

4168 — — , Who were the Kin Tartars? Chin. Recorder, II, p. 315.

4169 — — , The Tartar languages, Phoenix, I, p. 6, 12.

4170 — — , Mongol and European common words; ibid, II, p. 149.

4171 MACHMUDOF, Practical exercises in the Tartar language. Kazan, 1857, 8vo. (in Russian).

4172 SCHIEFNER, A., Ueber die unter dem Namen Geschichte des Ardschi Bordschi Chan bekannte mongolische Märchensammlung, Mél. as., III. St. Petersburg, 1858.

4173 PAUTHIER, G., Rapport sur deux médailles en cuivre jaune. Paris, 1860, 8vo.

4174 — — , De l'alphabet de Pa-sse-pa. Paris, 1862, 8vo.

4175 — — , Sur l'alphabet de Pa-sse-pa et de la tentative faite par Khoubilai Khan pour transcrire la langue figurative des Chinois, J. as., 5. sér., XIX, p. 5; also Paris, 1862, 8vo.

4176 WYLIE, A., Sur une inscription mongole en caractères Pa-sse-pa. Paris, 1862, 8vo.

4177 JUELG, B., Märchen des Siddhikür, oder Erzählungen eines verzauberten Todten. Ein Beitrag zur Sagenkunde auf buddhistischem Gebiete. Kalmückisch und deutsch. Leipzig, 1866, 4to.
See H. C. von der Gabelentz, Ztschr. d. D. M. Ges., XX, p. 455.

4178 — — , Mongolische Märchen. Erzählung aus der Sammlung Ardschi Bordschi. Mongolisch und deutsch. Innsbruck, 1867, 8vo.

4179 — — , Die neun Märchen des Siddhi-kür nach der ausführlicheren Redaktion und die Geschichte des Ardschi Bordschi Chan. Mongolich mit deutscher Uebersetzung und krit. Anmerkungen. Innsbruck, 1868, 8vo.

308

See H. C. von der Gabelentz, Ztschr. der D.
M. Ges., XXI, p. 297; XXII, p. 743.
4180   BOWRA, E. C., Mongol and Mogul, Tatar and Tartar, Notes and Queries, I, p. 57.
4181   DENNYS, N. B., A short vocabulary of the Mongolian language in the dialect chiefly used on the northern borders of China; ibid, I, p. 132.

c. Tibetan Language and Literature.

4182   GEORGII, F. AUGUSTINI ANTON. Eremitae Alphabetum Tibetanum, missionum apostolicarum commodo editum. Romae, 1762, 2 vols., 4to.
Topography of Tibet and itineraries from this work translated into German by J. C. Fabri, Samml. von Stadt,-Land-und Reisebeschreibungen. Halle, 1783, p. 207-314.
4183   Alphabetum Tibetanum sive Tungutanum. Romae, 1773, 8vo.; ed. J. Chr. Amadatius.
4184   PAULINUS, a S. BARTHOLOMEO, Musei Borghiani Velitris codices M. S. Avenses, Peguani etc. Accedunt monumenta inedita et cosmogonia Indico-tibetana. Romae, 1793, 4to.
4185   CSOMA de KOEROES, Translation of a Tibetan fragment, with remarks by H. H. Wilson, J. R. A. S. of Bengal, I, 1822.
4186   — — , Origin of the Shákya race, translated from the La or the 26th vol. of the Do class in the Kagyur; ib., II, 1833.
4187   — — , Note on the origin of the Kala Chakra and Adi Buddha Systems; ib., II, 1833.
4188   — — , Extracts from Tibetan works translated; ib., III, 1834.
4189   — — , Essay towards a dictionary Tibetan and English. Calcutta, 1834.
4190   — — , Tibetan and English dictionary. Calcutta, 1834, 4to. (See No. 4210.)

4191 — — , Grammar of the Tibetan language. Calcutta, 1834, 4to.
  See Chin. Repos., III, p. 185 ; IV, p. 40.
4192 — — Analysis of a Tibetan medical work, J. of R. A. S. of Bengal, V, 1835.
4193 — — , Abstract of the contents of the Bstangyur, As. Res., XX, 1836.
4194 — — , Analysis of the Dulva, a portion of the Tibetan work entitled the Kahgyur; ib., XX, 1836.
4195 — — , Analysis of the Sher-Chin, Phal-chhen-Dkonseks-Dode-Nyang-Das and Gyut, being divisions 2 to 7 of the Tibetan Work entitled Kahgyur; ib., 1836.
4196 — — , Interpretation of the Tibetan inscription on a Bhotian Banner taken in Assam, J. R. As. Soc., of Bengal, V, 1836.
4197 — — , Notices on the life of Shakya, extracted from Tibetan authors, As. Res., XX, 1836.
4198 — — , Translation of a Tibetan Sloka, J. R. As. Soc. of Bengal, V, 1836.
4199 — — , Enumeration of historical and grammatical works to be met with in Tibet; ib., VII, 1838.
4200 — — , Notices on the different systems of Buddhism extracted from Tibetan authorities; ib., VII, 1838.
4201 — — , Remarks on the notice of amulets; ib., IX, 1840.
4202 On the language and literature of Tibet, Quarterly Orient. Magaz., IV, 1825.
4203 On the great Tibetan Kanjur in 98 vols., edited under Kienlong; ibid, VII, 1826; and J. as., X, p. 138 ss.
  Mongolian translation of the same : Rémusat Rech., I, p. 217 (No. 4145.)
4204 MOORCROFT, W., On the scripture of the Tibetans, As. Journ., 1826.
4205 BURNOUF, E., Sur la littérature du Tibet, J. as., X, 1827.

4206 HODGSON, B. H., Notice sur la langue, la littérature et la religion des Bouddhistes du Népal et du
Bhot ou Tubet, J. as., 2 sér., VI, 1830, 2 plates.

4207 — — , Remarks on an inscription in the Banja
and Tibetan characters, taken from a temple on
the confines of the valley of Nepal, J. R. A. S. of
Beng., II, IV, 1833, 1835, plate.

4208 — — , Essays on the languages, literature and
religion of Nepal and Tibet. London, 1874, 8vo.
See Lit. Centralbl., 1875, No. 17.

4209 WILSON, H. H., Notes on the literature of Thibet,
Gleanings in Science, III. Calcutta, 1831.

4210 KLAPROTH, J., Observations sur le dictionnaire
tubétain imprimé à Serampore, Nouv. J. as., VI.

4211 Das Herz (die Quintessenz) der zum jenseitigen Ufer
des Wissens gelangten allerheiligst Vollendeten.
Eine tibetanische Religionsschrift. Leipzig, 1835,
8vo.

4212 Prayers in Tibetan. Smon-lam-btschu-tham-abyor-
bai-smon-bsongo-ba. Leipzig, 1835, 8vo.

4213 SCHMIDT, I. J., Ueber die Begründung des tibetischen Sprachstudiums in Russland und die Her-
ausgabe der nöthigen Hilfswerke, Bull. de l'Acad.,
I, 1836.

4214 — — , Ueber die Heroen des vorgeschichtlichen
Alterthums; ibid, II, 1837.

4215 — — , Die Thaten des Helden Bogda Gesser
Chan. St. Petersburg, 1839, 8vo.

4216 — — , Grammatik der tibetischen Sprache. St.
Petersburg, 1839, 4to.

4217 — — , Grammatika tibetskago yasuika. St. Petersburg, 1839, 4to., XIII, 333 pp.

4218 — — , Tibetisch-Deutsches Wörterbuch. St. Petersburg, 1841, 4to.

4219 — — , Tibetan-Russian Dictionary. St. Petersburg, 1843, 4to.

4220 — — , Der Index des Kandjur herausgegeben.
St. Petersburg, 1845, 4to., II, 251 pp., lithogr.

4221 — — , Der Weise und der Thor, aus dem tibetischen. Mit Text. St. Petersburg, 1845, 2 vols., 4to.

    'See No. 4234.

4222 — — und BOETHLINGK, O., Verzeichniss der tibetischen Handschriften und Holzdrucke im asiatischen Museum. St. Petersburg, 1847, 8vo.

4223 FOUCAUX, P. É., Specimen du Gya Tch'er Rol Pa (Lalitâ Vistâra), Partie du Chap. VII, contenant la naissance de Çakya Mouni. Texte tibétain trad. en français. Paris, 1841, 4to.

    See Brockhaus in Neue Jen. Lit. Zeit., 1842.

4224 — — , Le sage et le fou, extrait du Kanjur, revu sur l'édition originale et accompagné d'un glossaire. Paris, 1842, 8vo.

4225 — — , Ryga Tch'er Rol Pa (Lalitâ Vistâra) ou développement des Jeux, contenant l'histoire du Bouddha Çakya Mouni, trad. sur la version tibétaine et revu sur l'original sanscrit. Paris, 1847-49, 2 vols., 4to., Texte tibétain et traduction avec 6 planches.

    See A. Schiefner Mél. as., I, 1852; B. de St. Hilaire, J. des Sav., May to October 1854; Jan., Febr., April 1855.

4226 — — , Parabole de l'enfant égaré, formant le Chap. IV, du Lotus de la Bonne Foi, publiée pour la première fois en sanscrit et en tibétain et accompagnée d'une traduction française. Paris, 1854, 4to.

4227 — — , Le tresor de belles paroles, Choix de sentences composées en tibétain par le Lama Saskya Pandita, trad. en français. Paris, 1858, 8vo.

4228 — — , Grammaire de la langue tibétaine. Paris, 1858, 8vo., XXXII, 227 pp.

4229 — — , La guirlande précieuse des demandes et des reponses publiée en sanscrit et en tibétain et traduite en français. Paris, 1867, 8vo.

4230 Das ehrwürdige Mahajanasutra mit Namen: das

unermessliche Lebensalter und die unermessliche Erkenntniss. St. Petersburg, 1845, 25 Blätter in fol., lithogr.

4231 SCHIEFNER, A., Eine tibetanische Lebensbeschreibung Sakyamuni's, des Begründers des Buddhathums. St. Petersburg, 1849, 8vo.

    See O. Boehtingk, Bull. hist. phil. de l'ac. de St. Pet., V.

4232 — — , Tibetische Studien, Mél. as., I. St. Petersburg, 1851.

4233 — — , Das buddhistische Sûtra der 42 Sätze, aus dem Tibetischen übersetzt; ibid, I, 1852.

4234 — — , Ergänzungen und Berichtigungen zu Schmidt's Ausgabe des Dsanglun. St. Petersburg, 1852, 4to.

    See Schmidt No. 4221.

4235 — — , Ueber die logischen und grammatischen Werke im Tanjur. St. Petersburg, 4to.

4236 — — , Ueber eine eigenthümliche Art tibetanischer Composita, Mél. as., III, p. 12-16.

4237 — — , Buddhistische Triglotta, d. h. Sanscrit-tibetisch-mongolisches Wörterverzeichniss. St. Petersburg, 1859, fol.

4238 — — , Carminis indici 'Vimalaprasnatta raratnamala' versio tibetica. Petropoli, 1859, fol.

4239 — — , Târanâthae de doctrinae Buddhicae in India propagatione narratio. Petropoli, 1868, 8vo.

4240 — — , Târanâtha's Geschichte des Buddhismus in Indien, aus dem Tibetischen übersetzt. St. Petersburg, 1869, 8vo.

    See Wassilyeff No. 2913, 4254.

4241 — — , Barathae responsa tibetice cum versione latina. Petropoli, 1875, 4to., IV, 46 pp.

4242 SCHLAGINWEIT, E., Ueber das Mahayama Sutra Digpa thamchad shag par terchoi, ein buddhistisches Beichtbuch aus dem Tibetanischen uebersetzt und erläutert. Sitz. b. d. Bayer. Ak., I, II, 1863, 1864.

4243 — — , Tibetische Inschrift aus dem Kloster Heinis in Ladak. Mit Textbeilage; ibid, II, 1864.

4244 — — , Die Tibetischen Handschriften d. Kgl. Hof und Staatsbibliothek zu München; ibid, II, 1, 1875.

4245 JAESCHKE, H. A., Brief an den Akademiker A. Schiefner. Bull. de l'ac. de St. Petersb., VII, 1864.

4246 — — , A short practical grammar of the Tibetan language. Kyelang, 1865, 8vo.

4247 — — , Romanized Tibetan and English dictionary. Kyelang, 1866, 8vo.
   See Notes and Queries, III, p. 96; The Phoenix, I, p. 11.

4248 — — , Ueber die Phonetik der Tibetischen Sprache. Monatsber. der Kgl. Preuss. Ak. d. W. Berlin, 1867, p. 148 ss.

4249 — — , Probe aus dem Tibetischen Legendenbuche die 100000 Gesänge des Milaraspa. Ztschr. d. D. M. G., XXIII, p. 543 ss.

4250 — — , Tibetisch-Deutsches Wörterbuch. Leipzig, 1874, 8vo.

4251 FEER, L., Textes tirés du Kanjur, Tchandra-Sutra, Surya-Sutra, Tchatur-Gatha. Paris, 1864, 8vo.

4252 — — , Le Tibet, le Bouddhisme et la langue tibétaine, Rev. or. et am., IX, 1864.

4253 — — , Le Sûtra en 42 articles. Textes chinois, tibétain, mongol authographiés. Paris, 1868, 8vo.

4254 WASSILYEFF, W., History of buddhism in India, translated from the Tibetan. St. Petersburg (in Russian).
   German by Schiefner, No. 2913, and No. 4240.

4255 SUMMERS, J., The story of Ying Patchan from the Tibetan.

4256 CLARKE, H., Tibetan affinities of the palaeogeorgian language, The Phoenix, I, p. 54 ss.

4257 — — , The Phrygian, Etruscan and Caucaso-Tibetan; ibid, I, p. 151 ss.

d. Corean Language.

4258 GUETZLAFF, K., On the Corean language, Chin. Rep., 1832. See As. Journ., N. S., XI, 1833.

4259 The Corean Syllabary, Chin. Rep., II, 1833, p. 135.

4260 MEDHURST, W. H., Translation of a comparative vocabulary of the Chinese, Corean and Japanese languages, to which is added the 1000 character classic in Chinese and Corean, accompanied by indexes of all Chinese and English words. Batavia, 1835, 8vo.

4261 HOFFMANN, Tsiän-dsü-wen sive mille litterae ideographicae; opus sinicum origine cum interpretatione Koraiana. Lugd. Bat., 1833, 4to.

4262 SIEBOLD, P. F. von, Lui Hö sive vocabularium sinense in Koraïanum conversum, opus sinicum origine in peninsula Kôrai impressum annexa appendice vocabulorum Kôraianorum japonicorum et sinensium comparativa. Lugduni Batavorum, 1838, fol.

4263 ROSNY, L. DE, Vocabulaire Chinois-Coréen-Aino, expliqué en Français et précédé d'une introduction sur les écritures de la Chine, de la Corée et de Yeso. Paris, 1861, 8vo.

4264 — — , Aperçu de la langue Coréenne. Paris, 1864, 8vo., 70 pp.

4265 Corean writing in H. Wuttke, Geschichte der Schrift, I, p. 421-428 (No. 835.)

4266 PUZILLO, Opuit Russko-Koreiskago slovara (Essay of a Russian-Corean dictionary). St. Petersburg, 1874, 8vo., XV, 730 pp.

XVII. Geography, History, Ethnography of Extraprovincial China.

4267 WILLIAMS, S. W., Descriptive list of the largest towns and divisions in extraprovincial China, Chin. Rep., XIII, p. 561 ss.

4268 — — , Topography and division of extraprovincial China; ibid, XX, p. 57 ss.

4268a HOWORTH, H. H., The northern frontagers of China, Journ. R. A. S., Vol. VII, part 2; VIII, part 2.

a. Manchuria.

4269 VERBIEST, P., Voyage à la suite de l'empereur de la Chine dans la Tartarie orientale, Phil. Transact., 1686; also in Du Halde, Descr., T. IV (No. 2018); and Bernard's Recueil de Vóy. (No. 1457), Vol. IV.

4270 WITSEN, N., Noorden en Oost Tartarye. Amsterdam, 1705, 2 vols., fol.

4271 AMIOT, Notice des pays de la Tartarie, in Eloge de la ville de Moukden. Paris, 1770, p. 314 ss. (No. 4097.)

4272 JONES, W., Discours sur les Tartars. Paris, 4to.

4273 BROUGHTON, W. R., A voyage of discovery to the North Pacific Ocean. London, 1804, 4to.
German in Weimar. Bibl. der neust. Reisebeschr., XIX.
French: Paris, 1807-8, 2 vols., 8vo.

4274 MUELLER, Ueber den Amur. Büsching's Mag. f. Hist. und Geogr., II.

4275 KLAPROTH, J., Notice sur l'origine de la nation des Mandchoux, Mém. rel. à l'Asie, I, p. 411-454. From the Tung-hua-lu. See Klapr. Verz., p. 62.

4276 — — , Voyage à la montagne blanche, trad. du Mandchou; ib., p. 455.

4277 GORSKY, W., The origin of the ancestors of the present reigning Ching dynasty and the names of the Mantchu people, R. Eccl. Mission, I, 1852, No. 2 (in Russian.)

4278 WILLIAMS, S. W., Notices of the Sagalien river, Ch. Rep., XIX, p. 289.

4279 — — , Klaproth's account of the long white mountains of Manchuria.

See above Klaproth, No. 4276.

4280 PETERMANN, A., Die neusten russischen Erwer-
bungen im chinesischen Reiche. Mitth., 1856,
p. 175-186.

4281 TRONSON, J. M., Some observations on the coast
Tartars and their homes, Transact. Ch. Br. R. As.
S., VI, 1859, p. 121-135.

4282 WASILYEFF, W., Description of Manchuria and
details on the Manchus. St. Petersburg, 1863,
8vo. (in Russian).

4283 FLEMING, G. and MICHIE, Travels on horse-
back in Mantshu-Tartary. London, 1863, 8vo.,
illustr. See Lit. Centralblatt, 1868, p. 167.

4284 ANDREE, R., Das Amurgebiet und seine Bedeutung. Leipzig, 1866, 8vo.

4285 CHILKOFSKY, Trip on the Sungari in 1866, Is-
wjästiya of J. Russ. G. S., 1868 (in Russian).
See Petermann's Mitth., 1868.

4286 WILLIAMSON, A., Notes on Manchuria, Journ. R.
Geo. S., XXXIX, 1869, p. 1-36.

4287 Côte de la Mandchourie (map). Paris, Depôt de la
Marine, 1870.

4288 PALLADIUS, O., Notes of a journey from Peking
to Blagowestschenk through Manchuria, "Sapiski" Imp. Russ. Geo. S., IV, 1871 (in Russian.)
See Morgan, E. D., The recent journey of the
Archimandrite Palladius through Manchuria, Transl. from the Russ., Proc. R.
Geo. S., XVI, 1872, p. 204-217.

4289 HOWORTH, H. H., The ethnology of Manchuria,
"Phoenix" II, p. 19.

4290 — — , Origin of the Manchus; ibid, II, p. 58;
also J. R. A. S., Vol. VII, part II.

4291 On Manchuria, "Phoenix," II, p. 130.

4292a ROSS, J., Notes on Manchuria, Chin. Rec., VI,
1875, p. 214-221.

4292b — — , The Rise and progress of the Manjows;
ibid, VII, p. 155-168, 235-248.

b. Mongolia.

4293 BERGERON, Traité des Tartars.

4294 PETIT DE LA CROIX, Histoire du grand Ghenghiz Can. Paris, 1710, 8vo.

4295 D........, Histoire généalogique des Tatars, traduite du mscr. tatare d'Abulgasi Bayadur chan. Leyden, 1726, 8vo.

4296 RUBRUQUIS, Voyage en Tartarie in Bergeron, Rec. des Voy., I. Leyden, 1729, 4to.

4297 STRAHLENBERG, P. J., Nova descriptio geographica Tartariae magnae cum delineatione totius imperii Rossici, imprimis Sibiriae, 1730.

4298 — — , Nord-und Osttheil von Europa und Asia. Stockholm und Leipzig, 1730, 4to.
　　　English: London, 1738, 4to.; French: Paris, 1757, 2 vols., 12mo.

4299 D'ANVILLE, La Tartarie chinoise. Paris, 1732.

4300 — — , Nouvel Atlas de la Tartarie chinoise et du Tibet. Paris, 1737, fol.

4301 GAUBIL, P., Histoire du Gentchiscan et de toute la dynastie des Mongoux, ses successeurs, conquérants de la Chine. Paris, 1739, 4to.

4302 GUIGNES, J. DE, Mémoire historique sur l'origine des Huns et des Turcs. Paris, 1748, 12mo.

4303 — — , Histoire générale des Huns, des Turcs, des Mongols et des autres Tartares. Paris, 1756-58, 6 vols., 4to.; also St. Petersburg, 1824, 4to., with supplement by J. Senkowski.
　　　German by J. C. Dähnert. Greifswald, 1768.

4304 PALLAS, P. S., Sammlung historischer Nachrichten über die mongolischen Völkerschaften. St. Petersburg, 1776, 2 vols., 4to.

4305 VISDELOU, C., Histoire de la Tartarie, Herbelot Bibl. Or., 1777, IV, p. 47; Edition 1776 Suppl. p. 18-133.

4306 BRION DE LA TOUR, Carte de la Tartarie chinoise

dressée d'après les observations du P. Mailla. Paris, 1779.

4307 SOKOLEF, N., Reise längs der Mongolischen Grenze, etc. Pallas, N. Nord. Beitr., III.

4308 HUELLMANN, K. D., Geschichte der Mongolen bis 1206. Berlin, 1796, 8vo.

4309 IGUMENOF, Notice of Mongolia, " Siberian Messenger," 1819 (in Russian).

4310 Verfassung und politische Lage der chinesischen Mongolei. Neue geogr. Ephemerid., III, 1818.

4311 REMUSAT, A., Relation de l'expédition de Houlagou Khan, Journ. Asiat., 1823, p. 287 ss.

4312 — — , Recherches sur la ville de Karakorum avec des eclaircissements sur plusieurs points de l'histoire et de la géograghie de la Tartarie pendant le moyen age. Paris, 1825, 4to.

4313 — — , Mémoire sur les relations politiques des princes chrétiens avec les empereurs Mongols. Paris, 1827, 4to.; also in Mél. As., I.

4314 — — , Sur l'histoire des Mongols, d'après les auteurs Musulmans, Nouv. Mél. As., I, p. 427.

4315 — — , Observations sur l'histoire des Mongols orientaux de Senang setsen. Paris, 1832, 8vo.

4316 D'OHSSON, Histoire des Mongols depuis Ghengis Khan jusqu'au Timurlanc. Paris, 1824, 2 vols., 12mo.; Amsterdam, 1835, 4 vols., 12mo.; ibid, 1852.

4317 SCHMIDT, I. J., Forschungen im Gebiet der Völker Mittelasiens namentlich der Mongolen und Tibeter. St. Petersburg, 1824, 8vo.

4318 — — , Die Volksstämme der Mongolen, Mém. Ac. de St. Petersb., 6. sér., II, III.

4319 KLAPROTH, J., Beleuchtung und Widerlegung der Forschungen über die Geschichte der Mittelas. Völker des Herrn J. Schmidt. Paris, 1824, 8vo., map, plates. See No. 4317.

4320 — — , Examen d'un extrait d'une histoire des Khans Mongols de J. J. Schmidt, Mém. rel. à l'Asie, I, 1826 ; Schmidt's answer, ibid.

4321 — — Sur les Tartars, Mém. rel. à l'Asie, I, 1826.

4322 — —, Rapport sur les ouvrages du Père Hyacinthe Bitchourinski relat. à l'histoire des Mongols, VII, 1831.

4323 — —, Carte de la Mongolie, du pays des Mandchous, de la Corée et du Japon. Paris, 1833.

4324 HYACINTH, Bitschurin, Sapiski v Mongolii (Memoirs on Mongolia). St. Petersburg, 1828, 2 vols., 8vo. (in Russ.)
German by K. F. von Berg. Berlin, 1832.

4325 History of the eastern Mongols, As. journ. & monthly Reg., N. S., I, 1830.

4326 STEWART, J. C., The Mulfuzat Timury or autobiographical memoirs of the Moghul emperor Timur. London, 1830, 4to.

4327 On Mongolia and its inhabitants, As. Journ. & Mthl. Reg., N. S., X, 1833.

4328 GUETZLAFF, K., The Mongols, their conquests, etc., Chin. Rep., III, 1834-35, p. 441.

4329 PLAN-CARPIN, Relation des Mongols ou Tatars. Paris, 1838, 4to.

4330 ERDMANN, F. von, Vollständige Uebersicht der ältesten türkischen und mongolischen Völkerstämme. Kazan, 1841, 8vo.

4330a — —, The ancestors of Genghizkhan. St. Petersburg, 1841 (in Russian.)

4330b — —, On the history of Genghizkhan. St. Petersburg, 1849 (in Russian.)

4331a — —, Temudschin der Unerschütterliche, nebst Einleitung und Anm. Leipzig, 1862, 8vo., XIV, 614 pp. and 7 pp. tables.
See Ztschr. d. D. M. G., XVIII, p. 376.

4331 SCHOTT, W., Aelteste Nachrichten von Mongolen und Tataren, Hist. Krit. Abhandlung. Berlin, 1846, 4to., 30 pp.

4332 — —, Die letzten Jahre der Mongolenherrschaft in China, Berl. Ak. d. Wiss, 1850, p. 502.

4333 — — , Ueber die Heldensage von Geser Chan. Berlin, 1851, 4to.

4334 PALLADIUS, O., Ancient Mongolian traditions concerning Genghis Khan, Russ. Eccl. Miss., IV, 1865 (in Russian.)
Translation of the Yüan-t'shau-pi-shy.
See Chin. Recorder, V, 1875, p. 83.

4335 EDKINS, J., A visit to the agricultural Mongols, J. N. Ch. Br. R. As. Soc., II, 1866, p. 99-111.

4336a OSTEN-SACKEN, Fr. v. d., Report on the Russian consulate at Urga and explorations made in Mongolia, "Iswestija" Imp. Russ. Geo. Soc., 1869.

4336b DESMAISONS, Le Baron, Histoire des Mogols et des Tartares par Aboul-Ghazi Behâdour Khan, publiée, traduite et annotée. St. Petersburg, 1871, 2 vols., 8vo.

4337 WENYUKOFF, M. J., Map of Northwestern Mongolia with a memoir; ibid, VII, 1871, No. 7.

4338 DAVID, A., Journal d'un voyage en Mongolie fait en 1866, Bull. Nouv. Arch. des Mus., VII, 1871, p. 17-83, maps.

4339 — — , Voyage en Mongolie, Bull. Soc. Géogr. Paris, 1875, p. 5-45, 131-176, map.

4340 PARKER, E. H., A month in Mongolia, Phoenix, I, p. 51, 71, 95; II, p. 113, 120.

4341 HANEMANN, Fr., Bemerkungen zur Karte der westlichen Mongolei, Petermann's Mitth., 1872, p. 326-330, map.

4342 RADLOFF, W., Ein Ausflug in die westliche Mongolei. Köln. Zeit., 8th May, 1872.

4343 HOWORTH, H. H., Jinghis Khan, "Phoenix," II, p. 138.

4344 — — , The eastern Mongols; ib., II, p. 4.

4344a — — , The origines of the Mongols, Journ. R. A. S., Vol. VII, part 2.

4345 PRZEWALSKY, Physico-geographical sketch of the country between lake Dalainor in Mongolia and the northern boundaries of the Chinese province of Kansu, "Iswestija" Imp. Russ. Geo. Soc., July, 1872 (in Russian).

English in "Ocean Highways," Nov. 1872.

4346 — — , FRITSCHE, H., Geographische, Magnetische und Hypsometrische Beobachtungen angestellt von Kapt. Prschewalsky auf seinen Reisen in Centralasien während der Jahre 1870-73, Peterm. Mitth., 1874, p. 206 ss.

4347 — — , Mongolia and the country of the Tanguts. St. Petersburg, 1875, 2 vols., 8vo., maps. See Peterm. Mitth., 1876, p. 7-15, map.

German extracts by H. von Barth. Ausland, 1876, No. 5, p. 83-85, 109-113, 131-34; Zeitschr. f. Ethnol. Berlin, 1875; Die Natur, 1876, No. 8.

4348 Notes from the journal of a trip into Mongolia, Chin. Rec., IV, 1873, p. 187, 231.

4349 Neue Reisen in die Mongolei. "Ausland," 1873, No. 42.

4350 ELIAS, NEY, Narrative of a journey through Mongolia, July, 1872 to January, 1873, Journ. R. Geo. Soc., XLIII, 1873, p. 108-156, map.

See "Ocean Highways," June, 1873.

Italian in Cosmos di G. Coro, II, 1874, No. 2, 3.

4351 HERNANDEZ y FERNANDEZ, E., Viaje a la Mongolia, aventures de una familia española en la estepas del Asia central. Madrid, 1874, 2 vols., 8vo.

4352 FRITSCHE, H., Reisen durch die östliche Mongolei. "Ausland," 1874, No. 16.

4353 Hoinos (Gilmour, J.), Mongolia's two neighbours, Russia and China, Chin. Rec., V, 1874, p. 66-71.

4354 — , Norbo's Marriage; ib., p. 126-131.

4355 — , Mongol toilet; ib., p. 262-266.

4356 — , Whisky in Mongolia; ib., VI, 1875, p. 42-46.

4357 — , Mongolian Camels; ib., p. 181-197.

4358 — , How to travel in Mongolia; ib., p. 323-337.

4359 — , Thieves in Mongolia; ib., p. 401-409.
4360 PADERIN, Journey to Karakorum, "Iwestija" Imp.
  Russ. Geo. Soc., IX, 2. p. 355 ss.
4361 PFIZMAIER, A., Geschichte der Mongolenangriffe
  auf Japan, Phil. Hist. Cl. K. K. Ac. Wiss. Wien,
  1875; also sep. Wien, 1875, 8vo., 98 pp.
4362 MARTHE, J., Russisch-mongolische Beziehungen
  und Erforschungen. Zeitschr. Ges. f. Erdk. Berlin, X, 1875, p. 81-109.
4363 VAMBÉRY, H., Ein ungarischer Sprachforscher in
  der Mongolei, " Globus," XXVIII, 1875.
4364 KOHN, A., Die Mongolen; ibid, No. 24.

c. Central Asia.

(Turkestan, Dsungaria, etc.)

4365 GAUBIL, Journal de la Mission chinoise chez les
  Tourgouth Tartares en 1712, Souciet, Observ.
  Math., etc., I, p. 148-175.
    German in Müllers Samml. Russ. Gesch., I,
    p. 327 ss.
4366 — — , Des pays du Tsevang-raptan; ib., I, p.
  176-180.
4367 UNKOWSKY, J., Neueste Historie der östlichen
  Kalmückei, Müller's Samml. Russ. Gesch., I,
  1732, p. 123 ss.
    French in De Guignes. Hist. des Huns, IV,
    p. 102 ss.
4368 Berättelse om Ajukiniska Calmukiet, etc. (Notices of
  the Ajukian Calmucks, etc.) Stockholm, 1744,
  8vo. (in Swedish).
    German by Schnitscher in Müller's Samml.
    Russ. Gesch., IV, p. 275-364.
4369 AMIOT, Monument gravé sur la pierre en vers Chinois composé par l'empereur pour constater à la
  posterité la conquête du Royaume des Eleuths
  vers l'année 1757, Mém. Conc., I, p. 325-398.

4370 — , Position des principaux lieux du Royaume des Eleuths; ibid, I, p. 399.

4371 — , Monument de la transmigration des Tourgouthes; ibid, I, p. 401-418.

4372 — , Notice du royaume Hami; ib.

4373 ISLENIEV, Mappa fluvii Irtisz partim meridionalem gubernii Sibiriensis perfluentis cum pristino territorio stirpis Kalmucorum Songariae. Petropoli, 1777.

4374 CHAPPE D'AUTEROCHE, Voyage en Sibérie, etc. Paris, 1768, 2 vols., fol.

4375 SIEVERS, Reise von Tarbagatai zum Saisonnor und oberen Irtysch ins chinesische Reich, in Pallas N. Nord. Beitr., VII, 1786.

4376 WAHL, Vorder-und Mittelasien. Leipzig, 1795, 8vo.

4377 GLADWIN, Ayeen akbery or the institutes of the emperor Akbar. London, 1800, 4to.

4378 BERGMANN, B., Nomadische Streifereien mit den Kalmücken. Riga, 1804, 4 vols., 8vo.

4379 MOORCROFT, W., Plan of a tour to Chinese Tartary, Trans. R. As. S. of Bengal. Calcutta, 1812.

4380 — — , Expedition into Tartary, As. Journ., XIII, 1822; XIV, 1823.

4381 — — , Notice of Khoten, Journ. Geo. Soc., I, 1831.

4382 PANSNER, Map of Central Asia. St. Petersburg, 1816, 9 maps.
      See Klaproth, Mém. rel., III, p. 295.

4383 HUGH MURRAY, On the ancient geography of Central Asia, Trans. R. Geo. Soc. of Edinb., VIII, 1817, p. 171-202.

4384 T(RAILL), G. W., Letter from a gentleman proceeding on a public mission into Tartary, Quart. Journ. Lit. Sc. & Arts, VII, 1819.

4385 HAMILTON, Fr., Account of a map of the route between Tartary and Amarapura by an ambassador from the Court of Awa to the Emperor of

China. Edinburgh Phil. Journ., III, 1820.

4386 REMUSAT, A., Histoire de la ville de Khotan. Paris, 1820, 12mo.

4387 — — , Mémoire sur plusieurs questions relatives à la géographie de l'Asie Centrale. Paris, 1825, 4to.

4388 — — , Voyages dans la Tartarie, dans l'Afghanistan et dans l'Inde, Rev. d. deux Mond., V, 1832.

4389 STAUNTON, G. T., Narrative of the Chinese embassy to the Tourgouth Tartars. London, 1821, 8vo.

4390 GERARD, A., Journal of an excursion through the Himalayah mountains from Shipke to Chinese Tartary, Edinb. Journ. of Sc., I, 1824, map.

4391 KLAPROTH, J., Voyage à Khokand fait 1813 et 1814 par Ph. Nasarov, Mag. Asiat., I, 1825.

4392 — — , Notices géographiques et historiques sur Khokand, Badakhchàn et autres pays voisins; ibid, I, p. 81-123.

4393 — — , Notice sur les Amazones de l'Asie centrale; ib.

4394 — — , Troubles de la Dsoungarie, trad. du chinois; ibid.

4395 — — , Voyage dans l'Asie centrale par Mir Izzet Ullahen, 1812; ibid, II, p. 35 ss.
German in "Hertha," VI, 1826.

4396 — — , Voyage de Bukhtarminsk à Gouldja ou Ili, capitale de la Dzoungarie chinoise, par Poutimstev 1811; ibid, I, p. 173 ss.

4397 — — , Remarques sur les peuples qui habitent la frontière chinoise, sur les Tartares tributaires à la Russie et sur les Soïouts et Mongols soumis à la Chine, recueillies de 1771 à 1781 par Jegor Pesterev; ibid.

4398 — — , Notices sur les troubles survenus récemment dans l'Asie centrale, Journ. As., X, 1827, p. 310 ss.; Nouv. J. As., I, p. 147, 319.

4399 — — , Carte de l'Asie centrale, dressée d'après

les cartes chinoises par ordre de l'empereur Khien-Loung, par les Missionaires de Péking et d'après un grand nombre de notices extraites et traduites de livres chinois. Paris, 1835.

4400 ZWICK, H. A., und J. G. Schill, Reise von Sarepta in verschiedene Kalmückenhorden, etc. Leipzig, 1827, 8vo.

4401 HYACINTH, BITSCHURIN, Opisanie Dchungarii i wostotschnago Turkistanu. St. Petersburg, 1829, 2 vols., 8vo. (Description of Dsungaria and Eastern Turkestan, in Russian).

4402 — — , Istoritscheskoye obozrenie Oiratov ili Kalmykov (Researches into the history of the Oirats or Kalmyks. St. Petersburg, 1837, 8vo. (in Russian).

4403 — — , Istoria narodov obitavschikh v srednei Azii v devnia vremena (History of the nations which inhabited anciently Central Asia). St. Petersburg, 1851, 3 vols., 8vo., 1050 pp., map.

4404 DAVIS, Sir F., Notices of western Tartary, Transac. R. As. Soc. London, 1829.

4405 HUMBOLDT, A. von, Ueber die Bergketten und Vulkane Innerasiens. Poggendorf, Ann., vol. 94, 1830.

4406 — — , Mémoire sur les chaines de Montagnes de l'Asie centrale, Nouv. Ann. de Voy., IV, 1830.

4407 — — , Asie centrale. Paris, 1843, 3 vols., 8vo., maps.
German by W. Mahlmann. Berlin, 1844, 2 vols., 8vo.

4408 MILES, The Shajrut ul atrak or genealogical tree of the Turks and Tartars. London, 1830, 8vo.

4409 GRIMM, Karte von Hochasien. Berlin, 1832.

4410 GUETZLAFF, K., History and conquest of the Huns, Chin. Repos., III, p. 211.

4411 — — , History and wars of the Turks; ibid, III, p. 256.

4412 WATHEN, J., Notices of Chinese Tartary and Ko-ten, Journ. R. As. Soc., Dec. 1835; Chin. Rep., XII, p. 225.

4413 GENS, Nachrichten über Chiwa, Buchara, Chokand und den nordwestlichen Theil des chinesischen Staates bearbeitet von G. von Helmersen. St. Petersburg, 1839, 8vo.

4414 WOOD, J., Personal narrative of a journey to the source of the river Oxus. London, 1841, 8vo.

4415 DUBEUX, M., Tartarie, Beloutchistan, Boutan et Nepal. Paris, 1848, 8vo.

4416 VIVIEN de St. MARTIN, Mémoire analytique sur la Carte de l'Asia centrale et de l'Inde construite d'après le Si-yu-ki. Paris, 1858, 8vo.

4417 WASSILYEFF, W., History and antiquities of the oriental part of central Asia from the 10th to the 13th century. St. Petersburg, 1857, 8vo. (in Russian).

4418 WALICHANOFF, Tschokan Tschingisowich, Outlines of Dsungaria, "Sapiski" Imp. Russ. Geo. Soc., 1861 (in Russian.)

4419 — — , On the state of the six great eastern cities of the Chinese province Nanlu; ibid.

4420 SKATSCHKOFF, K., The Russian commerce at Tschugutschak (Tarbagatai), Russ. Industr. Messenger, 1862 (in Russian.)

4421 TORRENS, Lieut.-Col., Travels in Ladak, Tartary and Kashmir. London, 1862, 8vo.

4422 ATKINSON, Mrs., Recollections of Tartar steppes and their inhabitants. London, 1863, 8vo.

4423 SEMENOFF, P. P., Djungaria and the celestial mountains, Journ. Imp. Russ. Geo. S., 1865. English by J. Michell, Journ. R. Geo. S., XXXV, 1865.

4424 JLJIN, Chart of Central Asia. St. Petersburg, 1865 (in Russian).

4425 MONTGOMERIE, T. G., On the geographical position of Yarkand and other places in Central Asia,

Proc. R. Geo. S., 1866, X, No. 4; Journ. R. Geo.
S., XXXVI, 1866.
4426 RADLOFF, W., Das Ilithal in Hochasien, Peterm.
Mittl., 1866.
4427 KHANIKOFF, N. DE, Note sur le voyage dans
l'Asie centrale d'un officier allemand au service
de la compagnie anglaise des Indes Orient. Bull.
Soc. de Géo. Paris, 1866, p. 341 ss.
    See Rawlinson, Proc. Geo. S., X, 1866;
    Khanikoff's answer, ibid; Peterm. Mittl.,
    1867.
4428 WENYUKOFF, M. J., On the Pamir region and the
Bolor country in Central Asia, "Iswestija" Imp.
Russ. Geo. S., 1866 (in Russian).
    See Proc. R. Geo. Soc., X, 1866, No. 4.
4429 — — , Materials to a sketch of the Russian frontiers in Asia, 9th : The district of Tienshan. Wo-
jenny Sbornik. Febr. 1873 (in Russian).
4430 — — , Notes on the population of Dsungaria,
"Iswestija" Imp. Russ. Geo. S., VII, 1871, No. 7.
4431 JOHNSON, W. H., Report on his journey to Ilchi,
the capital of Khotan in Chinese Tartary, J. R.
Geo. S., XXXVII, 1867, p. 1-47, map.
4432 PAUTHIER, G., Relation du voyage de Kieou dans
l'Asie centrale, Journ. As., 1867.
4433 RAWLINSON, Sir H. C., On the recent journey of
Mr. W. H. Johnson from Leh in Ladakh to Ilchi,
Proc. R. Geo. S., XI, 1867, p. 6.
4434 — — , On trade routes between Turkestan and
India ; ibid, XIII, 1869, No. 1.
4435 BOWRA, E. C., The Hounoi and the Hsiungnu,
Notes and Queries, I, p. 2, 13.
4436 — — , The Ouigours and the Nestorian Christians ; ibid, I, p. 42.
4437 EITEL, E. J., The Uigours ; ib., II, p. 59.
4438 MAYERS, W. F., Comparative tables of geographical names in Central Asia ; ib., II, p. 163.
4439 SSEVERTSOFF, N. A., Excursion in the western

part of the Celestial mountains from the western frontier of the Transilian territory to Kaschkent, "Sapiski" Imp. Russ. Geo. S., I, 1867 (in Russian).

See Peterm. Mitth., 1869, p. 380.

English by R. Michell, J. R. Geo. S., XXXIX.

4440 — — , Travels in Turkestan and the Tienshan mountains. St. Petersburg, 1873, 8vo. (in Russian).

4441 — — , N. Sewerzow's Erforschung des Thianschan Gebirgssystems 1867, nebst kartographischer Darstellung desselben Gebiets und der Seenzone des Balkasch-Alakul und Siebenstromlandes nach den originalen und officiellen Russischen Aufnahmen von A. Petermann. Gotha, 1875, 4to., 2 Hefte, 2 maps.

4442 POLTORATZKY, The country between the Tchou and Syr rivers, "Sapiski" Imp. Russ. Geo. S., I, 1867 (in Russian).

French by P. Völkel in Bull. Soc. Géo. Paris, Dec. 1869, p. 433 ss.

4443 PRINTZ, A., Account of an excursion to the Chinese town Chobdo in 1863; ibid, 1867 (in Russian).

4444 SPOERER, J., Die Seenzone des Balchasch-Alakul, das Siebenstromland mit dem Ilibecken, Peterm. Geo. Mitth., 1868.

4445 HELMERSEN, P. A., Journey of Lieut. A. Nesnajew from Ust Kamenogorsk to Chobdo in 1771, "Iswestija" Imp. Russ. Geo. Soc., IV, 1868 (in Russian).

4446 Die neusten russischen Forschungen in Centralasien, Peterm. Mitth., 1868.

4447 HELLER von HELLWALD, Fr., Die Russen in Centralasien. Oesterr. Mil. Zeitschr. Jan., Febr., March, Jul., Aug. 1869.

4448 — — , Neue Forschungen in Central Asien. "Ausland" 1872, p. 241-248, 265-270, 289-294.

4449 — — , Die Russen in Centralasien. Eine historisch-politische Studie. Augsburg, 1873, 8vo.

4450 — — , Centralasien. Leipzig, 1875, 8vo., maps, illustr.

4451 FORSYTH, T. D., On the transit of tea from N. W. India to Eastern Turkestan, Proc. R. Geo. S., July 1869.

4452 — — , Gesandtschaftsreise nach Kashgar, "Globus," XXV, 1874.

4453 THONNELIER, J., Dictionnaire géographique de l'Asie Centrale, offrant par ordre alphabétique les transcriptions en caractères mandchoux et chinois des noms géographiques. Paris, 1869, 4to.

4454 OSTEN-SACKEN, Fr. von der und F. J. RUPRECHT, Sertum Thianschanicum, Botanische Ergebnisse einer Reise im mittleren Thianschan, Mém. Ac. Imp. d. Sc. St. Pétersb., VI, sér., XIV, 4, 1869, 4to.

4455 SHAW, R. B., A visit to Yarkand and Kashgar, Proc. R. Geo. S., XIV, No. 2, p. 124-137.

4456 — — , Letters from Mr. ——; ibid, XV, No. 3, p, 175-180.

4457 — — , Visits to High Tartary, Yarkand and Kashgar and return journey over the Karakorum pass. London, 1871, 8vo., 2 maps, illustr.
German by J. E. Martin. Jena, 1872.
See Peterm. Mitth., 1872.

4458 — — , Our communications with Eastern Turkestan, "Ocean Highways," Aug. 1872, map.

4459 — — , Results of his observations taken during his journey to Yarkand in 1870, calculated by W. Ellis, Journ. R. Geo. S., 1871, p. 373-392.

4460 — — , Central Asia in 1872, Proc. R. Geo. S., 1872. German in Peterm. Mitth., 1873, No. 1.

4461 — — , Miscellaneous notes on Eastern Turkestan, Pr. R. Geo. S., XVII, 1873, p. 195 ss.

4462 Geographical researches on the western Russian-Chinese frontier, " Iswestija" Imp. Russ. Geo. Soc., VI, 1870 (in Russian).

4463 HAYWARD, G. W., Journey from Leh to Yarkand and Kashgar and exploration of the sources of the Yarkand river.

4464 PESCHEL, O., Ueber den steinernen Thurm der Ptolemäischen Geographie. "Ausland" 1870, No. 15.

4465 VAMBÉRY, H., Das Dach der Welt, "Globus," XX, 1871, No. 12.

4466 IBRAHIM KHAN, Route from Kashmir to Yarkand in 1870, Proc. R. Geo. S. London, XV, 1871, p. 387-392.

4467 MARTHE, F., Russische Arbeiten über Centralasien aus dem Jahre 1870, Zeitschr. Ges. f. Erdk. Berlin, VI, 1871, p. 440-475.

4468 LANKENAU, H. von, Eine Reise längs der Russisch-Chinesischen Grenze vom Altai bis zur Tarbagataischen Gebirgskette, Aus dem Tagebuche der Generalin B. mitgetheilt, "Ausland," 1872, No. 29, 32.

4469 NETSCHOWOLDOFF, Reisen an den Grenzen der Dsungarei, "Globus," XXII, 1872, No. 2, 3.

4470 MEER IZZUT OOLLAH, travels in Central Asia in the years 1812-1813, Transl. from the Persian by Capt. Henderson. Calcutta, 1872, 8vo., 100 pp.

4471 A Russian embassy in Kashgar, "Ocean Highways," Nov. 1872.

4472 PHILLIPS, G., An ethnographical table of Central Asia, in Doolittle Handb., II, p. 201-210.

4473 — — , Geographical names in Tartary; ibid, p. 552-555.

4474 SCHEPELOW, A., Report of his explorations of the Mussart pass in the Thianshan, "Iswestija" Imp. Russ. Geo. S., 1873, No. 4 (in Russian).

4475 DELITZSCH, O., Das Reich Kaschgar oder Tschity-Schehr "Aus allen Welttheilen," Jan. 1873.

4476 — — , Die centralasiatische Frage; ib., 1873, p. 181 ss.

4477 SCHARNHORST. C., Astronomische Ortsbestimmungen am Thianschan, "Iswestija" Imp. Russ. Geo. S., IX, 1873.

4478 Central Asia, "Ocean Highways," March 1873, map.

4479 Our neighbours in Central Asia, China and Turkmania. St. Petersburg, 1873, 8vo., 138 pp (in Russian).

4480 Ein Blick auf Centralasien, "Globus," XXIV, 1873, No. 22.

4481 SCHOTT, W., Zur Uigurenfrage, Mon. Ber. K. Preuss. Ac. d. Wiss. Berlin, Nov. 1873, Jan. 1875.

4482 PADERIN, Journey from Uiassutai to Urga, "Iswestija" Imp. Russ. Geo. S., 1873.
Italian in "Cosmos" di Guido Cora, II, 1874, p. 73 ss.

4483 CHAPMAN, Sketches in Eastern Turkestan, Ill. Lond. News, 1874.

4484 WALKER, J. T., Map of Turkestan. Dehra Dun, 1874.

4485 — — , Sketch map illustrative of Sir D. Forsyth's mission to Kashgar, Geo. Magaz., May 1875.

4486 Eastern Toorkestan, Edinb. Review, April 1874.

4487 RIALLE, Girard DE, Mémoire sur l'Asie centrale. Paris, 1874, 8vo.

4488 SCHLAGINWEIT, E., Englische Forschungsreisen in Centralasien, "Globus," XXV, 1874, No. 23, 24.

4489 SCHLAGINWEIT-SAKUENLUENSKY, H. von, Die Pässe über die Kammlinien des Karakorum und des Künlün. Abh. K. Bayr. Ac. d. Wiss. München, XII, 1874; also "Ausland," 1875, p. 413-416, 434-437.

4490 SCHUYLER, E., A month's journey in Kokand in 1873, Proc. R. Geo. S., XVIII, 1874, No. 4.

4491 — — , A journey in Turkestan. New York, 1874, 8vo.

4492 Generalkarte von Centralasien. Wien, K. K. Mil. Geo. Inst., 1874.

332

See H. Kiepert, Zeitschr. Ges. f. Erdk. Berlin, 1874, p. 442-468; Schmidt, Russ. Rev., 1875, p. 587-593.

4493 TAYLOR, B., Central Asia. New York, 1874, 12mo.
4494 SOSNOWSKY, Report on the expedition to Buluntochoi, "Iswestija," Imp. Russ. Geo. S., 1875, map.
4495 SOSNOWSKY'S Forschungen in der Dsungarei 1872, "Globus," XXVII, 1875, No. 16.
4496 KER, D., The mineral wealth of Central Asia as bearing on Russian progress, Geo. Mag., Jan. 1875.
4497 GREGORJEW, W. W., Die russische Politik in Hinsicht auf Centralasien, Russ. Rev., 1875, No. 3.
4498 STUART, A., Le Chemin de fer central-asiatique, "L'explorateur géogr. et comm.," 1875, p. 396 ss.
4499 BOGDANOWITSCH, E., Exposé de la question relative au chemin de fer de la Sibérie et de l'Asie centrale. Paris, 1875, 8vo.
4500 KAULBARS, Baron A. W., Materials to the Geography of the Tienshan collected during the journey of B. K. in 1869, " Sapiski," Imp. Russ. Geo. S., V, 1875, map (in Russian).
4501 TERENTYEFF, M. A., Sketches of centralasian Russia; ibid, IV, 1874 (in Russian).
4502 DEBELAK, J., Die centralasiatische Frage, Oesterr. Milit. Zeitschr. 1875; also separately. Wien 1875, 8vo., 105 pp., map.
4503 KOHN, A., Die mohammedanischen Tataren in Nordasien, "Globus," 1875, No. 23, 24.
4504 BRETSCHNEIDER, E., Notices of the mediæval geography and history of Central and Western Asia, drawn from Chinese and Mongol writings and compared with observations of western authors in the middle ages, 2 maps, Journ. N. C. Br. of R. A. S., VIII, 1876; also Shanghai and London, 1876, 8vo. IV, 233 pp. See Shanghai Evening Courier 1876, 15th June; and Ch. Rec., VII, p. 301.

d. Tibet.

4505 Historica relatio de regno et statu magni regis Mogor in "De rebus Japonicis, Indicis, etc." a J. Hayo Scoto, Soc. Jes. Antwerpiae, 1605, 8vo.

4506 ANDRADA, A. DE, Nuovo descubrimento do Grao Cataya ou dos Reynos de Tibet. Lisbon, 1626, 4to.

> Italian: Rome, 1627; Naples, 1627, 8vo.
> Spanish: Madrid, 1628; ibid, 1645, 4to.
> French: Gaud, 1627, 8vo.; Paris, 1628, 8vo. Flemish: Gent, 1631, 8vo. German: Augsburg, 1627.

4507 Histoire de ce qui s'est passé au royaume de Tibet dans l'an 1626. Paris, 1639, 12mo.

4508 RAY, Th., Descriptio regni Thibet. Paderborn, 1658, 4to.

4509 BERNIER, Fr., Voyages et description des Etats du grand Mongol. Amsterdam, 1699.

4510 CARTROU, Histoire générale de l'empire du Mongol. Paris, 1715, 4to.

4511 DESIDERI, P., Notes sur le Tibet, 1716, Lettr. Édif., XV, 1722.

4512 D'ANVILLE, Carte générale du Thibet ou Boutan, etc., dressée sur les cartes et mémoires des Jesuites en Chine et accordée avec la situation constante de quelques pays voisins. Paris, 1733.

4513 FRANCESCO ORAZIO della PENNA di BILLA, Missio apostolica Tibetana-seraphica. Das ist neue durch Päbstliche Gewalt in dem grossen Tibetanischen Reich von denen P. P. Capucinern aufgerichtete Mission. München, 1740, 4to., 2 vols.

4514 — — , Relazione dello stato presente della missione del gran Regno del Tibet. Roma, 1752, 4to.

4515 Relazione del principio e stato presente della Missione del vasto Regno del Tibet e altri Regni confinanti. Roma, 1742, 4to.

4516 Representacion hecha por el R. Procurador General de Religiosos menores Capuchinos a la Sagrada Congregacion de Propaganda Fide, Sobre el Estado actual de la Mission de Tibet, trad. del Toscano por el Dr. D. Ant. Mar. Herrero. Madrid, 1744, 4to.

4517 Translation of a letter from the Tayshoo Lama to Mr. Hastings, governor of Bengal, received 29th March 1774, Philos. Transact. R. Soc., XLVII, 1778.

4518 STEWART, J., Account of the Kingdom of Thibet, extracted from the papers of M. Bogle. Philos. Trans., LXVII, 1778.

4519 PALLAS, P. S., Nachrichten von Tybet aus Erzählungen Tangutischer Lamen und den Selenginskischen Mongolen, Neue Nord. Beitr. I, 1781.
French by Reuilly. Paris, 1808, 8vo.

4520 Mémoire sur le Thibet et sur le Royaume des Eleuthes nouvellement subjugués avec une relation de cette conquête, Lettr. Éd., XXXI, p. 212 ss.; Nouv. Ed., XXIV, p. 5-56.

4521 HAKMAN, Nachricht betreffend Erdbeschreibung von Tybet; Neue Nord. B., IV, 1783.

4522 SAUNDERS, Reise in Thibet, Fabri's Collection of Travels. Halle, I, 1785.

4523 Nachrichten von Tibet; ibid, p. 207-314 (Translated from "Alphabetum Tibitanum," No. 4182.)

4524 TURNER, S., An account of a journey to Tibet, As. Res., I, 1788.

4525 — — , Copy of an account given by Mr. Turner of his interview with the Teshoo Lama at the Monastery of Terpaling; ib., I, 1788.

4526 — — , An account of an Embassy to the court of the Teshoo Lama in Tibet, containing a narrative of a Journey through Bootan and Part of Tibet, to which are added views taken on the place by Davis and observations botanical, mineralogical and medical by R. Saunders. London, 1800, 4to.

German: Hamburg, 1801, 8vo. French: Paris, 2 vols., 1802, 8vo.

4527 Reise eines Engländers im Gefolg des Dalai Lama, "Minerva," 1792, No. 12.

4528 Journey of the Teshoo Lama to Peking; Chinese account by Amiot, Mém. Conc., IX, 1794, p. 446-454; English in Dalrymple Orient. Rep., II, p. 275-285; Indian account by Gossein Porungheer in Dalrymple Orient. Rep., II, p. 145-164. Both accounts English in Turner, No. 4526, p. 443 ss., p. 457 ss.

4529 Voyages en Thibet par le P. Andrada traduits par J. P. Perraud et J. B. L. Billecoq; Relation de Thibet extraite des papiers de M. Bogle traduite de l'Anglais par Perraud; Extrait du voyage de M. Bogle au Boutan et Thibet traduit par Billecoq; Relation de l'entrevue de M. Turner avec le Tachou Lama, traduit par Perraud; Voyage au Thibet redigé d'après le recit de Pourungi par M. Turner. Paris, 1796, 16mo.

4530 MOORCROFT, W., Journey to Lake Mánasaróvara in Undes, As. Journ., 1816, p. 375-532.

4531 — — , Letter to John Fleming de dat. Leh, 25 April 1822, Transact. R. As. Soc., I, 1824.

4532 — — , Moorcroft and his companions, As. Journ., XXII, 1824.

4533 — — , Papers of the late Mr. Moorcroft., J. R. Geo. Soc., I, II, 1832.

4534 — — and TREBECK, G., Travels in the Himalayas, Ladakh and Kashmir in 1819-25. London, 1841, 2 vols., 8vo., maps.

4535 KLAPROTH, J., Mémoire sur le cours du Yaro Dzangbo Tchou ou du grand fleuve du Tubet, Mag. As., I, 1826, p. 302-329.

4536 — — , Déscription du Si-dsang ou Tubet d'après la grande géogr. impér. de la Chine et le dictionnaire géogr. de l'Asie centrale publié à Peking 1775; ibid.

4537 — — , Route de Tching-tou-fou en Chine à travers le Tubet oriental jusqu'à Hlassa; ibid.

4538 — — , Mémoire sur les sources du Brahmapoutra et de l'Irouaddy, Ann. de Voy., nouv. sér., VII, p. 263-304.

4539 — — , Voyage de M. Csoma de Körös dans la haute Asie; ibid, IX, 1826.

4540 — — , Notes sur le Tubet par P. Hippol. Desideri, recueillies par N. Delisle, J. As., VIII, 1831, p. 117.

4541 — — , Notice sur H'Lassa, capitale du Tubet, Nouv. Ann. de Voy., XI, 1829, plan.

4542 — — , Breve notizie dal regno del Tibet dal fra Frenc. Orazio della Penna di Belli 1730, publié d'après le manuscr. autogr. de l'auteur. Paris, 1835, 8vo.

4543 HYACINTH (Bitchurin), Opissanie Tibeta v nynieschnem yevo sostoyanii (Description of Tibet in its actual state, translated from the Chinese Weitsang-t'u-chih) (in Russian). St. Petersburg, 1828, 8vo., map, ill.

French by Klaproth. Paris, 1831, 8vo.

4544 CSOMA DE KOEROES, Geographical notice of Tibet, J. R. As. Soc. of Bengal, 1832; Ch. Rep., XIII, p. 505.

4545 LLOYD, J. A., Note on the white satin embroidered scarf of the Tibetan priest, with a translation of the motto by Csoma de Körös, Journ. As. Soc. of Bengal, V, 1836.

4546 — — , Narrative of a journey to the Burenda pass. London, 1840, 8vo.

4547 MORRISON, J. R., Chinese rule over Tibet, Chin. Rep., VI, p. 494.

4548 PEMBERTON, R. B., Report on Butan. Calcutta, 1839, 8vo.

4549 GRIFFITH, Journal of the Mission which visited Butan 1837-38 under Pemberton, As. Journ. of Bengal, VIII.

French by C. O. d'Ochoa. Paris, 1840.

4550 GERARD, A., Narrative of a journey from Sooba-
thoo to Chipke, J. As. Soc. of Bengal, XI.

4551 GUETZLAFF, K., Description of Tibet from native
books, Ch. Rep., IX, p. 26.

4552 — — , Tibet and Sifan, Journ. Geo. Soc., XX,
p. 2, 1850.

4553 VIGNE, G. T., Travels in Kashmir, Ladak, Iskar-
do, the countries adjoining the mountain course of
the Indus and the Himalaya, north of the Punjab.
London, 1842, 2 vols., 8vo., plates.

4554 NEUMANN, K., Tübet. Ausland, 1846.

4555 PAVIE, T., Le Thibet et les études tibétaines, Revue de deux Mond., N. S., XIX, 1847.

4556 CAMPBELL, Itinerary from Phasi in Tibet to Lassa,
Journ. Geogr. Soc., April 1848.

4557 CUNNINGHAM, Notes on Tibet, Journ. As. Soc.
of Bengal, 1848.

4558 STRACHEY, H., Narrative of a journey to the lakes
Cholagan and Cho-mapan in Tubet 1846. Calcutta, 1849.

4559 VEUILLOT, E., Le Thibet et les missions français-
es dans la Haute Asie, Rev. de deux Mond., VI,
1850.

German in "Ausland," 1850.

4560 PRINSEP, H. T., Tibet, Tartary and Mongolia.
London, 1851, 8vo.

4561 SCHOBEL, T. R., Tibet and India beyond the Gan-
ges. London, 8vo., plates.

4562 THOMSON, T. D., Western Himalaya and Tibet.
London, 1852, 8vo., map.

4563 HILARION, Relations of China to Tibet, Russ.
Eccl. Miss. Peking, I, 1853 (in Russian).

German in Abel und Mcklenburg, Arbeiten
der Russ. Gesandtsch. zu Peking, I,
1858 (No. 882.)

4564 KRICK, Relation d'un voyage au Thibet en 1852, et
d'un voyage chez les Abors en 1853 suivie de

quelques documents de Renou et Latry. Paris, 1854, 12mo.

4565 FOUCAUX, P. E., Le Thibet oriental, Rev. de l'Or., August 1856, p. 113-135; German in "Ausland," 1856, No. 4.

4566 SCHLAGINWEIT-SAKUENLUENSKI, H. von, Klimatologische Bilder aus Indien und Hochasien. "Ausland," 1865, No. 43.

4567 — —, Ueber die mittlere Temperatur des Jahres und den allgemeinen Character der Isothermen in Indien und Hochasien, Monatsb. K. preuss. Ak. d. Wiss. 1865, August.

4568 — —, Die thermischen Verhältnisse der tiefsten Gletscherenden im Himalaya und in Tibet. Ber. K. Bayr. Ak. d. Wiss. München, 1866, p. 290.

4569 — —, Vergleich hydrographischer Daten aus dem Oestlichen Tibet. "Ausland," 1871, No. 38.

4570 — —, Zur Fauna im Salzseegebiete des westlichen Tibet; ibid, 1871, p. 1006, 1031, 1055.

4571 — —, Die Salzseen des westlichen Tibet nebst allgemeiner topographischer Erläuterung Hochasiens. 2. Jahres b. d. geogr. Ges. München, 1872; p. 21-40.

4572 SCHLAGINWEIT, E., Neustes aus dem östlichen Tibet. "Ausland," 1866, No. 42, 43.

4573 — —, Die Könige von Tibet, Abh. Bayr. Akad., X. München, 1866.

4574 — —, Die deutsche Herrnhuter Mission in Tibet, "Globus," XIX, 1871, p. 335.

4575 BENNET, A., Rough notes of a visit to Daba in Tibet, Aug. 1865, Proc. R. Geogr. Soc. London, 1866, X, p. 165.
   See Zeitschr. Ges. f. Erdk. Berlin, 1866, p. 447.

4576 CHEETHAM, J. F., The Tibetan route from Simla to Srinagar, Alp. Journ., III, 1867, p. 118.

4577 SMITH, H. U., A trip to Thibet, Kylas, etc., Proc. R. Geo. Soc., XI, 1867, p. 119.

4578 MONTGOMERIE, T. G., Report on the Trans Himalayan explorations during 1865-67, Dohra Doon, 1868, 4to.; also Journ R. Geo. Soc., XXXIX, 1869, p. 146-187.

4579 — — , Route survey from Brit. India into Great Tibet made by a Pundit; ibid, 1868, map.
German in Peterm. Geo. Mitth., 1868, map.

4580 — — , Report on the Trans Himalayan explorations made in 1868, Proc. R. Geo. Soc., XIV, p. 207.

4581 STEWART, J. L., Notes of a botanical tour in western Tibet, Transact. Edinb. Bot. Soc., X, 1868-69.

4582 KINLOCH, A., Large game shooting in Tibet and the North West, containing description of country and of the various animals to be found, together with extracts from a journal of several years shooting. London, 1869, 4to.

4583 COOPER, T. J., On the course of the Tsan po and Jrawaddy and on Tibet, Proc. R. G. S., XIII, 1869, p. 392 ss., map.

4583a MAYERS, W. F., Illustrations of the Lamaist system in Tibet, drawn from Chinese sources, J. R. A. S., new series, Vol. IV; also London, 1869, 8vo., 24 pp.

4584 Extraits de lettres de M. A. Desgodius missionaire apost. au Tibet, Bull. Soc. Géogr. Paris, 1869, p. 317 ss.; 1870, p. 227 ss; 1872, Oct., Nov.

4585 GREGORY, J., Account of an attempt by a native envoy to reach the catholic missionaries of Tibet, Proc. R. Geogr. Soc., XIV, 1870, p. 214.

4586 CAMPBELL, A., Notes on Eastern Tibet, "Phoenix," I, p. 83, 107, 142.

4587 The Moravian Mission in Tibet; ibid, II, p. 170.

4587a HORNE, C., On the methods of disposing of the dead at Llassa, Thibet. J. R. A. S., Vol. VI.

4588 DESGODINS, A., La mission du Thibet de 1855 à 1870. Paris, 1872, 8vo., map.

4589 Zur Naturgeschichte des östlichen Tibets, "Globus," XXI, 1872, p. 332.

4590 Versuche zur Eröffnung Tibets; ibid, XXIV, 1873, p. 206.

4591 The discovery of the lake Tengrinor, Geogr. Mag., 1875, p. 41-44; also "Ausland," 1875, No. 22; "Globus," XXVII, 1875, No. 16.

4592 MARKHAM, C. R., Travels in Great Tibet and trade between Tibet and Bengal, Proc. R. Geo. Soc., XIX, 1875, p. 327-347; also Geo. Mag., 1875, p. 129-135.

4593 — — , The narratives of the mission of George Bogle, B. C. S. to the Teshu Lama and of the Journey of Thomas Manning to Lhasa. London, 1876, 8vo., maps, illustr.

4594 Aus Nepal und Tibet. Ausland, 1876, No. 5, p. 91-93.

e. Corea and Liukiu.

4595 HAMEL van GORCUM, H., Journael van de ongelukige Voyagie von t'Jacht de Sperwer gedestineert na Tayovan in t'jaar 1653, hoe t'selve Jacht op t'Quilpaarts Eyland is gestrant: als made een pertinente beschryvinger der Landen, Provintien, Staten ende Forten leggende in t'Coningryk Coree. (Journal of the unhappy voyage of the Yacht "The Hawk" destined to Formosa, how the same Yacht was stranded to Quilpaart's Island, with a pertinent description of the countries, provinces, towns and forts situated in the Kingdom of Corea). Rotterdam, 1668, 4to.
French: Paris, 1670, 12mo.; also in Rec. des voy. au nord, IV, 1718 (No. 1457.)

4596 Wahrhaftige Beschreibung dreier mächtigen Königreiche Japan, Siam und Korea. Nürnberg, 1672, 8vo.

4597 GAUBIL, Sur les isles que les Chinois appellent isles de Lieou Kieou, Lettr. éd., XXVIII, p. 355; Nouv. Ed., XXIII, p. 182-246.

4598 Nachrichten von der Halbinsel Corea in Asien. Wiss. von Literat. und Volk, 1796, No. X.
4599 Corée, Nouv. Lettr. Édif., V, p. 259-345.
4600 LEOD, J. M., Narrative of a voyage in H. M. S. "Alceste" to Corea, Lewchew, etc. London, 1817, 8vo.
4601 HALL, B., Account of a voyage of discovery to the west coast of Corea and the Great Loochoo island. London, 1818, 4to.
    German in Weimar. Bibl. d. neuest. Reise-beschr., II, p. 19.
4602 KLAPROTH, J., Aperçu général des Trois Royaumes Corée, Loutchou, Yéso. Paris, 1832, 8vo. (with a Corean Vocabulary.)
4603 SIEBOLD, Archiv zur Beschreibung von Japan. Leiden, 1832, fol.
    Pt. VII contains notes on Corea by J. J. Hoffmann.
4604 Missions en Corée, Ann. de la Prop. de la Foi, 1839. See Chin. Rep., VIII, 1839, p. 567.
4605 ANDRÉ KIMAI KIM, Voyage à la Mandchourie et en Corée, Ann. de la Prop. de la Foi, 1847.
4606 Carte de Corée, d'après l'original dressé en 1840 par André Kim et apporté par M. Montigny, reduit par V. A. Malte Brun. Paris, 1844.
4607 BÉLCHER, Sir E., Narrative of the voyage of H. M.S. "Samarang" to Corea. London, 1848, 2 vols., 8vo.
4608 ROCHE-PONCIÉ, J. de la, Carte de la presqu'ile de Corée. Paris, 1848.
4609 SMITH, G., Lewchew and the Lewchewans. London, 1853, 8vo.
4610 The reports of the Loochoo Mission society. London, 1853, 8vo.
4611 Bericht eines Chinesen über die Liukiuinseln. Neumann's Zeitschr. f. allg. Erdk., I, 1856, p. 262.
4612 RICHARDS, J., Notes on some places visited during a surveying expedition round the coasts of Japan

and Korea in the summer of 1855, T. Ch. Br. R. As. Soc., V, 1856, p. 109-124.

4613 WILLIAMS, S. W., Political intercourse between China and Lewchew, J. N. Ch. Br. R. As. Soc., III, p. 81-93.

4614 HALLORAN, Eight months' journal kept on board of H. M. sloops during a visit to Loochew. London, 1856, 8vo.

4615 YOUNG, A., On Korea, Proc. R. Geo. Soc., IX, 1865, No. 6.

4616 Materials to the geography of Corea, "Iswestija" R. Geogr. Soc., II, 1866 (in Russian).

4617 ROSTAING, VTE DE, Note sur une récente exploration du Hang Kyang en Corée, Bull. de la Soc. de géo. de Paris, Fév. 1867, p. 210, map.

4618 KNIGHT, S., Corea, Notes and Queries, II, p. 38.

4619 PFIZMAIER, A., Nachrichten von den alten Bewohnern des heutigen Corea. Sitzb. Kais. Acad. d. Wiss. Wien, 1868.

4620 — — , Der Feldzug der Japaner gegen Korea im J. 1597; ibid, 1874, No. 15-17; also separately. Wien, 8vo., 98 pp.

4621 — — , Darlegungen aus der Geschichte und Geographie Korea's; ibid, 1874, No. 21 ; also separately. Wien, 1875, 8vo., 56 pp.
See Siebold's Nippon Archiv.

4622 Deuxième supplément aux instructions sur la mer de Chine, 2o. partie contenant des renseignements nautiques sur la côte ouest de la Corée. Paris, Depôt de la mar., 1868.

4623 Côte occidentale de Corée. Paris, depôt de la Mar., 1868-70 (maps).

4624 ROSNY, L. DE, sur la géographie et l'histoire de la Corée, Rev. Orient., 2. sér., VI, 1868; also separately. Nancy, 1869, 8vo., 22 pp.

4625 Corea, Pinyang inlet and Tatong river approach, London, Hydr. Off., 1869 (map).

4626 West Coast of Corea, Washington Hydr. Off., 1869 (map.)

4627 HELMERSEN, P. A., Notices on Corea, "Iswestija" Imp. Russ. Geogr. Soc., 1869 (in Russian).

4628 Corean Archipelago, southern portion, London, Hydr. Off., 1871.

4629 West Coast of Corea, Merc. Mar. Magaz., Dec. 1871, p. 359.

4630 MAYERS, F. W., On Corea, Edinb. Rev., No. 278, Oct. 1872.

4631 La Corée, Revue Britann. 1873; also Journ. off. de la Repl. Franç., 7th Febr. 1873.

4632 Die Halbinsel Korea und die Koreaner, "Globus," XXIV, 1873, No. 9 ss.

4633 Japan und Korea, Evang. Miss. Mag. Basel, July, 1873, p. 262-289.

4634 ZUBER, H., Une expédition en Corée, Le tour du monde, XXV, 1873, p. 401-416, map.

4635 MARIA, LOVERA di, Posizione delle isole Liuschotten e Liu Kiu; Còra's Cosmos, 1873, p. 48.

4636 SATOW, E., Notes on Loochoo, As. Soc. of Japan, 1873.

4637 DALLET, Ch., Histoire de l'église de Corée précédée d'une introduction sur l'histoire, les institutions, la langue, les moeurs et coutumes coréennes. Paris, 1874, 2 vols., 8vo., map.
See Petermann's Mitth., 1875, p. 113.

4638 ROSS, J., Visit to the Corean Gate, Chin. Rec., V, p. 347-354, 1874.

4639 BRIDGE, O. A. G., A glimpse of Corea, The Fortnightly Review, Jan. 1876.

INDEX OF AUTHORS.

E

356

L

364

366

370

www.ingramcontent.com/pod-product-compliance
Lightning Source LLC
Chambersburg PA
CBHW030901270326
41929CB00008B/525